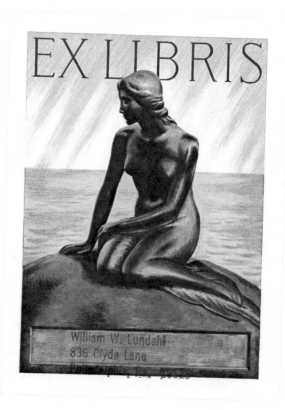

EX LIBRIS

William W. Lundahl
836 Clyde Lane

MANAGING THE SMALL BUSINESS

Managing the Small Business

JOHN B. KLINE, J.D.
University of Colorado

DONALD P. STEGALL, D.B.A.
University of Colorado

LAWRENCE L. STEINMETZ, Ph.D.
President
High Yield Management, Inc.

THIRD EDITION • 1982

RICHARD D. IRWIN, INC.
Homewood, Illinois 60430

ISBN 0-256-02508-8

Library of Congress Catalog Card No. 81–84889

Printed in the United States of America

1 2 3 4 5 6 7 8 9 0 MP 9 8 7 6 5 4 3 2

Preface

A number of new textbooks on small business management have been written and published in the past few years. The majority of these have appeared since the revised edition of *Managing the Small Business* was published in 1976.

It is apparent that a number of authors and publishers feel that the small business area is growing and needs the benefit of additional resource materials. We agree with this philosophy and have attempted to revise this edition so that it will better serve the needs of students for the 1980s.

In the present revision, we have attempted to maintain the strong points of the previous editions and to strengthen those areas that were deficient. In this effort, a number of individuals have contributed suggestions and comments and a number of students have indicated their feelings about text coverage, problems, and questions.

Even though some extensive changes have been made in the manuscript, it is our opinion that the task of operating a small business now is not a great deal different from the task it was at the time we wrote the first edition. Each functional activity—such as marketing, finance, accounting, and management—is essentially the same, though some of the techniques and procedures have changed. Our efforts have been to maintain a strong basic operational format and supplement this with updated knowledge and reference data.

A number of changes have been made from the previous editions:

1. A chapter on *Franchising* has been added to reflect the growing importance of this form of business activity, and in particular, its relationship to small business.
2. A series of cases has been included to be used in connection with the chapter material and to supplement the questions and short problems.
3. Some basic changes have been made in writing style, explanations, and the general level of word usage.
4. An effort has been made to remove redundant material that appeared in previous editions.
5. A selected list of Canadian reference materials has been added as Appendix B.

We are indebted to a number of individuals who gave us help and assistance with the cases, editorial work, typing, and manuscript preparation. Those who are deserving of special mention are Martin Schmidt, Linda Gerwig, and Nanci McCutcheon at the University of Colorado and Nadene Fournier and Daniel Graham at Dalhousie University in Halifax, Nova Scotia. In addition, there are many individuals across the country whose small business operations provided ideas and inspirations that in one way or another have become a part of this text.

Consistent with our desire to present the best possible treatment of small business management, any and all comments, criticisms, suggestions, and reactions of those who study and use this third edition are solicited and will be sincerely appreciated.

John B. Kline
Donald P. Stegall
Lawrence L. Steinmetz

Contents

organization. Factors affecting choice of legal form. Summary guidelines for selection of legal form. Follow-up action and details.

Kinds of laws, statutes, and administrative regulations that affect small businesses. Examples of administrative agencies. Kinds of administrative agency coverage at state levels. How administrative agencies investigate and control small businesses. The right to challenge administrative action. Control of the business via licenses, permits, franchises, and certificates. Legislative overkill in small business controls. The Uniform Commercial Code and how it affects and controls small businesses. Control of small business by means of leases, franchises, and license agreements. How small business transactions with the public are controlled. Laws governing advertising and pricing. Laws governing relationships with employees. Regulation of competition, products, and credit. Taxation—personal and business.

Advantages of operating a small business. Shortcomings of operating a small business. Constraints on operating a small business. Determining whether you are ready to start a business.

Developing the information base. Framework of opportunities. Buyer's and seller's goals. Paths to ownership. Summary—motives of buyers and sellers. Buying an existing business. Selling a business.

Preparing and using a prospectus. Making up the prospectus. Proposing a new versus an existing business. The pretesting process. Sequence and format of the prospectus. The bargaining and selling process.

CASE STUDY: Why I think I can make a go of opening a skin-diving shop, 116

Development of franchising. The scope of franchise operations. Starting and operating as a franchisee. The franchisor in the franchise relationship. State and federal laws regarding franchising. Future of franchising.

CASE STUDY: Norman Smith's second career, 131

Key factors in location selection. Advertising. Building images.

CASE STUDY: The Yellowstone Angler, 157

1

The role of small business managers

Since the days of the early settlements on the Eastern seaboard of North America, the American economy has felt the impact of a never-ending variety of small business operators. Most of the individual businesses that were started had a short life, many less than a single year; others prospered and continued a successful life over a span of several decades. Some of these businesses were started and operated to fill a distinct and apparent need for an essential feature of daily life; such as a bag of flour or a ferry ride across a sizable river. Such choices were relatively easy and required very little detailed or astute analysis to determine their possible success. Others were much more complicated and difficult.

During the development of North America, the advent of the Industrial Revolution substantially changed the employment options of many persons within the work force. Large firms employed many people, but small businesses were created and operated as a parallel to industrial and agricultural employment.

A further development was the increasing activity of that unique—or at least somewhat different—type of person known as the entrepreneur. Many attempts have been made to define the criteria that identify the entrepreneur, but such descriptions by no means exactly determine who is or is not that person. Nevertheless, the entrepreneur is generally recognized as being a person who generates action, detects opportunities, and identifies them as the basis for new forms of enterprise. Innovation is applied in ways not previously considered. Technology is used to establish new frontiers in business operations and techniques. Each of these is an example of some of the ways in which the entrepreneur will develop and capitalize on ideas. It is probably fair to say that entrepreneurs have somewhat greater talents than the average small business person and tend to involve themselves with activities that have broader horizons relating to growth, size, and ultimate power over business operations.

The early American entrepreneurs were just as essential and just as vital to the economy as they are now. Starting in Revolutionary times, they provided the stimulus for capital investments in trading companies, development of western lands, and canal and railroad companies. They have been an important factor in economic development ever since.

Most small business persons have a dream of ultimate success and the rewards of financial well-being, respect, power, and perhaps fame. Many people dream of the ultimate success that comes from operating a small business; therefore, we should consider the reasons that people start small businesses and the difficulties they encounter in starting and operating their own enterprises.

WHY START A BUSINESS?

Fortunately for those who try to "make it on their own," the larger segment of the population has an aversion to risk. They prefer the security and comfort of working for someone else. The regular paychecks, paid vacations, seniority and job security, and a good program of fringe benefits are too inviting.

But every so often an individual comes along who turns a deaf ear to security. What are the reasons for doing so? Are some reasons better than others? Instead of asking why start a small business, might it be more appropriate to ask why not?[1]

It appears the most successful small businesses are started by those who simply are unhappy with their present standard of living and desire to make more money. The dollar is a powerful stimulus to those bent on the better things in life. So it seems that those who want to make money try harder.

---

[1]Some of the ideas expressed in this section were based on comments made by Gordon B. Baty in *Entrepreneurship, Playing to Win* (Reston, Va.: Reston Publishing, 1974), chap. 1.

The second best chance for success appears to rest with those who desire to reap the benefits of their professional competency directly instead of selling it to an employer. They realize the value of their ideas and wish to gain professional recognition by accepting full responsibility for their development.

Beyond the desire to make money or to exploit one's professional competency, other reasons for going into business are far less likely to generate success. They include the following:

1.   The desire to be one's own boss; to work when one wants to work; to look up to nobody.
2.   The self-made objective that it is necessary to succeed in entrepreneurship to "prove" one's abilities.
3.   A social consciousness that compels one to do something for science, or technology, or society, or whatever the cause.
4.   An involvement because of real or imagined talents outside one's present job or profession.
5.   A vindictive attitude, expressed in the desire to "give it to the competition."

Of course, in reality, human motives are mixed. In any particular case, the reason for selecting entrepreneurship as a way of life will be some combination of justifications—any of those cited above and any based on the individual's unique background, training, or experience. But in the final analysis the question is whether the reason or reasons justify the costs, sacrifices, and risks of being on your own.

The premise of this book is that the central objective of the small business venture is to make money for the owner-manager-entrepreneur. All else should be secondary, regardless of the motive. To the extent the owner-manager seeks to accomplish a variety of objectives, energies are diluted. If the firm does not survive, no objective is fulfilled. Thus, all efforts should be directed to keeping the firm alive, and that means making money.

This is not to say there is something inconsistent with proving one's abilities and making money; or doing something for society and making money; or creating competition and making money. It is simply a matter of recognizing that only those ventures that profit will make any lasting contributions to society, technology, or the competitive system.

WHY NOT START A BUSINESS?

For those with the talent and ambition to become successful entrepreneurs, the Why? should be complemented with Why not?; i.e., Why not start a small business? From this point of view, the reasons reflect the advantages of entrepreneurship.

1. At no time and in no place has the climate for new small business been so good. Venture capital is more plentiful today than at any time in the past, and things keep getting better. Commercial banks, investment bankers, commercial finance companies, and others have become increasingly aware of the essence of capitalism reflected in entrepreneurship.

2. People tend to overestimate the difficulties and problems in starting a new business. Given some minimum level of talent, the more important ingredients are initiative and drive, particularly in view of the professional services available at reasonable cost, on either a part-time or full-time basis. Inventors, consultants, lawyers, and vendors are ready and waiting to help design, manufacture, and package a product to the entrepreneur's specifications.

3. The American economy, like no other, provides distribution channels to accommodate virtually any type of product. Commission representatives, distributors, wholesalers, and jobbers of every description stand ready to service the entrepreneur in almost any conceivable distribution effort.

4. There are vast numbers of skilled, competent individuals in the economy's labor force waiting for "the right move." To the extent the entrepreneur needs help, it can be bought. In today's world it is not unethical even to buy the competition's talent. No stigma is attached to changing jobs. That segment of the labor force with talent and expertise is more mobile than ever. It is not uncommon for professionals to join a small business for part ownership instead of cash, an arrangement that can be to the advantage of both parties.

5. Government is becoming increasingly helpful to small business. The federal Small Business Administration not only represents a potential source of funds, but also provides a wealth of information and assistance in its regional offices across the nation. At the regional and local levels, various development authorities and small business investment corporations offer assistance. The tax structures are also designed to provide incentives to the small business.

6. Finally, the personal and professional risks of entrepreneurship are usually overestimated. Leaving the security of being an employee and investing some amount of capital in a small business is not an irreversible position. In a complete failure, the entrepreneur loses his or her investment and has to find another job. But the experience has undoubtedly been of great personal and professional value. This is not to say that risk-taking does not involve a cost. But most things worth doing at all involve risk.

In summation, it seems many people with ability fail to take that first step into entrepreneurship because they have overestimated the hazards and underestimated the potential advantages. Furthermore, small business failures can be traced to a number of basic causes that can be avoided with a little foresight.

Tote Board High-Profit Race Track				
Odds	Race results	Win	Place	Show
1. 30:1 6. —	1st (8) Entrepreneur	96.00	42.00	12.00
2. 16:1 7. 8:1	2nd (3) Corporate manager		14.00	6.90
3. 4:1 8. 30:1	3rd (9) Real estate investor			4.20
4. 60:1 9. 3:2				
5. 20:1 10. 10:1				

WHO ARE THE ENTREPRENEURS?

The words *entrepreneur* or *entrepreneurship* appear repeatedly in the foregoing section. We have taken for granted that entrepreneurs are those who start businesses: this is generally conceded to be true, but entrepreneurs do much more. The important point is that there is a considerable difference between merely operating a business, as opposed to applying an endless variety of special talents and ideas to the total assortment of circumstances associated with smaller business.

In general, some of the traits of the typical entrepreneur are the following:

1. A strong belief in one's own ability to surmount all obstacles and get the job done.
2. A willingness to accept considerable risk if the odds are right.
3. A restless striving for the bigger or more ambitious result. The minimal, low-level operation is of little interest.
4. A driving tenacity to overcome the usual and less than unusual difficulties.
5. A shrewd sense of timing and the ability to respond to necessary and critical time factors.
6. An inherent restlessness to explore, improve, modify or discard, and start over; i.e., being unwilling to accept stability in a business operation.
7. The strong desire to control one's own fate regardless of the risk or ultimate chances of success or failure.

The foregoing listing is by no means a complete analysis of the entrepreneur, but rather is shown to indicate some of the basic traits possessed by such individuals. The important fact is to recognize that entrepreneurs are an important part of the small business scene and are responsible for a substantial number of those enterprise activities that turn out successfully.

It is important to recognize the difference between being an entrepreneur and just an operator of a business. Entrepreneurs generally have talents that can be applied in a variety of ways to a number of different business operations. In contrast to this, many people who are operating smaller businesses are lacking the ability and scope of knowledge and understanding that successful business management requires. This is the case when operating the smaller, rather traditional type of enterprise as well as operating the larger and more complex enterprises. The entrepreneur, moreover, will generally have the breadth of knowledge and ambition that permits the creation of enterprises that are difficult and complex but ultimately can have a very substantial success. In this regard success might be profit, growth, market share, etc.

SMALL BUSINESS FAILURES

In contrast to the special talents and abilities that give entrepreneurs a better than average chance of success, we find that many newly formed small businesses will fail. Since the late 1960s Dun & Bradstreet have reported for the United States a fairly steady rate of business failures, somewhere in the neighborhood of 10,000 firms per year. Furthermore, they show that the failure rate will include over 50 percent of the representative businesses in the first five years of their existence.

Year after year the record on business failures shows that in 9 out of 10 cases, the cause of failure is managerial inexperience or ineptitude. Among the major problems that plagued the bankrupt firms, insufficient sales generally headed the list, followed by competitive weakness, problems with receivables, or poor credit management.

Unfortunately, the general attitude of many entrepreneurs is that extra cash is the answer to almost every problem. The evidence shows, however, that if a company has everything but good management, it may prosper for a while but it is doomed to eventual failure. On the other hand if the firm's strongest asset is management, it will succeed one way or another.

Businesses that fail, both large and small, seem to repeat the same management errors. Thus, one of the best ways for the entrepreneur to learn management skills is by studying the mistakes of others. Bank of

America's *Small Business Reporter* publication entitled "Avoiding Management Pitfalls" cites the following eight areas of management incompetency that generally lead to small business failure.

Downgrading the need for experience

Most small businesses are founded on the abilities of one person: the owner-manager. If this individual lacks the necessary skills and versatility to either perform or supervise the tasks of finance, accounting, marketing, production, personnel work, and other aspects of management, the venture is destined for failure.

In the new firm, the best remedy for lack of experience is adequate training prior to entrepreneurship and the acquisition of people that add the necessary elements to the abilities of the management team. In the going concern the owner-manager must detect the missing parts of his/her experience and close those gaps with knowledgeable employees, partners, business consultants or counselors, and possibly an emergency self-development program.

Poor record-keeping

Poor financial records create problems in every facet of the small business, yet the need for a good accounting system is frequently overlooked. A study of 10 unsuccessful small businesses showed all had accounting systems so imprecise that the state of the business remained unknown even to the owners. In contrast, a similar study of 10 successful ventures revealed complete accounting systems and well-informed managers who knew how to use the financial date in running the company.

Although a knowledgeable accountant can set up an effective system and keep it going, the entrepreneur must understand the financial information derived from the system and be able to use it in decision making.

Poor cash management

The failure to maintain a stable and adequate financial position is a serious management error. A cash-poor firm has little or no bargaining position, and must waste a good deal of time struggling to appease creditors.

The nearsighted entrepreneur often allows capital to reach dangerously low levels. Bills cannot be paid with machines, or inventory, or accounts receivable; nor can these assets provide funds in an emergency.

In the new firm the problem is one of undercapitalization—simply not putting enough capital into the venture to get started properly. In the going concern, on the other hand, too much capital can get tied up in fixed assets, slow-paying receivables, or obsolete inventory if growth is not properly controlled.

In dealing with the cash flow problem the entrepreneur should consult with the accountant as well as with the banker. After studying the firm's records and financial statements these advisers can suggest ways to control costs and conserve cash. Furthermore, the manager should ask the accountant for instructions in proper budgeting and money management techniques to accomplish cost and cash control.

Failure to plan

Professional business consultants generally agree that one of the most frequent causes of small business failure they observe is the lack of planning. The rapidly changing marketplace of today demands forward-looking strategies. Well-formulated plans permit the entrepreneur to take better advantage of opportunities as they arise and head off management difficulties before they become too serious.

Planning is not simply thinking ahead. It involves the establishment of objectives and determination of methods for reaching the objectives. Without these elements the entrepreneur is merely indulging in wishful thinking, not planning.

Misuse of time

The typical entrepreneur has too much to do in too little time. A normal work week may average 50 to 60 hours. Experience shows that in many cases owner-managers spend as much as half their time on trivial matters, and leave vital jobs undone.

Good management of time requires learning to control the job rather than letting the job control the person. The objective is to work smarter, not harder. Proper management of time is a matter of self-discipline. Effective managers put first things first; they rank duties according to importance.

A critical aspect of time management involves delegating appropriate jobs to subordinates to free the entrepreneur from the routine, operational duties. A manager who fails to delegate properly can become so involved with everyday activities that important jobs, like planning, are often rushed. A further problem is the perfectionist, who rationalizes reluctance to delegate by claiming the employees are incompetent. Such persons are afflicted with the "I can do it better and faster myself" malady.

Inattention to marketing

Sales is the secret to success in any business venture. The best of products, personnel, and physical plant is of little use without customers. Unfortunately, some entrepreneurs have the false impression that their products or services will sell themselves. They dislike the thought that the product or service must be marketed.

The truth is, few things sell themselves. An organized and vigorous marketing program is essential to build customer awareness. Some view poor sales as an isolated problem rather than as a symptom of an inadequate marketing effort. In such cases, the entrepreneur attempts to stimulate sales through price cutting, aggressive sales tactics, or advertising gimmicks. But these short-run measures will not work unless the solution fits the specific marketing problem. Reduced prices are not a substitute for a poor location, and advertising will not sell an obsolete product.

An objective analysis of the firm's products or services, its present marketing effort, the competitive situation, and the genuine needs of customers will show the ways to solve sales problems.

Ignoring the human factor

Many entrepreneurs encounter serious personnel problems. They complain about poor workership, absenteeism, long coffee breaks, and the failure of employees to follow directions. Experience shows that malcontent workers not only waste time and materials but also tend to drive away customers. Some 70 percent of all customer losses can be attributed to poor service and employee indifference.

Most employee difficulties result from poor personnel administration. Too many entrepreneurs spend all their time worrying about production, sales, and finance and solve personnel problems on a crisis basis. A loyal and efficient work force can be built only if adequate attention is given to the hiring, training, and managing of employees.

Failure to assume the proper role

The success or failure of any business venture depends on the quality of management. The same capital, materials, and machinery that produce profits for one may generate losses for another.

The skills and talents required to be a good manager change as the company changes. The managerial know-how necessary to run a one-man operation in the early years is much different from the needs of a growing firm 5 or 10 years down the line.

As the firm grows to new stages of development the entrepreneur must adapt his/her role to the changing situation. The transition from operator to manager to executive must be smooth. If the entrepreneur sticks with the comfortable, familiar jobs, organizational growth and personal growth are both slowed.

SUMMING UP

This rather brief introduction to small business management should provide a means of starting to think about the obstacles that face those who start and operate small businesses.

These initial thoughts might best be focussed on identifying and learning about the three following topics.

1. The necessary operational aspects of a small business.
2. The contributions of the manager and/or owner (most often the same person) to the success of the enterprise.
3. The causes of business failure.

Much of the following text will be concerned with the various aspects of point 1 in the foregoing list. In conjunction with point 2 we will be showing and describing the efforts of management and in particular, our favorite person, the true entrepreneur. And finally, the root causes of failure will be examined and assessed in proportion to their risk factors or impact on the business operations of the entrepreneur.

We will attempt to devote an appropriate amount of space and consideration to the functions that we feel are most important in small business firms. Remember at all times: this is a book on small business management. The capable entrepreneur is a strong manager; while his/her style may be unique and methods unorthodox, there is no doubt that managerial talent is the reason for success.

Those who ignore the standards of good business practice and operate on the basis of trial and error are destined to fail. They go from crisis to crisis, always struggling with the same basic problems.

QUESTIONS

1. Which of the motives for becoming an entrepreneur seems to produce the most success? What is the second most successful motive?

2. What are the distinct advantages of entrepreneurship as you see them?

3. Year after year, what is the most common reason for small business failure?

4. Would you agree with the statement that if the entrepreneur can make it through the first five years, chances for success improve?

5. Although many entrepreneurs have the general attitude that extra cash will cure all ills, what is the real key to success in small business?

6. Discuss briefly each of the eight most common pitfalls endangering success in small business.

PROBLEMS

1. Examine, by interview if possible, three or four very successful small businesses in your community. Identify the factors in each case that appear to contribute to the firm's success.

2. Try to get some idea of the small business failure problem in your community. Attempt to examine some recent failures and identify the underlying causes as you see them.

3. Go to the nearest library that represents a government documents depository and survey the materials published by the Small Business Administration on small business failures and factors contributing to success in small business.

4. Read your local newspaper and look for an article or legal announcement pertaining to a small business failure. Follow-up and interview someone who can describe to you the reasons for the failure.

BIBLIOGRAPHY

Baty, Gordon B.   *Entrepreneurship: Playing to Win.* Reston, Va.: Reston Publishing, 1974. This book is an excellent treatise on entrepreneurship. It is required reading for anyone who aspires to operating his own business venture.

Bylinsky, Gene.   *The Innovation Millionaires.* New York: Charles Scribner's Sons, 1976. A fascinating series of short chapters that review the career and developmental efforts of outstanding entrepreneurs. Each person who is reviewed in this book is a source of inspiration for anyone who would like to think and dream about the chances of possible business success.

Klatt, Lawrence A.   *Managing the Dynamic Small Business Firm: Readings.* Belmont, Calif.: Wadsworth Publishing, 1971. Another winner. This book is a collection of articles that provide sound advice to the entrepreneur. It is highly recommended.

Vesper, Karl H. *New Venture Strategies.* Englewood Cliffs, N.J.: Prentice-Hall, 1980. This book should be read by every person who aspires to starting and/or running a business. The role and importance of the true entrepreneur are developed from a variety of positions and viewpoints.

2

Sponsors and sources of help for small business

The world of small business operation and management is often a very lonely existence, even though there are about 11 million small businesses. When one is small, and especially if located in a remote community, one may have the company of others but not much of anyone to turn to for help.

Fortunately for the small business entrepreneurs and managers there are agencies, companies, financiers, and advisers who do make it their business to help small business operators. This help may take the form of financial assistance or advice about sales, advertising, accounting, merchandising, or other activities. Many supporters expect adequate return for their efforts, but expect that the small business will be equally benefited in the process. Others help because small business is a part of the economic system and deserves its share of the available expertise. Others are benevolent in their efforts and derive personal satisfaction in helping others to succeed.

Support for small businesses tends to develop from the following kinds of sources:

1. U.S. Small Business Administration.
2. Minority enterprise agencies and associations.

3. Small business investment companies.
4. Venture capital firms.
5. Franchisors.
6. Trade associations.
7. Bureaus of business research.
8. Economic development associations.
9. Commercial banks.
10. A variety of federal, state, and local governmental agencies.
11. Colleges and universities.
12. Consulting firms.
13. Manufacturers interested in their dealers and distributors of their products.

SMALL BUSINESS ADMINISTRATION

The Small Business Administration (SBA), which is now a permanent agency of the U.S. government, has been in existence since 1953. During this period of nearly 30 years, the SBA has engaged in a wide range of activities. Because the SBA is an important factor in small business activity, the more important agency activities are summarized under a number of categories following this introduction.

For the purpose of making loans and providing financial assistance to small businesses the SBA specifies business size which in general does not exceed the following criteria:

1. Wholesale—Annual receipts up to $9.5 million, depending on the industry.
2. Retail or service—Annual receipts from $2 million to $8 million, depending on the industry.
3. Construction—Annual receipts of not more than $9.5 million, averaged over a three-year period.
4. Manufacturing—From 250 to 500 employees, depending on the industry.[1]

The prospective entrepreneur or owner must realize that the above listings are a means of establishing operating and maximum sizes for types of direct loans and *do not* limit assistance through other methods such as participation loans or guaranteed loans through banks or other agencies.

---

[1] *Federal Register Vol.* 46, no. 7 (January 12, 1981): 19–21. These size limitations and the forms of SBA assistance are, without doubt, in revision at the time of this writing. The reader is encouraged to check the latest SBA information for an absolutely accurate source of information.

FORMS OF SBA ASSISTANCE

The SBA provides many kinds of assistance to operators of small businesses. These include the following:

Financial assistance

Businesses needing financial assistance can contact an SBA office for advice. The agency may help in providing information to enable the individual or company to secure a conventional loan. If this seems unlikely, SBA may consider a participation loan with a bank or guaranteeing a bank loan up to 90 percent. A direct loan might be made if funds are available, but most SBA loans are made in cooperation with banks. The funds obtained can be used for construction, expansion of the business, acquiring machinery, equipment, supplies, and materials, and for use as working capital.

Under the loan guarantee plan, the SBA can guarantee up to 90 percent of the bank loan or $350,000 (whichever is less) at an interest rate set by the bank, within limits set by the SBA. These limits vary from time to time.

Economic opportunity loans

The SBA extends economic opportunity loans to disadvantaged business men or women to enable them to own their own businesses. These loans are made available only to families whose income is too small to finance a business and to whom conventional financing is not available because of social or economic disadvantages. Each applicant must prove some ability and is expected to have some money or other available assets.

State and local SBA development companies

State and local SBA development companies are formed to promote business within a state. Through these companies loans are made available, ordinarily equalling loans obtained from other sources. Such loans are underwritten by local people who put up money to finance community development.

Disaster loans

The SBA also lends money to persons who have suffered losses resulting from disasters such as storms, floods, hurricanes, volcanic eruptions, and earthquakes. It also offers loans to alleviate hardships brought on by urban renewal and compliance with new legislation. Because disaster loans are so variable, no details can be given here. The loan may be handled by the SBA but be dependent on action by some other federal agency. A presidential proclamation or action by a presidential cabinet secretary may authorize loans to assist the recovery of businesses that have suffered a disaster.

Lease guarantee program

Under the lease guarantee program the SBA will insure a lease obtained by a business person who otherwise lacks the credit rating necessary to qualify for a lease on more desirable premises. Special conditions are involved in this program, but the SBA has made many such guarantees and the program should be investigated by the business operator who needs a good or improved location.

Procurement assistance

The SBA is charged with the responsibility of making sure that small businesses participate in certain federal government contracts. Often the contract is written with a specific "set-aside," which must be filled by some small business. Often these set-asides are subcontracts let by the prime contractor to the smaller business. There are a number of activities associated with the procurement assistance program which help the smaller business: meetings and seminars are held to inform firms how to bid; efforts are also made to inform small firms of pending contracts and to sell surplus property to small businesses.

Management assistance

A number of different programs have been devised by the SBA to provide direct management assistance to small businesses. In training programs SBA conducts courses, conferences, problem clinics, and workshops. The courses are set up to help formulate policies, identify objectives, and help guide the organization of other functional activity useful in any business. Conferences deal with particular and specific topics, whereas clinics are concerned with various types of problem solving. Workshops also concentrate on problems and problem solving.

SCORE

The Service Corps Of Retired Executives (SCORE) is made up of ex-business executives who offer their services to help small business operators. A SCORE participant visits the entrepreneur, spends some time with him/her, and makes some suggestions based on the executive's background of experience and knowledge.

The SCORE group are not paid consultants, nor do they recommend engaging any specific firms to implement their suggestions. They may, however, suggest that certain help be obtained, which may include the services of a professional consultant such as a CPA, lawyer, arbitrator, or negotiator.

MINORITY ENTERPRISE AGENCIES AND ASSOCIATIONS

Minority business enterprise

The federal government is placing increased emphasis on ownership of businesses by members of minorities. Growing dedication to helping minority groups is a part of an effort to improve the economic position of all minorities, in particular by enabling them to assume an expanded position in the areas of business activity.

Toward accomplishing this goal, several aid programs have been initiated, and some direct funding of business enterprises has been tried. A Task Force on Education and Training for Minority Business Enterprise published the following findings:

1. There is an alarmingly high failure rate of minority-owned business-es. This failure rate is attributed primarily to poor management and business skills of the owners and managers of these enterprises.
2. There is a chronic shortage of trained minority talent available to

meet the pressing need for owners, managers, and business techni-
cians in the growing number of new and expanding minority
business firms.

3. Management and business skills are critical elements in the survival
    and successful growth of minority business enterprises.

4. Education and training programs designed to provide needed
    management and business skills must become an integral part of the
    national strategy to expand minority business ownership.

5. Entrepreneurship as a career opportunity for minority youth is
    given inadequate attention within the existing educational system.

6. There is a wide range of existing national, state, and local resources
    that can be enlisted to support or conduct minority business
    enterprise education and training programs for existing, potential
    and future entrepreneurs.

The task force further stated that at the time of publication of their
report no single federal agency had the ultimate responsibility for
minority business education and training development. It stressed
further that the need is urgent and that steps should be taken without
delay to correct the existing deficiencies.

Tables 2–1 and 2–2 illustrate the employment and income patterns of
minority persons today and what might be expected up through 1990. It
can be seen that minority groups family incomes are very low in
comparison to the average family income in the United States.

Office of minority business enterprise

The federal government provides most of the technical assistance to
minority groups through the Office of Minority Business Enterprise
(OMBE). These efforts are primarily devoted to such things as local
business development organizations, business resource centers, trade
associations, and other joint programs with state and local government
agencies. Their activities include the counseling of minority business
persons, packaging of loan applications, and providing management
and technical assistance to minority firms. In spite of these efforts much
more is needed, and it seems reasonable that the programs of OMBE
will continue to provide help.

Limited SBICs

Limited SBICs are small business investment companies that specialize in providing equity loans, long-term loans, and management assistance to small business concerns owned by socially or economically
disadvantaged persons. To qualify for this assistance, a business must
be at least 50 percent owned and managed by individuals from disadvantaged groups.

Figure 2–1
Labor force and participation rates, 1960–1975, and projections to 1990, by race, sex, and age

	Total labor force (millions)						Participation rates (percentage)					
	1960	1965	1970	1975	1980	1990	1960	1965	1970	1975	1980	1990
Total	72.1	77.2	85.9	94.8	104.0	116.6	59.2	58.8	60.3	61.0	62.0	63.5
White	64.2	68.6	76.4	83.9	n.a.	n.a.	58.8	58.5	60.2	61.1	n.a.	n.a.
Male	44.1	45.9	48.8	51.6	n.a.	n.a.	82.6	80.4	79.7	78.1	n.a.	n.a.
Female	20.1	22.8	27.5	32.3	n.a.	n.a.	36.0	37.7	42.0	45.4	n.a.	n.a.
Negro and other races	7.9	8.6	9.5	10.9	n.a.	n.a.	63.0	62.1	61.1	58.7	n.a.	n.a.
Male	4.8	5.1	5.5	6.1	n.a.	n.a.	80.1	77.4	74.7	70.3	n.a.	n.a.
Female	3.1	3.5	4.0	4.8	n.a.	n.a.	47.2	48.1	48.9	48.7	n.a.	n.a.
Male	48.9	50.9	54.3	57.7	62.1	67.3	82.4	80.1	79.2	77.2	77.4	76.7
16–19 years	3.2	3.8	4.4	5.1	5.2	4.3	58.6	55.7	57.5	60.2	62.0	62.6
16 and 17 years	1.3	1.6	1.8	2.1	2.1	1.6	45.9	44.1	46.7	48.5	50.4	50.7
18 and 19 years	1.8	2.3	2.6	3.1	3.1	2.7	73.1	68.3	68.8	72.0	73.1	73.1
20–24 years	4.9	5.9	7.4	8.2	8.9	7.5	88.9	86.2	85.1	84.5	84.5	82.7
25–34 years	10.9	10.7	12.0	14.5	16.9	19.1	96.4	96.0	95.0	94.1	94.3	93.7
35–44 years	11.5	11.5	10.8	10.6	11.9	16.9	96.4	96.2	95.7	94.9	94.7	94.0
45–54 years	9.6	10.1	10.5	10.5	9.9	10.9	94.3	94.3	92.9	91.9	90.5	89.3
55–64 years	6.4	6.8	7.1	7.0	7.3	6.7	85.2	83.2	81.5	74.7	73.8	69.2
65 years and over	2.4	2.1	2.2	1.9	1.9	1.9	32.2	26.9	25.8	20.8	19.4	16.2
Female	23.2	26.2	31.6	37.1	41.8	49.3	37.1	38.8	42.8	45.8	47.9	51.4
16–19 years	2.1	2.5	3.3	4.1	4.2	3.7	39.1	37.7	43.7	49.0	51.3	54.9
16 and 17 years	.8	1.0	1.3	1.7	1.7	1.4	28.6	27.5	34.6	39.9	42.4	46.4
18 and 19 years	1.3	1.6	1.9	2.4	2.5	2.2	51.0	48.6	53.4	58.0	59.7	62.3
20–24 years	2.6	3.4	4.9	6.1	7.0	6.7	46.1	49.7	57.5	64.0	67.5	74.7
25–34 years	4.2	4.3	5.7	8.5	10.6	13.6	35.8	38.5	44.8	54.4	58.4	66.0
35–44 years	5.3	5.7	6.0	6.5	7.6	11.8	43.1	45.9	50.9	55.7	58.1	63.4
45–54 years	5.2	5.7	6.5	6.7	6.6	7.8	49.3	50.5	54.0	54.3	56.3	59.9
55–64 years	3.0	3.6	4.2	4.2	4.6	4.5	36.7	40.6	42.5	40.7	41.6	42.2
65 years and over	1.0	1.0	1.1	1.0	12.1	1.3	10.5	9.5	9.2	7.8	7.7	7.2

n.a. = Not available.
Source: U.S. Bureau of Labor Statistics, Special Labor Force Reports.

Figure 2–2
Weekly earnings of full-time wage and salary workers in 1975 dollars, 1970–1975

	1970	1972	1973	1974	1975
All workers	$130	$144	$159	$169	$185
Male.	151	168	188	204	221
16–24 years.	112	119	136	146	149
25 years and over	160	178	203	219	235
Female	94	106	116	124	137
16–24 years.	88	96	103	111	117
25 years and over	96	110	121	131	146
White	134	149	162	173	190
Male	157	172	193	209	225
Female	95	108	117	125	138
Negro and other races.	99	115	129	140	156
Male	113	129	149	160	173
Female	81	99	107	117	130
Occupation					
Professional and technical	181	192	212	228	246
Managers, administrators	190	214	238	250	274
Sales workers.	133	151	163	172	189
Clerical workers	109	121	130	140	150
Craft and foremen.	157	172	195	211	223
Operatives.	115	126	140	150	164
Operatives, except transport	n.a.	119	132	141	157
Transport equipment operatives . . .	n.a.	152	169	180	198
Nonfarm laborers	110	123	138	149	154
Private household workers	38	40	39	50	54
Other service workers	87	104	111	117	123
Farm workers.	71	80	96	107	111

n.a. = Not available
Source: U.S. Bureau of Labor Statistics, Special Labor Force Report, no. 143, Usual Weekly Earnings of American Workers, 1971, and unpublished data.

Amendments to the Small Business Investment Act of 1972 increased the potential operating conditions for the limited SBICs. By the end of 1972 there were 53 licensed limited SBICs, with private capitalization of $18.4 million. So far the effort is limited in terms of potential minority business effort. Progress, however, is being made and undoubtedly will continue.

SMALL BUSINESS INVESTMENT COMPANIES

One form of venture capital investment firm is the small business investment company (SBIC). This form was generated by the Small

Business Investment Act of 1958, and as of 1974 there were about 700 licensed companies. Of these, about 450 are active and include not only companies with small groups of local investors but also firms that are quite large and publicly traded. About 80 of the total are owned by commercial banks.

An SBIC may invest up to 20 percent of its capital in a single small business, based on the original minimum private investment of at least $150,000. If the firm specializes in venture capital financing and is capitalized at more than $500,000, it may quality for SBA-direct or SBA-guaranteed loans aggregating up to $20 million.

The loans made by these firms are usually in excess of $75,000 and financing must be made for at least a five-year period. Many of the investments have been made in companies that are engaged in scientific or technological development and innovations.

The SBICs are permitted to make long-term loans, purchase stock in the company, acquire debt securities, or combine equity and loan financing. Companies which wish to obtain loans cannot have assets over $7.5 million, net worth of $2.5 million, or annual profits (two-year average) of over $250,000.

As is apparent from the foregoing, SBICs are sources of financing for the larger small business. The SBICs are also interested in companies which have a definite growth potential, not the firm that is in a conventional industry or business with a stablized business activity. Some proven track record, with an established profit pattern and growth potential, is usually necessary before an SBIC will consider a loan to an enterprise. Many experts on small business matters feel that SBICs do not really help the true small business, such as the start-up business.

VENTURE CAPITAL FIRMS

The term *venture capital* has been used in discussing SBIC activity in the previous section. The indication is that those firms are venture capital sources and do provide capital under somewhat more risky circumstances than conventional financiers do.

There are, however, many other venture capital firms, or private groups, that do provide help to the new or growing small firm. As explained previously, venture capital is nearly always placed in a business situation that represents short-term stability and substantial long-term growth potential.

Entrepreneurs, prospective business operators, and promoters of suitable firms and potential business propositions should not overlook venture capital sources. These may only exist locally, or they may have to be discovered by the entrepreneur. In a sense, substantial investors in a newly formed corporation are venture capitalists, but they invest only if the odds are right.

A newly formed business, or one to be expanded, can be used to solicit support. Depending on the nature of the idea or proposed activity, the venture capitalist will base a decision to back a firm on the elements of risk versus the potential of payoff. Venture capitalists do take sizable risks, but not without commensurate possibilities of substantial rewards. They are considered to be very expensive sources of funds for small business operators by many people who are knowledgeable in small business finance.

In securing aid for small business from the venture capitalist, the owners and operators must make sure they do not relinquish too much for the support received. Combinations of high interest rates, a share of the profits, having seats on the board of directors, and take over agreements are all a part of the bargaining used by venture capitalists. The reason that an entrepreneur or owner wants to have their own business must not be conceded to the venture capital firm as a condition of getting into or furthering the business.

Bankers, SBIC managers, and others in financing institutions are all potential sources who can suggest possible venture capital sources. Smart owners of small businesses do not, however, turn quickly to venture capital firms as a source of financing.

FRANCHISING

The subject of franchising is included here because, if properly administered, franchising can be a solid basis on which a business can be started. This is notwithstanding the fact that franchising is under considerable attack for practices that are not in the best interests of the franchisee. Chapter 8 covers franchising more thoroughly.

It is important to recognize that the principles on which franchises are based are fundamentally sound. Growth in the past 25 years is substantial testimony to the fact that the franchise industry has been a growth industry and in the period of rapid growth and expansion it developed many opportunities which were exploited by the franchisees. The franchisor provides to the franchisee the knowledge of the business in accounting standards and performance, merchandising, and product or service quality. In addition, they add expertise and economies of scale in purchasing, promotion and advertising, financing, and other elements necessary to a streamlined, efficient program. The franchisee provides cash flow to the parent organization, investment of money into the franchise, and works hard as the boss in making the business a success. With these inputs from both sides the franchise is supposed to be an unbeatable combination.

Franchising has failed in many instances for several reasons. These can be summarized for both sides as follows:

Where franchisors fail

1. Selling franchises only, with little thought given to the actual businesses to be created. Often a fraudulent practice which has been difficult to control.
2. Too rapid an expansion of franchised outlets in order to generate cash from franchise sales. This left many franchises with very little guidance and direction.
3. Saddling the franchisee with too restrictive a set of operating controls and conditions. These are often stringent and abusive and defeat the teamwork needed for success.
4. A lack of follow-through once the franchise is established.

Where franchisees fail

1. Assuming that the franchise system itself will make up for a lack of business training and managerial ability.
2. A blind belief in numbers and multipliers. Many franchisees have believed facts and figures which were encouraging but—unfortunately—inflated.
3. A failure to seek competent legal and business advice regarding the franchise agreement and its operating conditions.
4. A lack of understanding of the nature of business and what is required for success, such as an understanding of basic cost accounting, budgeting, and adjustment to fluctuating cash flows.

Based on what has been said, why even consider that a franchise is a supporting element for small business? The answer is that a great many small businesses are now being conducted in a successful manner under the franchise system. Reputable and ethical franchisors such as McDonald's hamburgers, Ben Franklin variety stores, and True Value hardware stores are examples of firm names that support a large number of franchisees who for the most part are satisfied with the franchise conditions. Firms such as these, and others, go to great lengths to make sure that their franchisees succeed. They know that they make money only if their retail and service outlets succeed. Otherwise, profits and reputations go downhill.

TRADE ASSOCIATIONS

Nearly every segment of small business activity is a part of some identifiable related business activity. These might be hardware stores, variety stores, retail sporting goods stores, food wholesalers, florists, and many, many others. Most of these identified groups are represented by trade associations, which in turn may have an assortment of helpful materials for their membership.

Quite often the association publishes a newsletter or monthly magazine, such as *Selling Sporting Goods, Tack 'N Togs Merchandising,* and *Professional Carwashing Magazine.* These tend to run heavily to advertising, but at the same time do contain feature articles and information from the constituent membership that is useful to the operating manager or owners. Some associations have training programs and educational materials, but in general their published materials tend to run heavily to pragmatic how-to-do-it materials. In addition, meetings, workshops, and other get-togethers are used to disseminate ideas and workable examples to the membership.

The principal value of the trade association and its efforts would be to expose the entrepreneurs to the kinds of owners and managers that represent the industry and the manner and methods that are used by these people in operating their businesses.

In running a business a prospective small business owner should take advantage of the appropriate trade association for the business and its efforts. Initially the dues may seem to be more than one can afford, but in all probability the benefits from the membership are well worth the cost.

There are so many trade associations that it is impossible to give space to even a few of them within this chapter. The entrepreneur or manager should consult a directory of trade associations to find out which ones to join. The best such sources would be found through the American Society of Association Executives' publication on *Who's Who in Association Management* or the book *National Trade and Professional Associations of the United States and Canada.*

BUREAUS OF BUSINESS RESEARCH

Bureaus of business research are found in many states, often at universities. The research materials developed by bureaus of business research are quite often ideal for the small business owner or operator. Many reports and studies are generated on a regional or industry basis without regard for direct economic benefit to the bureau. In addition, the majority of publications are by law or policy available to the public if they are state funded. The cost is often very low, a fraction of what would be charged by a private agency. In addition, specific questions will often be answered if the knowledge has application to a group, rather than a single business. As an example, the Bureau of Business

Research at the University of Colorado publishes a *Directory of Manufacturers in Colorado*. This has been sold to the public in recent years at a nominal price and provides a source of company names, principal executives, and number of employees. No other publication duplicates it in the State of Colorado. It is invaluable as a reference and mailing list and has a steady sale each year.

Again, as in the case of trade associations, it is impossible to enumerate the listing of these business bureaus. An interested entrepreneur or manager should write to the nearest bureau of business research and ask for the list of available publications on state economic activity. It is also a good place to inquire about the possibility of special studies which would be useful and which might be financed by federal or state agencies or a particular trade association.

ECONOMIC DEVELOPMENT ASSOCIATIONS

This category of helpful supporters of small businesses includes a mixed bag of organizations. These may be land development companies that are building and promoting industrial parks, railroad land development companies that wish to develop plant sites, and perhaps municipally financed industrial development districts, promoted by the local community or county.

A wide range of possibilities exist through these development associations. They provide useful building or operating sites, building and lease-back of factories, warehouses, etc., and in some cases arrangements for financing and employee help.

These kinds of associations are well-enough established and available on a broad-enough scale that they warrant investigation by a new or perhaps established entrepreneur or owner. The average person is usually unaware of the extent to which these associations exist and the kinds of help they provide.

In Colorado, the Colorado Economic Development Association is one of the largest, best known, and most successful organizations primarily devoted to the cause of minority business people. Other associations throughout the United States are also working in behalf of certain types of businesses or groups of individuals. The prospective small business person should find out if an economic development firm or association has services available to help the business venture. If such an opportunity exists, it is very likely that the total services available through the association will include guidance, counseling, and management assistance. What is available probably goes much farther than what is provided by many other supporting organizations.

COMMERCIAL BANKS

A number of the larger commercial banks, particularly those which have a number of branches, are engaged in certain programs for the smaller business. The best known of these is the *Small Business Reporter*, a publication series of the Bank of America in San Francisco, California. The *Reporter* is divided into "Business Profiles," which relate to particular kinds of business; "Business Operations," which analyze functional segments of a business; and "Professional Management," devoted to the professions.

The publication of the *Small Business Reporter* series are made available from time to time and can be obtained on a subscription or single order basis.

Other banks and banking chains publish information or newsletters which are helpful in preparing the business man or woman who is seeking loans. They also deal with subjects such as accounting statements, budgeting, and general management topics. The newsletter and bulletin materials are more general in nature but are often free and provide a good economic analysis of business activity and results in selected areas of business such as agriculture, retail sales, manufacturing, and the tourist industries.

Some banks even offer free seminars and educational programs for their clients. Picking a bank should involve consideration of the *nonfinancial* help that one might obtain from the bank, as well as the loan assistance the bank gives.

FEDERAL, STATE, AND LOCAL GOVERNMENT AGENCIES

As mentioned early in this chapter, there are many sources of help and information which are provided by federal, state, and local governmental agencies. In addition, there are private organizations which are specifically operated for business ventures on a smaller scale.

It is not possible to review and analyze even a small portion of these organizations within the scope of this chapter, but their existence and services should be investigated by anyone who might use their help. Typical of some of these organizations are state departments of commerce and industry or industrial development. Municipalities have local development commissions and chambers of commerce. At the federal level, cabinet-level organizations publish a great deal of material relating to the business operations that are affected by their activities and actions.

In the past several years much has been done in the area of help and guidance for minority groups. Speical agencies can be found which are

Figure 2–3
Banks provide useful data for their customers

EMPLOYMENT PROFILES OF EACH STATE

Analysis of this chart shows the economic compositions of the labor force in each state. In this way, an accurate picture of the economic forces at work within each state emerges for use in your planning.

You will note, for instance, that 13% of Wyoming's labor force is employed in mining— nearly double the percentage of any other mountain state. 5% of Nevada's workers find jobs in manufacturing — ¼ the rate for the Rocky Mountain Region as a whole.

Colorado's employment composition is diverse but with heaviest emphasis on manufacturing, trades, and services.

PERCENT DISTRIBUTION OF TOTAL EMPLOYMENT IN EACH STATE: 1970 – 1971

	Colorado		Arizona		Idaho		Montana		Nevada		New Mexico		Utah		Wyoming		Total Mountain States	
	1970	1971	1970	1971	1970	1971	1970	1971	1970	1971	1970	1971	1970	1971	1970	1971	1970	1971
CONSTRUCTION	7.0%	7.6%	8.5%	9.3%	6.2%	6.2%	5.8%	6.0%	11.8%	10.9%	8.3%	8.5%	5.8%	6.0%	7.3%	7.6%	7.6%	7.9%
FINANCE, INSURANCE, REAL ESTATE	7.3	7.3	7.3	7.6	5.5	5.5	6.1	6.3	5.0	5.2	6.1	6.2	6.2	6.4	5.3	5.1	6.6	6.7
MANUFACTURING	21.2	20.3	21.2	19.2	25.9	25.6	17.4	17.0	5.3	5.3	11.4	10.8	21.3	20.7	9.9	9.7	18.6	17.8
MINING	2.6	2.4	4.2	4.4	2.1	1.9	4.2	4.1	2.4	2.2	8.1	7.9	5.1	5.0	14.6	13.2	4.3	4.2
MISCELLANEOUS NON-MANUFACTURING	1.4	1.5	2.0	1.9	1.9	2.1	1.7	1.7	1.4	1.4	1.4	1.7	1.5	1.4	2.1	1.9	1.6	1.7
RETAIL TRADE	23.2	23.2	23.4	23.6	24.8	24.5	27.5	27.4	19.6	19.6	25.8	26.1	23.3	23.5	26.9	27.2	23.8	23.8
SERVICES	21.8	22.4	21.5	22.2	18.0	18.8	21.9	22.2	43.4	44.1	24.9	25.0	21.0	21.8	18.9	19.9	23.3	23.9
TRANSPORTATION AND PUBLIC UTILITIES	7.6	7.4	5.5	5.6	6.6	6.7	7.9	7.8	7.0	7.1	7.9	7.7	7.1	6.9	9.3	9.3	7.0	7.0
WHOLESALE TRADE	7.9	7.9	6.4	6.2	9.0	8.7	7.5	7.5	4.1	4.2	6.1	6.1	8.7	8.3	5.7	6.1	7.2	7.0
TOTAL	100.0	100.0	100.0	100.0	100.0	100.0	100.0	100.0	100.0	100.0	100.0	100.0	100.0	100.0	100.0	100.0	100.0	100.0

This table provides a comparison among the eight states and a comparison of employment categories within each state. In six of the eight states, manufacturing, retail trade and services are the three largest employment sectors. From 1970 to 1971, the number of jobs in Colorado increased by 3 percent. Construction, service industries and retail trade were the most rapidly growing employment sectors in Colorado in 1971.

Source: *Jobs/Colorado* (Denver: Colorado National Bank).

helpful and which can often provide direct financial help to the smaller business. These are in addition to the better-known activities referred to earlier in this chapter.

COLLEGES AND UNIVERSITIES

Numerous college and university programs around the country are being conducted for the benefit of owners and operators of smaller and rapidly growing businesses. Many educational institutions have specific training seminars designed for people interested in buying and selling smaller businesses, managing smaller and rapidly growing retail and manufacturing firms, supervisory courses in managing small business-es, and even such esoteric subjects as pricing strategies for small manufacturing firms.

Small business management seemingly is the backbone of the economy of the United States, and because of that there is much interest by colleges and universities who feel that they have a mandate to provide education to the needs of the public. It should not be thought, however,

Figure 2–4
Statewide business activity shows small business vitality (Idaho, 1975)

NEW DEVELOPMENT REVIEW

BOISE: The J. R. Simplot Company is negotiating with officials of the Soviet Union for the sale of a potato processing plant to be located in Russia . . . Ground breaking ceremonies took place in January for a $12.5 million addition to St. Luke's Hospital . . . A second Keystone Pizza opened at 4091 W. State . . . Bank of Idaho will build a new 4,240 sq. ft. branch on Bogus Basin Road . . . Safeway has opened a new 25,000 sq. ft. store at the Cole Village Shopping Center . . . Continental Air Conditioning, distributor of the Carrier Line, will open a 10,000 sq. ft. warehouse and branch office . . . Topping out ceremonies were held at One Capitol Center, Idaho's tallest building . . . C. Anthony opened a new 12,000 sq. ft. store at Cole and Ustick Roads . . . Smiths' Food King announced opening its fourth store at Boise, a 27,000 sq. ft. structure at Overland and Cole Roads . . . Morrison-Knudsen is constructing a 75,000 sq. ft. office building to house its engineering and mining staffs.

CALDWELL: A new family restaurant, Fiesta Time Cafe, has opened at 114 S. 7th . . . Mr. C's, specializing in floor coverings, is a new retail facility at Kimball and Arthur Streets.

COTTONWOOD: The Cottonwood Saleyard, owned by Urban "Shorty" J. Arnzen, serves Idaho livestock men between Council on the south to St. Marie on the north, as well as some from southeastern Washington state.

It takes four full-time employees and 18 part-time employees to service the average 250 stockmen and buyers at each weekly sale.

Sales volume for the Cottonwood enterprise exceeds $500,000 on large sales. In 1973, a total yearly volume was in excess of $12 million.

This livestock auction yard has been in operation since 1943 and previously it was a shipping point on the railroad to Camas Prairie.

DUBOIS: Construction has begun on a new courthouse.

IDAHO FALLS: DeMott Tractor Company moved into its new 16,000 sq. ft. facility . . . A new Shakey's Pizza Parlor is completed at 475 E. Elva . . . Spencer Opal Mines has opened the Opal House at 685 N. Gatemile, specializing in Idaho opals . . . A new $120,000 Country Kitchen Restaurant is now in operation.

MERIDIAN: Bob and Denise Casper opened Bob's Sew and Vac Center . . . Dana Welker established Beyond Repair, a ski equipment sales and repair shop.

MOSCOW: The Orogrande Lodge of Orogrande, Idaho is now owned by the Orogrande Company of Moscow. Purchase price was $250,000. The lodge will provide year-round recreation services and plans are under way for an additional 30 units.

MURTAUGH: The A. E. Staley Manufacturing Company has its potato starch plant in operation.

OROFINO: Orofino Industries, Inc. is open and manufacturing sport coats.

POCATELLO: Idaho's first Ernst Home Center is scheduled to open in March. The 44,000 sq. ft. home improvement center will carry more than 45,000 items geared for the do-it-yourselfer . . . $200,000 has been made available to a seven county southeastern Idaho area to hire unemployed persons in·local government under the Comprehensive Employment Training Act . . . Howard Carlson has opened Carl's Steak House . . . Dellart Floral moved to its new location at Third and Center . . . Checker Auto Parts at 655 Yellowstone is a new business . . . Hilton Inn will build a new 15-unit motel on a 14-acre site on Pocatello Creek Road.

POST FALLS: Clare-Pendar has been awarded a contract by Western Electric Company to construct a new line of modern telephone operator push-button switches.

PRIEST LAKE: Mrs. Jane A. Rea has founded Jarae's of Idaho, a shop specializing in all kinds of crafts and do-it-yourself projects . . . The Northern Light Craft Company, opened by Brian Conley, features handmade items by local artists.

REXBURG: A new 24,180 sq. ft. Safeway store is now open for business.

RUPERT: Three units of the planned nine unit Minidoka Medical Clinic have been completed.

Figure 2–4 *(concluded)*

SALMON: Cook's Silver Spur, specializing in sports equipment, is in its new $50,000 facility . . . A 12-unit, $185,000 apartment complex has been completed.

SANDPOINT: Mr. and Mrs. Bill Greenwood have opened Greenwood Sales and Service, an appliance store.

Source: *Idaho Image,* January–February 1975; Idaho Division of Tourism and Industrial Development, Boise, Idaho.

that public educational institutions are the only ones interested in problems of small business management. Many private universities have specialized programs designed for those who are interested in entrepreneurial jobs.

CONSULTING FIRMS

Because of the number of owner/managers of small businesses in the United States who have problems in operating their businesses successfully, many consulting firms have evolved who have the particular interest of the management problems of small businesses. These firms not only concern themselves with the traditional, people management problems, but they also concern themselves with marketing, finance, accounting, purchasing, salesmanship, and other managerial problems of managing the small business.

The Yellow Pages of the telephone directory in practically any major city in the United States lists consulting firms that specialize in offering consulting services to operaters of small businesses.

MANUFACTURERS INTERESTED IN THE DEALERS AND DISTRIBUTORS OF THEIR PRODUCTS

One final source which should be mentioned to those interested in owning and managing small businesses is that help and a lot of valuable—and free—advice is available from or through manufacturers and suppliers to operators of small businesses.

This help is offered because manufacturers and suppliers of products and services that are bought by the owners and managers of small businesses often want their customers to be financially solvent. This is not predicated upon some altruistic feeling, but because of a very simple, self-serving motivation. If indeed a manufacturer of, say, dried foods wants to sell the company's products through sporting goods stores, it is to the advantage of that manufacturer to have customers—i.e., sporting goods store owner/managers—to be able to pay for the merchandise bought from the dried foods manufacturer. Therefore the manufacturer of the dried foods is motivated to provide educational help along the lines of how to successfully manage the smaller sporting goods business. Often the manufacturers provide this help at conventions, retreats, shows, and other places where their customers (in this case, the sporting goods retailers) congregate.

Indeed, some professional speakers, trainers, and educators in the United States live virtually on fees from manufacturers who hire them to train and educate their retail customers.

This form of help for small business is not limited solely to retailers, but is more commonly found as a service manufacturers provide to their retail customers than in any other area of small business management. But virtually any large business which supplies small businesses is motivated to provide managerial help to their customers, and many do so willingly.

QUESTIONS

1. Enumerate the various forms of support available for people who want to run small businesses.

2. For purposes of an SBA loan, what is the annual sales or receipts size specified by the SBA for wholesalers? Retail or service industry? Construction industry? Manufacturing industry?

3. What is an economic opportunity loan?

4. Why should disaster loans be classed as a form of support given to the small business owner/manager by the Small Business Administration?

5. What is SCORE? Explain.

6. What is a limited SBIC? Explain.

7. What is a venture capital firm? Why does your text say that this might not be the most desirable source of help for an owner/manager of a small business? Explain.

8. What is the usual reason for franchisors to fail?

9. When franchisees fail, what are the common reasons? Explain.

10. How do manufacturers who are interested in their dealers and distributors often provide help to owner/managers of small business? Explain in detail.

PROBLEMS

1. Put together a proposal for a small business and develop in detail what source of sponsorship you might use to bankroll and otherwise get started in your small business. Make sure to develop in detail that information which you would feel it necessary to present to a person or organization whom you appealed to for help in starting your business.

2. Develop a prepared statement which you would want to give to a franchisor indicating why you feel as a prospective franchisee a

business which you propose is likely not to fail. Develop detailed information as to why you feel that your proposed franchise operation will be a success.

BIBLIOGRAPHY

Baumback, Clifford M. and Joseph R. Mancuso. *Entrepreneurship and Venture Managment.* Englewood Cliffs, N.J.: Prentice-Hall, 1975. A readings book with limited text comments. Valuable as a framework reference book which follows the stages of the business through start-up, growth, stability, and decline.

Connellan, Thomas K. *How to Grow People into Self-Starters.* Ann Arbor, Mich.: The Achievement Institute, 1980. A book designed primarily to emphasize how someone can realize support and help someone's personnel while trying to run a small business.

Klug, John R. *The Basic Book of Business.* Boston: CBI Publishing, 1977. This book is written for the individual wanting to start and operate a small- to medium-sized business (particularly one under 500 employees). It is not a textbook but a book of applications designed only for one purpose: to help the business get going.

Mancuso, Joseph R. *How to Start, Finance, and Manage Your Own Small Business.* Englewood Cliffs, N.J.: Prentice-Hall, 1978. This book covers everything from raising capital and preparing an effective business plan to profit disbursement and even the issuance of public stock. Very good for understanding who might help sponsor your small business.

3

The appropriate form of ownership

Every business activity is conducted within a legal framework. It might be a partnership or corporate form created to accomplish a limited purpose or a broad range of objectives. If no action is taken by the business operators to create a specific legal form, then the law recognizes that a proprietorship or some form of partnership exists.

THE INFORMATION BASE—FACTS AND JUDGMENTS

In selecting the best legal form, the prospective entrepreneurs should consider the following factors.

1. Ownership—How many owners will there be? Will their ownership be equal?
2. Management—Will the owners also manage the firm?
3. Financing—How much money is needed to start or purchase the business and what sources might provide it?
4. Liability—Is it desirable to separate the assets of the business from the personal assets of the business owners?
5. Incentives—Will the business be able to provide the incentive

33

necessary to attract the managerial talent needed for growth and success?

6. Taxation—What legal form will minimize the total tax load imposed on the business?
7. Retention of income—Which form will provide the maximum income?
8. Protection—Will the asset values developed in the business over time be preserved if key persons become unavailable because of illness or death?

A COMPARISON OF LEGAL STRUCTURES—PROPRIETORSHIPS, PARTNERSHIPS, AND CORPORATIONS

SOLE PROPRIETORSHIP

Advantages

1. *Easily created and terminated.* The sole proprietorship can be brought into existence without many formalities and is easily terminated.
2. *Direct, undiluted action.* The ownership, control, and management are vested in one person.
3. *All rewards to owner.* The owner works for himself or herself and determines his or her own destiny.
4. *Flexibility.* The owner is free to adopt change readily.
5. *Minimum regulation and taxation.* A proprietorship is generally free from control.

Disadvantages

1. *Unlimited liability.* The owners must be prepared to satisfy business debts with their own personal assets if the business is unable to meet its obligations.
2. *Capital limitations.* Equity capital is limited to the assets of the owner. This can be a serious restriction on growth and expansion.
3. *Perils of the individual.* If the owner dies or becomes seriously ill, the business is immediately jeopardized.

GENERAL PARTNERSHIP

Advantages

1. *Pooling of resources.* The partnership is useful in bringing together two or more persons who as a group have more business potential than as individuals. Ideas, managerial talent, money, and fixed assets are frequently combined to produce a successful business.

"Oh yes, I like the car fine—but what else does he have I might want?"

2. *Ability to obtain capital.* The combined financial resources of all the partners stand behind the negotiations for business borrowing.
3. *Simplicity and incentive.* Each partner is motivated by knowing that the success of the partnership is in part due to his or her own efforts. This encourages the partners to place the success of the business above their own self-interest.
4. *Limited regulation and taxation.* A partnership, much like a proprietorship, is subjected to a minimum amount of regulation, and the partners are taxed on their own individual incomes.

Disadvantages

1. *Unlimited liability.* All the partners are liable for the actions of each other.
2. *Tenuous existence.* The partnership is subject to many eventualities that may terminate or disrupt its operation. It may be terminated by the death, insanity, or incapacity of a partner. Furthermore, serious disagreements may be insoluble.
3. *Independence on management harmony and coordination.* The equality of

the partners is simple in theory but sometimes more difficult in practice. Partners may not agree on certain matters, or division of work assignments may prove awkward.

4. *Problems in share liquidation.* A partner's share is not easily disposed of except by agreement with the other partners. Attempting to dispose of a share to an outsider without proper valuation can be a problem.

CORPORATION

Advantages

1. *Limited liability.* The liability of a stockholder in a corporation is limited to the amount invested in the stock.
2. *Legal entity.* The corporation is a legal entity. It may own property, is not affected by the death or withdrawal of its stockholders, and is entitled to due process and equal protection under the Fourteenth Amendment of the Constitution.
3. *Ready transferability of ownership.* The shares of stock can be sold or transferred at will.
4. *Obtaining capital.* Forming a new corporation with a salable idea can provide opportunities to sell stock to a variety of investors. Later, a corporation that has achieved some stability can usually bargain more effectively for a substantial amount of capital than either a proprietorship or partnership.
5. *Employee benefits.* The corporation has a better chance to create incentives for employees. Stock ownership, bonuses, pension plans, insurance programs, and other fringe benefits and the tax advantages that accompany such programs are more easily provided by the corporate form of organization.

Disadvantages

1. *Legal formality and cost.* Creating a corporation may require considerable time, effort, and expense. In addition, the corporation is subject to considerably more control and more exacting compliance with regulations than the proprietorship or partnership.
2. *Doing business in other states.* Before a corporation can transact business in another state, it will ordinarily have to file a copy of its charter with that state. In addition, it will probably have to designate an agent to represent it in the event it is sued in that state.
3. *Possible division of ownership and management.* Through stock sale, the majority ownership of the corporation may be divided among absentees. The board of directors may wisely control management, or through apathy or neglect may allow the business to be managed by those who are ineffective or lacking in motivation.

4. *Protection of minority interests.* One or more stockholders holding the majority of stock will control the corporation. Minority stockholders are without recourse against the group except in cases of unlawful acts.

OTHER LEGAL FORMS OF BUSINESS ORGANIZATION

The three forms of business organization discussed above are those most commonly used by the small business person. Other legal forms may be used from time to time and are discussed below.

Limited partnership

As the name implies, the limited partnership is a partnership with certain limitations. In most respects the limited partnership is very similar to the general partnership, but it provides an opportunity for one or more partners to be designated as special or limited partners. The purpose of the limitation is to permit certain partners to invest in the business and to be given the protection of limited liability to the extent of their investment. Such protection, however, is available only if the limited partner does not take an active part in the management.

Joint venture

The joint venture is a form of partnership that is created for the express purpose of bringing together several individuals to engage in a business activity that is very specialized and exists for a limited, specific purpose. For example, a joint venture may be formed for the purpose of producing a play, engaging in oil exploration, or constructing a major project such as a dam or airfield. The joint venture operates very much as a partnership, although a number of states have limited the acts of the various participants and their ability to bind each other.

The business trust

A business trust is a form of legal organization in which a trustee manages the business through a trust relationship. The business is controlled by the trustee, who operates it for the benefit of those who have transferred their property for this purpose. The ownership of the principals is represented by trust certificates, which entitle these people to participate in the profits of the operation.

Subchapter S corporations

A business may elect to be classified as a corporation but be taxed as a partnership. In this way the advantages of limited liability can be achieved, but the burden of double taxation can be avoided.

This election is possible only if certain conditions are met. Generally, the business must be a domestic corporation, have only one class of stock outstanding, and have 25 or fewer shareholders.

FACTORS AFFECTING CHOICE OF LEGAL FORM

Prospective business operators make most decisions that affect the internal operations of their business according to their own wishes. In many areas of operations this is permissible, but in selecting the legal form, it is more difficult. There are many conditions from outside the business that are important and may cause the prospective entrepreneurs to change their choice of legal form.

1. *Initial capital and financing plans.* Few businesses are financed entirely from internal sources. Both equity capital and conventional loan sources are usually needed and will impose restrictions to protect their interests. Thus, financial investment interests may force a change of legal form.
2. *Changing benefits and obligations of owner-managers.* Prior to the final selection of a legal form the business owners should consider their future life together. Attempts should be made to look ahead and anticipate how and in what manner the personal destiny of each member of the group will be affected by a particular legal form. At this point the legal structure and its effect on the prospective owners is reassessed through serious and thoughtful discussions.
3. *Taxation and government regulations.* Small business owners are generally aware of the impact of government on their business in a general sort of way. The initial choice of legal form may not be influenced greatly by problems included under this category. But before long, taxation and regulations become more important. Owners begin to search for relief, possibly through a change in legal form.
4. *Exploitation.* People, time, money, and products can all be exploited under the right circumstances, and a variation in legal form may be useful for this purpose. Incentive ownership, franchises, market position, and many other operating techniques will often convince the management of a need for a different legal form for their operation.
5. *Growth, expansion, merger, and sale.* Any of these factors may demand a shift to another legal form. In fact, a change is often mandatory to achieve the full value of the proposed course of action.

SUMMARY GUIDELINES FOR SELECTION OF LEGAL FORM

Sole proprietorships

1. Easily formed—few legal requirements.
2. A minimum of special operating requirements—usually very little more than for the individual.
3. No limitation on personal liability.
4. Ownership or partial interests can be eaily transferred.
5. Capital acquisition depends on the personal ability of owner. All assets—personal and business—are one and the same.
6. The business is terminated at the death of the owner.
7. Proprietor and the business taxed as a single entity.

General partnerships

1. Easily formed with little required formality. A partnership agreement is recommended to safeguard individual interests.
2. Characterized by the "concerted action" of all partners. This applies to all activities as well as ultimate dissolution.
3. All partners have unlimited liability.
4. Capital acquisitions depend on the combined financial standing of the partners.
5. Death of any partner brings dissolution.
6. Each partner taxed on their individual income.

Limited partnerships

1. Should have a formal agreement indicating the role of both general and limited partners.
2. Limited partners must not assume a management role in the business; otherwise they may be held to be general partners. Limited partners are investors only.
3. Continuity and liability of the general partners are the same as for general partnerships. Limited partners' activities are separate and do not change an otherwise general partnership.
4. No special tax liabilities.

Corporations

1. Require formal processes of formation and operation. Start-up costs probably begin at around $300.
2. Provides easily divisible ownership, limited liability and continuity of existence—all of benefit to entrepreneurs.
3. The only viable form if substantial equity financing is needed. Very attractive to use in exploiting unknown opportunities.
4. Corporate taxation imposed along with subsequent tax on stock-

holders' income. Not always bad, but usually not a desirable condition.

5. Advantage of Sub chapter S are available anytime corporate status is contemplated by a small business venture.

Joint ventures and trusts

These legal forms are not used nearly as often as the previous ones outlined. Consult with an attorney if special requirements indicate their possible use.

FOLLOW-UP ACTION AND DETAILS

It is not possible in a textbook of this kind to explain all the various operating provisions of the legal forms available. Any prospective entrepreneur who plans to start a small business should review the Uniform Commercial Code, the Uniform Partnership Act, and the Model Business Corporate Act.

The services of a competent attorney—who understands the objectives of the proposed firm and the needs and intentions of its participants—are required whenever business relationships are being created. This should not be just *any attorney*, but rather an individual who can provide the answers that give the participants insight into what may happen under varying sets of circumstances.

The operational features of the three major legal forms are briefly compared in Table 3–1. This table summarizes the conditions that prevail in most jurisdictions but should be used only to get a quick feel for the differences among the three forms. Details and specific requirements must be established for each business within its home state and in any other state where it operates.

SUMMARY

The legal status chosen is one of the most significant steps in the ultimate success of a business. The selection of the best legal form depends on the ability of the entrepreneurs to understand the advantages and disadvantages of the various forms from the standpoint of both the business owners and those who support it from the outside.

The process of investigation and evaluation is related to the future. The correctness of the selection of the legal form can be judged only over a period of time. If the owners analyze, choose, and implement their choice wisely, the enterprise will have a strong framework to support the operations that follow.

Table 3–1
Legal form comparison summary

	Proprietorship	Partnership	Corporation
Creating the business	Simple acts of any business activity. May require a business license.	By acts of doing business or written formal agreement and business license.	Requires formal process and filing of documents.
Ownership	Sole control.	By agreement, or equally among each partner.	By amount of stock ownership.
Duration of existence	Lifetime of owner.	For duration of partners' lives. Partners may be replaced and substituted.	Continuous, in compliance with law of state incorporation.
Business names	A Christian name, or filing a *doing business as* (dba) statement.	Christian names or filing a *doing business as* statement.	Registration required of the trade name and trade marks.
Fees required	No standard fees. May require a *retailer's* or similar license, or personal certification.	No formal fees. May require a license and registration for out-of-county or state operations.	Fees for registration and stock issued. Fees and registration for out-of-state operations.
Annual requirements	Renewal of licenses and registrations.	Renewal of license and registrations.	Annual reports and franchise taxes, as to all states of registration.
Taxation	Based on taxable income generated in each state for state taxes. Federal tax on net total income.	Taxable income by states for state-generated income. Federal tax on each partner's taxable income.	Corporation tax on state-generated income. Federal and state taxes on shareholders' salary and dividend income.
Termination of business	At will of proprietor—no formality.	No particular formality. Partners should publicize termination to avoid further liability.	Should be terminated by formal declaration. Shareholders' rights are protected until formal "winding-up" is accomplished.

Note: Individual states may vary the circumstances of ownership.

QUESTIONS

1. How are the interests of management and outsiders treated when the legal form of a business is being considered?

2. How can the successful operation of a business be converted to capital gains?

3. How can the legal form of business affect the success with which employers capitalize on employee talent and performance?

4. What legal form would be most useful in providing incentives for employees who are in the managerial group?

5. Considering the many potential difficulties associated with a partnership, why are so many businesses started and operated as partnerships?

6. What are the potential dangers that threaten a proprietorship from a management and ownership standpoint?

7. How is a partnership able to increase its bargaining power for capital as compared to the opportunities available to a proprietorship?

8. What particular caution must be exercised by a limited partner in a limited partnership?

9. What things are of such importance to a partnership that they should be recorded in some minimum form of written agreement?

10. *a.* What might be the consequence of management's not complying with the legal formalities required by state incorporation laws?

    b. What rights would stockholders and creditors have if legal formalities were not complied with?

PROBLEMS

1. Obtain a copy of the Uniform Partnership Act and read it carefully. Analyze in particular Part IV, "Relations of Partners to One Another."

    Answer the following questions, which involve circumstances that are covered by the act in one or more sections:

    a. What obligations are assumed by a partner who joins an existing partnership?

      b.   How is it possible to determine what benefit is due a partner who has carried on personal activities in addition to partnership activities?

      c.   Why is it particularly important to distinguish between partnership investment and partnership loans made by one or more partners?

      d.   What action might be taken by the beneficiary of a deceased partner to insure that the partnership interest is fully realized?

2. Purchase a copy of the *Tax Guide for Small Business* issued yearly by the Internal Revenue Service of the U.S. Treasury Department. Review carefully chapter 1, sections 1, 2, 3, and 4. Observe that these sections are primarily provided to assist the taxpayer in properly meeting his income tax liability.

    Examine carefully the provisions that apply to each of the legal forms in regard to the following:

      a.   How income is determined for an individual within each of the three legal structures.

      b.   What determines the way in which various items are valued and what establishes the basis for a given interest.

      c.   Gains or losses arising from transactions outside the normal business operations of the enterprise.

      d.   The determination of values assigned to an individual at the time a business is divided, liquidated, changed to a different legal form, or changed in some significant way.

BIBLIOGRAPHY

Baumback, Clifford M., and Kenneth Lawyer. *How to Organize and Operate a Small Business.* 6th ed. Englewood Cliffs, N.J.: Prentice-Hall, 1979, chap. 9.

Frantz, Forrest H. *Successful Small Business Management.* Englewood Cliffs, N.J.: Prentice-Hall, 1978, chap. 2.

Moreau, James F. *Effective Small Business Management.* Chicago: Rand McNally College Publishing, 1980, chap. 3.

Redinbaugh, Larry D., and Clyde W. Neu. *Small Business Management.* St. Paul, Minn.: West Publishing, 1980, chap. 4.

4

Laws, regulations, and taxes affecting small business

Wherever a business is operated it will be subject to an assortment of legal restrictions and controls. In the United States the federal government exercises control through its power to regulate those activities that are "federal in character." The most prominent of these is the control exercised over interstate commerce. Control of interstate commerce extends to a wide variety of activities, such as transportation, radio and television broadcasting, product shipments across the state lines, and other forms of business that in some way are interstate in character. Other business activity is also specifically controlled at the federal level, but is of lesser importance to the average independent entrepreneur.

At each level of government, a mixed pattern of laws, regulations, controls, and taxation is applied to all forms of business. Controls continue at state levels, then by counties, and ultimately within the smallest political unit, usually a municipality. Considerable inquiry and investigation of the applicable laws is mandatory if an enterprise is to be operated successfully.

KINDS OF LAWS, STATUTES, AND ADMINISTRATIVE REGULATIONS THAT AFFECT SMALL BUSINESSES

The legal framework controlling business is based on federal, state, county, and municipal laws, statutes, and administrative actions.

Laws are based on the old English common law or updated versions adopted since the colonial days of the 1700s. Laws may thus be based on the precedent of the various case decisions making up the common law, or on statutes enacted by the U.S. Congress or state legislatures.

Statutes are laws that are the result of formal action by a properly constituted governmental body. Characteristically, many federal and state laws, including much of the common law, will be codified and included within the U.S. Code or the official statutes of the various states.

Administrative regulations are issued by administrative agencies at federal and state levels. These agencies are created by legislative action, and operating within the statutes that created them, they administer and control business by issuing rules, regulations, and directives. As lawfully established extensions of the more formal legal bodies, they can exercise a wide range of control over particular segments of business activity.

EXAMPLES OF ADMINISTRATIVE AGENCIES

A number of well-known federal agencies govern business activity. The following are typical administrative agencies; the area of interstate commerce that each agency controls is briefly indicated.

Securities and Exchange Commission. Regulation of the creation and sale of securities used to finance business enterprises. Very exacting controls are imposed in an effort to prevent fraudulent activity.

Interstate Commerce Commission. Regulation of railroads and trucking; including rates, equipment standards, safety, and many other aspects of surface transport.

National Labor Relations Board. Jurisdiction over wages, hours, and conditions of work, and the rights of workers to engage in collective bargaining.

Many other federal agencies affect the operation of certain businesses. Anyone contemplating the operation of a business will need legal advice regarding the effects of federal government regulations on that particular business.

KINDS OF ADMINISTRATIVE AGENCY COVERAGE AT STATE LEVELS

Administrative regulation and control is far more extensive at state levels than at the federal level. The following is a partial list of the typical kind of agencies that govern at state levels. (The list includes agencies existing in the state of Colorado.)

Division of Air Pollution Control (Department of Health)
Bond and Securities Division (Department of Treasury)
Coal Mine Inspection Division (Department of Natural Resources)
Colorado Land Use Commission (Executive Branch)
Division of Employment (Department of Labor and Employment)
Division of Water Resources (Administered by the state engineer)
Department of Health
Industrial Commission of Colorado (Department of Labor and Employment)
Public Utility Commission
Sales Tax Division (Department of Revenue)
Unemployment Compensation (Department of Labor and Employment)
Water Pollution Control Commission (Department of Natural Resources)
Workers' Compensation Claims (Department of Labor)

Agencies at state level govern a wide variety of businesses and also control the qualifications of persons who engage in certain business activity. The following *partial listing* of occupational categories from the state of Colorado is again typical of the control exercised by state administrative agencies.

Abstractors	Cosmetologists	Physical therapists
Accountants	Detectives	Plumbers
Architects	Electricians	Practical nurses
Attorneys	Insurance brokers	Professional sanitarians
Bankers	Land surveyors	Real estate salespersons
Barbers	Nursing home attendants	and brokers
Cemetery workers	Outdoor advertisers	Shorthand reporters
Chiropractors	Pesticide applicators	Theatrical agents

Regulation at the county and municipal levels is very similar to that applied at state levels. Typical areas of coverage are building codes, land use and zoning, public health and safety, taxation, licensing and franchising certain kinds of business, and a wide variety of other activities that are similar in scope.

HOW ADMINISTRATIVE AGENCIES INVESTIGATE AND CONTROL SMALL BUSINESSES

Administrative bodies, through their various officials, will conduct investigations and hearings. Some of these will involve an actual issue or complaint that has been brought by an individual or business. In other cases the investigation will be instituted at the option of the administrator and will be done for the purpose of investigating a particular practice or issue. It is interesting to note that various court actions brought against administrative bodies through the years have tended to confirm a pattern of rather broad powers on the part of these agencies. As an example, outside of actions conducted by the National Labor Relations Board, administrative agencies can solicit expert testimony without the necessity of abiding by the strict rules of courtroom procedure.

If a particular business is affected by some direct action on the part of an administrative agency, the owner is entitled to notice of hearing and an opportunity to appear and present his/her views properly. If, on the other hand, a particular business owner's company is merely one of a *class of business* that is being investigated, the owner may not be given the opportunity to present that company's case, although some hearings are frequently quite broad in scope. Most administrative bodies desire a good cross section of opinion and want to avoid the criticism that they have taken action on incomplete information or lack of sufficient testimony by interested parties.

THE RIGHT TO CHALLENGE ADMINISTRATIVE ACTION

There are two primary areas in which administrative action has been challenged. The first of these occurs when legislation sets up the agency and prescribes the duties and particular specific regulations for which the agency will be responsible. The agency may be challenged at this time because the law lacks clarity and definiteness so that a particular business or business person does not know exactly what rules and regulations must be followed. Such vagueness has been particularly troublesome in the qualification of certain professional and semiprofessional people. Occasionally it is the indirect aim of a state legislature to restrict entrance into a given activity and to attempt to implement this intention through the establishment of control exercised by the administrative body. Individuals have successfully challenged nebulous and indefinite restrictions repeatedly in such instances.

A second kind of situation in which administrative agencies are challenged involves the exercise of discretion on the part of the administrative organization. If the action of the particular administrative individual or group has been arbitrary or capricious or has been carried out without proper regard to the facts, then the individual or business that is the subject of this action has a legitimate basis for complaint. However, if the action of the administrative body has been properly conducted, with proper notice, hearing, consideration, and investigation, the business person normally has very little chance of success in attacking the process.

CONTROL OF THE BUSINESS VIA LICENSES, PERMITS, FRANCHISES, AND CERTIFICATES

Lawful business activity is conducted with the permission of one or more levels of government. Quite frequently a *license, permit, franchise,* or *certificate* grants the privilege of conducting a business. While these terms have somewhat different meanings, in essence they will produce the same end result. Licenses and permits are generally thought to be rather freely granted, whereas the terms *franchise* and *certificate* may be reserved for activities that are severely limited in scope, restricted to a limited number of establishments, and based on certain lawful discre-

This is where the decisions are made.

tionary determinations exercised by those granting the privilege. Thus, a city may grant a franchise for the operation of a taxicab service or a garbage hauling service.

Where personal qualifications are involved, society—through its lawmakers—seeks to achieve some degree of control over the standards of performance of different groups of people by requiring them to obtain licenses or permits. Professional people must meet rather extensive requirements involving training and education, and they must take an examination before they are qualified to be licensed. The reasoning here is that they are engaged by the public to perform critical services that demand a considerable degree of intelligence and knowledge. Furthermore, the activities of professionals, which may be matters of life and death, are determined on the basis of knowledge very rarely possessed by the individual to whom the service is rendered. The client or customer is entitled to some reasonable level of competence.

LEGISLATIVE OVERKILL IN SMALL BUSINESS CONTROLS

Controlling business activity through the licensing of individuals provides a very interesting insight into the conduct of business and the effect of the legislative process. Every state legislative session will produce a surprising number of new bills related to business licensing and control. Although it may appear that much of this legislation is proposed as a means of raising standards in certain areas of business activity, in reality the main purpose may be nothing but restriction on the number of persons engaged in such activity and holding back the number of the new competitors to be licensed. It is for this reason that the actions of legislatures in controlling small businesses has been termed *overkill*. Much arbitrary and unreasonable legislative action aimed at personal licensing and control has been found to be unconstitutional.

THE UNIFORM COMMERCIAL CODE AND HOW IT AFFECTS AND CONTROLS SMALL BUSINESSES

Over a long period of time, commercial transactions developed particular characteristics tending to segregate them into categories according to their function. The more common of these were sales, negotiable instruments, and contracts. Eventually business transactions became well established and the laws applying to them were standardized in forms such as the Uniform Negotiable Instruments Act and the Uniform Sales Act, which were adopted by many states.

Ultimately it became apparent that more equitable and consistent results would be reached if the majority of commercial transactions were covered by one master uniform act. Through the efforts of the American Law Institute and the National Conference of Commissioners on Uniform State Laws, a comprehensive body of law—the Uniform Commercial Code—was formulated. Adoption of the code by the states began in the early 1950s and has now been effected in all states.

In Article 1 of the official text the following purposes of the act are stated:

1. To simplify, clarify, and modernize the law governing commercial transactions.
2. To permit the continued expansion of commercial practices through custom, usage, and agreement of the parties.
3. To make uniform laws among the various jurisdictions. The code contains 10 sections, 2 of which, the first and last, deal with general matter, the other 8 being devoted to the various areas of commercial transactions. These areas of coverage are classified as follows:
   a. Sales.
   b. Commercial paper.
   c. Bank deposits and collections.
   d. Letters of credit.
   e. Bulk transfers.
   f. Warehouse receipts, bills of lading, and other documents of title.
   g. Investment security.
   h. Secured transactions, sales of account, contract rights, and chattel paper.

Anyone who is considering a business venture should secure a copy of the Code and read it over carefully. Many business law textbooks reproduce the Code and are good references to use along with the Code to obtain legal information about typical business documents and transactions.

CONTROL OF SMALL BUSINESS BY MEANS OF LEASES, FRANCHISES, AND LICENSE AGREEMENTS

Let us define some terms. A *lease* will ordinarily involve an interest in real property, whereas *franchises* and *license agreements* are negotiated with other business organizations for the purpose of establishing certain rights and duties affecting the conduct of business.

People considering the lease of a building or other business property should consider very carefully what duties and obligations are involved under the lease agreement. Lessors will be interested in provisions that will protect their property, ensure an adequate return, and protect them from actions of lessees that might place them in a position of liability. Lessees are interested in getting a lease that will permit flexibility of operations, compensation terms that are consistent with the business operation, rights of sublease or relinquishment as conditions warrant, and allowances for improvements to the premises that are necessary from time to time. The lessees as business operators should understand that a lease, being an interest in land, will allow rather broad privileges in the use of the property. Conditions of the lease must be very carefully complied with, because any substantial violation may allow the lessor to regain possession. Lease payments, agreement to comply with certain duties such as the payment of taxes, renewal of licenses, and compliance with municipal restrictions should be carefully observed by the business operator.

If one is to be involved in franchises and license agreements, one should study them to determine what is being furnished by the franchisor and what is included in the price being paid under the agreement. Important considerations are the kinds of controls the franchisor will exercise and the restrictions that are placed on the business. Other considerations will involve the amount of assistance provided to the business, the cost of such assistance and whether or not it is mandatory, the quantity of products or materials to be maintained, and what sales volume is necessary to maintain the franchise. The small business owner should know what options are available to the business if the operation does not prove successful for any reason, predictable or unpredictable.

Constraints via ownership of real property

The term *real property* usually means land or buildings or both. Real property ownership may be a desirable condition for the operator of a small business. If real property is bought or sold, the legal steps necessary in the transaction should be handled by the firm's legal representative.

Ownership of real property under a proprietorship ordinarily in-volves no legal complications; however, in the case of a partnership or corporation, care should be taken not to create complications at the time of liquidation or sale of the property or dissolution of the corporation or partnership. In all three cases, too, care should be taken not to assume obligations that will commit too much of the firm's resources to property ownership.

Opportunities to use and develop property are broader when the property is owned as opposed to most privileges under a lease. Many small business operators are less efficient in property management than a professional who specializes in this activity.

How patents, trademarks, and copyrights affect and control small businesses

A *patent* gives someone the exclusive right to make and sell something. The benefits of a patent are available through various arrangements. A business person may patent something on his or her own, which will require the services of a patent attorney, preparation of appropriate exhibits and reference material, and some period of time for research and perfection of the patent and the granting of it by the U.S. Patent Office.

Patents are often made available to business persons on a royalty basis through negotiations conducted directly with the patent holder. Patent rights to a particular product or process may be acquired by purchase or be used on a royalty basis, with payment on a percentage of dollar volume or quantity of output or production.

Trademarks are different from patents. A trademark is issued for the purpose of identifying the marks and symbols that are used by a particular manufacturer or producer. Protection is afforded by registration, and is achieved by actually using a mark or symbol in conjunction with a particular product.

Copyrights are more like trademarks than like patents. A copyright is issued to an author, composer, or artist, granting an exclusive right to the use of an original written, drawn, painted, composed, or photographed work. As of January 1, 1978, the copyright is issued for the lifetime of the author plus 50 years. For works published before January 1, 1978, the term of copyright is extended to 75 years from the date of first publication. Regulations governing the securing of copyrights are outlined in a pamphlet entitled *Copyright Law of the United States of America*. Regulations of the copyright office are issued by the Library of Congress, which controls the copyright process. In some cases, the long, extended use of a name in conjunction with a particular product will establish some proprietary interest in that name, although this is not something that can be predicted with any degree of accuracy nor is it something that can be counted on. The best way to establish a copyright, therefore, is to register it.

HOW SMALL BUSINESS TRANSACTIONS WITH THE PUBLIC ARE CONTROLLED

Relationships with individuals and businesses outside the firm are constant, continuous and amount to considerable volume over time. These business dealings often create problems. Thus a brief knowledge of how the small business operator's transactions with those outside the firm is controlled may be useful.

Agency

A business conducting transactions through an individual employed by the business is utilizing an agent. An agency relationship poses a considerable threat to the principal (the owners of the business) and to the organization because legally an agent is acting in behalf of the principal. Unless explicitly restricted, the agent is empowered to engage in a number of different activities that will obligate the principal. The principal must make sure that agents clearly understand their powers, the circumstances in which they must exercise particular care in their negotiations, and the nature of situations requiring them to refer negotiations back to the principal. Prospective customers must be informed of the existence of agency powers, of the specific types of power vested in different agents, and of alternation or termination of an agency relationship. Major responsibility for control of the agent is placed on the principal as the one who has created the agency relationship and is in the best position to control and regulate it. The consequences of agency dealing should be foreseen and steps taken to avoid unauthorized action by an agent. The reader should note that almost any employee is—to some extent—an agent of the business.

Contracts

All business activity is accompanied by contractual obligations. Business difficulties arising from contractual relationships usually involve a misunderstanding, a failure to perform because of inability or controversy, or unhappiness with subsequent events not contemplated at the time the contract was negotiated.

The most common type of contract negotiation carried on by the average business involves the sending of a purchase order, as an offer to buy, which is then accepted by the seller and becomes a contract. In recent years it has become customary for the buyer to use a basic contract form, which is then supplemented with special provisions pertaining to the particular contract. This somewhat tailored contract is then submitted to the seller; if the seller wishes to make changes or alterations the buyer is notified, and an amendment to the basic contract is prepared and submitted to the seller.

The seller negotiating with the buyer through a sales agent will use a sales order or sales memorandum as evidence of the negotiations between the seller's representative and the buyer. This is usually submitted to the seller's home office for review and preparation of the final contract.

Secured transactions

A secured transaction is used by a creditor who needs to establish protection to cover financial risk associated with a sale. Conditional sales, installment sales, and chattel mortgages are typically used for personal property sales, allowing the seller to retain some degree of protection to insure payment. Frequently the best protection is for the creditor to take a note from the buyer to insure payment of the obligation.

One variety of security arrangement is *field warehousing*. This three-party transaction includes a lender, a borrower, and a warehouse agent. Certain business operations develop sizable quantities of materials or finished goods that are not subject to the protection given by model and serial number identification and the use of chattel mortgages. Field warehousing ideally applies to these circumstances.

An area is set aside on the business premises; the property is placed there and marked to indicate that it is under a security arrangement with some lender, administered by a warehouse agent. Goods or inventory can then be added to or subtracted from the storage area, but only under the control of the warehouse agent. This avoids the risk to the lender that the particular business will pass a good title to unidentifiable goods. Lenders are protected and borrowers accomodated without the risk that goes with open-account loans, where the lender assumes the risk without security.

Sales transactions

Sales transactions involve a sale, delivery of the product, transfer of title to the product, and, sooner or later, collection of payment. Evidence of a cash sale, such as a sales slip or ticket, should be given the buyer. If an installment or time payment sale is made, then a more formal record should be prepared. In many states before merchants engage in install-ment selling, they must register with state authorities indicating their intention of doing so. When personal property is sold that can be identified in a specific fashion, such as a manufactured item with a serial number and model number, a chattel mortgage can be prepared and filed at the courthouse in the jurisdiction where the sale is made. This is a way of establishing a security interest in the product to ensure payment or repossession at a later date. Many merchants will take a note or a chattel mortge from a buyer at the time of a sale but will not enforce it against the buyer unless he/she becomes delinquent.

Warranties

A warranty is a seller's assurance about a product to a buyer. Warranties are either expressed or implied. An *expressed* warranty is a statement made on the seller's initiative; an *implied warranty* is attached to the transaction by law. Public policy has extended the obligation to buyers under implied warranty, and they are normally protected by assurance of what is known as "merchantable quality" or "fitness for a purpose." The business person should ascertain to what extent he/she is obligated under implied warranties, decide what he/she wishes to do with the express warranties, and be prepared to support the position taken. Liabilities under warranty are probably best handled by insurance; the insurance carrier will suggest ways to reduce potential liability. Negotiations conducted with suppliers should outline the warranty obligations of both parties.

Documents of title

Documents of title to some kinds of personal property facilitate handling, storage, financing, and sale. The two principal documents for business use are the order bill of lading and the negotiable warehouse receipt. Both of these documents provide evidence of title to personal property; the title to the goods can be sold, transferred, or pledged without moving the goods themselves.

The order bill of lading is ordinarily used in conjunction with a bank draft. The seller ships goods on a common carrier and forwards the original copy of the order bill, along with the bank draft, through his/her bank, to a correspondent bank at the point of delivery. The buyer must pay for the goods at the correspondent bank in order to get the original copy of the order bill (thus transferring title) and secure delivery of the goods. Sellers can thus insure payment before the consignee is able to obtain the goods. The negotiable warehouse receipt is issued against goods in storage and facilitates the process of sale, loan, or security arrangement. It is frequently used in connection with agricultural products and other types of materials stored in warehouses where some time will elapse before movement and use. Both instruments have rather specialized use, but in their appropriate place are very worthwhile.

LAWS GOVERNING ADVERTISING AND PRICING

Advertising

With care and judgment there is no need for the advertising program of a small business to generate any legal retaliation. Obviously, advertising must not be false or deliberately misleading, and it must not be defamatory in character. Advertised prices should be fairly stated and adhered to. Flagrant violations and various bait-and-switch tactics will sooner or later lead to reprisals by the better business bureau or legal action by the local district attorney.[1]

---

[1]Bait-and-switch is the technique of advertising a product at an attractive price and then refusing to provide the item to the responding customer. Instead, the customer is subjected to a deliberate attempt to sell a different, usually more highly priced, and practically always more highly profitable item.

The federal government has become increasingly strict in regard to advertising. Some questions still remain unanswered, but in general there must be a reasonable relationship between the product itself, the quantity of contents of the container, the size of the package, and the advertising that promotes the product. Many more advertising claims and their represented products are being reviewed by the Federal Trade Commission to determine truth in advertising. Stricter standards and more regulations are foreseen in the future. Problems concerning advertising can be avoided by telling the truth.

Pricing

For small businesses, legal problems relative to pricing are associated with so-called fair-trade pricing, selling below cost, and discriminatory pricing governed by the Robinson-Patman Act. Occasionally prices charged by small business persons will be questioned. They will usually know about fair-trade pricing because of stipulations laid down to them by the manufacturer or distributor who attempts to control the prices of products, and they will be advised by their attorney or accountant as to applicable state and federal laws. Many violations undoubtedly occur without the knowledge of the business person, or for such a short period of time that there are no repercussions.

Individuals operating businesses must not engage in price-fixing agreements or any conspiracy to fix prices, or use price as a means of destroying a competitor. Prices of many services are established by schedules that are accepted by business persons within a particular area. Prices of certain services are controlled by state boards in a number of states, or in some cases by a federal board; a business person cannot change this. Prices of things such as milk, haircuts, and taxicab transportation, for example, are frequently regulated.

LAWS GOVERNING RELATIONSHIPS WITH EMPLOYEES

The obligations and duties that an employer must assume in dealing with employees have changed substantially over the past 40 years. Regulations covering conditions of employment, minimum wage rates, and safety standards have been subject to substantial changes, for the most part in favor of the employee. Even employers who are not engaged in interstate commerce will likely be subject to state regulations that are not very different from those imposed by the federal government.

Federal Civil Rights Act of 1964

This act made it unlawful to base any condition of employment on a person's race, religion, age, sex, or national origin. A number of states, beginning with New York, had previously enacted such laws, which set the pattern of protecting employees from such arbitrary discrimination. The provisions of the act are administered by the Equal Employment Opportunity Commission.

Fair Labor Standards Act of 1938

The basic Fair Labor Standards Act established minimum wages, overtime regulations, and child labor standards for employees engaged in interstate commerce or the production of goods for interstate commerce. The act was amended in 1949, 1961, 1963, and 1966. The 1963 amendment, forbidding wage differentials based solely on sex, took effect in 1964. Failure to comply with the overtime regulations established under this law has often created problems for owners of small manufacturing firms.

Occupational Safety and Health Act of 1970

This is one of the most far-reaching and comprehensive acts passed in recent years, affecting many areas of labor-management relations. Its

coverage extends to over 60 million employees—all those whose activities affect interstate commerce. It requires that employers and employees comply with safety and health standards that are promulgated by the U.S. Department of Labor.

A provision of the act allows individual states to operate their own "approved" plans. There were, as of late 1974, 24 states operating their own approved plans, which must be at least as effective as the federal program. The degree of surveillance and control under the Act is increasing as additional officers are assigned to the tasks of enforcing the provisions of the federal act or the subordinate state plans.

Certain industries and substances are considered critical and are subject to particularly stringent controls. These are listed as follows:

Critical industries	*Critical substances*
Transportation equipment manufacturing.	Asbestos.
	Pesticides and chemicals.
Roofing and sheet metal.	Silica.
Food and kindred products.	Carbon monoxide.
Lumber and wood products.	Lead.
Heavy construction.	

Worker's compensation

Plans that are now established by statutes in every state provide that an employee, or certain specified relatives of a deceased employee, are entitled to recover damages for the injury or death of the employee. Recovery is possible whenever the injury arose within the course of the employee's work from a risk involved in that work. Recovery may be denied for a willfully self-inflicted injury or harm sustained while intoxicated.

There has been a widening of the coverage of these various statutes, which now tend to include occupational diseases such as lead poisoning, silicosis, injury from radioactivity, and black lung, which is brought on by years of exposure to coal dust in underground mining.

Employers may, through variations in state laws, comply with their provisions in one of three ways. They may post a bond consistent with the coverage required for their type of employment and number of employees; they can buy insurance from a private carrier; or they may enroll in a state-administered compensation fund.

Unemployment compensation

All states provide some method of payment to employees who are severed from their employment through the action of the employer, a joint action, or the sole action of the employee. Compensation is highest for a severance by the employer, less where there is a shared responsibility, and least if the action is entirely that of the employee. Where the employee is at fault, there will normally be some period such as 20 weeks, as a penalty, before benefits will begin.

The employee, to be eligible for benefits, must meet a number of requirements, such as a previous period of employment with a covered employer and have been paid wages in some multiple of the weekly benefit applied for. In addition, he/she must be able and available to accept a job and make a proper effort to comply with the rules of the agency that handles the unemployment benefits program.

REGULATION OF COMPETITION, PRODUCTS, AND CREDIT

The brief descriptions that follow are provided to alert the entrepreneur to some crucial areas of regulation. The basic pattern of laws and control are often established first at the federal level. Following that, state laws are often enacted that tend to extend the pattern of control over intrastate business.

Competition

The areas of regulation are primarily concerned with unfair competition, such as price cutting to destroy competition, kickbacks, false advertising, discriminatory selling, and reciprocity. The Federal Trade Commission is charged with enforcement of the federal laws under the Clayton Act and the Federal Trade Commission Act.

Many states have experimented with laws similar to the federal regulations. They attempt similarly to control the unfair aspects of competition, selling below cost (resale price maintenance laws), and activities in restraint of trade.

Products

The regulation of product standards is rapidly expanding. The Food and Drug Administration is charged with controlling the interstate shipment and sale of articles that may pose a hazard to the health and safety of consumers. Items such as cancer-producing substances, flammable articles, paints containing lead, and potentially hazardous toys are included among those that are so controlled.

At state levels the regulation and control are ordinarily assigned to the state board of health. Particular control is exercised over foods, water, meats, solid wastes, and noise. The extent of control is quite broad and necessitates that any potential business operator exercise care in searching out areas of regulation that may apply to the business. A corresponding level of regulations may also exist at municipal levels. These must also be determined and complied with.

Credit

The Truth in Lending Act was the direct result of efforts by the Board of Governors of the Federal Reserve System. It became effective on July 1, 1980, and regulates the conditions under which credit is extended to buyers. Controlled under the designation of Regulation Z by the Federal Reserve System, the act applies to businesses, professional people, tradespeople, or any individual or organization that extends or arranges credit for which a finance charge is or may be payable, or which is repayable in more than four installments. The act further concerns itself with finance charges and the annual percentage rate; open-end credit such as that extended by credit cards and revolving charge accounts; and real estate credit. The act does not set maximum interest rates, leaving that to the individual states.

Figures 4–1 and 4–2 illustrate what is acceptable for an open-end charge account and for a retail installment contract. Anyone who is involved with credit and installment selling with accompanying interest charges should be familiar with Regulation Z and should obtain the offical text and the manual published by the Federal Reserve System's Board of Governors (for samples of approved forms).[3] Particular applicable details can be reviewed with the company accountant or the firm's CPA.

TAXATION—PERSONAL AND BUSINESS

The success of any business will result in profits, which are then subject to taxation. Taxes are collected in a variety of ways, but the principal levy is imposed by the federal and state income taxes. Tax planning to avoid unnecessary taxation, primarily federal, will probably require the services of a good accountant as well as the advice of the firm's lawyer.

Minimizing or avoiding the tax burden is generally accomplished by some of the following means:

1. Keeping net income as low as possible to avoid the increasing percentage levied in each higher tax bracket.
2. Avoiding double taxation (first against corporation income and then against shareholder's income), which occurs in the corporate form of business.
3. Legitimately diverting business income into the expenses of salaries

---

[3]Board of Governors, Federal Reserve System, *What You Ought to Know about Federal Reserve Regulation Z—Truth in Lending* (Washington, D.C.: Government Printing Office, 1969).

Figure 4–1
An approved open-end charge account form

Any Store U.S.A.

MAIN STREET—ANY CITY, U.S.A.

(Customer's name here)

YOUR ACCOUNT NUMBER IS_____

TO INSURE PROPER CREDIT RETURN THIS PORTION WITH PAYMENT

BILLING DATES		To Your PREVIOUS BALANCE	We Added Your FINANCE CHARGE 50¢ MINIMUM	We Deducted Your		We Added Your PURCHASES
NEXT MO.	THIS MO.			PAYMENTS	CREDITS	

TRANSACTION NO.	DATE	STORE	DEPT. NO.	DEPARTMENT NAME	CHARGES	PAYMENTS & CREDITS

To Avoid Additional Finance Charges, Pay The "New Balance" Before Your Billing Date Next Month.	This Is Your NEW BALANCE	This Is Your MINIMUM PAYMENT	ANNUAL PERCENTAGE RATE %

NOTICE: SEE REVERSE SIDE FOR IMPORTANT INFORMATION

(REVERSE SIDE OF FORM)

PAYMENTS, CREDITS OR CHARGES RECEIVED AFTER YOUR BILLING DATE "THIS MONTH" WILL APPEAR ON YOUR NEXT STATEMENT. YOUR **FINANCE CHARGE** IS COMPUTED BY A SINGLE PERIODIC RATE OF   % (OR A MINIMUM CHARGE OF 50 CENTS FOR BALANCES UNDER $) WHICH IS AN **ANNUAL PERCENTAGE RATE** OF   % APPLIED TO YOUR "PREVIOUS BALANCE" WITHOUT DEDUCTING CURRENT PAYMENTS AND/OR CREDITS APPEARING ON THE FACE OF THIS STATEMENT.

DEPT. NO.	DEPT. NAME	DEPT. NO.	DEPT. NAME	DEPT. NO.	DEPT. NAME
1	MEN'S ACCESSORIES (Shirts, Ties, Socks, etc.)		(In this form of billing, this side of the statement contains a listing of all departments and a brief description of the merchandise sold in each.)		
2	MEN'S CLOTHING (Suits, Sportcoats, Outerwear, etc.)				

ANY STORE, U.S.A., MAIN ST., ANY CITY, U.S.A.

Source: Board of Governors, Federal Reserve System, *What You Ought to Know about Federal Reserve Regulation Z—Truth in Lending* (Washington D.C.: Government Printing Office, 1969).

Figure 4–2
An approved retail installment contract form

Seller's Name: _____   Contract #_____

RETAIL INSTALLMENT CONTRACT AND SECURITY AGREEMENT

The undersigned (herein called Purchaser, whether one or more) purchases from _____(seller) and grants to _____ a security interest in, subject to the terms and conditions hereof, the following described property.

QUANTITY	DESCRIPTION	AMOUNT	

Description of Trade-in:

	Sales Tax	
	Total	

Insurance Agreement

The purchase of insurance coverage is voluntary and not required for credit. ___(Type of Ins.)___ insurance coverage is available at a cost of $_____ for the term of credit.

I desire insurance coverage

Signed_____ Date_____

I do not desire insurance coverage

Signed_____ Date_____

PURCHASER'S NAME_____
PURCHASER'S ADDRESS_____
CITY_____STATE____ZIP____

1. CASH PRICE	$_____
2. LESS: CASH DOWN PAYMENT $_____	
3. TRADE-IN	_____
4. TOTAL DOWN PAYMENT	_____$_____
5. UNPAID BALANCE OF CASH PRICE	$_____
6. OTHER CHARGES:	
_____	$_____
_____	_____
7. AMOUNT FINANCED	$_____
8. FINANCE CHARGE	$_____
9. TOTAL OF PAYMENTS	$_____
10. DEFERRED PAYMENT PRICE (1+6+8)	$_____
11. ANNUAL PERCENTAGE RATE	_____%

Purchaser hereby agrees to pay to_____
_____ at their
offices shown above the "TOTAL OF PAYMENTS" shown above in _____ monthly installments of $_____(final payment to be $_____) the first installment being payable _____ 19____, and all subsequent installments on the same day of each consecutive month until paid in full. The finance charge applies from ___(Date)

Signed_____

Notice to Buyer: You are entitled to a copy of the contract you sign. You have the right to pay in advance the unpaid balance of this contract and obtain a partial refund of the finance charge based on the "Actuarial Method." [Any other method of computation may be so identified, for example, "Rule of 78's," "Sum of the Digits," etc.]

Source: Board of Governors, Federal Reserve System, *What You Ought to Know about Federal Reserve Regulation Z—Truth in Lending* (Washington D.C.: Government Printing Office, 1969).

or fees that may accrue to the benefit of the taxpayer. Family partnerships may accomplish this.

4. Converting ordinary income into capital gains.
5. Combining the choice of legal form and the firm's operational pattern to permit some discretion as to when income is taken out of the business.

Accomplishing any and all of the above usually requires the advice of a competent tax adviser.

Tax liability according to legal form

Different amounts of income will produce different total tax liability, depending on the form of business from which the income is derived. The following summaries are based on the Economic Recovery Tax Act of 1981 and are given just for ideas about how taxes can vary, depending upon legal form of the small business.

1. *Proprietorship.* Net taxable income determines the tax. Same as ordinary income tax to a worker.
2. *Partnership.* Same as the proprietorship, but the partner pays tax on his/her portion of partnership income only when the income is received.
3. *Subchapter S Corporation.* Same as the partnership, but may be based on a fiscal year that differs from the calendar year. Income can be taken as dividends in the more advantageous of two consecutive years.
4. *Corporation.* Taxation of income of the corporation and again on the dividends to the stockholder. Corporate income up to $25,000 reduces to 15 percent after 1982; $25,000 to $50,000 reduces to 18 percent; $50,000 to $75,000, 30 percent, $75,000 to $100,000, 40 percent; all over $100,000, 46 percent.) Stockholder then pays the personal tax on his own dividends.

There are many specialized facts and circumstances that will alter the tax liability of a business or individual. It is not possible in a text of this type to explore these even briefly: to do so would only lead to a series of questions that, when answered, would lead to others. The U.S. Tax Code is a testament to this.

One thing that may be of help in regard to taxes is to suggest that the small business owner consult periodically with an accountant, attorney, *and* estate planner to determine whether it is necessary to adjust the owner's net worth placements. Thus, if the net worth is vulnerable to tax it may be advisable to shift it to a protected position or perhaps donate gifts to children or charities.

The Economic Recovery Tax Act of 1981 substantially changed a great many features of group and self-employed retirement plans. For the self-employed small entrepreneur the provisions of this act provide opportunities for the creation of a self-financed retirement plan. Self-employed persons now may contribute $15,000 per year. Additional provisions and conditions make this an attractive arrangement for a person who wishes to set up a self-financed retirement plan. The provisions of the Economic Recovery Tax Act of 1981 should be reviewed with an accountant, attorney, or estate planner who is familiar with its coverage.

QUESTIONS

1. Differentiate between laws and statutes. Explain in detail.

2. List four examples of federal administrative agencies.

3. How is it that administrative agencies can hold control over small business? Explain in detail.

4. Does a small business have the right to challenge administrative action by administrative agencies? Explain in detail how.

5. What is a contract? Explain in detail.

6. What is the difference between a secured transaction and a sales transaction? Explain in detail.

7. In what way do federal laws govern the relationships of owner/ managers of small businesses with their employees? Explain in detail.

8. What does your text mean by legislative overkill and small business controls? Explain in detail.

9. Why is the Uniform Commercial Code important to an owner/ manager of a small business? Explain in detail.

10. Should anyone starting a small business be concerned about taxation of that business? Explain in detail.

PROBLEMS

1. Read your current newspaper and find a topical matter of how a state administrative agency ruling is having or has had an effect on a small business in your community.

Analyze carefully why and how the ruling has affected the business.

Develop in detail what you feel the local owner/managers of small businesses affected by that ruling can do to protect their rights and interests.

2. Contact the Better Business Bureau or the Chamber of Commerce in your area. Inquire as to the kinds of complaints that are presented to these organizations regarding false and/or misleading advertising and related unfair trade practices. Try to determine if certain firms are responsible for the majority of customer complaints.

3. Visit a local manufacturer and determine whether or not that business has been affected to any extent by the occupational safety and health act. Inquire about the following:

   a. The increased cost or investment required in the business to comply with the provisions of the act.
   b. How often the manufacturer is visited by compliance officers and the manufacturer's feeling generally about the compliance officer's efforts and activities in enforcing the act.

BIBLIOGRAPHY

Beckman, Gail McKnight; Walter F. Berdal; and David G. Brainard. *Law For Business and Management.* New York: McGraw-Hill, 1975. A book dealing with the kinds of transactions involved in starting and operating a business. Certain materials dealing with coverage of the Uniform Commercial Code are useful.

Bill, William R. (ed.). *Running the American Corporation.* Englewood Cliffs, N.J.: Prentice-Hall, 1979. Contains contributions from eight prominent authorities on regulations on how to run an American corporation. Provides an insightful look at the strictures that affect the business in the U.S. economy.

Liles, Patrick R. *New Business Ventures and the Entrepreneur.* Homewood, Ill.: Richard D. Irwin, 1974. Some very good basic materials on financing and taxation that are particularly relevant to the small business person. These materials illustrate situations involving legal complications and include supplementary comments.

Sheppard, C. S., and D. C. Carroll. *Working in the Twenty-First Century.* New York: John Wiley & Sons, 1980. Takes a look at the rules and regulations, laws, and procedures that will shape the future world of work and the strategies that will be required to make a smooth transition to that world of work. The book ties together the viewpoints of experts in business, labor, science, and the social sciences who present their visions of the constraints that will be placed on smaller businesses.

5

Should I operate a small business?

Individuals have many reasons for wanting to start their own business. If the typical small business owner were asked to explain the choice of a small business as a source of livelihood, probably the most common answer would be "to be independent" or "to make money." But these answers are often superficial. Much like the mountain climber who says he climbs mountains "because they are there," the small business owner may give the answer he/she feels the interviewer is seeking rather than the true answer, which lies deep within the man's or woman's character and personality.

Whether or not the typical small business owner has any true insight into his/her basic motivations, it is true that small business is usually chosen as a way of life because of certain appealing advantages. These advantages include: (1) being one's own boss, (2) doing something pleasant, (3) achieving job security, (4) aiding community development, and (5) enhancing personal status.

69

ADVANTAGES OF OPERATING A SMALL BUSINESS

Being one's own boss

The independence of being your own boss is the goal of small business ownership for many. Obviously, the freedom of action appeals to many individuals, but being your own boss means different things to different people. To some, it means being able to close up shop and go fishing when the urge strikes, while to others it means the freedom to do the work their way, without the need to satisfy the demands of another person. Whatever form this factor takes, there is no question that the desire for self-direction is an attractive advantage of small business for many.

Doing something pleasant

Owning a small business lets an individual engage in a line of work that he/she enjoys. Such freedom is closely linked to the independence of being one's own boss. However, the freedom to do something you like goes further than merely being able to determine when you want to

"If you don't get to work on time this morning, you're fired!"

do something. It also includes the freedom to elect not to do something and to tell others what to do.

Achieving job security

Many small businesses are started by persons who are seeking job security; that is, the lack of dependency upon an employer. In fact, one study found that one of every four small businesses are started by people who are unemployed at the time.

Although the number of people who start their own businesses because of the anticipated or real loss of a job is not known, there are always those who find themselves in jobs that for one reason or another, they don't like. When this happens, some are motivated to start their own business.

Aiding community development

Another advantage of operating a small business lies in public service. Many small business owners have started their enterprises because they feel a responsibility to shape and develop their community. The feeling of pride in providing the community with a particular product line or service is a motivating force to many.

Enhancing personal status

There is one final advantage that many people seek in small business ownership: the personal status and recognition that they feel will be theirs as independent, self-directed persons. Although some authorities feel that the image of the entrepreneur as the great inventor, promoter, or daring risktaker simply does not square with the facts, many people elect small business management in hopes of attaining such status and recognition.

SHORTCOMINGS OF OPERATING A SMALL BUSINESS

Choosing the field of small business certainly has its merits. But before jumping in head first, the disadvantages should also be considered.

Everyone's subordinate

One of the major disadvantages of operating a small business is the limited freedom one may have. Although the small business owner is not subject to an employer's demands, he/she is really *everyone's* subordinate.

The cliche "the customer is always right" contains more truth than fiction. Furthermore, money may have to be borrowed on the banker's terms, inventory delivered on the supplier's terms. In short, a small business operator may have to deal from a position of weakness much more often than from a position of power.

Paper work and record-keeping

Another problem in operating a small business is the paper work and record-keeping involved. Most persons who enter small business management recognize that there will be paper work, but many don't recognize the amount involved, particularly if the business is successful. Ordering new stock and keeping records of inventory, billings, payroll, collections, insurance, income tax, and employee withholdings are just a few of the necessary activities involving paper work. Although these tasks can be managed properly, they require a little care, which is often lacking in the small enterprise because for most, paper work is not very exciting. In fact, poor record-keeping is a major cause of small business failure each year.

The high potential for low income

Another disadvantage of operating a small business is the high potential for low income. While everyone expects to hit it big, the statistics indicate that a large number will earn only very meager returns, and an even larger number will fail.

Long hours and hard work

Final disadvantages of operating a small business are the long hours and hard work. Few people who succeed do so with short hours. Even fewer have plush working conditions. The overhead and other expenses in a small business usually do not allow for fancy offices and the latest in equipment.

CONSTRAINTS ON OPERATING A SMALL BUSINESS

Given the foregoing discussion of the advantages and disadvantages of operating a small business, we can draw two conclusions. First, an individual who chooses the life of a small business manager must recognize that this decision does not guarantee success. And second, although the individual who elects small business can control his/her environment to a very large degree, how this is done can make life a dream or a nightmare.

The following paragraphs deal with some additional factors that the successful small business owner must cope with.

The market for the product or service

Although most of the foregoing advantages are inherent in small business management, there are other factors that depend upon managerial talent. One of these is the ability of the small business manager to take some kind of action to gain control or influence over changes in the market. Consider the following example.

Bob Smith, a carpenter, lived with his wife and two children in a trailer park. One of his routine chores was to replace his bottled gas container as needed, since such service was not available in the park. Because Bob was a young, friendly individual, his neighbors didn't hesitate to ask him to pick up their bottled gas, as well.

Obviously, there was a need for a bottled gas distributing service in the area. Bob realized this need and quite profitably met it by (1) getting a franchise for the area from the local bottled gas distributor, and (2) informing his neighbor-customers that he was starting a business and would be charging for his services.

The fact that Bob recognized a market and captured it shows his perceptiveness. But the real test may come when natural gas is finally supplied to the area. Will Bob have the managerial ability to adapt in some way and survive?

The government

The activities of a city council or of other governmental agencies are sometimes important in determining the success or failure of a small business. Again, using Bob as an example, let's assume the city council suddenly gives rights to a public utility to install natural gas lines in Bob's sales area. Now what?

Because of his awareness or good business sense for the needs of others, Bob shifted his market to areas not served by the utility instead of attempting to fight city hall. As a result, he was able to maintain a profitable operation.

Other related problems

Continuing with our story of Bob, he soon ran into another management problem. A customer with a sizable bill was unable to pay so Bob decided to give the man (a bricklayer) the opportunity to work off the debt. Bob was a good carpenter himself, so he and the bricklayer put together a house construction crew and entered the business of speculative home building. The short-run result was that the bricklayer was able to pay his bill; the long-run result was a successful home construction business.

While the case in point may sound like luck to some, Bob's success was a combination of drive, energy, and determination. He had the business sense to perceive certain needs in the marketplace and the ability to satisfy those needs for personal gain.

DETERMINING WHETHER YOU ARE READY TO START A BUSINESS

By now the reader should be familiar with the role of small business in the American economy and the role of the individual in operating the firm. However, this knowledge is not enough for one to make the decision to open a small business.

Too many people enter their own business without knowing whether or not they are qualified to manage it. The usual rationale that lures a person into this trap is as follows: I know what it takes to be a small business manager, and I will look out for my own best interests; therefore, I will succeed.

Such logic is not always true. Although all systems may appear to be "go," one problem still exists—the selection of the manager. Although the natural reaction of most is to pick themselves to manage the business, such a decision may be the kiss of death. The manager selection process involves consideration of several important factors, which are discussed below.

Who is the entrepreneurial person?

Economic studies of all types have been conducted to evaluate the feasibility of new business formation. Large corporations are continuously investigating the opportunity, resources, and support elements needed in stimulating the development of new business opportunities. But the final decision is directly related to the existence of good management. The availability of capable managers is of minor concern to large corporations because they develop the people they need. But such is not always the case for the person wanting to start a small business. While big business recognizes the value of trained managers and will not expand operations unless they have qualified individuals to assume the task, people starting small businesses often fail to recognize the requirement for managerial talent.

The reason the need for managerial talent in small business is not always recognized is that small business usually does not expand in proportionally smaller increments, as large corporations do. Rather, a small business is either (1) started from scratch or (2) expanded into an area that will perhaps double its operations. Therefore, it can reasonably be said that small businesses need good, well-developed managerial talent the minute they open their doors, whereas large corporations can develop additional managers as they grow. In substance, the problem is that too often the assumption is made that the person who wants to start a small business is capable of leaping right in and becoming a *complete* manager of a *total* enterprise with little or no prior managerial training.

Because this fallacious assumption is often made, it is important to consider those characteristics that seem to lead to success in small business management.

Studies have shown there are significant differences between the typical small business person and the typical large business manager in the United States. The typical small business manager grows up in a family of working-class origins, more than half of them having fathers whose principal occupation was farming, clerking, selling, or unskilled, semiskilled, or skilled labor. Further, it has been found that nearly two thirds of the people who become successful entrepreneurs have had a poor, and oftentimes underprivileged, early family life. In fact, one of the reasons that blacks and other minority groups form an increasing percentage of successful small business persons is because of their backgrounds and the extraordinary achievement drives they have developed as a result of these backgrounds.

Education levels of enterprising people

It is frequently argued that to be successful in managing a business, one must be highly educated. But studies have found that the educational levels of small business entrepreneurs is quite diverse, being almost equally distributed among those with no high school education, those with some high school education, high school graduates, those with some college education, and college graduates. Thus, although a person's education may be helpful in succeeding as a small business manager, it doesn't guarantee success and, in some cases, is of no consequence.

Age and sex

Age is sometimes considered important by people in evaluating someone's managerial ability. The young tend to think the old are fixed in their ways and too conservative, while the old feel the young lack the experience to rely on when things get rough. Although both points of view probably possess elements of truth, studies have shown that age is *not* a relevant or differentiating criterion for success in small business management. Small business managers tend to be older (with a median age of 40 years) because of need, rather than ability, drive, or desire. In other words, when faced with unemployment, the young are more apt to continue their schooling than consider starting a small business. But for those who have reached middle age, starting their own business may seem to be the only reasonable alternative. Furthermore, starting a business usually requires capital—something the young do not always have and often cannot get.

Another influence on managerial success is sex. Like it or not, the fact remains that women in business are still discriminated against in some instances. This situation should eventually disappear, but for now it still demands consideration by those females who wish to manage their own small business.

Social attitudes of the entrepreneur

Although there are no specific combinations of background, education, age, or sex that seem to guarantee success in small business, a person's social attitudes may be an important ingredient.

For example, studies show that entrepreneurs and executives in established organizations tend to have different attitudes toward authority figures and interpersonal relations. The successful business executive usually has a positive attitude toward authority, whereas many successful entrepreneurs have little regard for authority figures. The entrepreneurs seem to have found outlets for their creativity, drive, and energy by creating their own businesses rather than in competing for recognition in someone else's business. In fact, one study found certain dominant traits in the typical small business personality: a middle-class social value system, a lack of social mobility drives—i.e., no desire to climb up the social ladder—and generally a task-oriented attitude.

In summary, the successful small business manager will often be from a middle- or lower-income family, with or without much education, but striving relentlessly in pursuit of certain goals and objectives. The successful manager of a small business believes in the demand for his/her product or service, and is willing to risk a great deal in pursuing independence.

Comparing yourself to the model of success

Awareness of the foregoing factors might help totally objective persons determine whether they are capable of managing a small business. The pitfall one must avoid is the rationalization of being "the exception" if, in fact, one doesn't fit the pattern. Because certain personality traits seem to distinguish successful small business managers from those who fail, let's look at the success model more closely.

Five personality characteristics are generally considered necessary for a person to succeed in managing a small business:

1. *Drive*—willingness to accept responsibility with vigor, initiative, and persistence.
2. *Thinking ability*—the capacity to think creatively and analytically.

3. *The ability to relate to people*—emotional stability, friendliness, cheerfulness, cooperativity, and tactfulness.
4. *The ability to communicate*—the capacity to comprehend, as well as speak and write well.
5. *Technical knowledge*—command of the facts and know-how necessary to provide the product or service offered.

Most important to recognize is that an abundance of one quality will not necessarily offset a shortage of another. Success is most probable for the small business person who rates high on all five factors.

CONCLUDING REMARKS

This chapter has discussed some of the pitfalls and problems encountered in operating a small business. Although successful small business managers tend to come from laboring-class families, there is little correlation between success and educational attainment, age, or sex. On the other hand, social attitude and certain personality traits are critical to success. Because it is difficult for one to be wholly objective about one's small business abilities, the decision to open up shop must be made only after the most careful deliberations.

QUESTIONS

1. What are the risks involved in a person's decision to become the manager of a small business?

2. How important is education to the probability of a person's success as a small business manager? Are any particular kinds of educational background more likely to assure the success of someone as a small business person?

3. Is there any pattern or stereotype that one might present as a typical personality of today's small business person? Explain your answer.

4. What kind of program would you use to evaluate yourself if you were thinking of starting your own small business? Develop such a plan in detail.

5. The desire to be independent or to make more money is often listed as a reason many persons want to manage their own small business. Are these reasons valid? Why or why not?

6. Is it true that the small business manager can always do those things that he/she likes and avoid doing those things that he/she dislikes doing? Why or why not? Explain your answer if you stated: "It depends."

7. What would be your reply to a person's statement that there is a major advantage to owning and operating a small business because of the feeling of public service that one receives from such activity?

8. What would be your comment to a person who states that "the successful entrepreneur has to be an inventor, promoter, and daring risk taker"? Present both your reply to this question and what you would anticipate someone's answer to your reply would be.

PROBLEMS

1. Sandra Smith is a good keypunch operator and has decided to open her own shop and provide keypunch services to local businesses. She has asked you to back her. What would you look for, what information would you ask Sandra for, and on what basis would you assess Sandra's probability of success in deciding whether to back her financially?

2. John and Maria Towne are both college graduates. John has his bachelor's degree in business and his wife has hers in art. Both of them are ambitious and have worked their independent ways up the corporate ladder in the companies where each had gone to work subsequent to their graduation from a small state college. John is now head bookkeeper in the company he works for and Maria has been promoted to senior buyer in the large department store for which she works.

   Both John and Maria have wanted to go into business for themselves for a long time. Both their families' backgrounds are entrepreneurial, and John's sister is a successful local distributor for a large cosmetics firm that sells door-to-door. John and Maria feel that they have what it will take for success if they open a fabric and upholstery shop. Maria knows buying and materials and John can certainly handle the bookkeeping.

   a. Do you think John and Maria will be successful? Why or why not?
   b. What would you, as their friend, advise them to consider before starting their own business?

c. Develop a list of five items that you feel are critical indicators for success to John and Maria's endeavor, assuming they pursue it.

BIBLIOGRAPHY

Baumback, Clifford M., and Kenneth Lawyer. *How to Organize and Operate a Small Business*. 6th ed. Englewood Cliffs, N.J.: Prentice-Hall, 1979, chap. 3.

Frantz, Forrest H. *Successful Small Business Management*. Englewood Cliffs, N.J.: Prentice-Hall, 1978, chap. 1.

Moreau, James F. *Effective Small Business Management*. Chicago: Rand McNally College Publishing, 1980, chap. 1.

Tate, Jr., Curtis E.; Leon C. Megginson; Charles R. Scott, Jr.; and Lyle R. Trueblood. *Successful Small Business Management*. Rev. ed. Plano, Tex.: Business Publications, 1978, part I.

6

Buying or selling a small business

Every day, across the United States and throughout the world, businesses are started, bought, sold, merged, inherited, or liquidated. Each of these events has an impact on the total structure of the small business scene. For any one whose interests include small business management, these changing patterns provide valuable data for study and review. What kinds of businesses are being bought and sold, and for what reasons? Within the changing framework, are there opportunities to buy or sell a good small business at a fair price?

This chapter is based on the idea that buying or selling a business are possible management alternatives that represent managerial responsibilities of all small business managers. Failing to explore a purchase possibility or selling out at less than full value are serious management errors. Realistic efforts should be made to prevent such mistakes.

DEVELOPING THE INFORMATION BASE

Prior to buying or selling a business, some effort should be made to analyze certain information about the contemplated transaction. Unless a careful effort is made, something vital may be overlooked. The emphasis here is on factors different from those that are involved when a business is started from scratch. Properly compiled, the information base can be used either as a source on which to rely prior to purchase, or as what a seller should know when approaching a potential buyer.

Economic census. The U.S. Bureau of the Census publishes a wide assortment of economic census information.[1] The 1977 series were developed on information gathered in 1976 and are the latest series now available. They are being repeated at five-year intervals for the years ending in "2" and "7," so the next full series will probably be available in late 1983. Individual censuses are available on the following subjects:

Retail trade	Mineral industries
Wholesale trade	Transportation
Selected service industries	Outlying areas
Construction industries	Enterprise statistics
Manufactures	

The census data will not give information directly related to any particular buy or sell situation. Rather, these business and economic censuses should be used to examine aggregate data and to identify trends, gauge potential markets, and forecast certain economic changes. These are valuable references that provide a wealth of valuable base data.

Key business operating ratios. The most available source of operating ratios on a national basis are the publications of Dun & Bradstreet, Inc., 99 Church Street, New York, N.Y. Operating data are published yearly and are available for periods within two or three years of the current time period. The data are included in pamphlets under the following titles:

1. *Key Business Ratios* (retailing, wholesaling, manufacturing, and construction).
2. *Cost of Doing Business* (corporations; partnerships and proprietorships).
3. *Terms of Sale* (manufacturing and wholesale lines).
4. *The Business Failure Record* (yearly).

The Dun & Bradstreet material, like the census information, is broad in scope but valuable as a basic reference to establish guidelines for review and comparison of specific situations.

---

[1] Most libraries will have information on the most current census publications. Availability and ordering information also may be acquired from the Publications Distribution Section, Social & Economic Statistics Administration, Washington, D.C. 20233.

Industry, agency, and geographical studies.   A wide range of these are available from sources too numerous to list. As a rule, the entrepreneur or manager should contact state university bureaus of business research (titles vary), trade associations, regional planning commissions, and other similar organizations. The objective is to obtain data that relate to the selected enterprise, so that valid judgments about "going value" can be established.

The foregoing is not intended as a substitute for information described in a later chapter dealing with research on a much broader scale. The emphasis here is on sources of data useful in making a judgment on the fair price of a particular business.

FRAMEWORK OF OPPORTUNITIES

The entrepreneur who begins an investigation of whether to buy or sell a business must identify several important factors. In this effort it is necessary to look beyond the more conventional analysis and probe deeply into some less recognized factors which are very significant in the ultimate transaction. The following ideas are offered to indicate how this investigation might proceed.

Customers

Customers are more than persons living in particular places with an average level of income. Why does a particular business have an opportunity to sell a customer something? What is it that provides the motive to buy? It is a well-known fact that people's wants are varied, with some products and services being in high demand, while others are scarcely noticed. There may be more than one principal reason for the demand. Possibly it evolves from a combination of function and desire; function being the performance characteristics of the product or service, and desire being a group of intangibles that give the buyer a sense of satisfaction and well-being.

Assuming that the functional aspects of products and services are readily understood, the following psychological relationships are offered as examples of another form of customer-oriented opportunities for small businesses.

1. *Status or prestige.* The notion that a product or service has quality, scarcity, uniqueness, or the proper endorsement will encourage status- or prestige-buying.
2. *Discounts and bargains.* Persuasion to buy is enhanced if the item is offered at a bargain price, or is thought to be a bargain.
3. *Health and vigor.* The emphasis that contemporary society places on

vigorous, energetic lifestyles encourages the purchase of a vast assortment of things.

4. *Service and accommodation.* Providing the extras has enabled many a small business to succeed. The use of contests, free delivery, and gift-wrapping services are typical examples.

5. *Protection and security.* Warranties, money-back offers, and liberal exchange policies are assurances that may encourage a buyer to select something without feeling irrevocably committed.

The smaller business is uniquely oriented to satisfy the combined needs of functional and psychological needs and desires. An alert entrepreneur can analyze and respond to situations that are difficult for a larger, more impersonal organization.

Market opportunities

The buyer or seller of a business will want to analyze the particular business from the standpoint of how market opportunities are being met. This is more than the conventional analysis of past success and the satisfying of certain easily identifiable needs. A more penetrating and broader analysis may reveal some untapped potentials. The following suggestions are offered in this respect:

1. Providing a brand new product or service, based on new technology, new needs, or new desires.
2. The creation of unique or innovative forms of merchandising a good or service.
3. Doing an existing job better and more efficiently than the competition.
4. Capitalizing on social and economic changes. Inflation, unemployment, scarcity, and customer attitudes create problems for many businesses but create opportunities for others.
5. Finding a niche in an expanding market not presently being served.
6. Using new technology to make a previously uneconomical product or service profitable.

These market opportunities should be evaluated in terms of what the small business can do better than larger organizations.

Thrust

The word *thrust* is used to identify the one or more characteristics of a particular business that are vital to its success. Understand that thrust is not necessarily a conventional feature or combination of features such as location, layout, and good management. On the contrary, it is often one or more intangibles that really carry the successful business forward.

When a business is being bought, care should be taken to identify the thrust forces and make sure that they are not lost in the exchange. Likewise, if the business is being sold and a strong thrust element can be maintained, this fact should be highlighted to enhance the sale.

Reputation

Most businesses that are being considered for purchase or sale will have been around for a while and will have a reputation among both existing and potential customers. A reputation based on existing customers will be reflected in past sales and considered as goodwill. On the other hand, a good reputation in terms of potential customers and increased sales volume is a strong plus factor. A good reputation is very possibly something that can be capitalized on under new management or circumstances, If it is identifiable, the business buyer or seller should attempt to assess its value and importance.

BUYER'S AND SELLER'S GOALS

When a prospective entrepreneur considers going into a business, the initial idea is often to start a new business. There is nothing wrong with this, but an effort should be made to determine whether or not a business can be purchased that provides certain advantages over the creation of a new enterprise. Sellers should also recognize that potential buyers may need to be contacted and presented with an attractive proposition.

Buyer's goals

A potential business buyer must give a lot of attention to his/her goals in business ownership before making the decision. If this task is performed with careful deliberation, the chances are these goals will be more realistic and valid than if considered under pressure.

Timing. Starting a business is often a fairly long-term project. An entrepreneur may plan, save money, and work to gain experience before actually starting. There is no reason why the process needs to be much different for a purchase. Preparation will still involve many of the same things, plus a decision to acquire what is right whenever it is found. The prospective owner may decide to look around casually or intently, depending on his/her own judgments. The idea might be to wait for a definite advantage in bargaining. Another aspect of timing might be to spend more money for a business that is some years ahead in development versus starting from the beginning with a lesser investment.

Exploitation. Opportunities are often exploited from an established base point or position. The prospective buyer may wish to exploit something, but cannot start from scratch. He searches and finds a going business where he can pursue his goal as a partner or stockholder. The goal of exploitation is met without having to wait to put together an entirely new venture.

Environment. The prospective buyer may desire a combination of geographical features, a community of a particular size, or a particular kind of a business of a certain size. Circumstances may be such that these things together are out of the question for a new business. However, they might exist in one or more businesses that may be available for purchase. Even though they are not known to be for sale, that does not preclude inquiry to find out whether acquisition is possible. As the old saying goes, "Anything is for sale if the price is right."

Seller's goals

The seller may never think of selling, but should not forget how fragile a small business is and the importance of working toward goals that will maximize achievement in one's life's work.

Motivation. A single business may be a life's work for several entrepreneurs. For others the stimulus of putting together something that grows and becomes successful is really what counts. The eventual large size and its heavy administrative work load may not be enjoyed. When the business reaches the point that it possesses the owner, it may be time to quit. The important point is that businesses do change. If goals can no longer be realized, it is time to sell.

Capital gains. A proprietor's goal may be to achieve financial independence. Once this is reached a successful business can probably be sold to realize substantial capital gains. Additional time may produce minimal increases, and there is always the risk that the owner will die or that other events may reduce the value of the business. The time to sell is when things are right and substantial capital gains can be realized.

Governmental intervention. Many small business operators are highly independent. They selected a small business because they can do things as they see fit and in their own style. Considerable freedom still exists for the small business because of exemptions from governmental control for firms with few employees or firms not in interstate commerce. But as the business grows, more and more government regulations and controls tend to apply. A reasonable action may be to sell and let someone else battle the bureaucracy.

Personal estate. Most business persons try to develop a personal estate plan. For some a desirable goal might be to leave their heirs the proceeds of their efforts rather than the business itself. This may be similar to the capital gains route, but more long-range. Plans may be to transfer the ownership over time to an employee or to the children. A sale may be made with a long-term payout. These possibilities often support the idea that business owners should pick their own time to sell, and not have it forced on them by circumstances beyond their control.

PATHS TO OWNERSHIP

Business ownership does not have to involve an outright purchase. There are ways in which it can be accomplished over time or through an arrangement that will include advantages for both buyer and seller.

The hired manager.   The hired manager may be an employee who is hired for the specific purpose of becoming the future owner. Under this arrangement the buyer works and gets a chance to find out more about the business, and the seller has the benefit of a serious employee who will view the job somewhat differently from the average employee.

It is important to understand the purpose of each party. The buyer is entitled to a period of time in which to consolidate plans to purchase the business. Being of potential ownership caliber, he/she has the right to expect some premium in compensation if the original options are not exercised. Once the options are exercised, the employee then has a self-interest and can move forward accordingly. The seller must realize the position of the prospective owner and the fact that the seller is best served by avoiding attitudes that will discourage a good prospective buyer.

Long-term buyers.   Many businesses, such as drugstores, insurance agencies, and abstract offices, are sold on the installment plan to an operating partner or stockholder. The owner can sell while the business is alive and well and the buyer can spread out commitments over several years. The selling owner can continue to work, train the new owner, receive income over time for tax advantages, and keep an eye on his/her remaining interest to make sure the enterprise is properly handled so that the final payout is not lost.

The option.   A purchase option may include a variety of arrangements that permit the buyer to extend the period of review and consideration. The option may include an employment contract for the buyer or perhaps a performance contract by the seller proving the worth of the business to the buyer. The sale might be based on the ability of the buyer to develop reasonable competence in running the firm, and to develop the feeling that the proposition is sound.

As in all options, the buyer must pay something for the privilege of having the right to buy, while still retaining the right to drop the option if things do not look good before the option expires.

Consultant.   A consulting service provides many opportunities for the consultant to learn the inner workings of businesses that employ outside advice. Considerable work with a firm may reveal an opportuni-

"Would you like to buy into my business as a partner? It's alive and doing quite well!"

ty that can be exploited best by the consultant. An element of trust and confidence is expected in such dealings, but this need not prevent the consultant from making a valid offer to buy some part or all of the business. The talents added may save a bad situation for the previous owner and provide a true opportunity to prove that the buyer's advice is sound when put to the true test of his/her own direction and control.

Partnerships. Most partnerships start with partners that contemplate an indefinite duration of their association. If a partnership continues, the time will eventually come when ownership changes are necessary. Prospective buyers may want only a partial interest initially and can decide later whether a regular partnership is agreeable to them.

SUMMARY—MOTIVES OF BUYERS AND SELLERS

Buyers should buy when they establish the fact that the purchase is clearly advantageous over starting a new business. Buyers can determine that businesses are for sale, that a particular business needs the right person to take it over, and that business is valuable only when provided with the right talent. What the buyer visualizes in the business is a potential to achieve results with new talent that outweighs the potential in starting something new.

Sellers sell to protect, perpetuate, revitalize, solidify, or liquidate. Sale is inevitable, but is timed to achieve maximum value ahead of decline, adversity, or failure. Superior buyers are attracted to a viable business, rewarding the owner for having foresight in selling when he/she can both provide and receive good value. Most businesses are not sold during the full bloom of their growth and vitality, but prudent appraisal suggests that selling at this time may be a wise move, showing foresight and good judgment.

BUYING AN EXISTING BUSINESS

At some point in time the serious would-be entrepreneur decides that the period of review and investigation is over. It is time to get busy and acquire the business that satisfies his/her needs and goals. Many things must be done before the obligation is assumed and the capital investment made.

The buyer should divide the acquisition process into two parts. The first relates to the personal situation and objectives. A satisfactory position must be achieved in each of the following:

1. To buy at the right price.
2. To minimize present and future taxation.
3. To get financial terms that are reasonable and within the buyer's ability to pay.
4. To maintain the momentum and vitality developed by the seller.
5. To eliminate or minimize any liabilities or latent difficulties that might carry over from the previous owner.
6. To get a sales contract, which protects the buyer's interests in the business from the seller or others, for a reasonable period of time.

If the buyer cannot buy and achieve the first five objectives, he/she may have second thoughts about going ahead with the purchase. It is also possible that the second stage of inquiry would not need to be completed if the six items mentioned could not be satisfactorily resolved. Considerable time and effort must be put forth on the analysis of the particulars of the business. However, before too much time and effort is expended, the buyer should approach the seller to determine whether satisfactory sale terms can be arranged. If they can, the buyer can then continue the detailed investigation, knowing that the efforts are not being wasted.

Figure 6–1
Classified ads help to locate buying and selling opportunities

Appraising the business

Some points in the following list will have been considered by the buyer before approaching the seller with a proposal. No attempt has been made to divide the list into which inquiries should be made before and which after the contract terms are determined. Each purchase is unique and subject to its own particular sequence and timing. Much depends on the nature of each party and the complexity of the transaction.

1. What is the past history as to the profits of the business year by year, going back at least five years?
2. Has the business gained or lost market position in the past five years?
3. What competitive changes have taken place, and has the business withstood these changes?
4. Is the location good? Is it decreasing or increasing in value?
5. If the lease and physical premises are good, how long can the location be retained?
6. Does cost analysis reveal proper balance in terms of expenditures, income, and return on investment?
7. Are the physical features of the business up-to-date and appropriate?
8. What products and product lines are represented?
9. Can favorable relationships be maintained with suppliers?
10. Are banking sources appropriate and adequate, and can they be maintained?
11. Does the business have strong management and supporting personnel, and can these be retained after the departure of the owner?
12. What community or trading area changes might possibly threaten the business?
13. Does the business have a strong identity with customers or clients, and can this be retained under new management?
14. Has the company been progressive in terms of meeting competitive demands regarding wage rates, pensions, bonuses, hospitalization plans, and the general well-being of the organization?
15. What prospects does the business have for increasing its share of the market and remaining competitive in the years ahead?
16. Why is the present management selling out?
17. Does the business have a strong support staff such as a lawyer, CPA, and consulting firm that can be retained if needed?

Financial analysis

Initially, financial analysis will be necessary to get a good grasp of what has happened to the business in the past. If the inquirer is lacking in the ability to analyze financial statements, then he/she should get professional help, preferably someone locally who has no conflict of interests and who can add information of an explanatory nature to the figures appearing in the statements.

Profitability. Nothing will be so important to the prospective buyer as the profit pattern of the business. Profitability will form the basis of much of the subsequent negotiations that may be conducted. If profits are relatively high, based on investment, then goodwill becomes important. If, on the other hand, profits have been low, consistent, and stable, then perhaps different factors assume greater importance.

Financial statement analysis requires comparisons over time, and any single period even up to one year may not be meaningful. As suggested earlier, three years may be an appropriate period; however, if statements are available for a longer period of time they should undoubtedly be reviewed. Sales trends, ability to withstand adverse conditions, growth, improved profit position, economies of scale, and general evidence of aggressiveness as shown in the statements are all items of vital concern. Much of the inquiry should be carried out in the presence of the existing ownership, and questions should be asked regarding the variances that appear.

In analyzing statements it is also important to consult related industry reference materials. Averages compiled by such businesses as Dun & Bradstreet, Eli Lilly, National Cash Register, and certain trade associations may provide background material with which individual line items can be compared.

Return on investment. Some part of profit is allocated to return on investment. In spite of the prime importance attached to profitability, the investment return figure, even though it be encouraging based on the general assessment of the business, is of no consequence unless compared to the asking price for the business. The rate of return calculation must include a reasonable valuation of all assets so that a proper relationship is established between the factors of investment and rate of return.

Analysis of past records should contemplate such things as follows:

1. What was the rate of investment return, and did it properly include allowance for ownership effort, time, and energy in addition to tangible fixed investment?
2. Were the past profits due to capable management or because the business was fortunate enough to have a good location and the benefit of successful nearby establishments?
3. Were profits increased by paying substandard wages, minimum withdrawals by the ownership, an unrealistic lack of adjustments in the accounting system, such as a failure to write off bad debts?

Computations for the future should examine:

1. Losses due to the department of the previous owner.
2. The time lag involved in the start-up under new management.
3. Higher prices that may have to be paid for goods and services until reputation and momentum are established.

Guidelines for analysis. Valuation and rate of return are always related. If valuation is too high, rate of return will be reduced, and vice versa. Start first with all tangible assets and determine the stated or book value, which should appear on the balance sheet. Physically inspect all such assets and reduce the stated value, if justified, to the true or representative value. Value all intangibles as accurately as possible. Compare the total to the investment and proprietorship interest. Rate of return from business operations is expressed as a percentage of total investment. Comparison to industry averages for similar businesses will point out whether the rate of return is higher or lower than average.

In analyzing a service business, intangible factors will frequently comprise a bigger portion of the total than the tangible factors. In such a case great care must be exercised in establishing the valuation, because the purchase relates to intangible values created by the previous ownership. After the business is purchased the values will decrease, at least temporarily. Substantial devaluation may thus be justified if the previous ownership is removed.

Tax considerations will probably require the services of a lawyer or tax accountant. Some negotiation and compromise will be needed to reach a fair accommodation of the interests of the buyer and the interests of the seller. The chapters on finance and accounting and the current *Federal Income Tax Manual* further treat problems of taxation.

Asset valuation

It is highly unlikely that the assets of any business are completely current and that they will fit exactly into the "fresh look" desired by the new management. The appraiser must take the seller's sale schedule, examine it in detail, and discount the figures as much as 10, 15, or perhaps 20 percent.

Inventory and equipment. Careful analysis must be applied to all aspects of the inventory, including its age, condition, quantity, balance, and its potential for sale. Quite likely the method of analysis will start with goods ready for sale. This analysis should be made as late as possible in the purchase negotiations.

In a wholesaling operation, similar analysis must be made of the inventory for sale, with particular attention given to sales potential, which requires review of recent sales to customers. An examination of the sales records may reveal that recent sales have been secured on the basis of special inducements so that present ownership could present a favorable picture to the prospective buyer.

Manufacturing and service businesses have different aspects regarding inventory, each of which is important to that type of operation. Manufacturing analysis will necessarily include an item-by-item check and evaluation of every part in the inventory, starting with basic raw materials and working through to final finished products. Rate of use, bad stock, obsolete items, and quantities held for repeat orders and spare parts will all be a part of this check. The inventory of service businesses is often difficult to value accurately because it is made up of a variety of things such as tools, equipment, franchised products, and spare parts whose value to a new owner is uncertain. Specialized tools and equipment can be extremely important and should be examined very carefully for conditions and their appropriateness to the contemplated service activity.

In addition to this, other equipment related to any individual business operation should be carefully examined and compared as to its *current value* to the new owner. If this equipment will not be utilized in the new business operation and has little sale value, it should be substantially discounted. Specialized equipment is particularly vulnerable to a loss of value, and even though the equipment is practically new it may not be disposed of at a figure approaching book value.

Mailing and customer lists. Many small business today conduct mail-order operations even though they operate a retail establishment. The mail-order name and address listings have value and, if bought on the open market, are quite expensive. Valuation of available lists will depend on how difficult it was to acquire the listings, how much they are worth to the business, and the use that has been made of them in the past.

Credit records. Most businesses will involve selling goods and services on credit, at least to some extent. Credit reports, credit records, and the historical analysis of experience with various accounts are important and may be considered a valuable asset to the business. They should be reviewed as to age and completeness and their appropriateness to the operation to be conducted in the future.

Goodwill. One of the most troublesome factors to deal with in buying a business is goodwill. Goodwill is very difficult to evaluate.

Goodwill is usually computed on the basis of the extra earning power of the business over and above a reasonable return on investment for that particular type of business. This may extend into the future from one to five years depending on the stability and established position of the firm.

Competition

Modern small businesses seldom enjoy a position of monopoly. Even though they are located in a community where they are the sole provider of certain products or services, it is unlikely that the population is willing to accept their product or service as the only one of its kind without considering competitive alternatives in another community. The business buyer is thus obliged to look carefully at the competition, whether it be a directly competing store in the area or the nearby mail-order catalog store operated by one of the major merchandising concerns. Records of the existing business will show very little regarding the extent of competition. When studying the competition of a prospective business, the buyer should determine first the number and location of the competitive businesses. Then he/she should ask the following questions: How aggressive are these business? What has been their past growth? Will these same businesses be competitive in the future? Are other competitors likely to be established?

Contracts, leases, and franchises

Any contractual arrangement should be carefully reviewed, preferably with an attorney. Careful study should be made to determine whether or not such arrangements have been properly drawn and what provisions have been made for the assumption of the business by the new management. A final check should be made just prior to the contract signing to make sure that all involved parties understand their privileges and obligations.

Confirmations

Many items involved with past operating records of business need to be confirmed with outside people. Examples are such things as invoices, sales records, title or lease arrangements regarding equipment, machinery, and inventory. Confirmation may be best handled by professionals such as a CPA or a business consulting service. Confirmation, in essence, should substantiate all things represented by the records, and any deviations should be presented to the owner for review and explanation.

Management and ownership

The existing management and ownership are always a plus factor in a successful business. There are times when they are so important that their removal from the business may cause serious problems for the new owner or manager.

It is probably desirable for the prospective buyer to assess the importance of the managers and/or owners and to think about how best to handle the transition with a minimum of difficulty. It may be possible to persuade some or all of the managerial staff to stay on with the new owner. Even the previous owner may stay through some period of time after sale, but it is usually better for the new owner or owners to plan to become self-sufficient as quickly as possible. The presence of two chiefs in any organization should not continue beyond a few months.

The buyer must be very thorough in all the negotiations with the seller, insist on a reasonable noncompetition clause in the sales contract, and should check out carefully the following items:

1. All tax statements and contracts that the owner filed or signed in the past five years.
2. A confidential character report and evaluation of the owner.
3. A review of the credit rating of the business by a professional reporting organization such as Dun & Bradstreet. This should probably include the past three to five years.
4. A record of all real estate transactions in the past three to five years, and the present ownership of all personal and company property.
5. A schedule of the assets of the business, from whom acquired, when, and their present ownership.

Computing the buyer's offer

The determination of the selling price for the business will vary from one situation to the next, but in general follows the outline set in Figure 6–2.

Figure 6–2
A formula for computing the selling price of a business

The following is a suggested formula for arriving at a price for a business. It is approached from the point of view of the buyer but should also be of help to the seller. Since all businesses are different, this cannot cover all types. It can only be a rough guideline to point up some of the key considerations.

Step 1. Determine the adjusted tangible net worth of the business (the total value of all current and long-term assets less liabilities).

Step 2. Estimate how much the buyer could earn with an amount equal to the value of the tangible net worth if it were invested elsewhere.

Step 3. Add to this a salary normal for an owner-operator of the business. This combined figure provides a reasonable estimate of the income the buyer can earn elsewhere with the investment and effort involved in working in the business.

Step 4. Determine the average annual net before-tax earnings of the business (net profit before subtracting owner's salary) over the past few years. Income taxes are excluded to make the earnings comparable with those from other sources or by individuals in different tax brackets. (The tax implications of alternate investments should be carefully considered.)

The trend of earnings is a key factor. Have they been rising steadily, falling steadily, remaining constant, or fluctuating widely? The earnings figure should be adjusted to reflect these trends.

Step 5. Subtract the total of earning power (Step 2) and reasonable salary (Step 3) from this average net earnings figure (Step 4). This gives the extra earning power of the business.

Step 6. Use this extra, or excess, earning figure to estimate the value of the intangibles. This is done by multiplying the extra earnings by what is termed the *years of profit* figure.

This years of profit multiplier pivots on these points. How unique are the intangibles offered by the firm? How long would it take to set up a similar business and bring it to this stage of development? What expenses and risks would be involved? What is the price of goodwill in similar firms? Will the seller be signing a noncompetition agreement?

Figure 6–2 *(concluded)*

> If the business is well established, a factor of five or more might be used, especially if the firm has a valuable name, patent, or location. A multiplier of three might be reasonable for a moderately seasoned firm. A younger, but profitable, firm might merely have a one-year profit figure.
>
> Step 7.   Final price = Adjusted tangible net worth + Value of intangibles. (Extra earnings × years of profit.)
>
> Here is how the formula described above might work in evaluating two businesses for sale:
>
> | | Business A* | Business B† |
> |---|---|---|
> | 1. Adjusted value of tangible net worth (assets less liabilities) | $100,000 | $100,000 |
> | 2. Earning power—at 10%‡—of an amount equal to the adjusted tangible net worth if invested in a comparable-risk business, security, etc. . . . . | 10,000 | 10,000 |
> | 3. Reasonable salary for owner-operator in the business . . | 24,600 | 24,000 |
> | 4. Net earnings of the business over recent years (net profit before subtracting owner's salary) . . . . | 40,000 | 30,000 |
> | 5. Extra earning power of the business (line 4 minus lines 2 and 3) . . . . | 6,000 | -4,000 |
> | 6. Value of intangibles, using three-year profit figure for moderately well-established firm (3 times line 5) . . . . . | 18,000 | None |
> | 7. Final price (lines 1 and 6) . . . . | $118,000 | $100,000 (or less) |

*In example A, the seller gets a substantial value for intangibles (goodwill) because the business is moderately well established and is earning more than the buyer could earn elsewhere with similar risks and effort. Within three years the buyer should have recovered the amount paid for goodwill in this example.

†In example B, the seller gets no value for goodwill because the business, even though it may have existed for a considerable time, is not earning as much as the buyer could through outside investment and effort. In fact, the buyer may feel that even an investment of $100,000—the current appraised value of net assets—is too much because he/she cannot earn sufficient return.

‡This is an arbitrary figure, used for illustration. A reasonable figure depends on the stability and relative risks of the business and the investment picture generally. The rate should be similar to that which could be earned elsewhere with approximately the same risk.

Source: Reprinted with permission from "How to Buy or Sell a Business," *Small Business Reporter*, vol. 8, no. 11, Bank of America, San Francisco, copyright 1969.

The buyer would generally prefer to purchase assets rather than stock or merchandise because of tax advantages. Increases in the value of assets over time are subject to capital gain whereas stock or merchandise produces ordinary income. A higher valuation of assets at the beginning results in a lower spread and eventual tax payment at the time the business is sold, if at that time asset value can be held down.

As implied above, sellers want the opposite results from the sale transaction. They would prefer to sell off the assets at a lower figure and reduce their tax liability, and shift buyers' payments to the stock or merchandise account, where no tax liability occurs. There are obviously limits to what can be done, but an attorney or accountant can advise what is proper under a particular set of circumstances.

Some difficulty may arise between buyer and seller in this area of valuations. The parties should plan to discuss the matter some time ahead of the final negotiations of sale.

Final negotiations

At the time of sale buyers must make sure that they are protected against subsequent action by the seller, creditors of the business, and taxing and regulatory authorities. To ensure protection, the buyers must make sure that the following matters have been resolved:

1. *Bulk transfers.* Compliance with the Uniform Commercial Code provisions requires the filing of a notice of intent to purchase and publication of such fact in an authorized newspaper.

2. *Release of liens.* An investigation with the proper state office should have revealed the extent of security interests of the seller and creditors of the business. A release of lien rights may be asked for from the creditors, to be obtained and furnished by the seller. If there is any doubt, the buyer should have an attorney handle this part of the transaction.

3. *Tax obligations.* All possible tax obligations should be checked and releases furnished indicating that sales and use taxes, income tax, withholding tax, unemployment taxes, and workmen's compensation payments have all been paid. Neglect of these obligations can result in an attachment against the business, but they may not come to light until long after the seller is gone.

A number of others things are necessary in the final contract. The buyer and seller should be represented by their own attorneys, who will work out the details of the final agreement. Much of what is necessary has been covered in various parts of this chapter.

Buying through a broker

The search for an appropriate business to purchase may be conducted through a broker. The broker should be able to provide advice, suggest possible businesses for sale, and give some help on analysis and evaluation. It is difficult, however, to assess clearly the basic motives and integrity of the broker.

If the broker represents the sellers, he/she looks to the seller for a commission and is obviously interested in making the sale. Great care must be exercised in dealing with brokers and no money paid or any agreement signed without consulting a competent attorney.

SELLING A BUSINESS

Throughout this chapter the principal emphasis has been on the problems associated with buying a business. The reasons are that this text is devoted to small business management and that management starts with ownership. In the sections dealing with buyer's and seller's goals, some ideas were presented which outlined differences in what buyers and sellers hope to achieve. Elsewhere reference is made to particular circumstances that are important to the seller. Most of the items of major concern for both parties have at least been mentioned and discussed.

Sellers should relate their situation to that of the buyer. Referring back through the chapter they can identify subjects in which the buyer's position is made known. Taking the opposite position, they can ask why the buyer is concerned about something and then decide what the seller should be prepared to do to meet this concern.

In most cases the seller will hope to achieve the following:

1. To sell when the business is sound and successful, and without pressure or duress.
2. To achieve maximum capital gains and the minimum tax liability.
3. To sell to a buyer who has a good chance of success and ample financial resources.
4. To sell without complications, leaving a minimum of loose ends such as second mortgages, carry-over obligations, and delayed settlements.
5. To achieve a sale that is a source of pride and pleasure for the seller.

QUESTIONS

1. What kinds of information should the prospective buyer be looking for when reviewing the information base?

2. How is it possible to know when you have found a genuine business opportunity?

3. How can you identify and measure the motives that lead a buyer to a purchase?

4. Is the factor of timing the purchase or sale of a business more critical for a small business than for a large one?

5. In what areas of business activity is a smaller business able to do a job superior to that of a larger competitor?

6. What are the ways to measure the thrust that propels a successful small business?

7. What are the hazards in acquiring a business over an extended period of time?

8. What precautions are necessary in analyzing the profitability of the smaller business?

9. How much investigation should be done before a prospective buyer makes known his or her intentions to the owner of the business being considered?

10. How should the prospective buyer handle the negotiations leading up to putting a value on goodwill?

PROBLEM

The early 1980s is a period of increasing problems in business operations and an increasing number of business bankruptcies and failures.

Review the financial notices in a metropolitan newspaper or a financial reporting paper that is published in a city of 100,000 population or over. Pick out the foreclosure sales, liquidations, and bankruptcy proceedings. Study these and then do one or more of the following:

a. Attend a foreclosure sale.
b. Investigate why a particular business failed.
c. Estimate the losses suffered by the creditors of the business that failed.

BIBLIOGRAPHY

Baumback, Clifford M., and Kenneth Lawyer. *How to Organize and Operate a Small Business.* 6th ed. Englewood Cliffs, N.J.: Prentice-Hall, 1979, chap. 4, 5, and 6.

Frantz, Forrest H. *Successful Small Business Management.* Englewood Cliffs, N.J.: Prentice-Hall, 1978, chap. 3.

Moreau, James F. *Effective Small Business Management.* Chicago: Rand McNally College Publishing, 1980, chap. 2.

Redinbaugh, Larry D., and Clyde W. Neu. *Small Business Management.* St. Paul, Minn.: West Publishing, 1980, chap. 2, 5, and 9.

7

Finding support and backing for your business

Any business venture will require the help of a number of individuals and organizations if it is to succeed. If the venture is the initial launching of the enterprise then a fully developed prospectus or plan for getting support is necessary. A subsequent major activity requiring outside help will be the negotiation of support. These two problems are addressed in this chapter.

PREPARING AND USING A PROSPECTUS

Preparing a prospectus often becomes the entrepreneur's "moment of truth," for the prospectus is the instrument through which the master plan for the business is made known and support is sought from those who can help. Whatever planning or preparation has taken place previously is of no consequence unless the plan can be sold and support obtained.

A prospectus, regardless of its style and format, must include all things that are necessary to convince those whose aid is solicited. A complete and comprehensive document is needed to launch the business; subsequent major business changes will also require their own special treatment. The complete presentation should include the following:

1. A clear and concise description of the business and the reasons that it is needed.
2. An emphatic statement of the major "thrust elements" of the proposal. The entrepreneur must explain how a particular opportunity will be exploited.
3. An exposition of the owner/manager's contributions to the business —skills, experience, time, effort, and commitment.
4. A sequential analysis and explanation of the manner in which success for the proposal will be achieved.
5. A candid analysis of the risks involved and how such risks or uncertainties will be dealt with.
6. Evidence of financial resources sufficient to support the proposed plan for a reasonable initial period.

MAKING UP THE PROSPECTUS

Considerable work must be done before the actual development of the prospectus is begun. For most individuals, this is their first effort in assembling and presenting information calculated to persuade an assortment of individuals that the proposition deserves support. To do this successfully, a number of factors must be analyzed and evaluated in terms of their importance to the final prospectus.

A self-serving checklist. To get started with the project it is necessary for the business person to arrange the effort in a logical manner. Initially, it is desirable to make a dry run through the required sequence, in a manner that will give maximum results for the effort expended. A format suggested for that purpose is outlined in Table 7–1. The inquiry can be conducted in the sequence indicated, until all topics have been covered. If during the process, the investigation reveals that a particular item is a serious stumbling block, additional time should be spent on that item before proceeding. If no resolution seems possible, a new approach can be taken, or the matter set aside until a new opinion or judgment can be applied, using different values and assumptions.

Table 7–1 has purposely been designed to maximize the return from the entrepreneur's effort. Section I, Personal factors, can be adjusted to apply to a variety of business situations and is preliminary to all other effort. Section II, Factual data, encompasses an analysis of existing data pertaining to a given business. Firm and reliable information exists and may be obtained with reasonable effort. In Section III, Judgment

Table 7–1
Sequence checklist for prospectus preparation

Initial inquiry	*I. Personal factors*
	1. Ability needed for the particular business venture.
	2. Experience in the proposed business or related business activity.
	3. Dedication to the demands of a business operation.
	4. Self-discipline required to live within the limits imposed by financiers, competitors, and customers.
Summary	
Second-stage inquiry	*II. Factual data*
	5. Zoning laws.
	6. Licenses, franchises, and permits.
	7. State and federal laws.
	8. Administrative regulations.
	9. Professional certification (personal licenses, etc.).
Summary	
In-depth analysis	*III. Judgment decisions*
	10. Appropriate legal form.
	11. Basic formula for success.
	12. Initial capital needs.
	13. Projected income and expense budgets.
	14. Competition amount and vitality.
	15. Physical features of operation.
	16. Commitments by investors.
	17. Your professional team lawyer, accountant, banker.
Final conclusion	

decisions, business people must force themselves to produce realistic answers to tough questions. Even so, it is desirable to work through the list without too much delay. Further investigation and inquiry should properly await the actual creation of the formal document. At this stage the checklist is the initial once-over that provides a foundation for later efforts.

The importance of sequence. The sequence used in presenting the facts in the prospectus is important. For example:

1. Personal goals, attitudes, and commitments must be dealt with first. While this information is subjective, no further inquiry is valid without a strong conclusion that the proposers of the venture can

personally apply themselves to the needs of the proposed enterprise.

2. Inquiry should proceed from at-hand information, through objective data, to the items that require the most in terms of time, money, and effort. Thus in Table 7–1, items 1 through 9 are rather quickly dealt with, while 10 through 17 need to be used only if a strong go-ahead is indicated.

3. A series of investigations should have overlapping value. Thus, if personal inquiry indicates a strong likelihood of success in one type of business, the probability of succeeding in a related business is fairly easy to estimate. Likewise, investigation into factual data will ordinarily furnish information applicable to a number of business situations. Where operational features of a business require analysis that is very difficult and the information obtained demands subjective interpretation, there is less chance of applying the information to another business opportunity.

4. Each factor, condition, and subjective judgment should be resolved and accepted before moving on to the next. Any one of these may remain in doubt for a time, but a clear indication of failure of any critical condition affecting the ultimate success of the proposed business is a warning to proceed cautiously. A different approach with some new ideas may develop answers that will provide added confidence and enable the analysts to continue with enthusiasm.

The three steps of analysis

Each stage of analysis will require its own special emphasis and concentration. The strength of the final prospectus will depend upon the care invested in all stages of the work from start to finish.

Personal factors. All persons who have a direct bearing on the ownership and management of the business must be included in the analysis of personal factors. Strengths and weaknesses must be dealt with—the strong points emphasized and the weak points reinforced to the extent they will not damage the overall results. Lenders and suppliers may be doubtful as to certain claims made for the abilities of the principals. Possible doubts should be discussed and efforts made to provide answers for the obvious questions that will come up from the lenders and suppliers.

Factual data. The factual data dealt with in Section II provide a chance for prospective business men and women to establish a real advantage. Within this area of the analysis there is a wide range of characteristics that have a bearing on the business being considered. If the prospectus is thin in other respects a strong case should be formulated from the factual base. There is virtually no limit to things which could be shown to have a bearing on a business in some form or other under certain conditions. This section can be exploited by applying some imaginative thinking. One is cautioned, however, about lying or misrepresenting data in this section.

Judgment decisions.   The final section of analysis is related to subjects requiring careful evaluation and ultimately judgmental decisions. Being highly subjective, these decisions will be questioned by those who are approached to support the prospectus. Often, the proponents of the venture will need considerable help—from outside advisers, if necessary—in formulating this section so that it is plausible and convincing.

At this stage of the analysis the banker will be able to advise on what a bank needs and wants from a prospective borrower. The accountant will advise as to the form and presentation of data in a manner that is acceptable to the business community. An insurance agent will discuss and advise as to the needs of the business in the casualty field, along with the hazards of business interruption or the loss of key personnel through accident or death. Other advisers might be a knowledgeable real estate broker, a management consultant, or a market research adviser.

There are some who may argue that the contact with outside individuals at this stage of business development is premature. There is some logic in this position, and the risk of disclosure at this point is real. The counterargument is that if no previous outside contacts have been made it is none too soon to start, and that some feedback from experts is needed to deal properly with the kinds of information that are typically dealt with in Section III. If funds are being solicited from investors, this is especially the case.

Presenting different kinds of prospectuses

Business operations vary widely, depending on the characteristics of the business and the individuals involved. These differences must be reflected in the prospectus in relation to their importance to the ultimate business objective.

In a retailing operation, it would be very important to present in considerable detail the results of investigation of such things as the location of the business, traffic patterns, particular product lines available to the business, and anticipated business activity by each department, along with inventory variations.

In contrast, a manufacturing concern might tend to emphasize the design and unique applications of its products, the plans to be followed in penetrating the market, the adequacy of production equipment, and proposed tactics for adjusting to varying competitive changes.

Operating characteristics of wholesaling center upon maximizing volume and service while minimizing costs, while service businesses are heavily identified with management. Wholesaling has diminished in importance in the field of small business while service businesses are now the fastest growing segment of small business activity.

Developing the right emphasis mix. In dealing with the problem of what to emphasize and why, the writing stages of the prospectus will require some careful thought and selection. In Table 7–2 a format is outlined that should help in identifying the various factors of concern and estimating their relative importance.

Care should be exercised in using 7–2: it is furnished only as a rule-of-thumb. The creators of the prospectus will struggle mightily at this point in the task, particularly if they do the job that should be done. It may take 5 drafts to get started and 10 rewrites. Whatever it takes, *it must be done well.* Sloppy thought and careless treatment of operational

Table 7–2
Characteristics of operational importance by type of business

Type of business	Degree of importance		
	First	Second	Third
Retailing	Product lines Location Traffic density Drawing power Layout Parking Leases Franchises	Physical facilites Labor restrictions Consumer credit Goodwill	Transportation facilites
Service	Franchises Liability Goodwill	Location Product lines Parking Environment	Layout Zoning Consumer credit
Service—retail	Location Liability Product lines Goodwill	Labor restrictions Zoning Traffic density Drawing power Environment Layout	Zoning Consumer credit
Manufacturing	Transportation services Zoning Layout Patents Labor restrictions	Location Parking Warranties Customer credit Liability	Traffic density Drawing power Layout Environment
Wholesaling	Low-cost facilities Layout Customer credit Product lines	Leases Zoning	Labor restrictions Locations Drawing power Environment

matters will quickly expose a prospective entrepreneur as lacking in an understanding of the basics. Don't let it happen. Rewrite it one more time if there is any question about its completeness.

Timing and presenting the prospectus

One of the essential talents of a winner is timing. In the case of the prospectus, timing is an integral part of the job.

In general, two aspects of timing are important. The first is the recognition of factors that are timely, such as the high interest rates and the ravages of inflation in the late 1970s and early 1980s. The other has to do with the actual timing of the prospectus itself. At what time will it be presented and considered? And to whom? Is it appropriate at that time, and if not, can it be reworked so that it is timely?

Understandable difficulties with timing are associated with such things as when to approach a given market, individual, or institution for money, meeting a change in a zoning deadline or a change in the balance of power of a regulatory board, such as a county planning agency.

It is particularly disturbing in the early 1980s to hear people say that "times are different," that small businesses are suffering from a lack of influence and bargaining power or from shortages of materials and fuel, or that all municipal and governmental actions are ill-advised. At any given time, one person's plight may be another's opportunity. Timing decisions should stay high on the list of possible late modifications of the basic plan and format.

Exploitation

Every prospectus must propose to exploit something. Exploitation in this context is not something bad but rather the process of capitalizing on opportunities. In general, these can include ability, people, products, time, knowledge, and wisdom, as well as opportunities of a more subtle nature.

As the prospectus takes shape, the goal of exploitation can serve to guide the planning and organizing around the underlying theme. Without it, the final prospectus may wander aimlessly and be lacking in strong dedication to a given objective. In pursuing any given exploitation goal, analysis should proceed step by step. It is important to provide answers to anticipated questions. What is the product or service good for? What unique application is available? How does this or that factor fit with the other factors? The thread of inquiry follows logically to develop the strongest case possible for the proposition. What you know is one thing; your proposed results must be conclusive in the minds of your supporters.

One cautious note: Sometimes the proposition may do the job so well that those exposed to it wind up using it for themselves. Be careful in areas where there is limited protection. Deal with reputable individuals and organizations. If necessary, withhold vital data until it is appropriate to reveal them. Reasonable persons will understand this concern for protecting essential information. This can be discussed in an honest and forthright manner.

Competition

Few business activities are free from competition. In theory, business without competition will adopt practices that are nonaggressive and will wind up the victim of its own greed and/or complacency. At any time competition might be described as aggressive, passive, feeble, dormant, and so on. The important thing is to realize that any threat or potential threat may generate action on the part of established competitors. The prospective business person should be careful not to misread the competitive signals, yet it is surprising how many business ventures are proposed on the assumption that competition is either decadent or nonexistent.

Potential supporters approached by the prospective small business person will weigh the element of competition very strongly, usually more so than the person proposing the business venture. Because of this, much time and effort must be spent to develop and analyze the competitive climate. Considerable investigation, personal observation, and inquiry will be required to develop fundamental data that are reliable enough to justify the application of analysis and judgment. Much of the latter will be concerned with the probabilities of human behavior, something which is difficult to predict.

A comparison of the various factors of competition by use of a matrix is illustrated in Table 7–3. This method requires the assignment of numerical values and is useful in developing a graphic display that provides a summary overview rather than one that is segmented or detached. As a valuable demonstration that one has investigated and thought out the potential impact of one's competitors, it should be included in the prospectus.

Table 7–3
New-entry competitor comparison table (arbitrary rating scale 0–100)

Value factors for comparison to proposed business	Established competitors*				
	A	B	C	D	E
Location	90%	75%	50%	60%	20%
Facility size	Large	Medium	Medium	Large	Small
Percent of existing potential market for new enterprise now served	20%	10%	12%	17%	5%
Total or partial competitor	Total	Noncritical lines and/or services	Total	Only critical lines and/or services	Partial and of no consequence
Managerial abilities	Strong	Strong	Average	Improving	Weak
Aggressiveness	80%	60%	15%	10%	5%
Momentum	Strong	Increasing	Declining	Unknown	Weak
Financial strength	Strong	Limited	Average	Vulnerable	Weak

*One or more of these may be mail-order or other nonresident firms.

PROPOSING A NEW VERSUS AN EXISTING BUSINESS

The prospectus soliciting support for setting up a new business will differ somewhat in format and emphasis from one seeking support in buying an existing business. Primary emphasis in this chapter is devoted to the new business. However, analysis should include comparison of the desirability of establishing a new business with that of taking over an existing business. Generally the importance or worth of each functional portion of a business will differ among businesses, so that the final judgment is based on a total evaluation rather than an item-by-item matching.

An accurate evaluation will establish a reasonable price that the prospective buyer is willing to pay to acquire an existing business. The amount offered will probably include something for goodwill; i.e., the amount of valuation in excess of a reasonable investment return. The values of a business that is unsuccessful or in financial difficulty will naturally be lessened.

Special attention should be given to items such as goodwill, valuation of assets, removal of successful or failing management, subsequent activity by the former owner, and subtle and obscure reasons that the business is being offered for sale. Occasionally a business might be acquired at a bargain, but this is a rare circumstance. An apparent bargain is perhaps the most dangerous condition with which to deal: it may encourage hasty or snap judgments instead of the careful application of logic and analysis.

THE PRETESTING PROCESS

It is reasonable to assume that the prospectus will be prepared, reworked, and edited by the principals in the business venture. In addition, it may be reviewed by friends, relatives, and others who are friendly to the cause. These critics, however, are not enough, as it is important that the prospectus be seasoned. The famous football coach Jock Sutherland, of the University of Pittsburgh, once said, "The time to play sophomores is when they're juniors." The same can be said for a given proposal.

Again, it may be prudent to secure professional advice—that of a CPA, an attorney, or others. If properly used, these experts are well worth the cost. Another approach is to test the prospectus with people who will not be asked to support the business. The testing process will be especially valuable in the following areas:

1. The master plan—is it good or bad? If bad, what needs to be corrected?
2. What is wrong with the format, content, age of the information, and graphic materials? *Lenders are particularly critical of outdated financial data or statements that are too optimistic.*
3. Possible realignment and adjustment—does there need to be a change in objective or direction? Is the sequence faulty or is logical development lacking? The first two pages of the prospectus are critical; they should probably be a short, hard-hitting, convincing resume.
4. Does the prospectus answer questions like these?
   a. What makes you think you can do this?
   b. Why should we risk our money on this enterprise?
   c. Where did you get this figure and those data?
   d. Why do you think your budgets are realistic?
   e. What is in it for me if I help you?

It is easy at this stage to become discouraged, but to do so is to lose the battle. Instead, review the criticisms and analyze them for valid objections. Avoid the assumption that these things are a direct attack on your ability or integrity. If you have picked your advisers well, their comments will be intended only to help.

SEQUENCE AND FORMAT OF THE PROSPECTUS

Time spent in perfecting sequence, readability, and format may be as rewarding as any other phase of preparing the prospectus; thus, the tendency to relax on these points should be repressed. In general, a good small business prospectus will proceed along the following lines:

1. Title page—including the date of the document, the proposed name of the business, and the names and affiliations of the principal officers.
2. Table of contents—if needed because of length or complexity.
3. Introduction—clearly and concisely outlining the proposed operation. This is very critical; two or three well-written pages will encourage and stimulate the reviewer, but a poor job may establish a mental image that defeats an otherwise sound proposal.
4. Functional anaylsis—step by step and in depth.
5. Summary and conclusions.
6. Supporting data—bibliography, exhibits, etc.

While the outline is simple, the chances that the prospectus will be accepted will be greater if it follows a sequence that is familiar to the business world.

Style of writing and readability are also important, along with proper word usage and correct spelling. This is not to suggest that the writer assume any particular style or method but rather that the chosen style be consistent and appropriate. It may be desirable to solicit editorial help from people who are familiar with business persons and their methods of communication.

The format used should represent the judgment of the people preparing the final document. Printing and photographic techniques are available that can accomplish whatever the entrepreneur judges will have the best effect on the audience. Relevant differences should be taken into consideration: for instance, a formal proposal by a consulting firm for a continuing governmental contract will differ from a proposal to a private risk capital source for funds to finance a new business producing complex manufactured products.

THE BARGAINING AND SELLING PROCESS

Before presenting the prospectus, a final step is to determine what limitations will govern the bargaining process with a lender. How much will the people proposing the business be willing to give up? How much will those who want to help expect to take for their efforts? What will they want? Mortgages, stock, guarantees, the right to be on the board of directors? The right to limit salaries? Initially, there will be no statements about what the proponents expect. They will be asking for support, without any accurate idea as to the kinds of answers they will receive. They must, however, decide the conditions under which they will accept outside support.

Ownership, profit, and interest rates

The most common issues of bargaining are related to the degree of ownership the owners are willing to relinquish to their supporters, their willingness to surrender part of the profits, and the rates of interest they are willing to pay. One or more of these areas in various degrees will probably be involved in the negotiations. *The important thing is to know the value of the proposition and whether these features are being settled in favor of the solicitors or those being asked for support.* If too much is given up by the entrepreneurs, the net effect is to reduce those who think they are small business persons to the status of low-cost management being exploited for someone else's benefit and profit. Unless the prospectus is evaluated before the negotiations begin, commitments may be agreed to that are more liberal than necessary or inconsistent with the anticipated operations.

In most cases all the support for a business venture will not come from one source. As each portion of the backing is committed there will be new conditions for those who follow, as the owners make adjustments in their own master plan. Master plan changes will also come about through negotiations that do not result in any agreement but point up circumstances which are objectionable. In such cases it will be necessary to reevaluate the prospectus and decide what changes in conditions are necessary.

QUESTIONS

1. What is a prospectus for a business? Why is a prospectus important for someone wanting to start a small business?

2. What are the various phases that one might go through in

preparing a prospectus? Which do you think is the most important? Why?

3. Will different kinds of businesses (wholesaling, manufacturing, retailing) require different information in their prospectuses? Why?

4. In presenting a prospectus to a potential backer of your small business, would it make a difference what you would do if you were proposing an expansion of an existing business or a development of a new business? Why do you answer the way you do? Explain in detail.

5. What do you think is the most important thing that a prospective investor might look at in evaluating your prospectus for a proposed business? Why do you say that?

6. In developing a prospectus, which do you think is more important: a clear and concise description of the business and the reasons that it is needed or a candid analysis of the risks involved and how such risks or uncertainties will be dealt with by the owner/operator of the business? Explain in detail.

7. What is a pro forma financial statement? Is this an important part of a prospectus?

8. What are the most important operational characteristics that one would want to present in a prospectus for a retailing business?

9. Why does this text use the term *exploitation* in relationship to the preparation and use of a prospectus? Explain.

10. Who should make up a prospectus? Why?

PROBLEMS

1. Consider the bookstore where you purchase your textbooks and other related material. Assume that you would like to start a business like that bookstore. Prepare a prospectus that you would present to a prospective backer of that venture.

2. Ask one of your professors for a sample copy of a business prospectus. Analyze critically that prospectus as to its completeness

and thoroughness in relationship to the material suggested and recommended in this chapter.

BIBLIOGRAPHY

Hayes, Rick Stephen. *Business Loans: A Guide to Money Sources and How to Approach Them Successfully.* 2d ed. Boston: CBI Publishing, 1980. This new edition of this very popular book is revised and expanded to include the latest developments in finding sources and support to finance your business. Designed to close the gap between lender and borrower, banker, and businessowner. An extremely comprehensive volume.

Credit and Collections: A Practical Guide. Boston: CBI Publishing, 1978. This book is a practical and readable source for credit managers and owners of small- and medium-sized businesses. Includes all the financial and nonfinancial analysis necessary to judge the credit worthiness of the customer.

Mancuso, Joseph R. *How to Start, Finance, and Manage Your Own Small Business.* Englewood Cliffs, N.J.: Prentice-Hall, 1978. This book is especially helpful to use in trying to write and develop a business plan. Five actual business plans and commentaries are included as examples of how others have written their business plans.

Rachlin, Robert. *Return on Investment: Strategies for Profit.* Englewood Cliffs, N.J.: Prentice-Hall, 1979. This book identifies strategies for setting long-term goals and revealing techniques for measuring competitive performance. Shows why the return on investment method of evaluation is one of the most reliable, accurate measurement techniques to evaluate financial performance and forecast market trends.

Case Study

Why I think I can make a go of opening a skin-diving shop

Review of the industry

The dive business and sport are both relatively new. The first aqualung was brought into the United States about 30 years ago. The first firm in the dive industry was U.S. Divers, which introduced the aqualung into the United States. The lung was developed in France.

In the beginning distribution in the diving industry was very mixed up. There were many methods of distribution:

Manufacturer to the individual.

Manufacturer to the retailer to the consumer.

Manufacturer to the jobber to the retailer to the consumer.

Manufacturer through mail order to the consumer.

Achieving sales in any diving business is dependent upon repair, service, and instruction. Any new outlet that doesn't offer these services will fail. Historically many dive shops have suffered and the industry has stayed in a state of unprofitability because nonbusiness people are trying to enter the industry, they continue to teach part time, sell equipment part time, and wait to enter the business full time. The entire industry has been in what appears to be a continual state of confusion because of this.

Several years ago a firm by the name of Scubapro entered the industry. Their intention was to gear their entire approach to the specialty dealer. There had never been franchising or price maintenance of any kind in the diving industry. The Scubapro Company at that time was one of the fastest growing companies of the diving industry.

At the present time the diving industry is divided into two groups of retail outlets; the specialty shop and the rest of the world. Most of the major manufacturers distribute to both types of outlets. There is also a large number of very small manufacturers who produce suits and other accessories such as underwater lights, etc.

The need for certification and lessons

In the United States, certification is needed by the consumer to get an air tank refilled. Refills are done almost exclusively by specialty dive shops. These shops require a card showing that the customer has completed a course. My shop is certified by one of the major certification programs.

Lessons are necessary to be a certified diver. The price for lessons fluctuates—$50 to $100 on the average. Standard course time is 6–8 lessons, requiring 3–8 weeks and including 22–40 hours of instruction plus an open-water check-out.

Frankly, I think most courses are geared to the hazards of diving, not the enjoyment. I intend to emphasize the fun of diving. The typical course is rather long and drawn out, running anywhere from five to eight weeks. A lot of time is spent on classroom lecture and pool workouts. To get a basic certification usually requires only one ocean or open-water diving outing.

The segment of the industry that I expect to outsell are courses which are run by part-time instructors. They are detrimental to the business in general. These instructors continue to make it appear difficult to dive just to satisfy their own ego.

My store will feature full-time professional instructors. I will teach people at their own rate, either fast or slow, and orient the teaching to solo diving. Furthermore, I feel that ocean work is far more important than pool work. I feel the key to my business growth is through instruction. The sales that I need will be directly geared to the number of students I can train.

Why I think I will succeed where others have failed

The typical dive shop owner has been in the business or at least dived for many years. Such people have been operating on a marginal basis. Many of them work at other jobs. They lack a professional approach in many respects. The shops are generally small and carry a limited amount of inventory; an inventory between $20,000 and $60,000 is not unusual. A very few have inventories of $200,000 or so, that I know of.

If one point stands out as a person enters most dive shops, it is the lack of organization and merchandising. Most of the stores do not look very professional. They have little merchandise, and what they have is not artfully displayed. I *will not* have those kinds of problems.

Size of industry

There are approximately 1,100 stores selling dive equipment in the United States. There may be about 450 of these which are of some quality and size and there are about 300 places to get air, called air stations.

Fashion has just begun to touch the industry. All indications point to a larger increase in diving by women. If this is to happen, a good dive shop must begin to cater to this new market. Diving in the past has had a very physical connotation. A diver was tough and willing to take great risk. This is just not true anymore. People can dive at any depth and with different abilities.

The professional diving shops around the country are slowly gaining ground in a large part due to the efforts of people who work toward upgrading their business and their teaching methods. I will be one of these people.

The most appealing potential of the entire industry, I have not yet mentioned. Resort development is, I feel, the key to the growth of diving. Diving in landlocked areas and cold water will attract a certain number of enthusiasts, but people who live in these areas will be very hesitant in continuing or purchasing equipment without the potential of and promotion of diving in warm water. This is why my resort location will keep my business from having the same problems as the shops in landlocked areas. My shop will be well done and have a first-class appearance. As I have pointed out, the consumer of today will be looking for more planned and controlled recreation. By developing a resort shop with qualified instructor personnel even an occasional diver can go on vacation and enjoy diving in my area.

Summary

I am sure you see the merits of my business plan, as explained in the foregoing. If you have any questions, please do not hesitate to ask.

QUESTIONS: The foregoing was a presentation made to a prospective financial backer of a skin diving shop. Do you think the person trying to start that small business received the money requested? Why or why not? Explain in detail how this presentation could have been made better. What kind of data, information, etc. should have been included?

8

Franchising

The term *franchising* brings to mind the typical operation that serves the public a limited range of quickly prepared foods. It is unlikely that there are very many individuals who have not been served in one or more of the outlets designated as a McDonald's, Burger King, Wendy's or a Baskin-Robbins ice cream shop. These are all highly successful franchise operations.

DEVELOPMENT OF FRANCHISING

Franchising began in the United States as a way for a manufacturer or dealer as a franchisor to project the image and reputation of the parent firm through the creation of a number of outlets to handle the firm's products. The creation of the franchise operated by the franchisee enabled the parent manufacturer or dealer to maintain an exclusive and controlled enterprise that would be solely devoted to the products of the parent firm.

Different kinds of franchising

The initial forms of franchises were involved with automobiles, farm implements, sewing machines, gasoline, and other products, and were generally known as *product distribution* franchises. The number of products distributed and the number of establishments operating under this form of franchising are very large. Many new franchises of this form will be created.

In the 1950s, a form of franchising known as *business format* franchising began to appear. This franchise form involves the use of a business format, management style, and some form of trademark or visual identification. This form has been used successfully by motels, convenience grocery stores, carpet cleaners, campgrounds, and in particular the fast-food outlets. A good part of the growth in this area paralleled the general increase in service businesses in the United States since 1950.

There exist several other variations, which are not as significant as the two previously mentioned. One in particular is the *business opportunity* venture. In this instance, the seller of the opportunity provides the items to be sold and secures locations and arranges for the method of sale, perhaps a rack or vending machine. There is no agreement as to the use of a trademark or a specific identified product associated with the seller.

Definition of franchising

Franchising is an arrangement for marketing or distribution in which a parent company, known as the *franchisor*, grants to the individual or smaller company, known as the *franchisee*, a right to do business in a prescribed way.

The particular terms of the relationship can vary a great deal but will include such things as the right to sell the parent company's products, to use its name, and to use a.standard form of architecture; the terms also will impose limitations as to contract expiration date and the scope of the business operations to be conducted.

The California Franchise Investment Law provides a definition that has been used as a model in similar franchise disclosure laws in 13 other states. The California law defines a franchise as:

> A contract or agreement, either expressed or implied, whether oral or written, between two or more persons by which:
> (1) a franchise is granted for the right to engage in the business of offering, selling or distributing goods or services under a marketing plan or system prescribed in a substantial part by a franchisor; and
> (2) the operation of the franchisee's business pursuant to such plan or system is substantially associated with the franchisor's trademark, service mark, trade name, logotype, advertising, or other commercial symbol designating the franchisor or its affiliate; and
> (3) the franchisee is required to pay, directly or indirectly, a franchise fee.

The identity-establishing things that the franchisor includes in the agreement will have a bearing on the ease with which the public will recognize a member of a particular franchise system. This is readily apparent in the case of McDonald's, Howard Johnson's, Kentucky Fried Chicken, Burger King, Pizza Hut, and many other fast-food outlets. An effort is made to maximize the impact on customers by identifying—with color, format, style, and service—aspects that are unique or special for the particular franchise system.

The scope of the franchise agreement is the principal subject of initial negotiations between the franchisor and franchisee. It is very important for any franchisee to understand what is being provided and at what price. This situation will be discussed more fully in a later portion of this chapter.

THE SCOPE OF FRANCHISE OPERATIONS

The very dramatic growth of franchising in the United States is summarized on a year-by-year basis in *Franchising in the Economy*, published annually by the U.S. Department of Commerce.

Starting in 1969, there was a steady growth of franchises at a rate in excess of 10,000 per year. From 1973 until 1975 a decline resulted from the petroleum crisis. In 1975 the upward trend resumed, at a slightly slower pace than the 1969 to 1973 period, but still at a rate of about 10,000 new establishments per year.

Various publications provide the following approximate figures as of 1978:

a. There were about 245,000 franchise business outlets *in* the United States.
b. There were some 17,000 franchise outlets *outside* the United States that were established and operated under direct control or under some arrangement with a U.S. parent company.
c. There were over 1,800 different franchise companies in the United States and Canada.
d. Canada constitutes the largest foreign market for U.S. franchisors and will continue to do so.
e. Franchisors based in Canada, France, England, and Japan will all enter the United States with their own franchise systems. Japan in particular, in the middle 1970s, experienced a rapid internal expansion of franchising.

It is not possible to include all the important facts relative to the scope of franchising in this chapter. The reader should look to the following two publications—both prepared by the U.S. Department of Commerce and available from the Government Printing Office, Washington, DC 20402—for current and informative data:

1. *Franchising Opportunity Handbook.* This publication lists franchisors and the scope and nature of their operations. It has other information that is valuable to the prospective franchisee and is updated regularly.
2. *Franchising in the Economy.* This is a companion to the book listed above. It contains more particular statistical data on franchising within the economic system of the United States. The publication is updated yearly.

Franchise advantages to the franchisee

The franchisor makes numerous advantages available to the franchisee immediately. The most significant of these are:

1. An established and familiar brand name and reputation.
2. Well-developed training programs and continuing services for the franchisee.
3. Access to market expertise in selecting a suitable site.
4. An established format for the real estate contracts, leases, construction contracts, etc.
5. Established operating manuals and accounting systems.
6. Aid in obtaining financing.
7. Promotion and advertising programs and the availability of merchandising materials.

Franchise disadvantages to the franchisee

Offsetting some of the advantages supplied by franchisors, there are some disadvantages:

1. The franchisee must pay for a number of different things provided by the franchisor. In some cases, there is reason to doubt the value of certain items.
2. The lack of follow-through by the franchisor in providing training and management guidance, particularly after the franchise is under way.
3. Failure of the franchisor to listen to, or be concerned with, a franchisee who wishes to be somewhat independent in his method of operation.
4. Threats and intimidation by the franchisor. At times a franchisee is coerced by a threat of losing the franchise or some other serious consequence.
5. Conditions in the contractual arrangements unfairly favoring the franchisor. These have been substantially changed by federal

and state laws enacted in response to complaints raised by franchisees.

It is readily apparent from a review of the two previous listings that the arrangements of the franchise system do not always engender a harmonious relationship. In general, a franchisor who is promoting and guiding a valid business operation has a great deal to gain in dealing legitimately with franchisees and using their efforts to his own advantage. Likewise, the franchisee must contribute his fair share of effort and determination to the success of the operation.

Many franchise arrangements fail because some detail of the overall system proves faulty. The idea may be all right, but that is a long way from being a successful operation. Franchise arrangements are sometimes viewed by the franchisee as a way of curing all the risks of being in business alone. This is naive thinking and indicates that people are inclined to believe what they want to believe.

It is important to emphasize at this point that nothing about a franchise system is foolproof. The franchisee is buying into an opportunity at some cost that must be related and compared to the cost of starting alone. If the values already established are sound and fairly priced, then the fees paid may be worthwhile.

Some features of a franchise are difficult to compare to those of a nonfranchise situation, but the comparison should be made with proper allowance for incommensurable factors.

STARTING AND OPERATING AS A FRANCHISEE

The prospective franchisee must analyze many circumstances before making a decision to go into any form of franchised enterprise. Some of these analyses require little time or effort and enable the entrepreneur to eliminate the consideration of unlikely or unsuitable propositions.

Franchise rate of return

Little data exist that will help the franchisee in making a judgment about the profitability of a given franchise. There are some indications that there should be an 18 to 25 percent return on invested capital before taxes, in addition to a managerial salary, plus a payback of the equity capital investment in no more than three years. These figures are arbitrary but they are not unrealistic; they would not hold true for a large service operation or for a substantial capital investment in real estate, where the payback is slower. Nevertheless, the franchisee should have every reason to expect results that compare favorably with those mentioned.

The prospective franchisee checklist

Many persons who contemplate operating a franchise are not well prepared to analyze carefully and thoroughly the conditions that are important to franchise success. The items listed in Table 8–1 should be evaluated before making a decision to go ahead with a franchise agreement.

The list in Table 8–1 is not as detailed or as comprehensive as criteria that appear in other publications. The reader is advised to obtain more detailed data if the answers to these questions do not disqualify the venture.

The important points in the list are sufficient to indicate that there are circumstances that are critical; these should be investigated in depth by any prospective franchisee. In general, the points emphasized apply to the different kinds of franchises and state the circumstances of prime importance. Additional inquiry will ordinarily involve a deeper probing of the basic statement to identify related topics that are important.

THE FRANCHISOR IN THE FRANCHISE RELATIONSHIP

This section outlines the reasons that there are franchisors and what they desire from the franchise arrangements. Knowledge of these reasons and desires makes it possible to understand how some of the circumstances of the franchise operation have developed. In general, these are soundly conceived and should work if both parties fulfill their avowed responsibilities. Unsuccessful franchisees, however, usually place the principal blame for difficulty on the franchisor. It is easier to blame those who have created and control the organization than to admit failure in operating a single outlet that has little influence on the entire system.

Franchise advantages to the franchisor

1. After the company has been formed, its growth depends on the income from franchise fees. The franchisor has a definite incentive to increase the number of franchisees.
2. The search for additional franchisees can be financed with the fees from established franchises.
3. Expansion can proceed rapidly once the venture is under way.
4. The cost of management can be kept low because franchisees are expected to be self sufficient, except for limited help from the franchisor.
5. The franchisor acquires the benefit of local expertise from the franchisees.

Table 8–1
Prospective franchisee checklist

1. Personal evaluation
   a. Why do you want to buy a franchise?
   b. Are you considering the right kind of franchise?
   c. Are you willing to work hard and for long hours?
   d. Do you have good health and physical stamina?
   e. Can you work under stringent rules and controls?
   f. Are you able to manage other people?
2. The franchise territory
   a. What franchise territories are allocated and how are they protected?
   b. Can you acquire additional adjacent territories?
   c. Is the territory big enough and wealthy enough to support the operation?
   d. Are there other comparable franchises operating in the territory?
   e. How will your location be selected and do you have any choice in its selection?
   f. What restrictions as to the territory and your premises are imposed by the franchisor?
3. The franchise contract
   a. Have you retained an attorney to study and evaluate the contract?
   b. Do you understand the terms of the contract?
   c. What do other franchisees say about the enforcement of the contract by the franchisor?
   d. Is the contract predominantly in favor of the wishes and dictates of the franchisor?
   e. Does the franchisor assure you that enforcement of the contract provisions will not be as harsh as stated in the contract itself? Can you rely on such assurances?
   f. Does the contract allow you to acquire additional territories, outlets, and privileges as your operations with the parent company grow?
   g. Do the contract conditions seem to be fair to both parties?
4. The product or services
   a. Is the product or service a proven quantity?
   b. Is it fairly priced to you so that it can be sold by you at a reasonable profit?
   c. Is it a fad or other short-lived item that may soon disappear from the marketplace?
   d. Can the franchisor supply it now and in the future, and does the franchisor produce it?
   e. Is it protected by a patent?
   f. Is it vulnerable to competition or replacement in the marketplace?
   g. Is it something that requires special skills or talents to develop its full potential?
   h. Is the item a necessity or something that is purely discretionary and subject to levels of discretionary spending?
5. The franchisor
   a. Who are the principals in the parent company?
   b. Are they persons of honesty and integrity or do they have a blemished personal history?
   c. Does the company exhibit managerial expertise backed up by solid accomplishments?
   d. Are company personnel free and open about company business dealings, plans for the future, and commitments to franchisees?
   e. Does the parent company want you to make a substantial profit?
   f. Can the company show solid evidence of a franchisee training program and continuing help to franchisees?
   g. What is the parent company's reputation among its franchisees?

6. There may be income from sources other than fees; such as products, materials, or management services.

Franchise disadvantages to the franchisor

1. It may be difficult to secure from the franchisees the cooperation and commitment required for success. This is a particularly diffi-

cult problem when the franchising operation is new and cannot cite the success of established franchisees to keep new owners in line.

2. State and federal laws are becoming more restrictive as to the operations of franchisors. No doubt much of the restriction is justified to protect the franchisees, who are subject to the control and manipulation of the parent company. Regardless of the reasons, this is an increasing problem for franchisors.

3. Franchisees are becoming more inclined to form associations and rebel against what they perceive to be unfair actions on the part of franchisors. This has encouraged franchise firms to form franchise advisory boards to deal with items that cause friction between the parties.

4. It is difficult to develop the type of management team that can deal effectively with the diverse group making up the franchise holders. It takes a perceptive and knowledgeable staff to handle the management.

Again, the listing here is brief, covering some major areas that affect the operations of the franchisor and the outlets that it controls. The franchisor has much to gain from the proper operation of a franchise unit. There is thus a tendency to push the franchisee and to try to achieve the benefits of a profitable operation. In doing this the franchisor may be over-zealous. The franchisor may also rebel against federal and state control and establish defensive procedures that restrict the operations of franchisees. This is done as a means of avoiding some possible but unforeseen liability that could arise from the franchise agreement.

The prospective franchisee should be very careful in his approach to a franchise arrangement. The nature of franchising adds substantial advantages to a prospective businessperson, *if* the right individual is matched with the right job. Unfortunately, the franchisor may be tempted to take on a franchisee simply because he/she can provide the initial financing. The prospect might unwisely be lured into becoming a franchise holder by the expectation of success and profits, regardless of his/her aptitude for the task.

All the franchise relationships are crucial and a bad beginning is a strong indicator of future grief.

The continuing relationship between the parent company and the franchisee requires commitment by both parties to uphold the bargain. The possibilities for success are apparent and the way to achieve them is known. Each party must respect the goal of the other in the joint effort required.

STATE AND FEDERAL LAWS REGARDING FRANCHISING

On January 1, 1971, the California Franchise Investment Law took effect; it was the first state law to regulate the offer and sale of franchises.

Prior to the offer and sale of a franchise in California, it must be registered by the Commissioner of Corporations and described by an offering prospectus. This prospectus must be delivered to the prospective franchisee at least 48 hours before the signing of any binding agreement or the payment of any consideration for the franchise.

The Commissioner of Corporations has broad powers under this law and can, as an example, require the franchisor to escrow funds from the franchisee if there is reason to believe that the franchisor will have difficulty fulfilling his/her obligations.

At the present time 16 states regulate offers and sales of franchises: Hawaii, California, Oregon, Washington, North Dakota, South Dakota, Minnesota, Wisconsin, Michigan, Illinois, Indiana, Rhode Island, Maryland, Virginia, Ohio, and Nebraska. There are some differences in the laws of these states, but any prospective franchisee could secure a copy of one of these laws to determine the nature of the protection afforded a franchisee in the regulated states.

In October 1979, the U.S. Federal Trade Commission promulgated the "Trade Regulation Rule Relating to Disclosure Requirements and Prohibitions Concerning Franchising and Business Opportunity Ventures." This rule requires a franchisor to disclose material facts about its business and its relationship to prospective franchisees. While these regulations do not cover all forms of franchise relationships, they impose quite detailed requirements on franchisors. A prospectus from the franchisor must be provided to the prospective franchisee, and a copy of all agreements to be executed must be provided by the franchisor at least five days before they are to be signed.

Through the Franchise Committee of the Midwest Securities Commissioners Association, the 16 states with franchise laws have developed the Uniform Franchise Offering Circular ("UFOC") and Guidelines. This consists of a uniform prospectus form, application for registration of the franchisor, consent to service of process and a salesman disclosure form. A section of the Guidelines describes the differences in the various states as to registration and disclosures.

Anyone who contemplates becoming a franchisee may already be subject to one or more of these laws and regulations. If so, then the prospective franchisee should investigate them to determine their bearing upon any franchise commitment.

FUTURE OF FRANCHISING

The development of franchising since 1960 has been one of the most dramatic success stories in basic business activity that the United States has ever experienced. There seems to be no reason why the use of the franchise form will diminish—in fact, it will probably at some time become a substantial part of business activity in almost every major country in the world. Regardless of the time it will take to reach into different cultures, habits, and business customs, it seems to have lost little vitality in the years of rapid growth since 1960.

The economic conditions of a country or of different parts of the world will have local effects on franchise growth, but the basic format seems to be firmly entrenched for years to come.

QUESTIONS

1. What was the initial incentive that led to the early franchise organizations in the United States?

2. Is there a considerable value to the combined features of a business format type of franchise as far as customer response is concerned?

3. Why should a state such as California feel it necessary to regulate franchisors by special legislation?

4. What particular kinds of businesses from foreign countries would be most likely to enter the United States as franchise organizations?

5. What steps should be taken by a potential franchisee to evaluate the service and product package of the parent franchise organization?

6. What conditions within a franchise agreement would be likely to cause friction between the franchisor and franchisee?

7. What questions are particularly important when a prospective franchisee is interviewing present franchise holders about their relationships with the parent company?

8. Is the requirement of a substantial up-front franchise fee a suspicious circumstance in securing a franchise from a relatively unknown firm?

9. Is the franchisor justified in demanding strict compliance with the franchise terms from the franchisee? Does such a policy conflict with the entrepreneurial spirit that is so desirable in small business managers?

10. Why do the regulatory laws provide that a franchisor must provide copies of the contract before the papers are to be signed?

BIBLIOGRAPHY

Church, Nancy J. *Future Opportunities in Franchising.* New York: Pilot Books, 1979. One of the Pilot Series of books which gives a good review of the future trends in franchising.

Directory of Franchising Organizations, New York: Pilot Books. Annual. A source book of the franchise organizations and their operations. Useful for reference data on names, addresses, and so forth.

Fels, Jerome L.   *Franchising and the Law.* Washington, D.C.: International Franchise Association, 1978. A good reference to determine the various legal questions that are of concern in franchising operations.

Norback, Peter, and Craig T. Norback.   *The Dow Jones-Irwin Guide to Franchising.* Homewood, Ill. Dow Jones-Irwin, 1978. A basic guide for the prospective franchise holder.

The Franchise Annual: Complete Handbook and Directory. St. Catherines, Ont.: International Franchise Opportunities. Annual. A source book that is very useful for the prospective franchisee in Canada.

Vaughn, Charles L.   *Franchising.* Lexington, Mass. D. C.: Heath, 1979. A basic, well-known book in the field of franchising. Has a variety of important data relative to various aspects of franchise operations.

Case study

Norman Smith's second career

In October 1979, Norman Smith was called at his home in Chicago and informed that his father had just died. The father had been a widower living on the family farm, which was located at the intersection of two state highways on the outskirts of Schumburgh, a town of some 8,000 people in western Kansas. In addition to the farm, the estate consisted of a 20-room, 3-story hotel with a local leased-premises restaurant on the first floor, along with a small real estate office and a beauty shop.

Norman had been left with the task of handling the family matters for his two married sisters who lived in Kansas City. They had no personal interest in the family estate except to be given their respective shares upon settlement.

After the father's funeral, the three children met in the cafe located in the hotel building and agreed that they would meet over the Christmas holidays to discuss what course of action should be taken in regard to the estate. Norman contacted his father's attorney and asked him to prepare an estimate of the values of the farm land and the building in town, along with other elements of the estate that were of little consequence. The estimates would be needed for his meeting later with his sisters in Kansas City.

Shortly before Christmas 1979, Norman Smith received a preliminary statement from the attorney in Schumburgh, which indicated that the farm comprised 1,120 acres of good-quality wheat land, and that it could be sold for around $300 per acre. It could also be leased out on a standard lessor-lessee arrangement without any difficulty. The farmhouse and the other farm buildings were of little value. The 1,120 acres were under an oil and gas lease to Morganeaux Oil Co., which operated four producing oil wells in the northwest section of the farm, a part of the Tokomo field. Royalties from the wells provided an income of about $100 per day.

The three-story hotel building in downtown Schumburgh had been built in 1925 and had been remodeled several times. It had a good heating and air conditioning plant, up-to-date furniture, and was adequate for the present trade, which consisted mostly of sales representatives, tourists who did not wish to pay higher prices at the major motel across the street, and a steady flow of people visiting the town on business or for treatment at the local hospital, which was well staffed and drew patients from a wide area around Schumburgh.

Upon receiving the letter from the attorney, Norman spent the next couple of nights studying it and trying to decide upon a good course of action. A few days later he called the attorney and asked for a few additional facts and estimates regarding the properties. He was unable to make any decisions and put the matter aside, planning to come back to it later.

Shortly before Christmas 1979, Norman again reviewed the attorney's correspondence and came to the conclusion that he would have to visit his sisters in Kansas City without any particular plan. He was 54 years old and had worked in Chicago for a large bank since graduating from the University of Kansas in 1950. His sisters were 51 and 48 years old, married, with families of their own. Both had jobs in Kansas City insurance offices and were not in need of additional income, although they had expressed the hope that their shares of the estate proceeds would enable them to retire within a few years.

Time for the meeting came, and Norman flew to Kansas City. He outlined the details to his sisters and asked what their preferences were. Nothing was mentioned in particular except it was agreed that nothing required immediate action, but some plan of action should be developed within a few months.

Upon his return to Chicago, Norman tried to address the problem. He knew from his banking experience that inherited farm land was an attractive hedge against inflation, and perhaps would become even more attractive in the future if the worldwide demand for wheat stayed high with resulting good prices. The hotel building would decline in value but presently was a good investment and would not require any additional investment for the time being. The estimated remaining life for the oil wells was 10 years with a steadily declining production over that period.

As Norman thought about his task, he formulated several possible courses of action. His first thought was that he was ready to leave Chicago. His children were grown and lived in the eastern United States. He and his wife had both grown up in Schumburgh and while they had not wished to remain there when they were younger, they realized that at this time moving back was not an unattractive idea. He could take an early retirement, return to Schumburgh, look after the farm and hotel, and out of his share of income and oil royalties be very comfortable. He could also get away from Schumburgh for extended periods, particularly in the winter, without any difficulty.

The idea seemed attractive, but Norman realized that it would be an abrupt change and that he really did not want to retire completely. He needed something to do for the next 10 years that was challenging, would involve his own efforts, and would perhaps allow him to create a substantial estate for his full retirement.

In connection with his position at the bank, Norman had dealt with financing programs for nursing and retirement homes. He had become aware of the increasing number of older people who would require such facilities in the future. He was also aware of the fact that many people living in rural areas would prefer to stay close to where they had lived and others would by necessity remain in their own local areas.

As Norman thought about nursing or retirement homes, he began to think how he might exploit such an idea for himself. He contacted his sisters and through their respective insurance company employers they obtained some further data on nursing and retirement home operations. They agreed to join Norman in an investment venture of some type.

The more that Norman investigated the idea the better he liked it. The town of Schumburgh was short of adequate care for both retirees and those who needed nursing care. There are differences in retirement and nursing homes as to operations, but there were examples where both were run concurrently in neighboring buildings. One or both seemed to be a possibility for a location in Schumburgh. Norman found that there are substantial tax advantages in erecting and operating new buildings, over the first few years. He realized that he was not trained or qualified as an administrator of a nursing or retirement home. He did, however, believe that he had an idea that would work. He could form a limited partnership in which he, his sisters, and an administrator would be the general partners. They would sell limited partnership shares to 15 to 20 persons at $10,000 each and then borrow additional money to build their first installation. One corner of the farm would be an ideal site, and land could be taken for that purpose. A suite in the hotel would be refurbished and become the partnership headquarters. As the operation developed and proved success-ful, additional installations would be constructed, using the partnership syndicate plan. When the attractive initial tax advantages diminished, the buildings could be sold and replaced by newer facilities.

QUESTIONS

1. Is it desirable in the 1980s to plan on career possibilities that involve a small business career after retirement?
2. Is it reasonable to think about a family partnership in which the parents join with some or all of their children in a joint venture?
3. What kinds of investments are particularly attractive to an individual who wishes to be self-employed? What kinds of investments are attractive to an individual who can interest limited partners who wish to participate?
4. Would it be feasible for a venture such as Norman Smith's proposed nursing and retirement home to eventually become a franchised operation?

9

Business locations, advertising, sales promotion, and image building

A suitable business location is one of the more critical factors in the ultimate success of any given enterprise. The costs of occupying, operating, and maintaining the building, or premises, will place substantial financial demands on the business. In many cases these costs are the largest item in the operating budget, requiring long-term obligations and commitment, and considerable investigation is necessary to determine whether a location can provide the home needed for the enterprise at an affordable price.

KEY FACTORS IN LOCATION SELECTION

Operators of small businesses, business consultants, financiers, and land use specialists have all expressed opinions about locations for business enterprises. For the most part their ideas are sound and should be used as conservative guidelines. Surprisingly, many businesses have succeeded even though they have defied the proved and accepted criteria. For the most part, however, a poor location will not contribute to a successful enterprise.

The factors that link the location of a business enterprise to its success are not the same from one location to the next. A comparison of locations will require that an assortment of factors be consolidated, evaluated, and compared. Usually the process involves an assignment of values on an arbitrary scale or index and the conversion of these values to dollar amounts for comparison.

When the prospective enterpreneur has decided what his personal criteria will be and understands the relationship between value and price, it is time to move on to the analysis of possible locations. The process involved is probably best divided into three main categories. These are:

1. Location and site analysis.
2. Supporting features.
3. Intangibles.

Location and site analysis

Each candidate location requires an examination of the following specific features:

1. Land (if vacant)—Size, shape, and elevations.
2. Land and buildings—Placement, frontage, exposure, access, etc.
3. Services and access—Streets, utilities, alleys, sidewalks, and parking.
4. Transportation facilities—Rail, truck, bus, and air.
5. Zoning and site use—Limited, controlled, nonconforming, etc.
6. Supporting services—Fire and police protection, garbage disposal, street lighting, security patrols.
7. Costs—Lease, rental, improvements, upgrading, and financing.
8. Carrying charges—Taxes, licenses, fees, maintenance, etc.

As indicated by the above list, the examination of the location or specific site is a fairly involved process. It is beyond the scope of this textbook to examine these features in any detail; the entrepreneur, however, will want to conduct a thorough inquiry and should seek professional advice for the more technical areas of evaluation.

The land itself can be observed, and if necessary, experts can be asked for necessary specific opinions. Soil conditions, underground water, and elevation changes can all be computed by competent engineering firms. Resurveys may also be necessary. Land and building combinations can also be studied and estimates made as to the cost of necessary changes.

Other physical features can be examined and evaluated. Streets, utilities, transportation access, and zoning regulations require analysis and evaluation but may not require expert opinions or judgments as to their relationship to the business.

Costs and carrying charges require computation and comparison. Some help from an accountant or other professional may be needed.

Comparison of possible locations

So far an attempt has been made to outline how a prospective business person would engage in the analysis of a prospective location. No decision can be made on the strength of the analysis of a single situation. Alternative locations, with strengths and weaknesses of features, values, and price, will have to be subjected to similar scrutiny.

Comparative analysis

It is unlikely that a given location can be properly analyzed and priced without comparison with other possible locations. No two locations will have the same advantages and disadvantages. The relationship between the value and the asking price will have to be estimated on the basis of a total of different characteristics for each site.

To begin with it will be helpful to review some basic publications dealing with those problems relating to site selection. It will seldom be possible to find references that apply directly to a given situation; instead, the prospective business operator should review several sources of data and then apply an adjustment or modification that brings the information in line with the circumstances being considered.

The National Retail Merchants Association of New York City is a good source of a number of operational manuals in the field of retailing. Many of these manuals discuss operating ratios and results as they apply to business operations. The data can be compared to an existing or proposed operation in terms of square footage costs, etc. The Urban Land Institute is also a good source of cost operating data for businesses, particularly for those operating in shopping centers.

When analyzing a possible location it may be desirable to know something about the value of a structure on the site or a structure to be constructed for the operator's use. If so, Boeckh's *Building Valuation Manual*, published by The American Appraisal Co. of Milwaukee, Wisconsin, or one of the valuation manuals published by Marshall & Swift of Los Angeles, California, will provide useful data. More detailed considerations relating to buildings are covered in Chapter 10

Weighting factors may be hard to establish, but they are generally applied within a framework which includes: (1) the specific type of business, (2) the different functional divisions of the business, and (3) the relationship and importance of the location. For each different business, functional feature, and location, the weight assigned will change. Even though such assignments are based on judgment, if they are applied with consistency by the same person, they will show differences even though the magnitude might be questionable. If honestly done they are of considerable value, particularly in developing information for the financial sources who will be asked to support the operation. Table 9–1 shows a location comparison rating sheet.

Table 9–1
Location comparison rating sheet

I. PRIMARY ACCEPTANCE OR REJECTION FACTORS				
Answer yes or no	*Locations under consideration*			
	A	B	C	D
1. Is this location available?				
2. Will zoning allow your proposed business?				
3. Does this site meet minimum business needs?				
4. Do existing structures meet minimum initial needs?				
5. Is the price of this location within your operating budget?				
6. Is the location fairly priced for your needs?				

A negative answer may be sufficient reason not to proceed with further investigation unless correction or modification can be achieved.

II. SITE VALUATIONS				
Use scale 0 to 100	A	B	C	D
7. How does this location compare with the best location available?				
8. What rating would you give the present buildings on the site?				
9. How would you rate your locational environment compared with the best environment existing within your trading area?				
10. How would you rate the adequacy of available parking for automobiles?				
11. What rating would be given to the nature and quantity of combined foot and auto traffic passing your location?				
12. What is the improvement potential of this location? Total	—	—	—	—

III. TREND ANALYSIS				
Brief answer as to conclusions	A	B	C	D
13. Has the location shown improvement through the years?				

Table 9–1 (*concluded*)

		(1)	(2)	(3)	(4)
14.	Is the owner and/or landlord progressive and coop-erative?				
15.	What major patterns of change are affecting this location:				
	a. Streets—speed limits—paving.				
	b. Shopping centers.				
	c. Zoning.				
	d. Financial investment.				
	e. Dynamic leadership and action.				
16.	What businesses have occupied this location over the past 10 years?				
17.	Have the businesses identified in item 16 been successful?				
18.	Why is this location now available?				
19.	Are a number of other suitable locations available?				
Compare the answer for each location and rank each by number from among those reviewed (1–2–3–4).		(1)	(2)	(3)	(4)

IV. PRICE-VALUE DETERMINATION

		A	B	C	D
20.	What is the asking price of each location?				
21.	What numerical total for each site is developed through questions 7 to 12?				
22.	Is there a negative answer to any question 1 through 6?				
23.	Do the answers to questions 13 through 19 develop a pattern which is:				
	a. Highly favorable.				
	b. Average.				
	c. Minimal.				
	d. Questionable.				
	e. Not acceptable.				
Ranking position of each location based on numerical totals and preferences as to subjective items in III and IV.		(3)	(2)	(4)	(1)

ADVERTISING

Advertising is the mass communication of information with the intent to persuade a sufficient number of people to become a firm's customers. Sales promotion is a broader technique that includes many forms of effort to develop a similar result; sales promotion is often considered to include advertising, but promotion may not refer directly to specific products at particular prices, whereas advertising is likely to do just that. Image building is a more subtle advocacy of persuasive notions that enhance the acceptability of a business in the minds of its customers. Some differences of opinion exist as to the foregoing distinctions, but they will serve our purposes for the discussions that follow.

Regardless of the differences suggested in the previous paragraph, all three of these activities have but one purpose: to build and sustain an adequate customer or client pool to maintain profitability.

Advertising strategies for the small business

Each small business will have the same problems in its advertising programs as virtually every other business, large or small. In general, the goal is to make the firm and its products known and to develop some need or desire for these products or services in the minds of consumers.

The initial decisions in regard to advertising are built around such questions as what to advertise, when, in what way, and to what market segments as potential targets. These are all important and vital questions for each individual firm.

Several established formulas for setting advertising budgets can be adapted to the needs of a particular small business. These are: (1) Percentage of sales, (2) Matching competitor sales, (3) Fixed-dollar expenditures, (4) Profit planning, and (5) Objective cost plan.

Percentage of sales is simple, direct, and easy to visualize. It is used by a number of retailers and has been successful in the past in connection with established advertising programs. It may be difficult to estimate sales in order to determine a percentage to use, but a budget based on estimated sales is often a good place to start. As time passes, adjustments can be made in the original budget.

Matching competitors' sales is another rather simplistic approach that nevertheless is defensible on the basis that you are competing for customers' attention with similar businesses. No one business will necessarily have any particular cost advantages, therefore you spend up to the level of your competition.

Fixed-dollar advertising is a very simple and direct way of allocating funds to a particular strategy or units available for sale. It is direct and easily understood, and it avoids some of the uncertainties that are involved with the other methods. It is also desirable in that it identifies something in particular, such as a new product line, and allocates funds to the advertising of those items as opposed to a more indirect approach with some of the other techniques.

Profit planning approaches the advertising expenditures from the standpoint of an analysis of the profit to be derived from a given level of sales. This technique is a good deal more elegant and sophisticated than are some of the other advertising budget techniques mentioned above. Because of this, it is also a good deal more time-consuming. However, it does force one to plan advertising expenditures and also to have a firm grasp of what net sales figures are likely to be, what the cost of goods sold and operating expenses are, and finally what anticipated earnings will be for the forthcoming advertising period.

Table 9–2
Ski Jackets, Inc.

Anticipated sales	$120,000	$200,000
Less operating expenses.	95,000	143,000
Subtotal.	25,000	57,000
Less desired profit.	20,000	35,000
Amount available for advertising	$ 5,000	$ 22,000

Basically the way the profit planning method works is that the small business person first determines what his or her gross profit will be at various levels of gross sales by means of break-even analysis. Once the gross profits are determined for the various levels of sales, the operating expenses are subtracted from the gross profit projections, thereby determining the amount of funds remaining for the advertising budget and the net profit for the period for each projected level of sales. As Table 9–2 shows, for an estimated gross sales of $120,000 with a hoped-for net profit of $20,000, there is only $5,000 available for advertisement; while at the estimated gross sales of $200,000 with a hoped-for profit of $35,000, there is $22,000 available for advertising expense. Obviously in view of the competitive picture of the ski jacket industry, Ski Jackets, Inc. would be well advised to plan for a profit of $35,000 and develop an advertising budget commensurate with that figure.

The above analysis also highlights one of the basic fallacies in the profit planning technique. That is while profit planning is nice, it may be impossible for Ski Jackets, Inc. to raise sales from $120,000 to $200,000 a year. Thus their advertising budget would be impractical at the $200,000 figure. Furthermore, these figures are nothing more than estimations, as are all break-even analyses, and are therefore not altogether valid. As mentioned above, they are also exceedingly difficult to determine. Therefore the profit planning technique, although more elegant and sophisticated in nature, is still subject to the shortcoming of being no better than the estimates that go into it and the practicality of such estimates.

Objective cost plans were developed to force management people to apply more rigorous analysis to the expenses and goals of an advertising strategy. The plan of operation is to (1) determine what the objectives are for the forthcoming program, (2) determine how these objectives might be met and (3) establish the cost necessary to meet these objectives. The process requires some very hard thinking by the owner or manager to set realistic objectives and then calculate the methods to be used and their cost.

Determining objectives might be fairly easy and straightforward, but method and cost are quite difficult. Like profit planning, however, it is a method that deals with the broad scope of the total advertising program as opposed to plans derived from some other criteria. It is one plan that should probably be considered by a number of smaller businesses as an initial approach to its advertising endeavors. After such review the manager can then select one of the other strategies as being more directly appropriate for the inherent advantages in any particular plan.

When the entrepreneur has had a chance to study and analyze the various plans suggested previously, it will be possible to make some initial judgment regarding the nature and direction of the firm's advertising progam. There are several important considerations in putting together an advertising program to do a good job.

Advertising programs

The advertising program selected will be based on several criteria depending on the particular nature of the firm and the wishes of the owner, such as those that follow:

1. The media forms that are available and the relative costs of each.
2. Markets to be reached based on the characteristics of the customers to be contacted.
3. A choice between an advertising agency or the preparation of the advertising material by the owner himself.
4. The mix of advertising to reflect budget changes, seasonality, adverse business conditions, etc.
5. The amount of help received from product and service suppliers.
6. The image or images to be projected.

Selection of advertising media

The small business with limited funds will have to choose carefully among media because of the costs involved. The available funds must be used to engage the most effective media to project the desired message to an adequate number of prospective customers.

The average customer is exposed to so many advertisements per day that it is a wonder that any limited effort can overcome the mass media efforts of just two major advertisers; Procter & Gamble and Sterling Drug. The fact is that customers can be reached by using the right program and engaging the right assortment of media.

Newspapers. Most small businesses rely on a daily or weekly newspaper for the majority of their advertising. Newspapers are generally local or regional in coverage and readership and provide a direct line of communication to the majority of those persons who are potential customers.

When buying newspaper space, it is wise to consider (1) the substantial discounts given for larger space commitments, either for a single issue or over extended periods of time; (2) the need to choose the proper news or feature section of the paper and the appropriate place on a page, and (3) the availability of good advertising personnel who can help to prepare the proper copy and layout of the ads to be used.

Telephone directory space. Telephone directories are related to newspapers and provide an advertising form that is relied on by a large number of small businesses. The use of the telephone as a part of most business transactions demonstrates that the telephone is a business necessity—it takes just one more step to make it a positive way to reach potential customers. The Yellow Pages are available on a column-inch or percent of page contract price that is added to the advertiser's phone bill. The principal decisions concern the amount of space to be contracted for and the number of alternative or auxiliary listings to be employed. The small business should undoubtedly allocate a consistent small portion of the advertising budget to this media form.

Direct mail.   Direct mailing pieces and other forms of direct contact materials such as handbills, Christmas cards, match books, and business cards are all particularly appropriate to a small business operation. Any form of direct mail carries a special message to a selected customer. This is squarely in line with the principal transaction objectives of many small businesses—specialized treatment and service for a limited number of select customers. To use direct mail effectively it must be carefully prepared and accurately targeted. Direct mail advertising pieces may convey article and price information, while the other forms might be used more in an image building effort. Direct mail is expensive and it may have little direct payoff. It should be used with the idea of maintaining a continuing awareness of the business in the minds of select customers. Direct mail is a good way to do just that.

Radio.   Radio advertising can be used very effectively by any number of small retail and service firms. In many areas where other media forms are not particularly appropriate, the radio may be most useful. Many areas do not have a newspaper that can provide coverage to a particular area or group of people. Such areas might be rural and not particularly responsive to advertisements in a small local paper. Other geographical areas, such as the suburbs around a large city, are difficult to reach in a direct way. In such cases, perhaps particular radio stations can be identified as having listeners who should be reached with advertising.

Other direct forms of advertising are available, such as billboard space, personal signs, and chamber of commerce literature. They are useful for a given situation but are not relied on in the same way as the methods previously listed. In some cases they are used more for purposes of image building than for direct advertising.

Developing good advertisements

In preparing the advertisements that will be used there are several objectives to be reached. The advertisement itself must be carefully and thoughtfully prepared so that the resulting copy will be effective.

How to write advertising copy.   In approaching the problem of writing copy for an ad, it is essential that the copywriter have a firm objective in mind. That is, he/she should have the answers to the questions "What am I selling?" "To whom am I selling?" and "What is the best technique for conveying my message?" Developing answers to such questions is not easy. It may seem ridiculous to say that some people don't know what they are advertising or selling, but the fact is that in writing advertising copy, many small business people aren't really aware of what they should emphasize. That is, many times they will emphasize the color or quality of a product when in fact the person reading the advertising would be more effectively swayed by an elaboration of the convenience of using the product.

Similarly, copywriters do not always know to whom they are addressing the ad. Many times they just feel that they are advertising at large and they thereby fail to focus on the specific audience that comprises the potential buyers for the product. Proper selection of the target of an ad is essential to effective copy writing.

In short, once the prospective customer is selected, the copywriter must decide on the best way to bring the product or service and the prospective customer together.

Principles of effective advertising copy. There are several principles for writing effective advertising copy. These principles state that the advertising copy should be (1) brief, (2) clear, (3) apt, (4) interesting, (5) personal, (6) sincere, and (7) convincing. It should be obvious that such requirements, if met, develop all the salient aspects of effective advertising copy.

Brevity. Brevity means conciseness. Each sentence is studied in detail; each word is considered for relevance, appropriateness, and meaning; all superfluous words are deleted; and, finally, the total advertising message is integrated into a hard-hitting appeal to purchase the product.

Clarity. Clarity means that the ad should be easy to understand. Basically, lack of clarity in advertising copy results from three faults: (1) the words that are used are not clearly understood by the advertising prospect; (2) the words are inappropriate, irrelevant, or poorly selected; or (3) the words that are selected are ambiguous, vague, or otherwise unclear to the subject.

Aptness. The third requirement for effective copy writing is that the copy be apt. In other words, the copy must fit the needs and wants of the prospect; it must be appropriate and relevant to the customer's terminology, thought processes, interests and desires. This requires that the copywriter not only have a good deal of insight into the customer's nature but also recognize that there are an infinite variety of human natures. Therefore, the copywriter must recognize that copy that is appealing to his/her own vanity, pride, and preferences may not appeal to others. Effective copy is written with the buyer's interest at heart and from the buyer's point of view, not with the seller's interests in mind and from the seller's viewpoint.

Interesting. A fourth principle of effecitve copy writing is that the ad be interesting. Unfortunately, what interests one person may not interest another. Basically the principle behind writing interesting copy is the appeal to people's emotions.

Personal. To be effective, advertising copy also must be personal. This means that the word *you* should be included—or at least implied—in the copy. For example, there is a good deal of difference between the effect of the general statement, "Anyone looking for a new car should visit Kline's Auto," and the statement, "If *you* want a new car, visit Kline's Auto for the best deal *you* can get."

Sincere and convincing. The final principle of writing effective advertising copy is that the individual must be sincere and convincing in writing the copy. To be sincere and convincing, the individual must be convinced of the worth, merit, quality, and value of the service or product. It is much easier to say that a product is guaranteed to last 15 years if the product is actually made to last for 15 years. Such sincerity, if obtained, will practically always be convincing.

Along with the preparation of the copy to be used, it will be necessary to decide how the advertisements themselves will be presented. If they are for newspaper use, they would obviously be different from that used for a direct mailing piece or other direct solicitation. Use will dictate changes in the direct message, the manner of presentation, and the particular characteristics of the audience to be appealed to.

Customer market analysis

It is necessary to examine in some detail the clientele to be reached by the advertisements. For a large firm an entire department might work full time on marketing analysis, including persons whose sole job is to determine the role and approach that advertising will play in selling the firm's products. While much of the actual work may be handled by an advertising agency, the firm itself must be satisfied with the results of the agencies' efforts.

If the smaller business uses an agency, the agency personnel will know how to conduct inexpensive market studies for the purpose of designing an advertising program. If not, the small business owner should consult specialized texts dealing with advertising. In general, the owner needs to know what geographical area can be reasonably served and what types of persons live in such areas, classified by population density, income levels, established shopping habits, competitive influences, etc. Much of this can be developed independently with a little guidance from a person who understands basic research methods.

Advertisement mix

The advertising mix denotes the kinds and proportions of media to be used. A typical budget might allocate 40 percent to newspaper copy; 10 percent to the Yellow Pages; 15 percent to direct mail, and the balance to a variety of other forms, such as a short-run joint sponsorship of sports news broadcasting on the local radio station.

Selection among the media will depend upon whether the various advertisements maintain a consistent pattern and produce the desired effect. Again, the services of an advertising agency may be desirable, but they are not mandatory. Frequently, it is good to concentrate in a few areas rather than to spread advertising too thin. At other times a rather broad mix is desirable. *The owner should be willing to experiment with different options* and should feel comfortable with the programs being used. Being comfortable does not mean being complacent. There must be a hard-hitting review to see whether the effectiveness of each ad has run out and to discontinue those that were not really worthwhile.

Advertising mix is understood as a strategy by most business people. A reluctance to act, either through neglect or lack of ambition, is the principal reason that such an advertising concept is ignored. Positive effort should be made by the entrepreneur and his advisors to install a system of analysis and review that will keep ideas coming and the appropriate changes made in advance of the need.

In general, advertising needs innovative, original, aggressive, astute, and creative efforts.

Cooperative advertising

If a firm conducts its business by distributing the products or performing services controlled by other firms or franchisors, then it should be able to secure advertising help from the parent firms represented. Sometimes this help is not forthcoming until the representative firm has attained some size (at which point the help may not really be needed) and has built up its own reputation, which is sufficient endorsement of the advertising being presented. If the firm does not have clout with its suppliers, help with the advertising effort should probably be sought anyway. It doesn't hurt to ask for assistance and even if the answer is no, there should not be any resentment held against the firm's manager. Manufacturers or service suppliers will have much to gain if their retail or service firm accounts are successful in their own promotional efforts and sales. There is no good argument against the need for customer sales personnel and service representatives to have the help they need to get the job done.

Winning battles in the world of advertising is demanding work, but essential and rewarding to any business person. It is one area of business operations where the ultimate payoffs may take a period of time to develop. It may also be very frustrating—what worked well last year fell flat this year. Fortunately, most smaller business owners realize the hazards in advertising and sales promotion. They can accept the facts, complain about them, and perhaps go broke for failing to act. On the other hand, they can realize the facts and accept them, get busy, and determine how best to do their advertising and then proceed to do it. It may not succeed, at least initially. At this point the owner should proceed to deal with the problems, formulate counteracting measures, and utilitze an advertising program that produces adequate results.

Sales promotion

Along with advertising, the small business owner will need to consider the broader aspects of sales promotion and developing the proper company image. It is difficult to make an absolute distinction between advertising and sales promotion, but for purposes of this discussion sales promotion goes beyond the direct cause-and-effect relations of advertising. In addition, it includes the continuation of the contact or exposure created by the advertising into some form of meaningful action that will help to complete the actual sales transaction with a customer.

What sales promotion should do

Very few products are sold without personal salesmanship; furthermore, personal salesmanship can promote many sales that otherwise would not have been made. It is therefore of the essence that the small business person realize that an advertising campaign is not a success and may even become a failure if it does not extend to, tie in with, and facilitate the actual sale of the merchandise.

Most successful business people know and recognize the need to advertise. Furthermore, they usually assume that their competitors have a product or service as good as their own at competitive prices. Therefore, they recognize that the primary purpose of their advertising is to get people to shop in their stores or sales offices, or to see their sales representatives. However, they also recognize that getting someone to look doesn't sell the product or service. The sale must still be made. Therefore, the effective advertiser will extend the advertising campaign to include the actual sale of the product (and any subsequent adjustments that must be made).

Extending an advertising program through the actual sale means a variety of things. For one thing, it means that the salesperson must know what is being advertised, at what price, and for how long. Further, it means that the salesperson must know all the products being sold thoroughly—inside and out, advantages and disadvantages, uses and limitations. Furthermore, good, effective selling means that the salesperson will know the same information about competitors' products and services. Thus, a good advertising program includes well-trained salespeople who know their product, what is said about it, and what can be said.

A thorough advertising program also means that the salesperson knows how to sell the product. Knowing how to sell a product is the very heart and culmination of any successful advertising program. It means that salespersons not only know their own and their competitors' products, they also know and understand the psychology of selling:

how to tie ads in with sales appeals, when to use the soft-sell approach or the hard-sell approach, how to employ any convincing demonstrations or gimmicks, how to size up customers' needs, and how to suggest companion sales, future sales, or alternative products.

BUILDING IMAGES

The third part of our concern for selling effectiveness has to do with images. These will be present and often are created without any conscious effort on the part of the owner. They are frequently detrimental or uncomplimentary. This last fact suggests that some conscious effort must be made to develop complimentary images that support the business.

Why worry about the company's image?

In order for a firm to *promote* a certain image, it is obviously necessary for the small business manager first to *establish* the desired image. Small business managers must know consciously what image they desire to portray to the public and to their own personnel. This requires, in turn, an understanding of how important an image is to the people involved. Generally, it is accepted that the image conveyed to the public is all-important. Since the image conveyed is so important, it must be recognized that a conscious, deliberate effort should be made by the business to sharpen or highlight the desired image in the minds of the public and the business personnel. It is not sufficient, as one writer has put it, merely to ". . . utter statements in somber tones about the need for better images." But it is, of course, asinine to try to develop an image that does not exist—e.g., the cut-rate firm that advertises in exclusive magazines in an endeavor to create an impression of superior quality. In short, a firm's image is all-important, but to be effective, this image must be within the realm of reason and practicality.

What images are made of

There are, of course, a variety of images that small business persons can attempt to develop for their businesses. They can develop an image of being exclusive—that is, being the sellers or providers of nothing but the best. They can develop an image of being inexpensive, perhaps appealing to people in the lower income brackets or people who feel that they do not need the durable or fashionable features of the best. They can develop an image of being innovative, providing the latest in fashions, styles, or designs, or they can develop the opposite image of being quite reserved and conservative, thereby appealing to a different clientele.

The objective of the whole image-building game is not necessarily to develop the *best* company image. Rather, it is that small business persons determine the *right* image—i.e., the image they wish the business to convey, and to whom. They can then try to establish such an image to the *appropriate* group. Thus, the small business might also attempt to establish different images for different groups of people if it can successfully isolate its market or clients with separate advertising campaigns or, more practically, by having different branch stores or service facilities.

Determining the image desired and conveying this image to the appropriate persons is very difficult. However, there are some characteristics of successful company images that the practical business manager can strive to achieve.

1. To begin with, an image is *synthetic.* That is, any image that is developed by a small business is deliberately planned and created to give a certain impression to particular people for a definite reason. Thus, almost any image desired can be *created,* and by the same token any image created can also be *changed* by deliberate effort.

2. An image must be *believable.* That is, images should be within the realm of the realistic. They should not be designed to convey something impossible or irrelevant. For example, it would be futile for a small business in a small country community to cultivate the impression that the store carries the latest Paris fashions. Most of the people in small, rural communities simply are too realistic to accept such a delusion, even if they would like to think that the designs of the top Paris couturiers are available to them.

3. An image is a vehicle or *means toward an end,* not an end in itself. In this sense the image is passive rather than active. In other words, image building is the development of a "likeness" of the organization; but in final analysis the organization is the likeness of the image. Thus, an image is constructed from actual circumstances that exist and that are brought into existence for purposes of image building. However, after a time, people will identify themselves in some relationship with the image constructed; then, actual circumstances begin to adapt to the image developed. Thus, when a business hires a public relations firm to develop a desired image, the firm is initially putting itself in the position of determining what image the business wants to develop, but once the image is built the business will necessarily have to comply with the image developed by the public relations firm.

4. Although passive, an image must be *alive* and *concrete.* That is, any image that is developed must be a vivid, almost tangible thought, feeling, or emotion. For example, consider the TV commercials for food or beverages in which taste or flavor is almost brought alive by the product that is portrayed—or the impression of elegance and good taste

suggested by a particular automobile ad. Similarly, the small business can make its image vivid—something that can be "felt" by employees, customers, and clients alike.

5. An image should be *simple*. Developing a corporate image requires the ability to simplify very complex thoughts. Just as the basketball coach knows that she must keep her game plans extremely simple so that all her players can understand and comply with them, so should the small business manager recognize that simple thoughts and actions should be used to convey an image to others. The small business can convey its image by simple, provocative slogans, advertisements, or jingles; by the thoughtful, quiet, and unassuming decor of an office; or by a friendly method of answering a telephone call.

6. An image should be *ambiguous*. In final analysis it must be recognized that although image building requires that several specific, deliberate steps be taken by the image builder, it must still be vague and ambiguous. To be successful an image must be something that can be perceived and accepted by a large number of observers. Such commonality of application for the corporate image necessarily requires that the image be vague or ambiguous enough so that each individual can see in it something with a special personal meaning. A wide range of people and personalities will be exposed to the specific stimulus of the image, and they will receive this stimulus in widely divergent lights and view-points. Sufficient ambiguity is therefore required for all people to receive the image in the *best* light. Thus, an image designed to be conservatively interpreted should still be ambiguous enough to avoid conveying the notion of a stuffed-shirt organization to large segments of the population.

Building your company image through your own image

The foregoing discussion was designed to highlight the factors that must be considered in building the image that a small business wants to convey. An additional aspect, however, must be considered by the owner of the small business and that is the factor of the owner's own personality. The small business person is always viewed as an extension of the business, and—no matter what is done—the firm will always be associated with the image of the owner/manager held by the general public.

The importance of this factor is probably best summarized in the old cliché "You can take the boy out of the country, but you can't take the country out of the boy." Likewise, the small business manager cannot effectively change personality to suit any image, and because the image conveyed will tend to permeate the entire organization, it must be recognized that to a large extent the owner/manager's personal image will determine the image of the company.

Knowing what image your small business projects

The question therefore arises: "How can one determine what one's own image is and develop a suitable image that serves the business well and will permit the maximizing of profit and growth for the firm?"

To answer this question, the small business manager should analyze his/her own personality by self-questioning, and thus determine the image to be conveyed. Basically these questions require a recognition of one's own driving needs.

Once the small business manager determines a desirable image to project through the business, then the question is how to establish this image and perpetuate it until such time that circumstances change and it is deemed advisable to establish a different image. This last is an extremely difficult proposition—to determine when to change an image so that one will keep in tune with the times.

Working toward a desired image

It is difficult to decide how to get started with the image-building program, but in general the following points should be stressed:

1. Developing an image that reflects the combination of temperament, personality, and integrity that the owner or manager believes in personally.
2. Deciding how the personal attitudes and beliefs of the owner can best be projected.
3. Anticipating obstacles on the part of customers that must be overcome or avoided.
4. Recognizing and using methods that appeal to people's preconceived notions or opinions.
5. Avoiding the task of changing someone else's firm conviction, but instead getting them to accept the position represented by you or your business.
6. Building upon ideas and actions that have lasting value as images.

The economics of developing a good image

It should be clear by now that in attempting to develop the desired reputation for a firm, the small business has a variety of things to contend with. For example, in order to build an image a small business person might take certain steps, such as decorating the store in an unusual way. The steps one takes—influenced of course by the type of business one is in—and how well one carries them out will determine how successful one is in building a company image. The secret is to choose the correct steps and those that one can afford financially. Thus a small business that is intent upon developing a particular reputation must know how to determine economically which of these decisions or steps can be justified, and therefore be considered. Actually, by use of a simple schematic device the small business can determine with relative ease the value, relevance, and importance of any of the decisions or steps to take. This method is presented in Figure 9–1. It should be obvious that any small business can generate a scheme similar to this figure, based on information relevant to the particular business.

In devising and utilizing such a figure, it can be seen that in determining what reputation-developing activity one intends to engage in, the small business owner must recognize two facts: (1) a dollar cost will be incurred for any reputation-developing activity; and (2) the dollar cost will increase at a progressive rate for the more complex, the more out-of-the-ordinary, the more bizarre reputation-developing activities. By charting these particular activities along a cost curve, the small business person can determine which activities are economically feasible for the firm and which are not. By way of general experience, it would appear that the financially uneconomical area is located somewhere between point A and point B. Beyond point B the incremental increase in cost far outweighs the incremental increase in favorable reputation that is promoted by the reputation-developing activity, while before point A the return far outweighs the expenditure. Therefore, as a matter of policy, the small business that has an image/cost curve like that in Figure 9–1 should be reasonably considerate in dealings with customers, and should neither sidestep nor appear to sidestep responsibilities to inform the public of the advantages resulting from dealing with that firm. However, there would appear to be little sense in attempting to win over a potential customer who is already antagonistic toward the small business or the area of activity in which the small business is engaged.

Typical successful image building techniques

A town of 12,000 people supports a small but highly fashionable ladies' ready-to-wear retailer. The manager continuously marks down *at random* odd items in the store without regard to their chance of sales at full price. He has developed a steady stream of shoppers who believe that his store is a "house of bargains." Actually there are not many bargains, but the image persists and results in the sale of many fully priced items.

A large hardware and appliance store allows its service department to develop its own policies in dealing with the public and provides incentive payments for sales over established volume levels. The service managers and the service representatives meet constantly and discuss their successes and failures and in general have decided that every service call should provide a plus factor for the customer. The department has developed an enviable image of giving more than their

154

Figure 9–1
Image cost curve

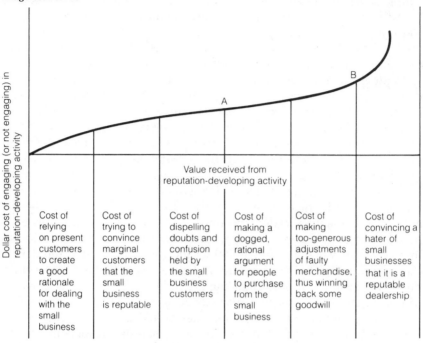

		Value received from reputation-developing activity			
Cost of relying on present customers to create a good rationale for dealing with the small business	Cost of trying to convince marginal customers that the small business is reputable	Cost of dispelling doubts and confusion held by the small business customers	Cost of making a dogged, rational argument for people to purchase from the small business	Cost of making too-generous adjustments of faulty merchandise, thus winning back some goodwill	Cost of convincing a hater of small businesses that it is a reputable dealership

(Y-axis label: Dollar cost of engaging (or not engaging) in reputation-developing activity)

competitors, even though their higher prices cover the additional costs incurred.

An office supply wholesale firm under new management analyzed the sales made by size, customer, cost, and other pertinent features. Even though the firm had been very profitable, it was decided that sales of less than $10 were not profitable and customers were notified that these would no longer be accepted. Even though the company's existence was not jeopardized, a number of customers were alienated and discontinued doing business with the firm. Subsequent analysis indicated that the abruptness of termination of such orders and the tenor of the notices given were largely responsible for the subsequent bad image and loss of customers.

SUMMARY

This chapter highlighted the efforts needed by the small business owner in projecting and maintaining the effective advertising, sales, promotional effort, and image building necessary for a successful firm.

The owner must accomplish these things at the same time, directing them toward a common goal with a series of efforts that are compatible with each other. In this way, the objectives of one will not ignore or counteract another, and customers can be appealed to with a variety of approaches. If the programs are properly administered, they will reach a greater number of people with the right message and produce a favorable response in the form of business for the firm.

QUESTIONS

1. What is the real purpose of advertising?

2. How does the small business person usually determine when to advertise? How does this person determine how much to advertise? Do these two things go together?

3. What considerations need to be made in selecting the appropriate advertising media?

4. What are the criteria that govern the development of good advertising copy?

5. Why is it important to experiment with different forms of advertising?

6. What is the connection between advertising and sales promotion?

7. How should a small business person work toward the right image?

8. What is the connection between the owner's self-image and the image that is developed in the business?

9. How should a small business person recognize the need to change or alter an existing image?

10. Are customers in the 1980s more critical of business practices and inclined not to accept attempts to develop desirable images of business enterprise?

PROBLEMS

1. Develop an advertising strategy for one of the following businesses:

   a. Automatic car wash.

156

    b. Record store.
    c. Jewelry store.
    d. Ethnic restaurant.
    e. Real estate firm.

2. Explain what you think would be a desirable type of image for the following businesses:

    a. Insurance agency.
    b. Foreign car garage.
    c. Public campground.
    d. Appliance repair service.
    e. Package delivery service.

BIBLIOGRAPHY

Walters, C. Glenn. *Consumer Behavior.* 3d ed. Homewood, Ill.: Richard D. Irwin, 1978. A basic text that is useful in understanding what motivates consumers and the ways for business persons to benefit from such knowledge.

Sandage, C. H., Vernon Fryburger, and Kim Rotzoll. *Advertising Theory and Practice.* 10th ed. Homewood, Ill.: Richard D. Irwin, 1979. A basic text that analyzes the fundamentals of advertising.

Kirkpatrick, C. A., and Frederick A. Russ. *Salesmanship.* 6th ed. Cincinnati: South-Western Publishing, 1976. A good text to complement those following on consumer behavior and advertising. Explains how and why sales are made and what is required to sell successfully.

Level, Dale A. Jr., and William P. Galle, Jr. *Business Communications.* Plano, Tex: Business Publications, 1980. The elements of communications and their relationship to the job of selling and sales promotion. Has developmental exercises to help in the skills of communication.

Case study

The Yellowstone Angler

As the end of 1980 was approaching, the Yellowstone Angler as a going business was finishing its first full season of operation as a small specialty fly fishing shop. The proprietor, George Anderson, had decided to go on his own, after spending seven years as an employee of Dan Bailey's Flies and Tackle in Livingston, Montana. The first year had been successful, but the real proof of the success of the firm would have to come in the next couple of years. With this in mind, George decided to review the past season and use the period following the Christmas holiday to firm up his plans for the course of his business for the next few months.

The locale

Anyone who has visited Livingston, Montana, and the surrounding area cannot help being impressed with the magnificent scenery and the many opportunities for the outdoor sports enthusiast. Located some 50 miles north of Yellowstone Park, Livingston is ideally situated as a location for shops such as Dan Bailey's and the Yellowstone Angler. Within 150 miles there are hundreds of miles of excellent trout waters comprising the upper river systems of the Yellowstone, Missouri, Madison, Green, and Snake rivers, and many natural lakes and reservoirs. Many serious fly fishermen spend time each summer in the region, and a number of them make Livingston their headquarters. It is not hard to understand the choice of Livingston as the location for the Yellowstone Angler.

The shop

The shop is located at 124 North Main Street, a short distance off Park Street, which is the former main highway through the city. The interstate highway bypasses the city, and customers need to know how to find the fly shop.

As a specialty shop catering to serious fly fishing enthusiasts, it is necessary to provide superior quality products and expert advice as to their use. George attempts to spend most of his time at the shop. In his absence his assistant can provide the necessary expertise and help with the miscellaneous duties when sales are slow. The shop carries one or more of the better quality lines of rods, reels, fly lines, specialty clothing, waders, wading shoes, float tubes, and an innumerable assortment of artificial trout flies. An attempt is made to secure flies that have been tied by expert tiers, particularly those who specialize in certain types, which are much in demand by discriminating fishermen.

The shop is attractive and tastefully decorated but is not nearly as large or as well stocked as other noted shops throughout the West. An attempt is made to do a good job with a carefully selected assortment of inventory— the same approach that should be taken by any individual in a specialty business.

The customers

Because it is a specialty shop catering to a relatively small proportion of fishermen, there is no way that the Yellowstone Angler can survive on local customers, or even those who live within a reasonable driving distance. In fact, the firm must attract business from many localities throughout the United States, and it must be able to do some of this by mail advertising. The late fall, winter, and spring are periods in which mail order business will be the mainstay of the firm. Livingston is approximately 8,000 in population and can provide some year-round business, but not a great deal.

As customers increase their knowledge about the area and the services of the firm, the pool of potential customers should grow. This growth will have to proceed at some reasonable rate to offset the loss of customers that constantly takes place for any smaller business.

Trends affecting the business

The availability of a potential customer pool depends upon several trends, some favorable and others unfavorable. Some of the favorable trends would be such things as the following:

1. The superior natural environment in the geographical area surrounding Livingston, which can support substantial fishing opportunities. This is also the case in some other states as well, along with a trend toward restricting waters to fly fishing only. This is often coupled with a program of "catch and release," as a fish caught on an artificial fly will normally survive if handled carefully and returned promptly to its natural habitat.
2. The growth of fly fishing as a prestige sport. This trend tends to attract persons who may not fish much but collect and admire high-quality equipment. They buy to satisfy their ego and are no small force in the higher-price market.
3. The development of the environmental movement. Many of the actions of environmentalists are not directly concerned with any particular resource, but anything that restricts changes in natural fish habitat will be a benefit to trout and other sport fish.

To counteract the favorable trends, there are many undesirable trends and developments that are diminishing the number of fly fishermen. Some of these are the following:

1. The need for energy and the relentless efforts of persons who stand to gain from energy development. Even with the best safeguards and technology available, it is reasonable to assume that opportunities to pursue the sport of fly fishing will diminish when the country is faced with urgent needs for energy and with the steady development of technical processes that pose a threat to pure water supplies.
2. Land-use changes. Highway building removes surface cover and increases sediment loads in rivers and streams. Homesite construction also brings substantial land displacement from rural to urban uses. Such land disturbance leads to silting, chemical leaching, and abnormal stream flows.
3. The loss of fishing waters to private ownership and control. Removal of fishing waters from public access limits the available fishing opportunities. This is an increasing problem as many fly fishermen attempt to protect and maintain their own select waters.

An evening spent in his office, thinking about the season stretching into 1982, revealed several things to George. There seemed to be no great problems in continuing to conduct his business successfully if he could maintain some growth among the dedicated fly fishing enthusiasts who were his principal source of revenues.

Other problems, or potential difficulties, did exist, and it would be necessary for George to anticipate these and make plans to accommodate such problems that might develop.

QUESTIONS

1. In what ways should specialty shops such as the Yellowstone Angler expand their operations into products that are peripheral to the main products sold?
2. Would it be reasonable to believe that the business of the Yellowstone Angler would be seriously affected by rising gasoline costs, or increases in air fares?
3. What forms of promotional efforts would be most beneficial in appealing to potential customers who are widely dispersed throughout the United States?
4. Is it true that dedicated enthusiasts of various sports and vocational pursuits are continually buying and replacing equipment in excess of actual needs? Can George take advantage of this practice in his business?
5. How can the Yellowstone Angler meet its needs to inject more capital into the business in order to finance a larger inventory and possible future mail order catalog business, yet have George retain complete ownership of the business?

10

The building and operating facilities

Choosing a location usually involves also choosing a building and its operating features. The problem of location is always of first priority because nothing can ordinarily be done to change the basic character of a location. The building, however, can be changed, along with its facilities. Practically, there are limits to what can be done, but every prospective business owner needs to examine combinations of locations, buildings, and facilities in order to know what is available and at what price.

The majority of small enterprises are started in existing buildings, which are adapted to the particular business. Beginning entrepreneurs usually start with little operating capital, hence prime locations, new buildings, and the most modern facilities are beyond their initial capabilities. Modifications and scaled down criteria frequently dictate that the firm's location and its facilities be adequate, but not much more.

Entrepreneurs initially tend to rent or lease for limited periods because they are uncertain about the possible success of the business and because they lack resources for fixed capital commitments. Many locations are adequate but do not include buildings and facilities that are suitable for the larger, better established, and more secure enterprise.

These modest locations are what the new business operator is looking for. Money spent on upgrading may produce results that are quite adequate at a cost much less than that of a better location with a better building, for which the entrepreneur would have to compete with a variety of businesses.

THE BUILDINGS PHYSICAL FEATURES

The building to be used for the proposed enterprise must be examined to assess its main physical features. These are characteristics of the actual structure that cannot be altered without considerable effort and expense. These principal features include:

1.	Space.	4.	Access.
2.	Configuration.	5.	Floor plan.
3.	Frontage.	6.	Compatibility.

Space. The actual space, generally floor space, is the basis on which the value of most buildings is calculated. Not all floor space is of equal value, but given a number of related characteristics, it is floor space that is acquired and used.

The floor space is good, average, or poor, depending on certain features that bear directly on its usefulness. Open space allows the space to be divided or partitioned. Columns, doorways, windows, and stairways restrict what can be done with the space available. If properly placed they enhance the space; if not, they detract from its usefulness. Physical proportions are also important. This includes the size of rooms, their widths, depths, ceiling heights, locations of doorways and windows, and the appropriateness of these to each other.

Configuration. Elements of configuration are related to the basic design and appropriateness of the building to a given purpose. As in the case of space, the physical features are very significant and in total determine the usefulness of the building to the tenant. Configuration would go much further than the features mentioned in regard to space. All systems would be included, along with the adaptability of the building to a given purpose, or for meeting a particular group of objectives. Another aspect of configuration is related to style and appearance—features that may have considerable importance in certain retail operations and service businesses.

Frontage. Frontage provides exposure and contact with customers and clients and, it is hoped, makes some lasting impression on those who become customers in the future. Some amount of footage along the street, mall, or highway usually is necessary. How much and where is not an easy question to answer. For some businesses in a shopping center, 10 or 12 feet may be all that is needed. For another business, 100 feet might not be enough.

Securing adequate and fairly priced frontage requires a correct assessment of the impact of frontage and its contribution to the proposed business.

Frontage that is too little, bracketed between substantially larger businesses, or ineffective because of bad design or door placement should be rejected. A corner, with frontage on two sides, is usually better, but a higher asking price may offset any advantage of a corner location.

Access.   Access, as a building feature, is a much more subtle element than access to a location. Obviously, the customer or client must be able to reach the building physically without difficulty and in a manner that does not vary too much from accepted standards of customers convenience.

Access in total includes the entire premises and accessibility in all respects. Elevators, stairways, partitions, doorway sizes, traffic flow

patterns, and zoning controls are all a part of access. Even the lighting and color schemes have an effect on the willingness of individuals to walk a certain corridor or seek out an obscure part of a building.

Floor plan. The considerations of floor plan for a basic structure are not ordinarily too difficult. Unless the floor space is badly arranged, with doorways in awkward places and poor placement of stairways and windows, an adequate floor plan should be possible. Sometimes an older structure cannot be altered to any extent without bringing the entire building into compliance with current building codes. If changes in plumbing, heating, wiring, or fire controls are needed to achieve a good floor plan, it may be better to look elsewhere for a suitable building.

Compatibility. If a building does not fit into its environment and provide what the entrepreneur needs at that location, it is not compatible. Differences in style and appearance are readily apparent, but they are not necessarily incompatible.

More serious problems arise from differences in elevation between the chosen site and adjacent or nearby buildings. Too much or too little setback may exist. Or the lighting system (interior and/or exterior) may create an unfavorable impression in the customer's mind.

Occasionally, an extreme design or appearance may be advantageous, but it is a risky approach. Novelty in floor plan can become tiresome and boring in the long run.

ZONING AND LAND-USE CONTROLS

The past 25 years have been a period in which zoning has become firmly established in the majority of business and residential areas across the United States. The past 10 years have seen a variation of zoning develop that is described generally as land use regulation and control. Whereas zoning applies in urban areas, land use is more generally applied to rural areas. Neither term is exclusive, but the distinction is commonly made in the context of controls over the uses of property.

The trends in zoning and land use in most cases are probably contrary to the long-range interests of small business owners and operators. Zoning and control tend to require compliance with a variety of conditions and regulations. Higher standards and tighter restrictions tend to raise the price of land, diminish the amount of land available for use, and increase the cost of buildings.

Buildings and other structures are affected in a variety of ways by zoning and land-use controls. The most important of these are described briefly under the following categories:

1. Building controls—Buildings for any use (business or other) are controlled as to the amount of land required for a given type of structure. Building height, setback, utility and street access, fire protection, construction features, and other related conditions are also controlled.

2. Designated uses—Building and locations for business are subject to strict control. Certain business operations may be conducted only in certain properly zoned areas. Other businesses, such as liquor stores, pawn shops, and even professional offices, may be controlled by administrative boards that enforce restrictions as to number and location.

3. Prohibited uses—Standards adopted by zoning boards and land-use agencies have become increasingly restrictive. As an extension of designated uses, many business activities are now prohibited in many areas or are subject to tight controls where they are permitted. For example, there are usually limits on the storage of gasoline within city limits and the generation of smoke, fumes, dust, and water pollution beyond certain limits is prohibited. Revolving beacons or flashing signs are often prohibited. Accessory buildings may not be allowed. Buildings may be restricted or prohibited in a floodplain or where unstable soil conditions exist. Finally, it is quite common to deny business use of a building unless adequate off-street parking is provided.

An example of business zoning classification is shown in Figure 10–1. The illustration is typical of zoning provisions for business where business activity is divided into several categories. Businesses covered in Figure 10–1 are of a nonindustrial nature and represent typical retailing and service establishments.

COVENANTS AND SOCIAL STANDARDS

Many business properties are not owned and controlled by those that use and occupy them. This is quite often the case for small businesses. The control of an owner or property manager may be quite restrictive and contrary to what the small business operator would like to do with the building and surrounding land area.

Property owners and agents exert control in ways that they think will maximize the return on their capital investment. If the market for commercial properties is tight, tenants and lessees can expect restrictions that favor the owner. If a single property or one-tenant building is involved, the restrictions may be arbitrary and overly restrictive. If the market is weak, the owner will be inclined to be more permissive in the negotiations. In a multiple-business use area, such as a shopping center,

Figure 10–1
Typical zoning provisions for restricted business areas

B–BUSINESS DISTRICT
(RESTRICTED BUSINESS AREAS)

11.1 USES PERMITTED

1. Uses numbered (1) through (9) as permitted in T—Transitional District;
2. Places for the conduct of any restricted business, not limited to the following: antique shops and art shops; banks; barber shops and beauty parlors; book and stationery stores; clothing shops; department stores; dry goods and variety stores; eating and drinking places; electrical and household appliance stores; florists; furniture stores; gasoline stations; gift shops; grocery stores; hardware stores; jewelry and craft shops; music, radio and television stores; newsstands; office supply stores; offices for business and governmental use; optometrist shops; package liquor stores; photographic studios, equipment and supply stores; public utility collection offices; shoe stores; sporting and athletic goods stores; indoor theaters; toy stores; travel bureaus; and watch repairing.
3. Public utility mains, and underground facilities; and
4. Accessory buildings and uses.

11.2 MINIMUM LOT AREA

1. on land where the principal building is *not* connected to *both* public water and public sewer facilities . . . 15,000 sq. ft.;
2. on land where the principal building *is* connected to *both* public water and public sewer facilities . . . no minimum requirement.

11.3 MINIMUM LOT WIDTH

1. on land where the principal building is *not* connected to *both* public water and public sewer facilities . . . 120 ft.;
2. on land where the principal building *is* connected to *both* public water and public sewer facilities . . . no minimum requirement.

11.4 MINIMUM LOT FRONTAGE . . . 40 ft. (minimum front lot line)

11.5 MINIMUM FRONT YARD . . . 60 ft.

(minimum distance of any building from the centerline of a street or highway, except as specified in Section XVIII)

11.6 MINIMUM SIDE YARD . . . 10 or 12 ft. (as amended Feb. 24, 1969)

(minimum distance of buildings from each side lot line or one half the distance between detached buildings on the same lot)

11.7 MINIMUM REAR YARD . . . 20 ft.

(minimum distance of any building from the rear lot line or from the centerline of an alley where one exists)

11.8 MAXIMUM BUILDING HEIGHT . . . 50 ft.

---

owners and property managers tend to adopt measures that they feel are consistent for the entire group of businesses. In general, they will favor the larger tenants over the smaller ones. Typically, signs and advertising on the actual building site are strictly controlled. This may not be a problem for a major retail store, but it is a serious handicap for a small business.

CONSTRUCTION FEATURES

The construction features of a building should be carefully investigated because in most instances a building's major characteristics cannot be changed without considerable expenditure. Items to be considered include:

1. Basic building materials and the method of construction. Newer buildings often use trusses for roof support to eliminate interior columns or load-bearing partitions. Combinations of concrete masonry and structural steel provide a very good building, particularly from the standpoint of maintenance, fire protection, remodeling, and ultimate expansion. Older buildings ordinarily do not have the advantages resulting from modern construction.

2. Service and equipment characteristics. Items in this category include the provision of an adequate electrical system—including many outlets, three-wire service for 220-volt or higher-voltage service, and adequate modern lighting fixtures—air-conditioning equipment, a good heating system, rest rooms, circulation and exhaust fans, and other equipment that may be necessary to the business operation.

3. Interior layout. Consideration here will vary widely from one type of business to another, but the building must include, within reason, a proper wall, ceiling, and floor arrangement which is needed for appearance, utility, and maintenance. The amount of floor loading that can be applied in a building with suspended floors must be computed to determine whether limitations exist on the storing of merchandise or the placing of machinery in particular places. Older buildings may have basements, balconies, or second stories that can be used, but they may be limited as to their usefulness. Many modern buildings are built on one level with no basement and have the advantage of a solid concrete floor, movable partitions, and limited window space. A building with these characteristics can be adapted to a variety of internal arrangements.

4. Appropriate design. Often undesirable design elements in a building can be concealed through remodeling to present the desired appearance. Small factories, offices, restaurants, and specialty mercantile establishments have been located in existing buildings where such remodeling has given a uniqueness and drawing power to an otherwise very ordinary business structure.

BUILDING IMPROVEMENT AND UPGRADING

A new building erected to suit the tenant will have been planned around appropriate major structural and site features. But in an older building, a new tenant will probably have to change a number of features, both inside and out.

Additions. Permanent additions to the structure are "attachments" and ordinarily cannot be removed at the end of the tenant's occupancy. These additions should be discussed and negotiated for with the owner, inasmuch as they usually benefit the property. Certain fixtures and equipment that are not attached normally remain the property of the tenant and may be removed at the end of the occupancy.

Exterior changes. Many older buildings need exterior changes, but often no more than a "facelift." This may be accomplished by building a false front, putting in new windows, doors, and trim, or perhaps merely getting a new paint job. Surface treatment is often inexpensive and can be dramatic in terms of changed appearance. A changed exterior appearance is a good idea for a new tenant, unless he/she is simply taking over an already highly successful business. Contemporary and modernistic appearances may be highly desirable in some cases, but not appropriate in others. Careful study of costs and payoff potential is necessary in any case.

Interior changes. Changes in the interior of a building are usually divided into two major categories; (a) structural changes and (b) decorative changes. If the basic structure is being altered, substantial problems may develop. Many building codes specify that basic structural changes require that the building be brought into conformity with the present building code. This can necessitate substantial modernization of electrical wiring, plumbing, heating, fire protection, etc. Minor changes, such as moving a partition, may be allowed, as will redecorating, painting, and the like.

Frequently, an ingenious new tenant can accomplish substantial improvement without incurring a great deal of expense. Floors, ceilings, doorways, and windows are subject to a variety of changes. Often the difference in cost between an adequate interior and something much better is very small.

INVESTMENT PLANNING FOR THE BUILDING

The total program involving the building and its facilities is a substantial long-term commitment for any business. The smaller business is faced with the same kinds of decisions as the large business, but on a reduced scale.

Either a new or an older building and its facilities will require a good comprehensive long-range investment plan. Initially the business needs a good building in which to get off to a good start. A conservative investment is prudent until the business proves that it can succeed.

If the business does well the first year, a long-range plan should be developed so improvements in the building and facilities keep pace with business growth. Provisions should be made to expand, move to a new location, build a new building, remodel, or redecorate as appropriate.

Once a year the capital investment program should be reviewed, including the investment in the building and its facilities. Depreciation rates, rates of inflation, and other economic data should be studied. Methods of financial analysis such as payback and discounted cash flow should be examined to determine the economic feasibility of alternative courses of action. Consult the chapters on financial management for details on this.

EFFECTIVE FLOOR PLAN

A good floor plan involves the proper utilization of floor space according to the needs of a particular business. Retailing, service, manufacturing, and wholesaling are all different and require specialized floor plans within the internal restrictions of the building. In a retailing operation, the floor plan is designed to promote sales activity; thus the needs and accommodations of customers are considered very carefully. In a manufacturing enterprise, the floor plan is designed for efficiency in the movement of materials, manufacturing sequences, and varying levels of product output and product mix. Service businesses and wholesalers likewise have individual problems requiring special consideration as to floor plan.

Retailing

In retailing, the floor plan is designed to be consistent with what is considered the most effective way to merchandise the particular product or products.

External features. The entrance to the store must be attractive and well placed in regard to the amount of frontage available. Many businesses have chosen to remodel so as to achieve offset entrances that provide more window display space. Some people like to have the outside display windows open to the interior of the store, whereas others prefer closed-back windows, which permit use of the area behind the window for display.

Internal features. Aisles should be designed so that customers will pass by a variety of merchandise, yet employees will be able to serve customers conveniently with adequate checkout points. Cash registers or service centers should be located at strategic points to aid employees in satisfying the needs of customers.

Floor space within a store is generally rated as being most attractive at the front and to the right, because of the phenomenon known as "right-hand reflex." This phenomenon is associated with the fact that most people are right-handed, and as a result, they habitually keep to the right and probably tour through a store in a counterclockwise pattern. Thus, merchandise that is located near the front and to right of the main entrance will be seen first by the most shoppers. A retail business conducted in a building with more than one floor must allow for the lower value of basement and upper-story floor space, as well as locations remote from main store entrances or internal aisle.

Service businesses

The floor plan for a service business should be oriented around a combination of service and sales because most service firms conduct some sales to complement the service activity.

Floor-plan analysis. The service business owner will need to develop a floor plan that promotes a smooth flow of orders and paper work and the fast and easy handling of parts and supplies. The convenient placement of telephones, catalogs, inventory, and eqiupment is very important.

On-site customer service. If the business deals with the public at the service site the floor plan must be set up so that service personnel can handle customers along with their service work. Walk-in trade, telephone orders, service-truck scheduling and dispatch, and other similar aspects of the business can all be worked into an efficient floor plan.

Manufacturing

By its nature, manufacturing lends itself to a more objective type of floor-plan analysis based on manufacturing methods and procedures.

Factory layout analysis generally begins with a study of the amount and shape of the available floor space and the existing openings such as windows and doors, as well as the loading docks, ceiling heights, and permissible floor loadings. A base floor plan can be drawn up including all physical characteristics of the building. In some cases, simple three-dimensional models might be used to get some idea of the height and space relationships that are possible in a particular building. The following checklist indicates the factor to consider in designing an effective floor plan for manufacturing.

Manufacturing floor plan checklist.
1. The products to be manufactured, with attention given to quantity and value.
2. The equipment to be used.
3. The relationship of eqiupment, personnel, materials, aisle space, and rate of production.
4. Product flow through the plant.

5. Provision for changes in product and equipment, and expansion possibilities.

Environmental considerations.   Lighting is a principal environmental factor in manufacturing. The amount of light, the placement of lights, the creation of shadows, the contrast present, and the type of light sources are all important for maximum efficiency. Color is another aspect of plant design that may affect the floor plan. For example, certain color combinations may be desirable in one area, but not in another. Layout should also include considerations of physical characteristics such as noise, heating, and air conditioning, all of which have an effect on the workers' environment and their degree of effectiveness.

Services support.   Service factors of importance in manufacturing include provision of adequate electrical current, the use of in-plant transportation equipment such as lift trucks, the efficiency of access to storage areas, and everything connected with moving materials through the manufacturing area. Plant storage of raw materials and finished goods will create a need for space, and reasonable allowances for them must be built into the floor plan.

The warehousing function in manufacturing demands special considerations. The type of warehouse storage needed, the kind of equipment used to move material, the frequency of movement, the possibility of congestion, the need for protection of certain materials, and the overall support of the manufacturing operation in an efficient manner are all considerations that need attention.

Wholesaling

Wholesaling is an operation that must be highly efficient in handling large volumes of goods. Problems can arise when warehousing operations are conducted in premises that may not be conducive to the most efficient operation. Warehousing for a wholesaler involves consideration of the following factors:

1. Ample low-cost space.
2. Access to rail and truck transport, loading and unloading docks, and proximity to the customers served.
3. Material-handling equipment such as fork-lifts.
4. Utilization of automation when appropriate, including such things as automatic conveyors, closed-circuit television, communication systems, and remote-control devices.
5. The proper environment for the goods in terms of temperature, humidity, ventilation, and so on.
6. Security, protection, and control. High-volume wholesaling operations entail the risks of loss, breakage, and theft. Therefore,

adequate insurance must be purchased and measures adopted to minimize pilferage.

SITE AND ENVIRONMENT

The surroundings of the building are considered *site* factors. The environmental features may extend for some distance, and may be under the control of other landowners. Environmental features can be important, even though they may be some distance away. (See Figure 10–2.)

Street, sidewalk, and service areas

The business site must be analyzed to determine its attractiveness to customers. Streets and sidewalks should be well lighted, and deliveries should be made at an entrance not used by the customers. Some attempt should be made to find out what standards and norms are expected by persons who visit the building and to adapt the premises accordingly.

Setback and frontage

In most communities, businesses will have a uniform setback from the street. Each business should effect some degree of individuality

Figure 10–2
America's main streets are changing with the times—A view of Main Street in Grand Junction, Colorado, showing the results of Operation Foresight.

Photo courtesy Grand Junction Chamber of Commerce

through design of the store front and the entrance. A particular theme or motif for the building front may do a great deal to enhance the site. The use of materials such as redwood, glass, plastic, corrugated metal, or wood shakes may create a unique appearance. In addition, an illuminated sign can be used that is complementary to the theme of the store front.

Complementary construction and appearance

Not all buildings and sites need to be complementary with the surrounding buildings or shopping areas. The mere fact that a building is different is not enough reason to reject it, but rather to examine it carefully and to determine whether its uniqueness will have persuasive effect.

Parking

Customers of today will not walk very far from their automobiles. Although this distance may vary, ordinarily it is limited to one or two blocks. Many businesses have flourished in remote locations because they are accessible by automobile. But others have suffered because they were located too far from good parking areas.

In some cases, merchants have joined together to buy and maintain parking lots, which are either free or metered. Other inducements to get customers into shopping areas have included free public transportation and the removal of parking meters on downtown streets. In any event, good, close parking is absolutely necessary to a successful business operation.

Environmental improvement

Any time a building and site is being examined for possible selection, it is important to consider the environment and determine what the needs and chances are for improvement. Environmental improvement can be accomplished only by a concerted effort on the part of all the business persons in the area. Leadership exercised by one or two members of the group will generate action by others to upgrade an area, bringing more customers and sales for everyone.

Building and site ratings

A good way to conduct an analysis of a building and its basic features is to determine what factors are important for a particular type of enterprises and then make comparisons between available possibilities.

Table 10–1 shows the relative importance of certain factors to different industries. If combinations of retailing, service, manufacturing, and wholesaling are contemplated, an integrated checklist can be devised from the table.

Table 10–1
Business building and site-rating table (by importance and type of business)

Factors	Retailing	Service	Manu-facturing	Wholesaling
Building feature				
Age	1	4	3	4
Space.	1	3	1	4
Configuration.	1	4	4	3
Appearance.	1	3	3	4
Frontage	1	4	4	4
Access	1	2	1	1
Interior utilization				
Floor space	2	3	1	1
Room dimensions	1	3	1	4
Ceiling heights.	2	2	2	4
Stairways, elevators.	3	3	1	1
Window space.	1	3	4	4
Utility services	3	1	1	3
Improvement potential				
Building exterior.	1	3	4	4
Building interior	1	3	2	2
Site	1	2	3	4
Surrounding.	2	2	3	4
Streets and walks	2	1	3	3
Access	1	1	2	1
Expansion	2	2	1	1
Site and environment				
Street and service areas . . .	1	2	2	3
Setback and frontage	1	3	4	4
Parking.	1	2	2	3
Surrounding businesses . . .	2	3	4	4
Area environment	2	3	4	4

Key to ratings: 1 = critical; 2 = very important; 3 = not ordinarily important; 4 = minimum
importance.

THE NEW BUILDING

At some point in the selection of a location and building, it may be prudent to consider a new building. Maybe several tenants can join together and construct a building, or space can be found in a building under construction by others. In any event, the possibility should be considered and perhaps pursued.

Construction. Construction features in new buildings include many materials and techniques that can be quite attractive. Better lighting, heating, air conditioning, and other elements of comfort and style can be incorporated. Communications and traffic patterns can be set up, and movable partitions can be designed that allow great flexibility.

Site planning. If a site has certain drawbacks, these can often be minimized at the time of construction. Screening, retaining walls, courtyards, and other methods can help to upgrade a site and make a new building even more attractive.

Services. Various forms of services that are important to most businesses may be easier to plan for in a new building. Standby power and fuel sources may be critical for a manufacturer. Adequate pure water may also be necessary. Delivery, trash disposal service, and police and fire protection are also of prime importance.

Parking. If a new building is located where there are a number of other businesses, then parking may be a problem. On the other hand, it is usually easier to plan for adequate parking in a new building situation.

WHEN TO REMODEL, EXPAND, OR MOVE

The factor of change is always present and eventually will bring about conditions that require modification in most business operations. Unfortunately, small businesses are usually slow to recognize change and to react to it in a positive way.

It is difficult to establish general criteria to determine when a small business should remodel, expand, or move. The following discussion will provide some guidelines.

Remodeling. A decision to remodel may be more of an act of faith than anything else. Even though a business continues to prosper, and return on investment seems to be holding up well, periodic remodeling and renovation may be necessary to keep the business in a competitive position. A checklist similar to the one employed when the business was established or acquired should be used to prepare a detailed and honest appraisal of the situation. Such an appraisal should probably be done yearly, with particular emphasis on factors of business appearance, competitive gain or loss, available funds for change, and a dedication to stay in business.

Expansion. The decision to expand a business operation may be easy to make. The need to expand is generally apparent in the volume of business being done. Planning for an expansion should include sales projections and estimates of the capital needed to accomplish the project.

Moving the business. In some instances, relocation of the business may be the only reasonable action for continued success. A decision to move is a critical one, and generally involves more risk and expenditure than either remodeling or expansion.

Much of the analysis regarding a move is similar to that of remodeling or expansion; emphasis must be given to certain subjective comparisons such as the value of a new building site versus that of the old one, and the expected sales volume at the new site versus that at the old.

QUESTIONS

1. Why is an older building often selected for starting a new enter-prise?

2. How would you estimate the value of the investment in a *new appearance* for a beginning business?

3. Do building codes place a burden on an entrepreneur who would like to utilize an older building?

4. How would you attempt to measure the impact of the surrounding environment on a beginning business?

5. Why is floor space alone a poor criteria in evaluating a building for a particular purpose?

6. How do you measure the relative value of a building located among many others along a business strip, such as an older highway or main street?

7. What precautions do you take in signing up to be a tenant in a new building with a number of other tenants, who are as yet unknown?

8. How would you analyze the problem of how long to commit a business in a lease or rental of a building?

PROBLEMS

1. Review the Yellow Pages of a phone book and pick out a business that, judged by its listing, is small and unusual as a business enterprise. Then go to the business with the intent of finding out the following:

    a. Your initial reaction to the environment and to the building itself (before entering the structure).
    b. The impression created by the exterior without knowledge of what is going on inside.
    c. The consistency of the interior appearance with the kind of business being conducted in the structure.

    d.   Those things about the building and facilities that strike you as being particularly good or bad.

Record your observations as quickly as you can after the actual observation takes place. First reactions are usually more important than later ones.

2.   Select a particular type of small business in retailing, services, manufacturing, or wholesaling. Identify at least five firms in that type of business within reasonable geographical proximity and of about the same size.

Prepare your own checklist of things you would like to observe in the type of business selected. Visit each of the firms and record what you have seen and any particular comments about each feature. Identify what you think are the strong and weak points of each operation.

BIBLIOGRAPHY

Baumback, Clifford M., and Kenneth Lawyer. *How to Organize and Operate a Small Business.* 6th ed. Englewood Cliffs, N.J.: Prentice-Hall, 1979, chap. 8.

Broom, H. N., and Justin G. Longenecker. *Small Business Management.* 4th ed. Cincinnati, Ohio: South-Western Publishing, 1979, chap. 10.

Frantz, Forrest H. *Successful Small Business Management.* Englewood Cliffs, N.J.: Prentice-Hall, 1978, pp. 37–53.

Moreau, James F. *Effective Small Business Management.* Chicago: Rand McNally College Publishing, 1980, chap. 5.

11

Insurance and the small business

The individual who starts a small business creates risk by entering a situation in which the outcome is uncertain. And although the desired outcome is success business statistics indicate that business failure is also a very real possibility.

The type of risk created when a business is started is basic to the free enterprise system and is termed *speculative,* or *dynamic,* risk. There are three possible outcomes in speculative risk situations: profit, status quo, or loss. It is the hope for a profitable outcome that motivates the small business owner to accept the uncertainty of speculative risk. If the motivation is not present, or if the outcome in a speculative risk venture proves unprofitable, the individual may seek a more secure position as an employee of someone else.

In addition to the creation of speculative risk, the small business venture also exposes the owner to what may be termed *pure,* or *static,* risk. Pure risk situations are those in which there are only two possible outcomes: loss or no loss. Although pure risks are often difficult to avoid, they may be assumed or transferred. Insurance is a social device for the *transfer* of certain pure risks, whereas speculative risks are, generally speaking, not insurable.

179

The purpose of this chapter is to provide the small business owner with a basic understanding of insurance and the management of pure risk.

CLASSIFICATIONS OF PURE RISKS

There are three types or classes of pure risk: property, liability, and personal. *Property* risks include the loss of tangible property because of such perils as fire, lightning, windstorm, hail, theft, and a multitude of others. In addition, loss of use, or added expense because of the loss of tangible property is also a property risk.

Liability risks involve the loss of existing assets or future income because the business owner is declared legally liable for actions that result in bodily injury or property damage to others. The possibility of legal liability covers a wide range of situations including such things as the distribution of a defective product, the maintenance of the business premises in a condition unsafe to the public, and actions of employees in dealing with customers.

Finally, *personal* risks include the loss of a person's income-producing ability through premature death, disability, sickness, accident, or retirement.

RULES OF RISK MANAGEMENT

Robert I. Mehr and Bob A. Hedges in their book *Risk Management in the Business Enterprise* cite what they consider to be the "rules of risk management." Although their guidelines for the management of pure risk may appear quite simple and perhaps intuitive, they do provide a useful framework within which risk management decisions can be made.

The *first* and probably most important of the three rules is "don't risk more than you can afford to lose." The treatment of pure risk involves determining how each individual exposure to pure risk should be handled. As a practical matter pure risk will be either assumed or transferred through insurance, and in deciding whether to assume or transfer the risk, the small business owner must estimate the maximum size of the potential loss. If the best estimate indicates a maximum potential loss so large that its occurrence would result in bankruptcy or serious financial impairment, risk assumption is not feasible. In other words, relating the maximum potential loss to the resources of the loss bearer will determine the importance of the risk exposure. Of course the maximum sustainable loss, as well as the resource base, will vary from firm to firm and from time to time in a particular firm.

The *second* rule of risk management is "don't risk a lot for a little." From the individual's point of view, insurance involves the exchange of a certain small loss (the premium) for the elimination (actually the transfer) of a potentially large loss. In implementing the second rule, the premium should be related to the potential loss and treated as a savings or cost. For example, if comprehensive physical damage insurance on a $4,000 automobile costs $35 a year, the savings or return if the insurance is not purchased and the risk is assumed equals $35/$4,000 or 0.875 percent. The owner is exposing a $4,000 investment to possible loss or damage for less than a 1 percent return and that is risking a lot for a little. On the other hand, a driver who pays $40 a year for auto collision coverage with a $50 deductible, when the same coverage with a $100 deductible would cost only $12 a year, is paying a cost of $28/$50 or 56 percent for the second $50 of coverage. Here, from a cost point of view, the car owner is paying dearly for a small return. In the first case, the purchase of insurance is consistent with the rule and in the second case it is not.[1]

The *third* rule of risk management is simply to "consider the odds." This general rule can be more specifically expressed in terms of three types of judgmental errors common to most amateur risk managers. First, there is the tendency to underestimate the chance of loss in connection with long-shot situations. This is particularly true if an individual is asked to risk a little for the possibility of a large return. However, as the amount of dollars risked increases, the possibility of loss becomes more important. For example, one might accept risking $1 in a gambling situation where the chances are only 1 in 50 of winning $100. On the other hand, the same person may reject risking $1,000 in a gambling situation where the chances are 1 in 5 of winning $5,000.

The second judgmental error is allowing the smallness of chance of loss to overshadow the largeness of the potential loss. When the risk taker senses that the chance of loss is very remote, there is a tendency to ignore the possibility of loss, even in those cases where the potential loss is large. An example of this would be the retailer who considers the possibility of a product liability suit so remote that he ignores the fact that judgments in such cases are very large.

Finally, the third error in judgment is somewhat the reverse of the

---

[1]The cost of 56 percent implicitly assumes that the insured has an average of one collision claim a year in excess of $100, which of course is unlikely. If one assumes the insured averages less than one collision a year, the cost of the second $50 of coverage is even greater than 56 percent.

second, that is, the case where the near-sureness of an apparent gain causes the size of the potential loss to be underestimated. People who insist on driving in excess of the speed limit violate this rule, as do jaywalkers, and people who, because they haven't had an automobile insurance claim in some time, rationalize that they would be saving money by not buying insurance.

PROBLEMS IN APPLYING THE RULES OF RISK MANAGEMENT

Despite the apparent common-sense nature of the rules of risk management, there are six potential problems one must consciously avoid in applying the rules. Unfortunately, the evidence shows that small business managers as a group are highly susceptible to these difficulties of application.

1. *The problem of objectivity.* It is human nature for most individuals to be conceited in various degrees regarding their own abilities. This seems to be particularly true of those who seek the independence of owning their own businesses. This type of person tends to overvalue gains and undervalue losses, which leads to a violation of all three rules.

2. *The problem of inadequate information.* Making decisions from a position of ignorance is dangerous; yet it is always easy to overlook the facts because of the time normally involved in gathering and interpreting information. A good example of this is the small retailer who does not realize the exposure to legal liability in not maintaining safe premises for customers. Furthermore, time is not taken to find out. A little effort in this direction can be well worth while. Trade associations, lawyers, the Small Business Administration, and several other sources of information exist that could prevent some sleepless nights.

3. *The problem of psychic income.* This problem evolves from the universal human tendency of overestimate potential gains and underestimate potential losses. It is "the dream of great things." Business failure statistics are in large part empirical proof of the urge for psychic income, that is, income that is produced only in the imagination. From an insurance point of view, the individual who gets involved in the psychic income problem is the same type of individual who tends to ignore static risks.

4. *The problem of oversight.* The person who has the problem of oversight maintains the idea that "it can't happen to me." More specifically, this takes two forms. Either the potential costs in any particular decision involving risk never appear as real as the

benefits, or the risktaker believes that the costs are not even associated with the gains. For example, the person who drives his automobile within the speed limit only when the police are sighted, does so because he may be caught and receive a speeding ticket; yet he ignores the high costs of disability or accidental death.

5. *The problem of risk aversion.* This problem is in a sense the opposite of the attitude represented in the first four instances. In this case, the individual is so sensitive to risk situations that decisions involving risk are all aimed at risk avoidance, the minimization of risk. The maintenance of such an attitude is costly for two reasons. First, opportunities that are basically sound may be rejected; and second, unnecessary costs may be incurred to transfer risk when such a decision is not warranted. In this regard, an important thought comes to mind—that is, the good business person doesn't necessarily seek to avoid risk, but only to control it intelligently.

6. *The problem of the inevitable error.* Finally, the small business owner must recognize that regardless of the time, effort, and money spent on risk control, the improbable will sometimes happen. Risk involves the possibility that some future event will occur, no matter how remote that possibility may seem. Of course, the most rational approach to this reality is simply to follow the rules of risk management.

METHODS OF HANDLING RISK

At this point it is appropriate to discuss the methods for handling static risk situations in the small business. They include risk avoidance, risk assumption, risk reduction, the shifting of risk, and risk transfer.

The avoidance of static risk is a possibility only when a choice is available, and in most instances this is not the case. For example, the possibility of fire or windstorm loss to a business building may be minimized, but cannot be eliminated. On the other hand, an example of a situation involving a choice is when the loss of large sums of money by theft can be avoided by management policy regarding the handling and transfer of funds—such as making several bank deposits each day or using an armored car service, for example.

Risk assumption is a second possibility and may be voluntary or involuntary. Involuntary risk assumption can result from ignorance, stubbornness, irrational reasoning, or lack of funds. Voluntary risk assumption, on the other hand, may be the best decision in a particular situation, or may be necessary because appropriate insurance coverage is simply not available.

Although the small business person rarely has the opportunity to self-insure, it is a means of risk assumption. Self-insurance involves the establishment of a fund within the business to handle the possibility of financial loss as a result of a particular peril or hazard. It is different from simple risk assumption, however, in that it involves estimating the potential loss for the period and earmarking funds intended to absorb the estimated losses. The problem in self-insuring is, of course, estimating the potential loss in some scientific manner, which requires a large enough number of units exposed to loss that the law of large numbers applies.[2] For this reason, it is not a feasible tool for risk assumption in most cases.

The reduction of risk involves taking steps to affect both loss frequency and loss severity. Reducing loss frequency involves an awareness on the part of the small business person and his/her employees that good housekeeping and proper safety precautions are effective in the prevention of loss. On the other hand, it is also important to take those steps that will minimize the amount of loss once the loss begins. Efforts to reduce risk are important, with or without insurance. With insurance, risk reduction programs may mean premium reductions; in other cases good risk reduction may eliminate the need for insurance altogether.

The most common way to shift risk is by contract. Such arrangements as subcontracting, surety bonds, and hedging are typical examples of shifting risk. Through subcontracting the person or persons contracted to perform a particular task will be responsible for adequate performance. In the case of surety bonds, the bonding company guarantees that a particular individual will perform in a prescribed manner. Hedging is accomplished by buying and selling goods for future delivery in such a way as to protect against a fluctuation in the market price.

Finally, risk transfer is accomplished by the purchase of insurance. It is important not to look at insurance as a substitute for handling risk if some other method is more appropriate. More will be said about this in a section on buying insurance.

---

[2]The law of large numbers, in probability theory, states that the larger the number of trials of a specific event, the more nearly the actual outcome will approach the expected outcome. The expectation may be based on opinion or theory (called "a priori"), as in flipping a coin, or on actual observation or experience (called "a posteriori"), as in the frequency of household fires in a particular city. For example, in flipping a coin, the change of its coming up heads is 0.5 and the more times you flip the coin the more nearly heads will result 50 percent of the time. In house fires, empirical evidence will indicate expected losses and also an expected variation from expected. As you increase the observations, however, the variation between expected and actual will narrow. From this brief explanation, it should be apparent that most business managers are not in the position to apply the law of large numbers, because their groups of units or exposures are not large enough to provide a reliable estimate of expected loss.

PRINCIPAL TYPES OF INSURANCE COVERAGE

After the small business owner has carefully examined his/her exposure to static risk, the basic insurance needs of the business must be determined. Those insurance needs common to most small business organizations are briefly described below.

Property insurance

A standard *fire insurance policy* is a necessity in any circumstance. It covers losses to goods and premises resulting from fire and lightning, and also losses caused by the removal of goods from the premises endangered by fire. In addition, most business owners consider it necessary to purchase an *extended coverage endorsement,* which extends the standard fire policy to include the perils of explosion, riot, vehicle damage, windstorm, hail, and smoke damage.

If the business operation is conducted on leased premises the owner must determine the extent of the owner's insurance coverage. Usually that policy does not include coverage for the tenant's inventory and equipment.

Burglary insurance will compensate the business owner for stolen property in cases of forced entry. (The major coverage excluded is the theft of business accounts.) Robbery insurance, on the other hand, will pay for losses of property if force or threat of violence was involved. Protection from loss of payroll and securities can also be added to the robbery contract if desired. In the case of small retailers, a combination policy called the *storekeeper's burglary and robbery policy* is tailored to cover small losses due to both perils at a premium that is considerably less than that for the more comprehensive crime policies assembled by an insurance agent.

One additional property contract that the small business owner may want to consider is *business interruption insurance,* which pays net profits and expenses in cases where a business is partially or totally shut down because of a fire or other insured cause. The total claim is based on an estimate of the income lost because of closure and the expenses that continue and must be paid despite the closure.

Casualty insurance

One of the most important insurance coverages the small business owner must obtain is *general liability insurance,* which covers the costs of defense and judgments obtained against the company because of bodily injury and/or damage to the property of others. In addition, under most circumstances this policy should probably include *product liability* coverage. The small business failure statistics are full of instances in which loss of a liability lawsuit forced bankruptcy.

In addition to the general liablity policy, all company-owned cars and trucks and their drivers should be covered by *automobile liability insurance,* and liability insurance should be carried on employees who use their own cars for company business.

Life insurance

The use of *life insurance* can benefit the business operation, as well as the heirs of a covered individual. To assure a measure of continuity and financial stability to the venture, the following options are available. In the sole proprietorship, life insurance can be used to provide cash for the survivors of the deceased owner and used to continue or dispose of the business. In the partnership or corporation, on the other hand, the proceeds of a life insurance policy can be used to fund a buy-sell agreement in the event of the death of a partner or stockholder. Finally, in certain instances, life insurance can be used to reimburse the firm for financial loss resulting from the death of a key person in the business, or to build up a sinking fund to be available upon that person's retirement.

Workers' compensation

Most states make workers' compensation programs mandatory. Such plans provide benefits to employees injured at their place of work, regardless of the legal liability of the company. The schedule of benefits is defined by state law and thus varies from state to state. Normally, however, the benefits include medical care and income payments for a disabled worker and his/her dependents. Certain classes of employees are often excluded, particularly those in agricultural or domestic jobs. Premiums are based on the employee's salary or wage level and the type of work involved. Hazardous jobs will carry a rate as high as ten percent of salary, whereas low-risk occupations may cost as little as one percent of salary.

Bonding

The small business owner can use various types of bonding arrangements to shift the financial responsibility for an employee or a job to a third party. The third party is known as a surety, and is either a licensed bonding company or an insurance company. A fidelity bond placed on an employee will reimburse the employer if the employee steals company funds. As a general rule, any person having access to company funds should be bonded, without exception. A surety bond guarantees the performance of a job. For example, a general contractor in the construction industry is reimbursed if a bonded subcontractor fails to complete a job according to the terms of the agreement that was made.

THE NONPROFESSIONAL RISK MANAGER

The proper management of static risk is a tough job for the untrained. In a typical situation, the small business owner is concerned with the allocation of some limited number of premium dollars in some optimal manner. He/she must select among the risk management tools of assumption, reduction, and transfer to achieve the maximum protection against static losses. In more specific terms, the task involves answering the following three questions:

1. What kind of insurance should be purchased?
2. How much insurance should be purchased?
3. From whom should the insurance be purchased?

In developing appropriate answers to these questions, the small business manager needs help, and a major problem stems from the fact that the insurance adviser is usually also the insurance salesperson. The insurance agent works on a commission basis, which means the more insurance the agent sells, the more income he/she makes. Thus, the unscrupulous salesperson would tend to recommend the purchase of insurance in instances where the risk may be more appropriately handled in some other way. In other cases, the agent who puts a priority on sales volume rather than satisfied clients may not be a good adviser simply because he/she has never taken the time to gain the knowledge required to properly analyze a particular firm's static risk situations.

It is fortunate that although such conditions do exist in the insurance industry, they are not widespread. The majority of insurance agents are competent, intelligent, and knowledgeable in their jobs. Such conditions do, however, suggest that the small business owner must treat the selection of an insurance adviser as a serious matter. This task is more clearly stated by saying the small business owner should know enough about insurance to:

1. Know when advice is needed.
2. Know whether the adviser is good.
3. Know whether the advice is good.

General principles of buying insurance

An insurance contract is a complex document that the layman finds difficult to understand. Furthermore, given the large number of contracts available and the scores of modifications that can be added, there are literally hundreds of combinations from which to choose. This can make buying insurance a perplexing problem if certain general principles are not adhered to.

As a general principle, the small business manager should buy insurance only when it is the most appropriate and least expensive means of achieving the financial security that is desired in the face of uncertain losses. Under what circumstances, then, is insurance the most appropriate and least expensive means available? Four important rules must be applied in answering this question.

Rule 1: This large loss principle. Insurance should be used on the premise that the probability of loss is less important than the possible size of the loss. In other words, if a situation exists where the potential loss could be large, the fact that the loss is highly improbable should be ignored. Since the small business owner must assume some risks and transfer others, it is rational to transfer those he/she cannot afford to bear. This is commonly known as the large loss principle.

Often the complaint is voiced that those who need insurance the most are those who can least afford it. To some extent this is true, because the need for insurance is based on the inability to withstand the possible loss if insurance is not purchased. So while those who need it can least afford it, they are the very ones that can least afford to be without it. Any potential loss that could lead to severe financial stress or bankruptcy requires insurance. Thus, in deciding whether to buy insurance the question is not, "Can I afford it?", but "Can I afford to be without it?" This situation, of course, is closely related to the first rule of risk management cited earlier: "Don't risk more than you can afford to lose."

Rule 2: Insurance is a last resort. Risk should be transferred through insurance only when absolutely necessary, because it is costly. Insurance always costs more than the expected value of a loss (i.e., the probability of loss times the potential loss) because the premium must also include the insurer's administrative and selling costs, plus profit. Thus insurance is economically feasible only when the probability of loss is low and potential loss severity high. If the probability of loss is high and potential loss severity low, the purchase of insurance is a mistake.

Unfortunately, people tend to want insurance in situations in which the probability of loss is high and loss severity relatively low. Such people fail to appreciate the true function of insurance, which is to guard against the catastrophic economic loss. A good example of this error in judgment is the purchase of full coverage when deductibles are available.

Unfortunately, it is easy to find cases in which the insurance industry has violated the large loss principle. The most common is the offering of full coverage in instances where deductibles should be used. Although there is nothing morally wrong with full coverage, it is certainly not the most effective way to spend the limited number of premium dollars that the small business manager typically has available.

Rule 3: If insurance is called for, buy adequate coverage. If the decision is made that insurance is the best means for handling a particular pure risk involving property, be sure the coverage is adequate. The reason for this rule is that all property insurance contracts contain what is known as a co-insurance clause. The co-insurance clause states that if the amount of insurance purchased on the property is less than some stated percentage (usually 80 percent), the insured will share all partial losses up to the face value of the policy.

For example, if a small business owner has a building with a current replacement value of $100,000, and the fire insurance policy purchased contains an 80 percent co-insurance clause, $80,000 of insurance ($100,000 times 80 percent) is required if full partial losses are to be collected. If only $60,000 of insurance is purchased in this instance, the company will pay only three fourths or 75 percent of a partial loss. The formula that determines how much the company will pay is as follows:

$$\frac{\text{Amount of insurance actually purchased}}{\substack{\text{Amount of insurance required, i.e.,}\\ \text{80 percent of current replacement value}}} (\text{Loss}) = \substack{\text{Amount}\\ \text{company}\\ \text{will pay}}$$

In the above case, if there is a $10,000 fire loss, the insurance company will pay

$$\frac{\$60,000}{\$80,000} (\$10,000) \text{ or } \$7,500 \text{ of the loss}$$

and the small business owner will have to absorb $2,500 of the loss.

Although co-insurance clauses of any percentage may be written into a property insurance contract, 80 percent is the most common. One good reason for the co-insurance clause is to encourage the small business owner to buy adequate insurance coverage on his/her property.

Rule 4: Buy the largest deductible the business can afford. Always ask the agent to compare the premium cost for different levels of deductible. Remember, a deductible in insurance simply means that the insured shares in the loss by paying the first $100 or $200 (or more) of every loss.

The rule in using deductibles is to determine the maximum amount of each loss the small business can absorb without a financial strain. In the long run, taking the maximum deductible affordable will mean substantial premium savings.

Selecting the agent and the company

The first step in deciding where to buy insurance is to focus on the agent, not the company. As previously indicated, the careful selection of an insurance adviser (agent) is a fundamental part of insurance buying.

A good agent has two primary qualifications: a thorough knowledge of insurance and a genuine interest in the needs of his client. Fortunately, one will find that the better agents usually represent the better companies.

Some agents are "independent," which means they represent several companies. Others, particularly in life and health insurance, represent only one company. Then there are insurance brokers, who can help in setting up an insurance program and acquire the coverage through any number of companies. The distinction between the agent and broker is that the agent represents and works for the company, whereas the broker represents and works for the client.

In choosing the company, there are four factors to consider: financial stability, claims service, company policy on cancellation, and premiums. As for financial stability, the layman should consult the evaluations of the Alfred M. Best Company, which can be found in most university, college, and public libraries. In the property and liability areas, *Best's Insurance Reports* and *Best's Key Rating Guide* are published annually. In addition to financial strength, the Best reports also rate efficiency of operations and caliber of management. The rating key is explained in each of the publications and can be easily understood.

As for life insurance, Best publishes *Life Reports* and the *Spectator Life Insurance Yearbook* annually. Both contain detailed financial and historical data on most life companies, and each company is rated. Again, a clear explanation of the ratings is provided.

In examining a company's claim services, there are two sources of information. Talk to the agent about claim-settlement procedures and, if possible, contact some of the company's policyholders who have recently had claims.

Finally, a knowledgeable and understanding agent is the best source of information on the company's cancellation policy and premiums.

Tip on insurance prices

In buying insurance, the small business manager must realize there are no bargains. Saving a few dollars in premiums may mean the difference between good service and average or poor service. The adage "You get what you pay for" applies to insurance as it does to anything else.

There is hardly an insurance policy in existence that some company cannot make a little broader for a higher premium. On the other hand, the same company can trim the coverage and reduce the premium. This does not mean that the cheapest insurance is always the poorest, nor the most expensive always the best. All it really indicates is that the broadness of coverage is an important determinant of the premium. In comparing price, be sure to consider the advice and service needed and whether these are adequately provided by the company selected.

QUESTIONS

1. Distinguish between speculative and pure risk. What are the three classes of pure risk?

2. What are the rules of risk management? Think of several examples in your own recent experiences when you have violated the rules.

3. What do you consider the most important problem you face in applying the rules of risk management?

4. Discuss the methods of handling risk and for each method give two examples of its proper application.

5. Review the principal types of insurance coverage a small business owner must consider buying.

5. What are the three basic problems the nonprofessional risk manager faces in managing static risk?

7. What is the large loss principle?

8. Why should insurance always be considered as a last resort?

9. What four factors are most important in selecting a company?

10. How should one compare premium rates in deciding what insurance company to buy from?

11. Explain how the co-insurance clause works in a property insurance policy.

PROBLEMS

1. Contact a local fire and casualty insurance agent and discuss with him the problems most frequently encountered in satisfying the insurance needs of small businesses in the community.

2. Contact two or three successful small businesses in your community and review their insurance programs. Ask the managers questions regarding why they do or do not have particular types of coverage.

3. John Smith owns a building with a current replacement cost of $200,000. He buys a fire insurance policy on the property with an 80 percent co-insurance clause, but the face value of the policy is only $120,000. Six months later, the building catches on fire and there is a $20,000 loss. How much of the loss will the insurance company pay? How much of the loss must John Smith absorb?

BIBLIOGRAPHY

Baumback, Clifford M., and Kenneth Lawyer. *How to Organize and Operate a Small Business.* 6th ed. Englewood Cliffs, N.J.: Prentice-Hall, 1979, chap. 15.

Broom, H. N., and Justin G. Longenecker. *Small Business Management.* 4th ed. Cincinnati: South-Western Publishing, 1979, chap. 22.

Frantz, Forrest H. *Successful Small Business Management.* Englewood Cliffs, N.J.: Prentice-Hall, 1978, pp. 273–280.

Tate, Jr., Curtis E.; Leon C. Megginson; Charles R. Scott, Jr.; and Lyle R. Trueblood. *Successful Small Business Management.* Rev. ed. Plano, Tex.: Business Publications, 1978, chap. 23.

12

Getting the capital you need

Once the prospectus has been put together, the manager of the intended new business venture must identify the firm's needs for capital and the best sources of that capital. The problem involves estimating those funds necessary to *promote* and *organize* the business, as well as those funds necessary for the *going concern*. In the going concern the problem is determining whether working capital and fixed assets are adequate and provided by the best possible sources. The importance of these decisions is demonstrated by the fact that inadequate capital is one of the most common causes of small business failure.

For purposes of this discussion the word *capital* refers to the total funds employed in the firm. The owner's contribution is called *equity*, and those funds provided by creditors represent *debt*. The sum of the debt and the equity therefore is the total capital of the business.

Although the standard financial ratios and data published by various organizations may prove helpful in estimating capital needs, it is hazardous to rely exclusively on such indicators. The manager should also make estimates (based on experience and knowledge of conditions in the line of business, and the particular market area where the firm is going to operate) of what the capital needs of the business will be.

ESTIMATING CAPITAL NEEDS FOR CURRENT ASSETS

The capital needed for operating a business is usually tied up in fixed and current assets. Current assets are such things as cash, accounts receivable, and inventory. Fixed assets are things such as land, building, machinery, and equipment. Let us now look at what capital we need for current assets.

Cash needs

In attempting to determine a minimum required cash balance, the amount of cash outflow that will take place before cash inflows begin can be estimated. This involves anticipating payments necessary for such items as labor, rent, supplies, utilities, and other expenses that will occur as soon as the business is open. To be on the safe side, a cash balance necessary to pay two or three months' expenses without figuring on any cash inflows during that period might be appropriate, because that much time may be required to achieve a satisfactory sales volume (and collection period if sales are made on credit). In addition, there is always the possibility of unexpected or hidden expenses. Both of these factors suggest that the cash balance in the initial period should be a generous one.

Investment in accounts receivable

A similar type of investigation is used to determine the investment requirement in accounts receivable. The problem is to anticipate the relationship between cash sales and credit sales, formulate the credit terms that are to be offered to customers, anticipate the paying habits of credit customers, and consider all the costs associated with administering the credit program.

Additionally, the manager must realize that once a credit sale is made, the account receivable may not be paid before the inventory must be replenished. Small businesses frequently get into trouble by not adequately providing for the volume of credit sales they make. They tend to think only in terms of sales volume. They fail to understand that as credit sales increase, the amount of working capital available to replenish inventory decreases until the cash is received for the credit sale, and inventory levels may decline drastically. Then, as a result of inadequate inventory, sales volume eventually declines. This sequence of events has ruined many otherwise successful business ventures.

Investment in inventory

In estimating the investment necessary in inventories, the types and quantities of products to be stocked must be considered. For the retail and wholesale business this presents the problem of first determining what is a reasonable and attractive selection of items to offer and then estimating sales of each item. For the manufacturer, the problem is usually how much and what kind of material is needed for the production operation.

In some cases suppliers will offer advice to their customers concerning reasonable inventory stocks. Turning customers away or shutting down production lines because of out-of-stock situations really hurts. On the other hand, the manager cannot expect to handle an infinite variety of items in order to avoid lost sales or production. Another factor important in determining appropriate inventory levels is the location of suppliers and the time required to replenish supplies.

The foregoing paragraphs cover what a business's capital needs might be for the current assets. As a general rule, the manager should err on the high side in estimating capital requirements for current assets. A common weakness in many small businesses is inadequate working capital and a disproportionate investment in current assets relative to fixed assets. Too much capital is tied up in assets that are difficult to convert to cash. The real danger arises if the business must depend on daily receipts to meet daily obligations. Then, when sales slump or unexpected expenses occur, the firm may be in serious financial trouble. Now let us, therefore, look at the capital needs for financing the fixed assets of the business.

Investment in fixed assets

In calculating the amount of investment required in fixed assets, price quotations on machinery, equipment, tools, furniture, and fixtures are available from suppliers. Land and building cost estimates may be based on prices asked by the sellers. The manager must realize the lack of flexibility associated with the purchase of fixed assets. As a general rule it is desirable to minimize fixed asset investment when possible. This often can be accomplished by borrowing on a long-term basis.

Frequently there will be a choice between leasing and buying fixed assets. For most small, new firms leasing arrangements are attractive. Leasing is, in essence, another form of borrowing. Leasing not only reduces the capital requirement in fixed assets, but provides a flexibility that is helpful if the business is more or less successful than originally anticipated.

The foregoing discussion has been concerned with determining the needs for funds in the new business venture. However, the same questions must be answered in situations in which the entrepreneur buys a going concern. In addition, it must be determined whether the purchase price of the going concern is reasonable, a problem considered in Chapter 6.

SOURCES OF CAPITAL AND CREDIT FOR SMALL BUSINESS

There are four basic means of generating funds for use in a small business: trade credit, reinvestment of profits, equity financing, and loans. Trade credit involves the purchase of goods, supplies, and equipment on credit from suppliers. Thus the business obtains its merchandise without having to pay for it until later as that business sells its products. The reinvestment of equity as a source of capital simply involves plowing some part of the profits back into the business. This is usually *not* a bountiful source of funds for a business starting out. The principal sources from which small businesses obtain funds are commercial banks, other financial institutions, and interested individuals. Equity financing involves selling ownership interest in the firm to someone as a partner or stockholder. Equity and debt (loan) financing are the biggest sources of capital with which to finance a business. Let us look first at equity financing and then at financing via loans or or debts.

EQUITY FINANCING

When the organizers of a small business provide required capital, they are engaging in equity financing. Recall that equity represents ownership, and shows up on the financial statement as net worth. Most of the funds to start up the typical small business will be obtained from equity sources.

As indicated, the provider of equity will usually demand some control over the management function. The source of equity funds will in part be determined by the legal form of organization. There are six potential sources of equity financing.

Sole proprietorship

The sole owner of a business keeps exclusive control over its management, but sources of equity are limited to personal savings, loans secured by real estate, stocks, bonds, or other personal property of high value, or funds supplied by friends, relatives, or customers of the owner without obligating the business.

Partnership

When two or more persons share the ownership and liabilities of a business, their sources of equity are much the same as in the single ownership situation. The only difference is that there now are more owners. Frequently, the person with a good idea (or experience and skill in management) and inadequate funds will join another individual who can provide the required capital. Sometimes this situation can create a happy merger of talents and money. Often it creates problems later, sometimes ruining the business.

The corporation

The corporation is formed by three or more individuals who apply to a particular state for a corporate charter. Ownership interest is represented by the number of shares of stock each person holds. A unique and attractive feature of the corporation is that each person's liability for the obligations of the firm is limited by his/her extent of ownership. The source of equity capital for the corporation involves the sale of capital stock to friends, relatives, stockbrokers, or any other interested parties. If the stockholders gain a voice in management through voting rights vested in share ownership (which is usually the case), raising equity through the sale of stock can jeopardize the entrepreneurs' control.

Small business investment companies

A number of companies have been licensed by the Small Business Administration to provide equity capital to small businesses and in some cases make long-term loans. A small business investment company (SBIC) will supply equity financing to sole proprietorships and partnerships that can qualify. In corporate organizations they will buy part of the capital stock outright. Some SBICs are also interested in the convertible debentures of small corporations. A convertible debenture represents an unsecured debt of the firm, convertible into common stock at some future date on terms specified at the outset. On the debt side, an SBIC will either grant outright loans of 5 to 20 years, or guarantee loans made to the business by a commercial bank.

Venture capital groups

It is not uncommon for groups of investors to form venture capital associations to provide equity capital to promising small businesses. They commonly prefer to deal with corporate organizations and either buy stock outright or invest in convertible debentures. Some people feel they are very greedy and very difficult sources from which to obtain capital.

Local or business development corporations

Development corporations are similar in many respects to SBICs. Private businesses and citizens form associations to promote business ownership, employment, and income in their own communities. They may raise funds through strictly private sources or through public subscription. They generally provide equity financing, but have been known to make long-term loans (5 to 20 years) and to guarantee commercial bank loans.

DEBT FINANCING

When the organizers are able to provide at least half of the capital needed through their own equity funds they generally seek the remainder from one or more debt sources. The creditors are not able to exercise any control over the management function as long as the debt agreement is adhered to. The loan contract, however, naturally stipulates certain conditions the borrowers must observe. Borrowed capital is indicated in the financial statement as liabilities. It is repaid, along with interest, out of profits and/or the sale of assets.

The sources of borrowed capital can be grouped, in terms of risk, into four classes. There are eight kinds of institutions in the four classes, and they provide more than 20 different types of financing.

Class 1 sources: Low risk, lowest cost

The Class I sources include commercial banks, life insurance companies, and savings and loan associations. They deal principally in short-term debt (less than one-year maturity) and intermediate-term

debt (three- to five-year maturity), though in some cases, longer-term debt can be arranged (beyond a five-year maturity).

Commercial banks. The commercial bank usually is the most economical source of borrowed capital available to the small business. It provides more debt to small business than any other source, either directly or through intermediaries (finance companies and trade suppliers) that borrow from the bank. Loanable funds come from customers' demand and time deposits, and loan policies are influenced by management decision as well as by government regulation. If at all possible, the small business manager should establish and maintain a good relationship with more than one commercial bank. The following list indicates the types of financing banks normally provide.

1. *Commercial loans:* These are the most common type of loan that banks make to small businesses. A commercial loan meets short-term seasonal needs; maturity is 90 to 180 days, and collateral may or may not be required.
2. *Term loans:* This bank loan arrangement normally provides funds for up to five years, on a secured or unsecured basis. The principal is repaid by periodic installments, and typically the business must adhere to certain conditions spelled out in a term loan agreement.
3. *Bank credit cards:* A retailer is able to offer credit to customers without financing the sale or assuming any credit risk through acceptance of bank credit cards. Visa and Master Card are the two most prominent nationwide plans. The cost to the retailer is sometimes as high as 5 or 6 percent of the sale price.
4. *Equipment financing and leasing:* Commercial banks will lend on equipment as collateral and can also arrange for the small business to lease equipment for negotiated periods of time.
5. *Real estate loans:* Banks make real estate loans to purchase, construct, or improve buildings, or to acquire land. These obligations are practically always secured by the asset financed, under strict agreement.
6. *Inventory distribution financing:* These bank loan arrangements permit manufacturers to distribute inventories to customers at times or in quantities most consistent with production schedules and capacities. The goods are produced and shipped to seasonal businesses long before the selling season starts. The manufacturers use *extended dating* in granting the customers credit, which means the invoice does not come due until late in the season. The benefits to the manufacturer are a reduction in inventory storage costs and the savings resulting from level production instead of seasonal production.

7. *Accounts receivable financing:* Commercial banks will lend money on accounts receivable pledged as collateral. However, such arrangements are made only on a recourse basis, which means that if accounts pledged become slow paying or bad, they must be replaced with good ones. Thus, the small business manager is left with all the problems and costs of collection.

8. *Factoring:* Several commercial banks maintain factoring departments, which will buy accounts receivable outright on a nonrecourse basis. This arrangement has the advantage of eliminating the costs of the credit and the collections function in the firm, but it may restrict sales if certain prospective customers are not acceptable credit risks to the bank. Also, factoring usually is more expensive than accounts receivable financing because the lender is assuming more risk.

9. *Other secured and unsecured loans:* These loans are made with or without collateral. Most often the real bases of the loan are the borrower's honor and financial strength, and the firm's potential for success. In other cases, valuable personal items, or the savings deposits of an individual or business, serve as security.

10. *Commodity or inventory loans:* Bank loans are made to manufacturers or wholesalers to purchase commodities (inventories) that are readily marketable, nonperishable staples. The goods serve as collateral.

11. *Floor planning:* This is a form of inventory loan that banks make to retailers on large consumer durables, such as automobiles and appliances. Titles remains with the bank, but possession is given to the seller. As the individual items are sold, the loan balance is reduced.

12. *Indirect collections financing:* This arrangement is used when a retailer generates a large volume of consumer sales contracts but prefers to retain the control and collection of the accounts. The commercial bank, in effect, purchases the contracts (receivables) at a discount but permits the firm to administer the credit program.

Life insurance companies. These institutions may provide debt financing, on a secured basis, to low-risk business firms that are well established. Their other function as a source of funds is to make long-term, low-interest loans to their policyholders, based on the cash value of the individual policyholder's contracts. Many insurance companies have so many resources that they regard a loan of $1 million as a "small loan"; because many small companies cannot invest that much money, as a minimum, they fail to qualify for insurance company loans.

Savings and loan associations. These institutions accept savings deposits from the public and use these funds to specialize in real estate loans. They are chartered and regulated by the state and/or federal governments. As a source of debt capital to small business, savings and loans provide two possibilities. First, the small business owner may obtain funds from a savings and loan by mortgaging or refinancing the family home or other real property. Second, all S&Ls can make real estate improvement loans to small businesses.

Class II sources: Moderate to low risk, low cost

The only institution considered to be in Class II is the Small Business Administration (SBA). This federal agency administers funds— appropriated by Congress and controlled by the Bureau of Budget—to assist small businesses. The SBA was established in 1953 to fill a need of small businesses for intermediate- and long-term funds (the average loan maturity is near five years).

As a prerequisite to obtaining a SBA loan, the firm must be unable to

qualify for private commercial financing. The SBA will service moderate to low risk needs at a relatively low cost. SBA loans are of five types and may be direct or made in participation with a commercial bank.

Direct loans. An amount up to $100,000 can be provided directly to a qualified small business if adequate collateral is available.

Bank participation loans. The SBA supplies up to 75 percent of the loan required or $150,000 (whichever is less), and the commercial bank puts up the remaining 25 percent.

Displaced business loans. These are SBA loans made to businesses displaced by federally funded programs such as urban renewal. The loan limit is 133 percent of the value of the business displaced or $350,000 (whichever is less).

Economic opportunity loans. Physically handicapped individuals and members of minority groups can acquire SBA funds for establishing a small business under the economic opportunity program.

Guaranteed loans. The SBA can guarantee up to 90 percent or $350,000 (whichever is less) of a business loan from a commercial bank at the lender's standard interest rate.

Class III sources: Moderate risk, moderate cost

The Class III sources of funds include leasing companies, inventory and equipment suppliers (who provide what is known as trade credit), and commercial finance companies. The inventory suppliers and commercial finance companies deal exclusively in short-term credit. The equipment suppliers and leasing companies provide intermediate-term credit (one to five years).

Leasing companies. These concerns lease buildings and/or equipment to small businesses at fixed rentals for negotiated periods of time. The principal advantage is reduction of initial capital requirements.

Inventory and equipment suppliers. One of the most important sources of funds to small business is the trade supplier. Since their customers' success contributes to their own, trade suppliers permit small businesses to buy inventory on credit or equipment on an installment basis. Certain manufacturers may also lend money to individuals or groups to establish dealerships for the manufacturers' products or to finance expansion. Inventory is normally financed for 30, 60, or 90 days, with discounts for prompt payment. Equipment is usually financed for up to five years with a 20 to 30 percent down payment required.

Commercial finance companies. These companies provide small businesses with funds for several purposes and under a variety of arrangements. Most of them deal with retail businesses. Inventory or equipment can be used as collateral. They also will finance accounts receivable on a recourse basis or will factor receivables (buy them outright) on a nonrecourse basis. Secured or unsecured commercial loans are also made to meet seasonal or short-term money needs for periods of 90 to 180 days.

Class IV sources: High risk, high cost

Only one source of funds realistically falls in the high-risk, high-cost group: the personal finance company. Because of the cost, it should be considered only as a last resort. Personal finance companies lend relatively small amounts to individuals on a secured basis, requiring repayment in installments over 3 to 36 months. Personal finance companies will take risks and accept types of collateral that commercial banks and other institutions will not.

Other sources of high-risk, high-cost funds are loans from what are best known as loan sharks. These lenders may be individuals or companies who are in the business of bailing out people who have made poor business decisions or for one reason or another get their businesses into a cash bind. Interest rates charged by these sources can be astronomical; usually the money is lent for a short time; and practically always the borrower harbors hard feelings toward the lender. Nevertheless, if failure of the business is the only alternative to using a loan shark, then these sources, too, can be and are used.

QUESTIONS

1. What factors should be considered in estimating what cash will be needed for financing of current assets in your business? Explain.

2. Why does your text explain the importance of investment of monies in accounts receivable? Explain.

3. What are the basic means for generating funds for use in a small business? Explain.

4. What is meant by equity financing? Explain in detail.

5. What is meant by debt financing? Explain in detail.

6. What are the lowest risk, lowest cost sources of debt financing in a business? Explain.

7. What are the highest risk, highest cost sources of financing for a small business? Explain in detail.

8. What is the best source of obtaining capital for a small business? Explain why you answered the way you did.

9. Explain the difference between a sole proprietorship, a partnership and a corporation.

10. What is meant by accounts receivable financing? Explain in detail.

PROBLEMS

1. Visit a local bank and discuss the financing of small business with one of the commercial loan officers. Does the bank make a point of providing some amount of venture capital to promising small businesses in the area? Ask for a copy of the loan application to see what types of information the bank requires of small business loan applicants.

2. Based upon the financial data provided to you from your instructor, put together a basic projection of how much money you will need to start the business which is represented by that financial data. Justify why you will need the sums of money which you think you will need, specifying what will be used for current assets, what will be used for fixed assets and what might be used for other requirements.

3. Contact the nearest office of the Small Business Administration and discuss it's role in financing small businesses in your community. Ask for the various application forms for an SBA loan and compare them with the information and data which your local banker requests from small business loan applicants.

BIBLIOGRAPHY

Buskirk, Richard T. *Handbook of Managerial Tactics.* Boston: CBI Publishing, 1976. This book is based on the author's premise that success in business depends more on the tactics used by managers than the basic merit of the plan. In short, he writes that tactics are the manager's tools, the means by which he or she gets the job done. Enumerates and describes how to go about getting the things that you want.

Butteriss, Margaret, and Karl Albrecht. *New Management Tools: Ideas and Techniques to Help You as a Manager.* Englewood Cliffs, N.J.:

Prentice-Hall, 1979. Shows how new management programs can be implemented and financed. Examines the advantages and disadvantages of diverse concepts showing how different approaches can be used to accomplish the same objectives.

Hayes, Rick Stephen. *Business Loans: A Guide to Money Sources and How to Approach Them Successfully.* 2nd ed. Boston: CBI Publishing, 1980. The author discusses banks, other private sector lenders, and government lending. He gives business people an idea of what kinds of loans are available, their definitions, and who grants them. The author also reveals the types of people the borrower is likely to be most willing to deal with.

Osgood, William R. *How to Plan and Finance Your Business.* Boston: CBI Publishing, 1980. This handbook is designed to be used by those starting new businesses and those already established. It describes the tools, techniques and terminology of getting the financing which you need to operate your business.

Case Study

The following case presents the financial data for Posey Sports, Inc.

Posey Sports, Inc., is a moderate-sized ski and bike shop located in a suburb of a large midwestern city. It is the sole ski retailer and bike shop in the fashionable suburb and is strategically located on one of the major arteries leading from the city to the ski slopes and bike trails. Consequently, it does a very good local business but also manages to capture business from customers who live far away.

The company has had several very good years, although it has suffered like other ski and bike retailers during winters of little snow and summers of too much rain. However, growth has been steady over the past years at an annual rate of about 10 percent. The managers of Posey feel that growth will continue next year at the same rate. However, like many entrepreneurs whose ventures have had several years of substantial growth, Posey's managers and owners are concerned about generating sufficient cash flow to meet operating costs, pay for advertising campaigns, and otherwise continue to operate efficiently and effectively.

Of a particular concern to the owners of Posey is the problem of liquidity and cash flow because in the past they have had to supply sizeable amounts of cash to tide them over until receivables came rolling in. The two partners who own the business (who happen to be brothers) are no longer in a position to make the large monetary advances to meet the business's cash requirements. The funds available for such purposes had been coming from an inheritance they had received. That cash source has finally been depleted, and outside cash is not available in sufficient amounts. Besides, the partners feel it is time the business was made to go on its own.

You are the operating manager of Posey Sports, Inc. While you are not an owner and do not carry the title of president, you have absolute authority to conduct the store's business as you see fit. The owners have told you that this power carries over to store finances, and that, as of today, their expectations of you are to run the business in its entirety, including its finances, with no input whatever (managerially or financially) from them from here on out.

You realize that you need to make a plan to acquire the capital you will need for the next year. Last fiscal year's P&L statement and balance sheet and next year's expected sales, by month, are given below.

QUESTIONS: How and where would you get the cash you will need for next year's operation? How much money do you need?

POSEY SPORTS, INC.
Income Statement
June 30, 19X1

Sales		$720,190.00
Cost of goods sold:		
Beginning inventory	$105,100.00	
Plus: Purchases	445,200.00	
Less: Ending inventories	120,300.00	
Total cost of goods sold.		430,000.00
Gross margin		$290,190.00
Less: Operating expenses:		
Fixed expenses		187,295.00
Variable expenses		96,187.00
Net profit before taxes		$ 6,708.00

POSEY SPORTS, INC.
Balance Sheet
June 30, 19X1

Assets

Current assets:		
Cash on hand	$ 5,585.03	
Accounts receivable	6,532.17	
Inventory accounts		
Ski department	60,073.61	
Bicycle department	6,338.94	
Tennis department	2,473.51	
Rental department	14,056.08	
Prepaid insurance	899.26	
Reserved.	—	
Other current assets	153.81	
Total current assets.		$ 96,112.41
Fixed assets:		
Land at cost.	50,000.00	
Building and improvements	97,194.14	
Less: Accumulated depreciation	50,000.00	
Delivery equipment	15,000.00	
Less: Accumulated depreciation	4,266.18	
Service equipment	7,505.62	
Less: Accumulated depreciation	2,734.98	
Furniture and fixtures.	6,033.40	
Less: Accumulated depreciation	1,180.54	

Office equipment	3,905.09	
Less: Accumulated depreciation	918.00	
Fixed assets—net.		164,343.01
Other assets:		
Organization expense	356.00	
Less: Accumulated amortization	260.91	
Total other assets		95.09
Total assets.		$260,550.51

POSEY SPORTS, INC.
Balance Sheet

Liabilities and Stockholders' Equity

Current Liabilities:			
Accounts payable—trade	$ 40,408.89		
Payroll tax accounts	755.74		
Sales tax accounts	473.47		
Accrued interest.	3,600.00		
Accrued property tax	1,327.22		
Accrued real estate tax	1,519.00		
Notes—current portion	95,322.48		
Other current liabilities	—		
Total current liabilities		$143,406.80	
Long-term liabilities:			
Note payable—bank	120,000.00		
Mortgage Payable.	43,267.30		
Less: Current portion	95,322.48		
Long-term—net liabilities		67,944.82	
Total liabilities.			$211,351.62
Stockholders' equity:			
Capital stock issued	18,600.00		
Retained earnings.	30,598.89		
Clearing account	—		
Total stockholders' equity		49,198.89	
			49,198.89
Total liabilities and stockholders' equity . . .			$260,550.51

Projected Sales For Next Year

July 19X2	$11,000
August	15,000
September	18,000
October	28,000
November	70,000
December 19X3.	90,000
January 19X3	53,000
February.	45,000
March	30,000
April	20,000
May	18,000
June 19X3	15,000

13

Financial management in the small business—Part 1

Managing any business from the financial point of view involves two basic objectives. The first is to insure that an adequate flow of cash is available to pay bills as they come due. The second objective is to make the business as profitable as possible. It is important that the small business manager recognize the dynamic aspects of accomplishing the objectives of liquidity and profitability. In the going concern the objectives are really never reached: they simply present a day-to-day problem.

FINANCIAL OBJECTIVES

The liquidity objective

Understanding cash flow within a business is vital to an understanding of the liquidity objective. The concept of cash flow involves the timing of cash receipts and cash disbursements. In the typical small business, sales are seasonal to some degree; thus at times cash inflows exceed outflows, but at other times cash outflows exceed inflows. As a result cash on hand will sometimes be excessive and sometimes inadequate. The timing problem in cash flow management can be visualized by imagining a situation in which cash inflows are always precisely equal to cash outflows. That is, every time an outflow of cash is called for, an inflow of cash is available. Under such conditions the need for cash on hand would be zero. Unfortunately, few if any businesses enjoy such a position. A typical cash flow cycle is illustrated in Figure 13–1.

Cash inflows. Cash is the common denominator of all transactions, and throughout the cash flow cycle attention remains focused on the cash account, or the cash reservoir. Cash flows into this reservoir intermittently from three sources: owners (in the form of equity financing), creditors (debt), and customers (income from sales). Cash may also flow into the cash reservoir, when needed, from the liquidation of short-term securities. These near-cash investments represent the profitable, temporary employment of cash that will be needed at some future date. (Of course, when the amount of cash on hand is excessive, the flow may be from the cash reservoir into near-cash investments.) The most regular flow in the cash flow cycle involves working capital. Working capital is defined for purposes of this discussion as total short-term assets. Thus, as shown in Figure 13–1, there is a continual flow of cash from the cash reservoir into inventories, from inventories

Figure 13–1
The flow of cash in the business firm

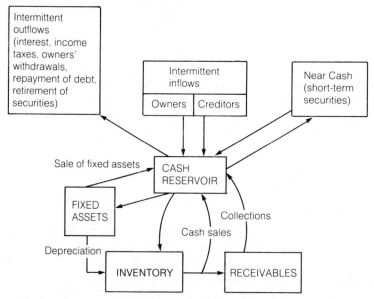

Note: Such expenses as supplies, wages, and selling and administrative expenses are paid in the general circulation of cash.

into receivables, and from receivables back into cash. To the extent that *cash* sales are generated, cash flows directly from the inventory reservoir into the cash reservoir.

Cash outflows. Two basic outflows occur. One is the outflow of cash in return for assets. The second involves cash payments made intermittently to parties outside the business for such things as principal and interest on debt, income taxes, and owner's withdrawals. In summary, then, Figure 13–1 depicts the flow of cash in the firm and reflects the nature of the liquidity objective; that is, to synchronize as nearly as possible cash inflows and outflows.

The profit objective

The liquidity objective is linked to the profit objective in that profitability is maximized only if every dollar is put to its most efficient use. In terms of the cash flow cycle, the profit objective involves the concepts of margin and turnover. In other words, the return per dollar of operating assets each time it goes through the cycle, coupled with the number of times it completes the cycle in some period of time, constitutes what is termed *earning power*. To clarify the profit objective, the factors that influence earning power are illustrated in Figure 13–2.

In more precise terms, the earning power of the business depends on

Figure 13–2
The relationships that determine the earning power of the firm

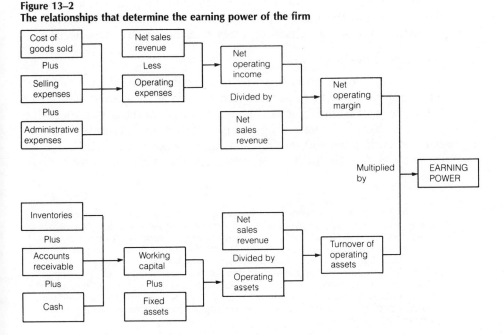

the operating margin multiplied by the turnover of operating assets. The margin equals net operating income divided by sales, with operating income defined as net sales revenue minus operating expenses. The turnover of operating assets is determined by dividing operating assets into sales, with operating assets defined as all those assets that are necessary in the operation of the business (i.e., working capital as well as fixed assets).[1]

The close relationship between the liquidity, or cash-flow, objective and the profit objective is now apparent. For example (as Figure 13–2 will show), if the cash balance is higher than necessary, operating assets are higher than they need be, turnover is less than possible and earning power is reduced. Obsolete inventory and accounts receivable that are uncollectible produce the same result. In terms of margin, if trade discounts are not taken, operating expenses are increased, and operating income, margin, and earning power are reduced.

It should be evident that the objective of the small business owner is to find that combination of margin and turnover that maximizes the earning power of the firm. This is not an easy task, for margin and turnover tend to move inversely. For example, an increase in the margin can be accomplished by increasing the selling price. But as price (margin) increases, sales (and turnover) may decline. And if the decline in turnover is more than proportional to the increase in margin, earning power declines. On the other hand, the small business owner may think he/she can increase turnover by reducing the selling price. However, if the decrease in the margin resulting from the price cut is more than proportional to the increase in turnover, earning power will decline.

Summary of the objectives

The objectives of good financial management should now be clear. First, cash flow must be adequate to meet bills as they come due. There is for every situation some best amount of cash necessary to meet this objective, based on the timing of cash inflows and outflows for some selected period. Second, the relationship between margin and turnover must be such that the earning power of the business is as high as possible.

---

[1]A simple example will help clarify the earning power calculation. Assume net sales income of $600, operating assets of $200, and net operating income of $60. In such a case, the net operating margin is $60/$600, or 10 percent, and the turnover of operating assets is $600/$200, or 3. Therefore, the earning power of the firm is 3 times 10 percent, or 30 percent. Remember that the net sales represent gross sales minus returns and allowances; net operating income equals gross sales minus operating expenses; and operating assets include the total investment in working capital and fixed assets. Another way to define operating assets is simply to include the value of all assets necessary in conducting the business operation. This would include everything from display cases and inventory to a typewriter and delivery truck.

Given the objectives, the functions of the manager from a financial point of view become evident. The responsibilities involve planning the needs for funds consistent with the objectives; acquiring the needed funds at minimum cost consistent with the objectives; and managing the use of the acquired funds consistent with the objectives.

FINANCIAL PLANNING AND RATIO ANALYSIS

The entrepreneur invests time, effort, and capital in the business venture, needs to have an adequate cash flow, and seeks an adequate profit in return. With these objectives, does the firm measure up to expectations? Some means for determining the operating efficiency of the firm must be devised.

One of the most helpful approaches to this problem is the examination of certain ratios and relationships evident in the financial statements of the firm—the balance sheet and the income statement. The quality of the firm's management can be revealed through an effective analysis of these ratios and interpretation of its financial statements.

Ratio analysis not only is useful to the owner as a tool in appraising the current position and past performance of the firm but is frequently employed by outsiders who wish to appraise the firm's financial position. For example, the banker wants to make a careful analysis of the prospective borrower's position before lending money. Trade creditors also will be interested in the financial position of the business in making a credit decision. Thus, whether or not the entrepreneur considers ratio analysis valuable as a tool for internal use, he/she often is asked to provide the information that ratio analysis affords to others.

Limitations of ratio analysis

The basic problem in using ratio analysis as an aid in performing the planning function, and in providing information for others, is understanding that ratios are of little value in themselves. Ratio analysis may suggest a problem, but ratios cannot explain the causes or seriousness of the situation. Thus, ratio analysis provides guides, not precise measurements, with which the manager can analyze the business operations.

The objective here is to identify a few ratios and relationships that are most commonly used to measure small business performance. It is suggested that these ratios be calculated and examined either monthly or quarterly and that emphasis be put on significant changes over time.

Standards for comparison

The small business manager may compare ratios within the firm on a historical basis and outside the firm with certain selected industrial standards. If the firm has operated for some time, historical standards can be easily established. In setting up these internal guides the manager must decide what level of performance is reasonably attainable in the particular situation. If there is a desire to supplement the historical guidelines with industrial indicators, the latter can be obtained from such sources as the Small Business Administration, Robert Morris Associates, Dun & Bradstreet, and the Department of Commerce.

Suggested framework for ratio analysis

There are two basic types of financial ratios: *operating ratios* and *structural ratios*. Operating ratios express relationships among various items in the income statement. The dollar figures in the income statement are converted to percentages that compare individual statement items to total net sales for the period. Net sales equal 100 percent and the other percentages are obtained by dividing each item's dollar amount by the net sales figure. These ratios reveal that part of each sales dollar is gross profit after inventory is paid for; they also show how the various expenses reduce this profit. Thus, operating ratios provide a closer examination of the expenses incurred in producing income and can be used as tools to decrease costs, improve efficiency, and increase profitability.

The second approach to ratio analysis involves the use of structural ratios. Structural ratios are those that show the relationships between various balance sheet items and those that compare an item on the balance sheet with one on the income statement.

Like operating ratios, structural ratios (expressed as percentages or ratios) provide the basis for comparisons of different periods within the firm's history or of the firm's experience with that of other businesses in the same industry.

Commonly used ratios

Money used for working capital in a business must be both adequate in amount and liquid in nature if the objectives of liquidity and profitability are to be accomplished. Analysis of the firm's cash flow reflects the overall efficiency of management, and the use of various ratios in the firm will point up such things as impending problems in cash requirements, the need to arrange additional financing before cash is exhausted, and the danger of overbuying and overexpansion. The following ratios are suggested to analyze the cash position of the firm.

Current ratio. The current ratio relates current assets to current liabilities and is intended to give some indication of the firm's ability to pay bills as they come due. Unfortunately, the current ratio alone can be very misleading as an indication of bill-paying ability. The reason is that inventories are included as a current asset, and certain portions of inventory may not be very liquid. In fact, an inventory problem resulting from overbuying or retention of obsolete items would not be indicated by the current ratio.

Many financial management textbooks state that a current ratio of 2:1, or more, is considered good. Reliance on rules of thumb, however, can be dangerous, and a current ratio of 2:1 is a good example. A cash-poor firm unable to pay its bills on time or unable to take advantage of trade discounts can have a current ratio of 2:1 or better. In fact, firms have been known to go bankrupt with a current ratio of 2:1.

Obviously, if the current ratio is low, the firm may encounter difficulty in paying bills. On the other hand, a current ratio that is too high reduces profitability. The difficulty arises out of the *timing* of cash flows, as discussed earlier. A high current ratio may represent excessive cash balances, excessive inventories, or some questionable accounts receivable. Thus, all one can conclude is that a current ratio that appears to be too high or too low demands further analysis.

Quick ratio. A second ratio that is helpful in evaluating past performance and the present position is the quick ratio. The quick ratio

relates current assets to current liabilities just as the current ratio, but on the asset side inventories are *omitted*. Thus the quick ratio gives a truer indication of the firm's ability to *pay* bills.

Cash is the most liquid asset. Accounts receivable represent sales that have been made, but until these accounts are collected they represent dollars that are one step removed from cash. Inventories, on the other hand, are stocked in anticipation of future sales that may or may not materialize. Thus, in terms of liquidity inventories are two steps removed from cash.

It follows that a more valid test of the ability of a firm to produce cash flow to meet current liabilities is the test that excludes inventories. The problem of obsolete and slow-moving inventory will not be seen in the current ratio, but it will certainly be evident in the quick ratio.

Average collection period. One of the most important indicators of current conditions in a business that sells on credit is the average collection period. The average collection period indicates how liquid the receivables are by indicating the average number of days each dollar of credit sales is outstanding. The calculation involves dividing the annual credit sales figure by 360 to determine the credit sales per day. Then the daily credit sales figure is divided into accounts receivable. The result is the average collection period expressed in days.

The average collection period proves most useful when watched over time. An average collection period that is increasing may indicate poor collection policies or an increase in slow-paying accounts. On the other hand, an average collection period that is too short may indicate that credit policies are too strict, and that potentially profitable customers are being turned away.

Inventory turnover. This ratio is the cost of goods sold divided by average inventory at cost. It tells the manager how rapidly dollars are flowing through inventory, and how current the inventory is.[2]

An inventory turnover that appears too low may indicate overbuying or a hard core of obsolete or slow-moving merchandise. An inventory turnover that is too high may indicate incomplete stocks and a frequent sacrifice of sales. Many of the financial problems of small business can be traced to poor inventory management. The inventory turnover ratio will be indicative of such problems.

Net sales to working capital. Known also as turnover of working capital, this ratio measures how actively the firm's cash is being put to

---

[2]Inventory turnover may also be calculated by dividing sales by average inventory at market price. Regardless of the formula used, however, it must be recognized that cost of goods sold cannot be related to the market value of inventory, nor can sales be compared with inventory at cost. The reason is that the markup on the cost of the goods to the selling price overstates the value of inventory.

work in terms of sales. Net working capital is defined as current assets minus current liabilities.

If the ratio of net sales to working capital is low, the manager should either reduce working capital or increase sales. On the other hand, a business with a high turnover of working capital is attempting to support too large a volume of business with its present level of working capital investment. Such a business may appear very profitable, but sales supported by a thin working capital position establish a balance of cash inflows and outflows so delicate that it may be easily upset by such things as a sudden loss of sales or a deterioration in the turnover of accounts receivable. The obvious solution in such a case is additional working capital, or a reduction in sales through price increases or tighter credit terms.

Other ratios worth considering

Another set of ratios useful to the small business manager consists of net worth ratios. Recall that net worth is the excess of total assets over total liabilities; it represents the owner's equity in the business.

Net worth ratios are valuable in comparing equity interests to credit interests, in evaluating profitability, and in analyzing investment in fixed assets. It is important that net worth in these ratios be defined as tangible net worth. Intangible assets such as goodwill, patents, and copyrights should be ignored.

Debt-to-net-worth ratio. One of the most important of the net worth ratios is the debt-to-net-worth relationship. It relates total debt to tangible net worth, which compares the dollars that creditors have contributed in financing the business to the dollars the owners have contributed. Creditors use this relationship to get some indication of the risk involved in lending to the firm. For instance, if the debt-to-net-worth ratio is 1:1, the assets can decline 50 percent in value before threatening the solvency of the business. On the other hand, if there are two dollars of debt per dollar of equity, a decline of only 33 percent in the value of assets would pose this threat.

Fixed assets to net worth. Some small business owners tend to over-invest in fixed assets. Particularly after a period of very profitable operations the urge is to modernize and expand, often in excess. The ratio of fixed assets to net worth monitors a firm's position in this respect.

Net profit to net worth. Finally, it is important to analyze profit in terms of net worth Net profit expressed as a percentage of net worth indicates the return on the owner's equity in the business. The value of such a figure is apparent, but it should not be confused with the earning power of the firm. Earning power, as previously explained, denotes the return on the operating assets of the business. Earning power indicates the efficiency with which the total assets of the firm are being utilized. The net-profit-to-net-worth relationship indicates the efficiency with which the owner's funds are being utilized. Whether or not a particular return to net worth is acceptable depends on the owner's appraisal of risk and a personal judgment as to what is adequate.

Summary and conclusions on using financial and ratio analysis

The foregoing discussion cites the more important financial ratios and relationships that should be periodically calculated, recorded, and analyzed to provide insight into the financial position of the firm. In using ratios, one must keep in mind the significance and limitations of each. Furthermore, in any type of analysis such as this, the manager must keep in mind the overall position of the firm.

The first step is to take particular care in selecting the standards for comparison, both historical and industrial. Then any variation from the norms demands explanation. Furthermore, marked differences that occur over time also require explanation.

As for historical standards, it is suggested that the ratios be recorded on a monthly basis over a two-year moving period. An analysis of such records should then reveal distinct patterns that will be helpful in establishing guidelines for performance.

Rules of thumb and standards quoted by outside sources are available, but such guidelines must be used with caution. Each business venture is unique, and despite many apparent similarities between two firms, subtle differences may limit the value of a comparison on a financial or operating basis.

The small business manager must be concerned with the most efficient use of funds, and the simple tools of ratio analysis provide a means for evaluating management policies. Despite its shortcomings, ratio analysis aids the financial manager in planning the needs for funds. Furthermore, ratio analysis can indicate when fund management policies should be altered to afford a more efficient and profitable utilization of the firm's financial resources.

CASH BUDGETING

Significance and preparation of a cash budget

Another principal financial management tool in the management of a small business is the cash budget. A cash budget represents the manager's plans for the future expressed in dollars and cents. The management of day-to-day financial operations involves anticipating the timing of cash receipts and disbursements. The cash budget is a prediction of future cash flows based on an expected level of sales volume; it will indicate when borrowing will be necessary and in what amount, and it will show when cash will become available to repay the loan.

A good cash budget is important because it charts the course of the business in maintaining its liquidity. Furthermore, the comparison of actual experience with the budget (once the operating results are in) provides a basis for improving future performance. The cash budget is concerned primarily with short-term needs of the business.

The first problem in constructing a cash budget is selecting the time period. The budget period must be long enough to permit effective planning. If it is too short, significant cash flows just beyond the period may be overlooked. On the other hand, if the period is too long, the chance of errors in forecasting is increased.

The second step in preparing the cash budget is to estimate sales. In predicting sales, the manager must consider internal factors as well as external factors. From an internal point of view, historical information on past sales in particular product lines is usually helpful. From an

external point of view, a number of factors should be considered. For instance, what would be the effect on sales of a change in price? What would be the effect on sales of additional advertising or changes in quality and styling? What would be the effect on sales of adding a product line? What would be the competitors' reaction to any action the manager takes to affect sales?

Having considered both the internal and the external factors, the sales forecaster requires a great deal of experience and good judgment to produce a reliable result. Remember, the cash budget is only as good as the sales forecast.

An example of the cash budgeting process

The first step in preparing a cash budget is to prepare a worksheet that will give total receipt figures for the firm month by month. Figure 13–3 shows the work sheet for the IKC Gift Shop. The receipt figures are based on the relationship between credit sales and cash sales and on the collection pattern of credit sales.

Figure 13–3
IKC Gift Shop worksheet

	June	July	August	September	October	November	December	January
Sales (forecasted)	19,000	17,000	21,000	33,000	29,000	45,000	55,000	25,000
Credit sales (60% of monthly sales)	11,400	10,200	12,600	19,800	17,400	27,000	33,000	15,000
Collections (75% of previous month's credit sales)		8,550	7,650	9,450	14,850	13,050	20,250	24,750
(25% of credit sales two months hence)			2,850	2,550	3,150	4,950	4,350	6,750
Cash sales (40% of monthly sales)			8,400	13,200	11,600	18,000	22,000	10,000
Total Monthly cash receipts			18,900	25,200	29,600	36,000	46,600	41,500

Given the total receipt figures, the cash budget can now be prepared. The cash budget is divided into two types of transactions. The operating transactions record the effect of the monthly cash inflows and outflows on the cash position. The financial transactions follow the operating transactions and record the adjustments necessary in the monthly cash balance to provide the funds to carry the firm through the budgeted period. The operating transactions for the IKC Gift Shop are shown in Figure 13–4.

As apparent in Figure 13–4, during the months of August, October, and November cash inflows are less than outflows, so that IKC cannot maintain its minimum cash balance requirement without making temporary additions to the cash balance. Thus, the questions are: How much cash will be needed? When is it needed? When can IKC expect to pay it back? These questions are based on the assumption that for a seasonal increase in inventory IKC will use debt of some sort, either trade credit from suppliers or a self-liquidating inventory loan from a commercial bank.

The answers to the questions of how much, when, and how long are

Figure 13–4
IKC Gift Shop operating transactions

Operating transactions	August	September	October	November	December	January
Cash receipts (from worksheet)	18,900	25,200	29,600	36,000	46,600	41,500
Cash payments: Purchases (70% of next month's sales)	23,100	20,300	31,500	38,500	17,500	16,100
Wages and salaries	2,000	2,200	2,200	2,400	2,400	2,000
Rent	600	600	600	600	600	600
Other expenses (2% of month's sales)	420	660	580	900	1,100	500
Total cash payments	26,120	23,760	34,880	42,400	21,600	19,200
Net monthly cash gain or (loss) (receipts minus payments)	(7,220)	1,440	(5,280)	(6,400)	25,000	22,300
Cash balance (end of month) (July 31, $11,200)	3,980	5,420	140	(6,260)	31,260	53,560

provided in the financial transactions section of the cash budget. The financial transactions for the IKC Gift Shop are recorded in Figure 13–5. Figure 13–5 provides all the information necessary to plan IKC's need for short-term funds. Assuming that the sales forecast is valid, IKC will have to borrow up to $12,000 over a five-month period, beginning in August. Furthermore, if the best source of such funds is a short-term bank note, the loan can easily be retired in late December and a handsome profit realized.

In summary, the cash budget is a useful technique for planning the needs for short-term, temporary funds. The usefulness of the cash budget in any particular situation, however, is dependent upon the reliability of the sales forecast.

BREAK-EVEN ANALYSIS

Scope and terminology

A third analytical technique the manager of the small business will find helpful concerns planning for profits and is termed *break-even analysis*. Break-even analysis examines the relationship between costs

Figure 13–5
IKC Gift Shop financial transactions

Financial transactions	August	September	October	November	December	January
Cash balance (beginning of month)	11,200	5,980	7,420	5,140	5,740	18,740
Net monthly cash gain or (loss) (from Figure 13–4)	(7,220)	1,440	(5,280)	(6,400)	25,000	22,300
Cash balance before financing	3,980	7,420	2,140	(1,260)	30,740	41,040
Borrowing required to meet minimum cash balance requirement (multiples of $1,000)	2,000	0	3,000	7,000	(12,000) Repayment	0
Cash balance EOM after financing	5,980	7,420	5,140	5,740	18,740	41,040
Cumulative borrowing	2,000	2,000	5,000	12,000	0	0

Figure 13–6

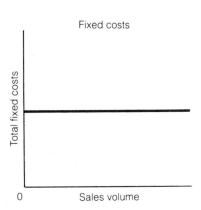

and revenues at various levels of sales. The purpose is to determine at what sales volume the firm begins to make a profit.

The first step in using break-even analysis involves classifying all the costs of operation as either variable or fixed. A variable cost is one that varies in direct proportion to sales; thus, the greater the volume of sales, the higher are total variable costs. A variable cost is graphically illustrated in Figure 13–6. The origin of the line is at zero sales because, by definition, if operations ceased variable costs would not exist. Variable costs that are common to most small businesses include hourly wages of employees and cost of goods sold.

A fixed cost is defined as a cost that does not vary with sales. Thus, a fixed cost exists regardless of sales volume. In graphic terms, it would appear as illustrated in Figure 13–6. Typical fixed costs in the small business include rent, mortgage payments, and lease payments.

Application

Once operating costs have been classified as fixed or variable, it is possible to analyze the reaction of revenue (and profits) to various sales volumes under existing pricing policies. The following illustration demonstrates the application of break-even analysis.

Cloverleaf Bottlers, Incorporated, produces and bottles soft drinks. The productive capacity is 500 cases a day. Fixed costs are $100 a day and variable costs are 60 cents per case. The soft drinks sell for $1 a case. Given this information, the level of output (i.e., the volume of sales) necessary for Cloverleaf to produce a profit can be determined. Figure 13–7 graphically gives the solution.

The fixed costs of Cloverleaf are represented in Figure 13–7 as a straight line at the level of $100, consistent with the definition of a fixed cost. The variable-cost line represents variable costs of zero at zero

Figure 13–7
Cloverleaf Bottlers, Incorporated break-even analysis

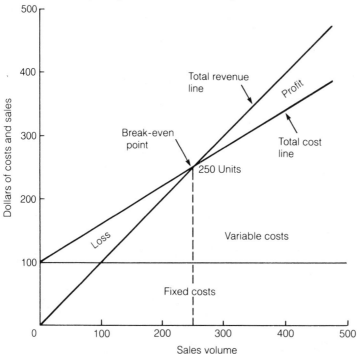

volume, and total variable costs of $300 at capacity. Superimposed on
the fixed-cost line, the variable-cost line also represents the total-cost
line, total cost being $100 at zero output (all fixed costs), and $400 at
capacity ($100 fixed plus $300 variable). The revenue or price line in
Figure 13–7 has its origin at zero and extends upward to $500 at capacity,
which represents the price of $1 per case.

The break-even level of sales volume is represented by the intersection
of the total revenue line with the total cost line and is defined as that
sales volume where total costs just equal total revenue. Notice that in
Figure 13–7, the break-even level of sales volume for Cloverleaf is 250
cases.[3] This can be checked by the following simple computation.

---

[3]The algebraic solution for the break-even point is obviously much more reliable than
reference to a graphic presentation. The formula $f + vx = sx$, where f equals fixed cost, v
equals variable costs per unit, and s equals selling price per unit, gives the correct result.
For example, in the case above:

$$\$100 + 0.60x = \$1.00x$$
$$0.40x = \$100$$
$$x = \$250$$

$$\text{Total income: } 250 \times \$1 \qquad = \$250$$
$$\text{Total expenses: Fixed costs} = \$100$$
$$\text{Variable costs} = 250 \times 0.60 = \$150$$
$$\$100 + \$150 = \$250$$

This means that any day on which Cloverleaf can sell more than 250 cases, the operation is profitable. On the other hand, a daily sales volume of less than 250 cases fails to cover total costs.

The value of break-even analysis is now apparent. The difference between the total cost line and the revenue line indicates profit or loss at any level of sales. The higher the break-even point, the less chance the business has of operating at a profit over the long run. The lower the break-even point, the more likely is profit over the long run.

Using break-even analysis in planning

To be used, the break-even level of sales volume must be related to the firm's normal level of operations and to what are considered normal variations in sales. For instance, in terms of the Cloverleaf example and a break-even level of sales volume of 250 cases, the important questions are: What is considered to be the normal or average daily sales volume, and what is the expected range of sales volume over time? In a seasonal business such as soft drinks, it may be that during certain times of the year a level of operation below the break-even point is expected. If, however, operations were to continue for an extended period of time below the break-even point, because of a loss of sales or an increase in costs, steps would have to be taken to shift the break-even level of sales volume or to increase the average daily sales if the business is to be continued on a profitable basis. In other words, with a break-even level of 250 cases, the firm is faced with the question: What is the probability that the firm will ever have to operate below the 250-case level? Furthermore, if operations for a time are below the 250-case level, how long is such a condition expected to continue, and what are the reasons for such a condition? Finally, if the break-even level appears to be too high relative to what is considered to be a normal level of sales volume, what steps can be taken to shift the break-even point? The answers to these questions are important, for the relationship between the break-even level of operation and the normal level of sales volume can have an important influence on the ability of the firm to borrow funds.

Limitations of break-even analysis

There are three principal limitations of break-even analysis. First, the analysis represents a short-run static relationship of costs to sales volume. The data used are historical, and any variation in conditions that affect costs will quickly change the relationship. Second, the relationships indicated in the simple graphic presentation used here are represented as straight-line functions, which probably will not hold true for all levels of operation. For instance, variable costs may increase as sales volume increases to high levels and approaches capacity. Finally, the graphic analysis assumes that regardless of sales volume, the price is constant. This may not hold true if price decreases are necessary to increase volume, or if a firm reduces price to maintain sales volume when business is slow.

Despite its shortcomings, break-even analysis provides the small business manager with insight into the relationship between costs, revenue, and sales—insight into the ability of the business to produce a profit.

SUMMARY

The role of the small business owner as financial manager involves planning the needs for funds, acquiring the needed funds, and managing the acquired funds. The planning of the needs for funds was the subject of this chapter.

An important aspect of the planning function is to examine the present financial position and the past performance of the firm. This chapter presented a framework of financial ratios that help satisfy this need and give insight into the potential of the firm. The ratios also expose problems of a financial nature that demand attention.

An indispensable part of the financial planning function is the cash budget. The cash budget represents a projection of cash inflows and cash outflows. It indicates those periods when borrowing may be necessary, what amount of borrowing may be necessary, and when funds will become available to retire the debt. Reliability of the cash budget depends on the accuracy of the sales forecast.

Finally, break-even analysis provides a valuable tool in planning for profits. It indicates the relationship between costs, revenues, and sales volume and thus the relationship between sales volume and profits. Furthermore, given some level of sales, break-even analysis shows the effect on profits of increasing or decreasing sales volume.

QUESTIONS

1. What is meant by the liquidity objective of a small business? Explain in detail.

2. What is meant by the profit objective of a small business? Explain in detail.

3. Why should you use a certain amount of reserve in making ratio analysis? Explain in detail.

4. List four ratios commonly used in analyzing the financial structure of a small business.

5. Explain the importance of the current ratio.

6. Differentiate between the current ratio and the quick ratio.

7. What is meant by the debt to net worth ratio? Explain in detail.

8. What does one need to know to make a cash budget for a small business? Explain.

9. How does break-even analysis tie in with the planning function in a small business?

10. What limitations affect the use of break-even analysis in attempting to control the finances of a small business? Explain.

PROBLEMS

1. You are the financial manager of ABC Company. The earning power of your company has shown a considerable change in the last 10 years and you want to find out why. So you proceed to make an analysis of the following:

Statement of Earnings
($000s)

	1971	1981
Sales	$100	$200
Cost of goods sold	(?)	(?)
Gross profit	(?)	(?)
Operating expenses	(?)	(?)
Net operating income*	$ 20	$ 80
Interest expenses	(?)	(?)
Taxable income	(?)	(?)
Taxes 50 percent	(?)	(?)
Income after taxes	(?)	(?)
Preferred dividends	(?)	(?)
Net income available to residual owners	(?)	(?)

*The company has no nonoperating assets or nonoperating income.

Balance Sheet Items

($000s)	1971	1981
Net operating assets*	$200	$300
All noninterest bearing liabilities	130	50
5 percent bonds....................	40	160
4 percent preferred stock..............	0	50
Common stock capital account..........	10	10
Capital in excess of par value	10	10
Earned surplus....................	5	15
Reserve for corporate expansion	5	5

* The company has no nonoperating assets or nonoperating income.

You computed the following ratios for the years 1971 and 1981:

	1971	1981
Operating ratio.	80%	60%
Gross margin	40%	55%

Based on the information given above, write on a piece of notepaper:

a. The unsupplied figures for the statement of earnings for the years 1971 and 1981.

b. Answers to the following questions:

The operating margin in 1971.	__?__	%
The operating margin in 1981.	__?__	%
Assets turnover in 1971.	__?__	times
Assets turnover in 1981.	__?__	times
Earning power in 1971	__?__	%
Earning power in 1981	__?__	%

c. Words to complete the following sentences:

(i). The change in the operating margin from 1971 to 1981 could be accounted for by _____.

(ii). The change in turnover from 1971 to 1981 could be accounted for by _____.

(iii). The change in earning power from 1971 to 1981 could be accounted for by _____.

2. Using the information shown below in the balance sheet, calculate the following:

Turnover of operating assets.

Average collection period (based on 360 days).

Gross profit percentage.

Inventory turnover (based on year-end inventory).

Debt to net worth.

Acid test ratio.

Balance Sheet

Assets		Liabilities and Capital	
Cash	$ .62,500	Notes and accounts payable.	$250,000
Accounts receivable	125,000	Common stock	200,000
Inventory	262,500	Retained earnings.	300,000
Plant and equipment.	300,000		
	$750,000		$750,000

3.   Following is certain information relative to the position and business of American Stores Company:

Current assets as of September 30:	
Cash on deposit	$12,000
Inventory	30,000
Accounts receivable	10,000

Current liabilities as of September 30:	
Inventory	30,000
Accounts payable	10,000

Recent and anticipated sales:	
September.	40,000
October	48,000
November.	60,000
December.	80,000
January.	36,000

Credit sales.   Sales are 75 percent for cash, and 25 percent on credit. Assume that credit accounts are all collected within 30 days from sale. The accounts receivable on September 30 represent the credit sales for September (25 percent of $40,000).

Mark up.   Gross profit averages 30 percent of sales.

Expenses.   Salaries and wages average 15 percent of sales, rent 5 percent, depreciation (a noncash expense) 1 percent, all other expenses 4 percent. Assume that these expenses are disbursed each month.

Net operating profit.   5 percent.

Purchases.   There is a basic inventory of $30,000. The policy is to purchase each month additional inventory in the amount necessary to provide for the following month's sales. Terms on purchases are 2 percent, 10 days; net 30 days. Assume payments are made in month of purchase, and all discounts are taken.

Fixtures.   In October $600 is spent for fixtures, and in November $400 is to be expended for this purpose.

On the basis is the facts given above, complete the following schedules on a separate piece of notepaper.

Schedule A—Estimated monthly dollar receipt

Item	September	October	November	December
Total sales	$40,000	$48,000	$60,000	$80,000
Credit sales	10,000	12,000	?	?

Receipts	October	November	December
Cash sales	$36.000	?	?
Collections on accounts receivable . .	10,000	?	?

Schedule B—Estimated monthly cash disbursements for
purchases

Item	October	November	December
Purchases.................	$42,000	?	?
Less 2 percent cash discount	840	?	?
Disbursements..............	$41,160	?	?

Schedule C—Estimated monthly cash disbursements for
operating expenses

Item	October	November	December
Salaries and wages.............	$ 7,200	?	?
Rent	2,400	?	?
Other expenses	1,920	?	?
Total.................	$11,520	?	?

Schedule D—Estimated total monthly disbursements

Item	October	November	December
Purchases.................	$41,160	?	?
Operating expenses	11,520	?	?
Fixtures	600	?	?
Total.................	$53,280	?	?

Schedule E—Estimated cash receipts and disbursements

Item	October	November	December
Receipts...................	$46,000	?	?
Disbursements..............	53,280	?	?
Net cash increase.............	?	?	?
Net cash decrease	$ 7,280	?	?

Include in Schedule F the amount (in round thousands of dollars) necessary to keep the Cash account above a minimum of $8,000 desired at the end of each month.

Schedule F—Financing required by American Stores Company

Item	October	November	December
Opening cash	$12,000	?	?
Net cash increase.............	?	?	?
Net cash decrease	7,280	?	?
Cash position before financing	$ 4,720	?	?
Financing required	4,000	?	?
Financing retired	?	?	?
Closing balance..............	8,720	?	?
	?	?	?

BIBLIOGRAPHY

Burstiner, Irving. *The Small Business Handbook.* Englewood Cliffs, N.J.: Prentice-Hall, 1978. Written in a nontechnical, easy-to-understand style. Designed as an informative guide to the small business manager wanting to know how to financially manage the smaller or rapidly growing business.

Hartley, W. C., and Yale Meltzer. *Cash Management: Planning, Forecasting, and Control.* Englewood Cliffs, N.J.: Prentice-Hall, 1979. This book explains carefully what cash flow is and how it behaves. It shows how operating managers and financial executives can most effectively measure, forecast, and control cash flow in the small business.

Hunt, Pearson; Charles M. Williams; and Gordon Donaldson. *Basic Business Finance.* Homewood, Ill.: Richard D. Irwin, 1974. A solid, basic finance book for anyone interested in the financial management of the small business.

Steinmetz, Lawrence L. *High Yield Management in the Small Manufacturing Firm.* Boulder, Colo.: Horizon Publications, 1978. An easy-to-read presentation of the financial problems often found in managing smaller, rapidly growing manufacturing firms.

Case study

Mike's Alpine Haus

Christmas Eve

It was raining as Mike Jones drove down the nearly deserted street. There was absolutely no snow, but it was December 24th, Christmas Eve. Mike had just left his downtown shop—Mike's Alpine Haus—at midafternoon and was on his way to a Christmas cocktail party being thrown by a local manufacturer of ski wear. As he pulled into the hotel parking lot he noticed Ozzie Wolfe, the manager of a department store ski shop, just getting out of his car.

Mike called to Ozzie to wait for him under the hotel marquee.

"Still no goddamn snow!" said Mike. "It's been seven or eight weeks since it snowed and that really wasn't much good."

"Mike, it snowed a little at the areas and that's what counts," said Ozzie. "The two little areas around here aren't much good, but they're better than nothing."

"Ozzie, it's snow here—in the city—that gets people in the mood. If there isn't snow on people's cars and yards and houses, they don't think about winter sports. It's tough to get people to think about having fun in the snow if winter is a drag, and believe me it's been a real drag for too long!"

Ozzie Wolfe smiled. He had once worked for Mike and after getting out of the army had gone to work for Greenfield and Watson, the city's largest department store. When G&W decided to upgrade its skiing department eight years ago, Ozzie Wolfe was made assistant manager. He became manager five years ago and since then winter sports sales had jumped from $825,000 annually to well over $3.5 million. Ozzie liked Mike, and he felt a little sorry for him since he knew Mike's business was off. Ski reps were notoriously gossipy about what was happening and many said Mike's sales had dropped by 8 to 10 percent each of the last few years. But Ozzie had warned Mike that he couldn't go head to head with department stores and discounters and expect to capture the lion's share of the ski business as he had done in the late 50s and early 60s. Ozzie had said that there was a place for the specialist, but he couldn't be all things to all people as he once had been.

The cocktail party

"Hey baby, what's happening?" It was the booming voice of Don Costa, the rep for Mike's biggest selling line of skis. "You're looking good, Mike," he said, "no snow keeps you out on the golf course at least."

"You shouldn't even know golf exists," replied Mike.

"He sells most of his skis on the golf course," broke in Ozzie. "How are you, Don, it's good to see you again. How's Martha?"

Almost like a slap in the face the realization struck Mike that Don, his most important supplier, and Ozzie Wolfe, his most aggressive competitor, had become good friends. How and why he didn't know, but he was afraid to guess.

A sunny day in January

It had been almost a month since the Christmas Eve cocktail party as Mike sat reviewing his October-November-December figures. He compared them with last year's numbers and wondered whether he would be able to hit last fiscal year's total of $934,300. He remembered how he had had really to cut prices on good skis and boots during February and March of last year and he dreaded the thought of practically giving away in the next 30 days some of the great new skis and boots he had bought for this year.

Mike looked at some other figures he had dug out of the file (see Exhibits 1 to 4).

Mike felt that if the year to date was any indication, he might sell only 800 pairs. He thought he had a total of 1,400 pairs in stock (not counting the 250 pairs of old skis he kept in the basement), and he hoped he could find a

Exhibit 1
Fiscal year total ski sales

Three years ago.	1,575 pairs
Two years ago.	1,422 pairs
Last year	1,200 pairs

Exhibit 2
Review sheet—Not official (October/November/December, both stores)

	This year	Last year	Two years ago
Total sales.	$298,245	$327,005	$350,990
Skis in dollars	47,150	64,416	76,560
in units	410	528	638
Boots in dollars	34,000	58,212	63,546
in units	400	588	714
Bindings.	13,108	16,350	17,940
Other ski hard goods. . . .	8,545	12,962	18,350
Ski clothing:			
Men . . . . ,	38,312	38,199	36,450
Women	85,540	80,030	83,392
Children	9,750	10,310	9,980
Tennis	8,666	4,319	6,130
Backpacking	19,383	12,017	6,519
Bicycles	10,693	3,766	2,525
All other merchandise . . .	10,440	8,650	10,655
Rental and repair	12,658	17,774	18,943

Exhibit 3

MIKE'S ALPINE HAUS
Income Statement for Both Stores Combined
August 1–July 31, Last Fiscal Year

Net sales		$934,300
Cost of goods sold:		
Beginning inventory at cost	$245,200	
Purchases	642,575	
	887,775	
Ending inventory	287,137	
	600,638	
Cash discounts taken	4,000	
Cost of merchandise sold		596,638
Gross margin		337,662
Operating expenses:		
Rent, insurance, and other administrative	103,500	
Salaries and commissions	143,858	
Advertising, promotions, and travel	33,703	
Taxes and interest	27,501	
Total operating expenses		308,562
Net profit		$ 29,100

Notes: All inventory valued at original cost.
Depreciation included in Administrative expenses is $14,700.
Rental income was $22,605.

way to work the inventory down to a comfortable level. Pursuing last years' figures further, Mike found some interesting cost–revenue relationships (see Exhibit 5).

Mike quickly tabulated about how many skis he had purchased for the current year and came up with 1,200 to 1,250 pairs. He wondered whether his sale of clothing was faring as badly as skis seemed to be. He found that he carried over about $47,000 of clothing (at retail) and that he had spent between $120,000 and $130,000 for new ski clothing for this year (at cost). He had hoped to sell around $230,000 worth of clothing during the year, but he felt sales had dropped off in January more than they should have. It was probably the lack of snow, he felt, but then some sales people had reported being out of some sizes.

It was late in the afternoon and he wanted to get away to ski for the weekend since he had a meeting with his banker on Monday. He looked at the payables journal on his way out of the office—it totaled $237,107.

QUESTIONS

1. How do you assess the financial conditions faced by Mike's Alpine Haus? What do you feel will happen to the business?

Exhibit 4

MIKE'S ALPINE HAUS
Balance Sheet
End of Last Fiscal Year

Assets

Cash	$ 4,400
Accounts receivable (employees and	
selected friends)	8,750
Inventory (at cost)	287,137
Other (prepaids, etc.).	6,040
Total current assets	306,327
Rental equipment	30,005
Trucks and shop equipment.	26,310
Fixtures	34,950
Buildings and improvements	210,300
Subtotal.	301,565
Less: Accumulated depreciation.	141,315
Net depreciable assets	160,250
Land (at cost)	88,925
Total assets	$555,502

Liabilities and Net Worth

Current liabilities:	
Accounts payable	$ 51,407
Note payable (bank)	67,000
Note payable (board member)	26,000
Total current liabilities.	144,407
Long-term loan from foundes estate	86,000
Net worth:	
Common stock	150,000
Surplus and retained earnings.	175,095
Total liabilities and net worth	$555,502

Exhibit 5
Last year ski inventory and purchases (pairs)

Cost	Inventory, July 31	Purchases for last year
less than $50.	233	150 (to use as price promotion)
50–75	106	260
75–90	14	300
90–110	126	350
Over 110	209	475
Totals.	699 (plus about 260 old skis)	1535

Notes: 1. 125 pairs returned to manufacturers.
2. Last year's sales: 718 pairs sold between August 1 and January 31. 502 pairs sold on sale after the end of January. Total sales of skis from January through April = $37,650.
3. Beginning inventory this year, 835 pairs.

2. What has been the most adverse effect of stringent competiton on the performance of Mike's Alpine Haus and the business's financial condition?

3. What are the key elements of Mike's cash flow problems? What should his forecasted cash budget look like?

4. Given the market and competitive conditions, what should now be the long-range financial goals and objectives of Mike's Alpine Haus?

14

Financial management in the small business—Part 2

The preceding chapter discussed planning the needs for funds. The purpose of this chapter is to consider the strategies used in acquiring funds and their proper use in operating the enterprise.

SHORT-TERM VERSUS LONG-TERM FUNDS

Earlier chapters have outlined the various sources of funds, planning for the needs for such funds, and the accounting and control procedures that monitor their use. It is now appropriate to examine the factors that influence the decision makers in selecting the sources of the needed funds.

The first important distinction to be made is that between *short-term* and *long-term* funds. In addition, distinctions are also made between *current assets,* such as inventory for sale, and *fixed assets,* such as buildings, machinery, and equipment.

In general, the short-term funds will come from different sources, be applied differently, and be managed according to a set of criteria different from those applying to long-term funds. Long-term financing of fixed assets will require that funds remain committed over a long period and not be subject to fluctuations that characterize the short-term funds. Quite realistically, the short-term funds are likely to be borrowed and the longer-term funds to be obtained primarily from equity sources, although a number of factors will determine the particular mix to be used.

Matching the source of funds with the use

The reason for financing a fixed or permanent asset with permanent funds is related to the cash flows obtained from the asset. Through the sale of a product or the performance of a service, the small business manager obtains a cash inflow that covers the direct costs of operation, the recovery of a portion of the investment in the fixed assets, and profit. However, because fixed assets are normally used for a number of years, the recovery of such an investment is a slow process. In such a case it would be unwise to promise to repay a creditor who has financed a fixed asset at a rate faster than cash inflows can be generated from the use of the asset.

Looking at the problem from the short-term side, the higher the proportion of temporary current assets employed, the greater the need for short-term debt. The argument against using long-term debt or equity to finance temporary current assets is related to the profit objective of the firm. That is, as inventories are sold and accounts receivable turn into cash, the excess cash should be used to reduce debt, for it would be unprofitable to pay interest on a loan when the borrowed funds were not being utilized. Furthermore, if temporary current asset needs were financed with equity funds, the use of this money in the off-season in cash or short-term securities would represent an unprofitable investment of owners' capital.

In summary, a principal objective of the manager in determining the appropriate source of funds is to finance temporary current asset needs with flexible short-term debt that will expand and contract with corresponding fluctuations in the assets. On the other hand, in financing fixed assets, long-term debt and equity are required because of the extended period involved in recovering the investment. However, matching the source of funds with the use of the funds is not the only factor that should be considered in solving the acquisition problem.

The importance of financial leverage in selecting a source of funds

One major decision regarding the source of funds is the possible use of financial leverage. Leverage properly used can increase the return on ownership capital, and every effort should be made to maximize the return on the ownership investment.

The approach to leverage is based on the fact that most enterprises will be financed by both equity investment and borrowed money (debt). If at any time, the use of debt can be employed to produce a profit in excess of the interest rate to carry the debt, then it is advantageous to utilize debt. Such an opportunity may, however, be accompanied by the risk that the income from the employment of borrowed money is not sufficient to cover the interest on the debt.

Proportions of debt and equity financing are not totally at the discretion of the borrower because some proportion of equity will always be necessary to secure certain remaining portions of debt financing.

For purposes of definition, financial leverage is being used any time a portion of the assets is financed with funds bearing a limited return. Let us now examine the ways in which financial leverage may be favorable, unfavorable, or neutral. The extent to which leverage is favorable or unfavorable depends on the level of income generated by the firm (see Example A and Example B).

Example A—no financial leverage

10 Ownership shares at $100 each.	$1,000.00
Income from the above amount before	
income taxes	60.00
Income tax rate of 48% = Tax liability	28.80
Earnings after tax	31.20
Earnings per share.	3.12

Example B—financial leverage

8 Ownership shares at $100 each	$ 800.00
Debt (interest at 5 percent)	200.00
Income from the above amount before	
income taxes	60.00
Interest on the debt	10.00
Earnings before taxes.	50.00
Income tax rate of 48 percent = tax liability.	24.00
Earnings after taxes	26.00
Earnings per share.	3.25

Realizing the importance of the income stream in determining whether financial leverage is favorable or unfavorable, it is apparent there is a break-even level of income at which (in terms of return on ownership shares) it is a matter of indifference what debt-to-equity ratio is used. Consider Example C.

Example C—financial leverage—mixed proportions

1.	Equity investment of debt and equity.	$ 800.00
	Debt (interest at 5 percent)	200.00
	Income minus debt payment	40.00
	Income tax at 48 percent	19.20

Example C—financial leverage—mixed proportions *(continued)*

Earnings after tax	20.80
Earnings per share (8 shares at $100).	2.60

or

2.

Equity investment (10 shares).	$1,000.00
(No debt investment)	—
Income before taxes	50.00
Income tax rate at 48 percent	24.00
Earnings after tax	26.00
Earnings per share.	2.60

or

3.

Equity investment	$ 600.00
Debt investment	400.00
Income.	50.00
Interest on debt	20.00
Income before taxes	30.00
Income tax rate at 48 percent	14.40
Earnings after tax	15.60
Earnings per share.	2.60

These examples show that it is a matter of indifference as to what the capital structure is in generating the ultimate return to the shareholder.

In conclusion, the decision to use financial leverage is largely dependent upon the expected level of income. In deciding on the use of leverage, the break-even level of income should be compared with the expected level of income. If it appears the chances are better than 50–50 that earnings before interest and taxes will exceed the break-even level, the manager might decide to use some financial leverage. However, the comparison does not tell how much financial leverage to use. The amount of financial leverage that should be used in any particular situation is directly related to the probability that earnings before interest and taxes will exceed the break-even level and the amount by which they are expected to exceed that level.

FACTORS IN A CHOICE OF FUNDS

Previous chapters have dealt with such things as the sources of help for the smaller business. In this regard, Chapter 2 is an introduction to the sources of funds with minimal detail as to actually acquiring funds. In Chapter 12 the authors are explaining the nature of funds as to the general sources and how they are employed in the business. Again, circumstances are reviewed in a general manner.

In the earlier parts of this chapter the nature of funds usage is examined from the standpoint of long-term versus short-term funds and the particular way in which each kind is employed in the business.

Thus, we know something about the individuals and firms who have funds and how the business operator should plan to use such long- or short-term funds.

Another step is the choice of funds based on the conditions of operation that the particular business must face. Thus, the owner/manager will attempt to secure funds that, overall, are most appropriate for his/her particular enterprise. The criteria to be used in selecting the source of funds for a business are concerned with (a) risk, (b) control, (c) flexibility, and (d) timing.

Risk is concerned with the matter of financial leverage that has previously been illustrated. If the debt funds can safely be used, then there is an advantage to their use. If not, there is risk because the owner must relinquish a prior claim on the income and the assets of the business in favor of the creditor or creditors.

Control is a matter of concern to an owner if there are other partners or stockholders. Once the decision is made not to organize the business as a sole proprietorship, then other persons will be involved in the business.

Flexibility means having as many alternative sources of funds open as possible. Such a position enhances the manager's bargaining power when dealing with a prospective supplier of funds. If the manager is already overextended in terms of debt a serious limitation is imposed on the availability of additional funds. Although debt funds may be generally available at attractive rates, it may be impossible to borrow. Prospective lenders are highly interested in the debt-equity relationship. Therefore, the small business manager must recognize the need for balance in the sources of funds, for it is this balance that provides flexibility.

Timing is closely related to flexibility, for an important consequence of flexibility is that it enables the manager to seize opportunities that minimize the cost of borrowing. Of course, in certain instances, funds will be needed and must be obtained even if they are relatively costly. But any time the manager is in the market for funds, the present costs of raising capital should be compared with expected future costs. It may be wise to delay a particular investment requiring borrowing if interest rates are expected to fall, because the cost savings from lower interest rates will be significant.

ASSET MANAGEMENT

Once the small business manager has planned the need for funds and selected the particular sources of funds that are most appropriate to meet those needs, there remains the continuing job of ensuring that the funds are employed efficiently.

Cash management

The problems related to cash management were dealt with in Chapter 13. The discrepancies that develop in the cash budget may arise from a variety of reasons, such as a strike, bad weather, or the financial problems of certain customers. Because cash is crucial to the continuing operation of the business, it is important to maintain some safety margin of cash to handle unexpected events. The amount will be based on the best judgment of the entrepreneur. The size of the cash balance will vary with the availability of such funds and the credit standing of the firm, which determines the extent to which funds can be borrowed. If the credit rating of the firm is good, funds should be available to cover most unforeseen events. If substantial quantities of cash are needed it may be possible to sell machinery and lease it back or sell accounts receivable.

Reasonable steps must be taken to safeguard incoming cash. Employees who handle cash should not be allowed to control all aspects of receipt and accountability. Division of duties in cash handling can provide some measure of control. Other safeguards such as bonding may be needed if the quantities of cash handled are substantial.

Fraud and embezzlement are potential threats and are usually detected among one or more long-standing employees—the ones who are trusted so they can operate more freely.

If the firm develops excess cash during some period of time, then such funds should be invested in high-grade commercial paper or U.S. Treasury bills. Other presently available forms of longer-term attractive investments do not restrict the withdrawal of funds and charge a reasonable recall rate for funds withdrawn ahead of schedule.

Management of accounts receivable

The small business owner of today will have to take an approach to the problem of accounts receivable different from that taken by a business person operating in the 1950s or earlier. The basic objective of extending credit and thus the implied conclusion that the sales potential will increase is balanced against the cost of the increased sales and the losses that accompany a more liberal credit policy.

One change over the years involves the use of the various credit cards; MasterCard, American Express, and Visa now are well known almost everywhere. Another change involves the use of consumer credit that has been established by banks and credit unions for the benefit of their reliable clients. Innovations in the granting of credit have made it possible for many individuals to buy on credit who might not otherwise do so.

If there are to be credit sales, then the owner must decide how to manage them. If the risk is shifted to a card company, delays and uncertainties in collections are removed in exchange for a 6 percent or 7 percent fee charged by the company for acceptance of the risk. In many instances the additional costs of such an arrangement are not resisted by the credit customer. It thus makes sense to utilize this and other credit arrangements that generate a higher volume of sales.

Inventory management

The investment of funds in inventory is one of the principal outflows of cash needed to maintain the activities of the business. Inventory is carried on the firm's books as an asset, but it is an expensive asset. It is subject to the risk that it may not sell as finished goods. The same problems are associated with the handling and control of inventory as of cash: What is the right amount to have on hand? When will you need it? How should you plan to use it?

Inventory management is the subject of many forms of analysis, and a variety of systems have been created for ordering, handling, and control. It is useful to divide inventory into classifications that differ in their nature and in their influences upon investment decisions. Some of these are the following:

1. Goods for resale.
2. Purchased raw materials for manufacturing.
3. Support materials for a manufacturer or service firm.
4. Work in process.
5. Safety stocks.

Inventory cost analysis is based on a series of operations. To begin with, there are costs associated with locating suitable suppliers or sources. Following this are the costs of placing orders, incoming transportation, inspecting, warehousing, manufacturing, finished goods warehousing, and finally shipment to a customer. At all stages it is necessary to provide—at a cost—protection against loss, theft, deterioration, and obsolescence.

For proper handling of all aspects of the inventory program, it is necessary to establish a cost for each activity performed as an inventory function—such as storage, transportation, and inspection—and for eventualities including stock-outs and fluctuations in prices. In addition, inventory is subject to a great deal of trade-off analysis—i.e., the determination that one type of investment is better than another, maybe at the same apparent cost.

Management of fixed assets

The investment of funds in fixed assets involves the commitment of dollars over an extended period of time, usually several years. Fixed asset investment is a form of deferred expense. A cash outlay is made at one point in time, but the cost of the outlay is charged to those periods in which the use of the assets is realized.

As in inventory management, there are certain costs to consider in determining the appropriate fixed asset investment. First, there is the cost of funds to purchase the fixed assets, as well as any tools or equipment needed to service the assets. Next, the cost of space occupied by the fixed assets includes depreciation charges, maintenance charges, rental costs, taxes, and utility costs. Some fixed assets, such as machinery, have certain service costs associated with their purchase. Typical machinery service costs include property taxes, insurance costs, maintenance costs, and depreciation. Finally, there is always the risk of obsolescence. In making the fixed asset decision, the small business manager is again involved in balancing all the costs associated with buying the fixed asset with the benefits from its use.

In deciding upon a particular level of fixed asset investment, the small business manager may have to consider the problem of safety stocks. For example, a department store must be built and stocked with furniture and fixtures in order to handle peak sales periods, but during slack periods much of the furniture and fixtures remain idle. There are several ways of minimizing this safety stock of fixed assets. The department store may have special sales at particularly slow times to attract customers, or may encourage consumers to shop early and avoid the seasonal rush.

The fixed asset investment decision, whether it involves the replacement of old equipment or the purchase of new equipment, is a capital budgeting decision, and the manager must relate the net investment outlay to the net benefits the outlay will produce over time.

In evaluating the management of both inventory and fixed assets, the manager should realize there may be idle stocks that should not be reduced to zero. Some stocks of inventories and fixed assets may be needed to allow for unpredictable changes such as a sudden increase in demand or the breakdown of a machine.

Because inventory levels can usually be adjusted quickly, anticipation stocks are accumulated largely to meet seasonal increases in demand. Stocks of fixed assets, on the other hand, cannot be readily changed and often must be accumulated well in advance of expected long-run increases in sales.

CAPITAL BUDGETING

Capital expenditures involve relatively large sums of money invested over relatively long periods of time; hence errors in evaluating fixed asset investment opportunities can cause serious consequences. Most firms, at any point in time, have several investment opportunities that could be undertaken. Capital budgeting is the means for evaluating investment opportunities in terms of profitability.

Capital budgeting is based on the assumption that capital should be employed in such a way as to provide the greatest return. Accepting the proposition that capital may not be adequate at any given time to finance all the projects that appear feasible, the manager must have some means of ranking opportunities in order of priority.

For example, suppose in a small manufacturing firm, the existing long-run investment opportunities include the development and introduction of a new product; the purchase of new data processing equipment to aid in administering the credit program; the replacement of the company's delivery trucks; expansion of sales promotion into a new territory; construction of a new office building; or the employment of several additional salespeople for a more intensive selling program in the existing market. In most cases it is unlikely that capital is available in amounts adequate to finance all six investments, regardless of their profitability. Therefore, some technique must be used to rank the proposals in terms of their desirability.

The remainder of this chapter establishes certain techniques for evaluating alternative investment opportunities.

The basics of capital budgeting

The approach to capital budgeting evolves around two conditions relating to the capital item under consideration. In all cases there are (a) the initial cash outlay and (b) the net annual inflows of cash. Thus, the investment decision requires that the initial amount of cash be known and that the net annual cash inflows be determinable.

To begin with, a typical situation might involve the necessity that an existing machine be replaced with a new machine. A new machine transaction will usually include the cost of the machine, shipping costs, and installation costs. To offset these would be the trade-in or salvage value of the old machine. At this point, it is important to realize that the depreciated value of the old machine makes no difference, nor does the fact that though depreciated it still has useful life left. All that counts is the net cost of the new machine, and the past history of the old machine is not a part of the decision.

Initially, we could use, as an example, an $8,000 machine, freight charges of $500, and installation costs of $500. If the old machine can be sold for $1,000, then the total initial investment is reduced by $1,000, leaving an initial cash investment of $8,000.

The most likely cash receipt in the replacement decision is the salvage value of the old machine. It is important to note, however, that the only concern in determining the initial cash investment is with cash flow.

Thus, certain costs are ignored. For instance, the old machine could be used for three more years; hence, it is likely to have a book value. It is unlikely, however, that the salvage value will be precisely equal to the book value. If the resale market is good, the old machine may sell at a price in excess of the book value. On the other hand, the resale value in the secondhand market may be considerably below the book value. Whatever the case, the only concern is with the cash inflow from the sale, regardless of the difference between the cash inflow and the book value. If the old machine sells for an amount less than book value the book loss should not be charged against the purchase of the new machine, for the loss involves no cash outflow.

The reasoning behind this procedure is simple. The loss (equal to the difference between the actual salvage value and the book value) has no relationship to the decision to buy the new machine. Whether the cost of the old machine has been recovered over the period it has been used is a matter of history. To charge this loss to the potential of the new machine is not good logic. The present decision should not be burdened with losses resulting from past decisions.

Getting back to the example, assume the old machine sells for $1,000; thus we have a cash receipt of $1,000 associated with the investment decision, and it is to be subtracted from total cash expenditures. Step one is now complete; it has been determined that the decision to replace the old machine involves an initial cash investment of $8,000.

Now for the second step: calculating the future net change in cash inflows resulting from the initial cash outlay. The old machine produces some cash flow; so in step two the only concern is with the change in this cash flow produced by the new machine. Assume the new machine will increase sales revenue annually by $18,000 and has an estimated life of three years. In order to produce the $18,000 of additional annual sales, however, advertising expenditures must be increased by $2,000 a year and an additional salesperson must be hired at a salary of $8,000 a year. So from the additional sales revenue of $18,000, additional expenditures of $10,000 a year are subtracted to arrive at a net change in cash inflow before taxes of $8,000.[1]

In determining the profitability of the replacement decision, an after-tax figure is preferred, thus the differential flows of cash must be adjusted for taxes. This is not as simple as it may sound, unless the depreciation rate on both the old machine and the new machine are

---

[1]In determining the annual net change in cash inflow, the manager must be very careful to consider *all* net changes in expenses. For example, the purchase of a new machine to replace a machine currently being used may involve a difference in maintenance costs. If so, the annual net additions to maintenance costs or the annual maintenance cost savings should be treated in the same manner as the added sales expense.

identical. If the old and new depreciations are the same and an income tax rate of 50 percent is assumed, the net annual cash benefit after taxes would be $4,000. But if there is a difference between the old depreciation rate and the new depreciation rate, the $8,000 before-tax figure must be adjusted for this difference before calculating the income tax liability.

For example, assume that the old machine was being depreciated $2,500 a year, and that the new machine is to be depreciated on a straight line basis at $3,000 a year ($9,000 ÷ 3); thus there is an additional depreciation charge of $500.[2] This reduces the addition to taxable income from $8,000 to $7,500, and applying the 50 percent income tax rate, it produces a tax liability of $3,750.

Step two is complete and produces the following conclusions: the new machine will produce a net addition to profit after taxes of $3,750 a year, and a net annual cash benefit after taxes of $4,250 a year as shown in the summary below. This is the first time that the net profit after taxes has been mentioned. It is used in one of the capital budgeting techniques to be described.

	Books	Cash flow
Net added cash inflow, years 1–3	$8,000	$8,000
Annual depreciation on old machine, $2,500		
Annual depreciation on new machine, $3,000		
Net change in depreciation	500	
Added taxable income	7,500	
Added taxes at 50 percent.	3,750	3,750
Net change in profit after taxes.	$3,750	
Change in cash flow after taxes		$4,250

The payback method

The first of three methods available to evaluate investment opportunities is called the payback method. It involves simply determining the length of time necessary for the sum of the net cash benefits to equal the initial outlay. In other words, the payback period is calculated by dividing the initial cash outlay by the annual cash benefits. In the example, with an initial cash outlay of $8,000 and an annual cash benefit after taxes of $4,250; the length of time necessary to recover the initial investment is 1.88 years, or about 1 year and 11 months.

The payback method is useful in two situations. First, if the firm is cash poor it may be most important that the initial investment be recovered as soon as possible. Second, if the firm is subject to rapid

---

[2]The new machine can be depreciated for tax purposes before considering the benefit of old machine salvage. In the example this means that the depreciable amount is $9,000.

technological change the manager may be interested in recovering the initial investment as soon as possible.

There are two major deficiencies in the payback method. First, it ignores variation in the rate at which net cash savings are realized. For instance, assume that two investment opportunities requiring an initial cash outlay of $12,000 have the following income streams: machine A produces $2,000 the first year, $4,000 the second year, and $6,000 the third year; whereas machine B produces $6,000 the first year, $4,000 the second, and $2,000 the third year. Although both machine A and machine B are paid for in three years the investments are not equally desirable. Based on the premise that money has a time value, and when recovered can be employed elsewhere, the machine that provides the larger sums in the earlier years is more profitable.

The second deficiency is that the payback method ignores any stream of income extending beyond the payback period. For example, assume that two investment opportunities both require an initial outlay of $9,000. In case A the net cash benefit is $3,000 a year for a five-year period, whereas in case B the net cash benefit is $3,000 a year for a three-year period. Although both investments are paid for in three years, the investment in case A is more profitable because of the longer income stream.

The average rate of return method

The average rate of return is the percentage of average annual net income after taxes to average investment over the life of the project. It is the basis of a second method of evaluating investment opportunities.

In applying this method in the example the average net profit after taxes of $3,750 per year represents the income stream. Assuming straight line depreciation, average investment is $4,500, or one half of $9,000. Thus, the average rate of return method produces a rate of return of about 83 percent.

There are three deficiencies in the use of the average rate of return method. First, because we average the annual income figure, the method ignores any differences in the flows on a year-to-year basis. Second, the duration of the income flow is ignored. And third, the method ignores the time value of money.

The net present value method

A more reliable method of evaluating alternative investment opportunities is the net present value method because it considers the time value of money.

The time value of money is a concept that recognizes that a dollar to be received a year from today (or anytime in the future) is less valuable than a dollar possessed today. This is true for three reasons: immediate pleasure is preferable to postponed pleasure; there is always the risk that the future dollar will not be received; and dollars possessed today can earn a return. Thus, the rational person would not ordinarily relinquish today's dollar in exchange for a promise that it will be returned in the future, unless some payment is to be received for its use in the form of interest. If the individual felt that foregoing immediate pleasure, plus accepting the risk that the dollar will never be returned, requires an interest charge of 20 percent, then today's dollar should be returned one year from now with 20 cents interest, for a total of $1.20. To put it another way, the present value of $1.20 to be received a year from now discounted at 20 percent is $1.

This introduces the problem to be solved in using the net present value method of capital budgeting. Initial cash outlays represent dollars that must be spent today. The income stream, on the other hand, represents dollars to be received at some time in the future. Therefore, in order to compare the two (and arrive at a valid conclusion as to the profitability of the investment opportunity), we must compare the present value of the dollars to be received in the future with the present value of the initial cash outlay.

In figuring the time value of money, a present value table such as Table 14–1 can be used. It indicates the present value of $1 to be received at the end of N years; discounted at a rate X. For instance, assume we want to know what amount invested at 20 percent will return $1 a year from today. Find the 20-percent column in Table 14–1 and go down to the line representing year 1. The present value of $1 to be received a year from now discounted at 20 percent is $0.833.

Similarly, $1 to be received at the end of two years, discounted at 20 percent, has a present value of $0.694. Taking this one step further, we can now determine the present value of a stream of cash benefits represented by $1 to be received at the end of year 1 and $1 to be

Table 14–1
Present value of $1

Years hence	4%	8%	10%	12%	16%	20%	24%	30%
1	0.962	0.926	0.909	0.893	0.862	0.833	0.806	0.769
2	0.925	0.857	0.826	0.797	0.743	0.694	0.650	0.592
3	0.889	0.794	0.751	0.712	0.641	0.579	0.524	0.455
4	0.855	0.735	0.683	0.636	0.552	0.482	0.423	0.350
5	0.822	0.681	0.621	0.567	0.476	0.402	0.341	0.269
6	0.790	0.630	0.564	0.507	0.410	0.335	0.275	0.207
7	0.760	0.583	0.513	0.452	0.354	0.279	0.222	0.159
8	0.731	0.540	0.467	0.404	0.305	0.233	0.179	0.123
9	0.703	0.500	0.424	0.361	0.263	0.194	0.144	0.094
10	0.676	0.463	0.386	0.322	0.227	0.162	0.116	0.073

received at the end of year 2 discounted at 20 percent. The answer is simply $0.833 plus $0.694, or approximately $1.53.

The net present value method of capital budgeting simply involves discounting the stream of future cash benefits to be received over time at a selected rate of discount and comparing the present value of the future benefits with the initial cash outlay.

The application of the net present value method is relatively simple. All the manager does is select a minimum acceptable rate of return, set the problem up by completing steps one and two (described above), then discount the stream of net cash benefits at the selected rate of discount.

The next step is to subtract the initial cash outlay from the present value of future cash benefits. If the answer is zero, the rate of return is exactly equal to the selected rate of discount; if the answer is negative, the rate of return is less than the selected rate of discount; and if the answer is positive, the return exceeds the minimum required.

Applying the present value method to the example used in the explanation of the payback and the average rate of return method, assume that a minimum return on the replacement machine of 30 percent is required. Thus, we go to the 30 percent column in the present value table and make the following calculations: the present value of the $4,250 cash inflow in the first year is 0.769 ($4,250), or $3,268; the present value of the $4,250 to be received in the second year is 0.592 ($4,250), or $2,516; and, the present value of the $4,250 to be received in the third year is 0.455 ($4,250), or $1,934. Thus, the total present value of the income stream is $7,718. Subtracting the initial cash outlay ($8,000) from this figure gives a negative result, which indicates the rate of return is less than 30 percent. The investment decision does not produce the return required and, on the basis of profitability, should be rejected.

The internal rate of return method

In this method, which is similar to the net present value method, a rate of return is projected that equals the present value of the cash outlays with the discounted present value of cash inflows over the life of the capital item at some demanded rate of interest. Trial and error is used between various rates of interest to find the rate that is acceptable in the time period allowed.

Evaluating the capital investment decision process

In many instances the small business person will not make the final decision as to a capital item on the basis of the calculations outlined earlier. Nevertheless, the basic elements of business operations today include such things as high interest rates, double-digit inflation, escalating replacement costs for machines and equipment, and a very low average yearly improvement in industrial productivity. These four items suggest that a more careful analysis and investigation of investment alternatives is warranted.

One of the problems associated with capital budgeting and the ranking of alternative investment opportunities is that the probability of realizing the anticipated income stream is not considered in the net present value method. Two projects with equal net present values may have different degrees of risk, and evaluation of this risk factor involves an estimation of the range of error that may be present in estimating the future income stream. That is to say, even though the net present value figures are the same in two cases, the probabilities of receiving the anticipated income streams may be different, and one proposal may be preferred over another on this basis.

It must also be recognized that none of the methods takes into consideration the nonmonetary aspects of the investment decision. There may be investments that are necessary, even though it is difficult to determine their net present values, or despite the fact they do not rank high among the various alternative opportunities. For instance, it may be that buying a new machine would be very profitable, but a parking lot for employees is necessary. So the machine purchase may have to be postponed and the parking lot built. In another case, it may be that additional advertising appears necessary to maintain the firm's share of the market, even though it is difficult to determine the effect of the additional expenditures on cash inflows.

LEASE AND RENTAL ALTERNATIVES

The opportunity to lease or rent a wide variety of machinery and equipment often provides a desirable alternative to the ownership of the same items. Our discussions to this point have dealt with ownership and the methods used to calculate the risks and rewards of such ownership. Today, however, the options of lease and rental are providing a way for businesses to stretch their available funds over a greater range of capital investment needs.

Lease or rental ordinarily costs 10 percent to 20 percent more than purchase, *on a computed basis.* The attractive advantages of lease or rental are the shorter time period of commitment to the item involved and the ability to write off lease and rental costs as current expense.

For our purposes, leases usually run for periods of one or two years, perhaps three, while rentals involve periods less than one year. Legally

they are no different although shorter periods require higher payments. In most cases the equipment provided is new or nearly new. Many options are available to serve the needs of the lessee, such as base leases (without maintenance or service), full service leases, leases with or without insurance coverage, maintenance contracts, etc.

Another advantage strongly favoring a lease is the relatively short time period that the lessee is obligated under the lease. A year or two is normally well within the range of predicted need and use for a piece of equipment. At the same time, interest rates and the income stream can be closely estimated in the short run. For periods beyond two or three years it is difficult to predict usage for a piece of equipment, and obsolescence is always an unknown factor.

To make a comparison between ownership and lease or rental the entrepreneur will use one of the methods previously outlined for comparing alternative investment opportunities. Additional items of a nonmonetary nature may be considered, and trade-off analyses also may be necessary. By using such an approach a reasonable judgment can be formulated.

TAX PLANNING AND CAPITAL INVESTMENT

It is not within the scope of this volume on small business to suggest ways for a given entrepreneur to minimize the tax liability of a business. It is necessary, however, to alert the reader to the fact that capital investments are closely linked with tax rates, tax payments, and the reduction of exposure to taxation. In today's business world, it is necessary to know what options are available and how they apply. One of the options is the combining or separation of business and personal assets.

Often, such decisions are made by simply taking a particular course of action. Once started, there is little chance that the processes can be changed or reversed. In other cases, managers are uninformed and pass up possible beneficial options.

Each entrepreneur must devote the proper time, effort, and money to insure that the applicable areas of taxation are understood in connection with the financial management plans for the firm.

In concluding, the small business manager's success will depend somewhat on the lessons learned from past experience and on the ability to assess current trends that will affect conditions in the future. Experience and good judgment play an important role in tax and investment analysis, and a periodic review of past investment decisions will help in making better decisions for future action. Many conditions are now much more uncertain than they have been in the past, so that the assessment process must be conducted more thoroughly and carefully to help avoid any serious miscalculations.

QUESTIONS

1. What are the advantages and disadvantages of employing financial leverage in the small business?

2. Discuss the factors of risk, control, flexibility, and timing as they relate to selecting a source of funds.

3. What is the principal problem associated with managing the cash account and what tool can be used in solving the problem?

4. Distinguish between controlling the level of receivables and controlling the acquisition of receivables.

5. What costs are associated with determining the appropriate inventory investment?

6. Discuss the two steps in setting up a capital budgeting problem.

7. Define the three capital budgeting techniques discussed in the chapter.

8. Explain what is meant by the statement "money has a time value."

9. What are the disadvantages or deficiencies in using the average rate of return method and the payback method in capital budgeting?

10. What is meant by the "nonmonetary aspects" of the investment decision? Give examples of some typical nonmonetary considerations.

PROBLEMS

1. Compute the following:

   a. The present value of $4,000 to be received at the end of five years, discounted at 8 percent.

   b. The present value of $2,000 to be received at the end of each year for five years, discounted at 10 percent.

   c. The present value of $3,000 to be received at the end of years 1 and 2, and $4,000 to be received at the end of years 3 and 4; discounted at 6 percent.

2. The information below pertains to three alternative investment opportunities:

	Investment A	Investment B	Investment C
Initial cash outlay	$5,400	$9,000	$12,000
Estimated economic life	3 years	6 years	6 years
Salvage value.	0	0	0
Differential cash benefit before depreciation and taxes			
1–3 years	$2,400	$4,500	$ 4,600
4–6 years	0	$3,500	$ 7,200
Annual straight line depreciation charge . .	$1,800	$1,500	$ 2,000

Assume the corporate income tax rate is 50 percent and rank the three proposals by using the payback method, the average rate of return on average investment, and the net present value method. How do you explain the differences in the rankings?

BIBLIOGRAPHY

Engler, George N. *Business Financial Management*. Rev. ed. Plano, Tex.: Business Publications, 1978. Good basic text that analyzes the subject of financial management. Useful as background information for financial decisions.

Soldovsky, Robert M., and Garnet D. Olive. *Financial Management*. Cincinnati, Ohio: South-Western Publishing, 1980. A good solid text dealing with the overall activities of financial management. Useful in connection with the topics of this chapter.

Ulbrich, Halley H., and Bruce Yandle. *Managing Personal Finance*. Plano, Tex.: Business Publications, 1979. This text on personal finance includes subsidiary types of financial decisions that are a part of the job of the financial manager.

Wert, James E., and Glenn V. Henderson, Jr. *Financing Business Firms*. Homewood, Ill.: Richard D. Irwin, 1979. A text that carries the subject of financial analysis into the realm of the business enterprize.

Case study

Forkavers

In 1946, upon returning home from duty in the U.S. Air Force, Rodney Forkaver had opened an office supply store. By 1955 the firm Forkavers had become a large and well-known establishment in a California town of some 30,000 population. The firm had no particular specialties but did carry a very extensive line of all basic office supplies, typewriters, and adding machines and a limited line of office furniture.

In 1966, Rodney Forkaver's son, Kevin, was finishing college and had decided to join his father in the business. Kevin had worked from time to time for his father, but he felt that his father was not committed to accepting him into the firm. By 1966, however, the firm was well established, was profitable, and could afford another ownership income to be taken from its operations. The elder Forkaver had thought it through and now felt his son should join him.

The decision was made and Kevin joined Forkavers as assistant sales manager with the understanding that he would be given the job of sales manager upon the retirement of Kenneth Haley, which was due to take place in another three years.

The business continued to prosper, and the elder Forkaver was approached by a number of his friends and business associates who asked him to invest in a variety of business endeavors. Some investments were made, but Rodney Forkaver was essentially conservative and was not inclined to invest except in things that he felt confident about and that involved ongoing operations that were familiar and not particularly risky.

During the late 1960s both the Forkavers observed the phenomenal growth and development of the high-technology firms that occupied "Silicon Valley" in the area around Santa Clara, California, which was to spawn the creation of many successful firms and the opportunity for many persons to become millionaires in a short time.

Having known several persons who were a part of the technology boom, it was tempting for the Forkavers to invest in newly created firms, knowing that the investments of several of their friends had been very successful. Rodney Forkaver, however, had prospered and was able to enjoy the fruits of many years of hard work by playing more golf and traveling with his wife for a month or two every year. He still retained controlling interest in the business and advised against these outside investments.

In the early 1970s, Forkavers became an even larger operation, taking on several lines of distribution for major manufacturers and setting up a large warehouse in San Jose, California, to service their operations, which now included six retail stores in the greater San Francisco-Oakland area of California.

By 1975 arrangements had been made for Kevin to succeed his father, who decided to retire and move permanently to San Diego. One of the last major joint efforts of the Forkavers was to establish a consulting and supply firm to provide a furnishing and decorating service to schools and office buildings and a furniture refurbishing operation to reclaim old office and commercial furniture. By 1978 these new operations were well established, and Kevin Forkaver felt pleased that the firm had done well. There had been some difficult times, but the conservatism of the elder Forkaver had carried over and protected the business against any serious financial difficulties.

By late 1978 the technology boom began to show signs of reappearing. At the same time, there was a substantial interest in companies exploiting resources such as oil, gas, uranium, and precious metals. Once again the chances to invest became apparent and Kevin Forkaver was reminded of a similar period some 10 years before—at that time he did not control the company; now he did.

The Forkaver firm was a leader, well entrenched and recognized as a progressive, successful business. Its store managers were well paid through salary and bonuses and were carefully directed by Kevin Forkaver. By 1979, the effects of the high interest rates and a cutback in building construction had reduced the total income of business and the profit by some 20 percent. The business was not seriously affected, but it was a sobering turn of events for a firm that had experienced a long, steady expansion. In thinking about this, Kevin Forkaver felt that it might be wise to either franchise his operation or sell some of his interest to the public and to key employees of the firm. If the franchise arrangement was selected, the present store managers could provide a beginning group who could help establish the new company. If a public stock offering were made, it would not be a dramatic type of business interest that was being sold, but rather a solid established business whose rate of return and growth were both somewhat above industry average.

The sale of stock would provide Kevin Forkaver and his key employees with stock, which would have some reasonable value and subsequent opportunity for resale. A franchise system could also be the subject of a stock sale in order to raise funds but would require a longer time and more steps in order to complete the final results. The Forkaver firm had been approached by one larger manufacturing firm that wished to exchange stock and integrate the Forkaver operation into its nationwide building products division. This offer, however, had been rejected.

Kevin Forkaver's attitude was that he should now have his chance to parlay his own business into something that would be more substantial and more beneficial to him in the long run. He felt strongly that Forkaver's should franchise or go public.

QUESTIONS

1. Are there strong reasons for placing a substantial family enterprise in a protected or more secure position before the principal owner dies or is unable to carry on the business?
2. Are there good reasons for choosing to go public versus establishing a franchise system?
3. Does the high rate of inflation tend to encourage people to invest in equity investments that have the potential of providing capital gains? Would this influence a decision by individuals in favor of a firm like Forkavers?

15

Accounting and financial
controls

The experienced entrepreneur knows there is a close relationship between good accounting practices and business success. To keep in touch with financial conditions on a day-to-day basis requires accounting information that is accurate, properly organized, and continually up to date. From another view, a good accounting system must be comprehensive enough to satisfy the purpose of financial control, yet easy to understand and interpret. Financial decisions based upon inadequate, unreliable, or confusing accounting information may lead to financial disaster.

WHAT MUST ACCOUNTING AND FINANCIAL CONTROLS PROVIDE?

The records that are developed and are the basis for accounting and financial controls have three fundamental objectives. Each of these will be outlined briefly as follows:

Current financial status. The current accounting records show developments as they occur and expose potential problem areas. Corrections can then be made before any substantial damage has been done. Such records also show the performance of the firm over time and provide the necessary information for the filing of tax returns. They also provide the basis for the various documents that must be filed with bankers and other outsiders, who may want a statement showing the present financial status of the firm in determining its credit standing.

Control of a firm's assets.   There must be a firm commitment on the part of an entrepreneur to manage his/her firm and not *be managed* by events that are out of control. The availability of every asset and the proper uses for each type of asset must be known. Furthermore, complete and accurate data will help to protect against the possibility of fraud, waste, and theft by employees or other persons associated with the business.

Business planning.   Every business must have adequate and up-to-date records as a basis for planning. Having come from past records, and over some period of time, the repeating updated records are the most valid data that pertain to that particular business. Such past records are the structural base used to make decisions for future periods.

THE ACCOUNTING PROCESS

Assets are what the business owns; *liabilities* are what a business owes. Cash, accounts receivable, supplies, furniture and fixtures, building, land, and equipment are typical assets. Typical liabilities include accounts payable, notes payable, and wages and taxes that have not been paid. The capital of the business is the owner's contribution and represents the difference between total assets and total liabilities. This is the concept upon which all accounting systems are based:

$$\text{Assets} = \text{Liabilities} + \text{Capital}.$$

To further clarify, there are two claims against the total assets of a business: liabilities represent the creditors' claims, and capital represents the owner's claim. It follows, therefore, that regardless of the transaction involved, liabilities plus capital always equal assets. For example, if the manager buys a delivery truck for $4,500 and pays cash, the cash account is reduced by $4,500, but the value of another asset (equipment) is increased by $4,500, and total assets remain unchanged. In another example, if a bank loan of $1,500 is paid, the asset cash is reduced by $1,500, but so is the liability bank-notes-payable reduced by $1,500, and the equation remains in balance.

Accounting transactions

In a double entry accounting system there are two parts to each combined accounting record.

In accounting terminology every business transaction represents a debit entry in one account and a credit entry in another account; thus total debits always equal total credits. Of course any particular account may have both debit and credit entries. Whether a particular entry is a debit or a credit will depend on the type of account and on whether the transaction increases or decreases the account. For example, when the manager bought the truck for cash, the amount paid for the truck was entered as a debit to the equipment account and as a credit to the cash account. And when the bank note was retired, the transaction was recorded as a debit to notes payable and as a credit to the cash account. Figure 15–1 shows the effects of debit and credit entries on the basic accounts and indicates the typical balance in each of the accounts. All records of an accounting system are based on this double entry concept.

Primary financial records

The financial records of a business begin with the documents that indicate the business transactions *as they take place*. These include such things as sales receipts, cash register tapes, petty cash slips, purchase orders, checkbook stubs, invoices, and monthly statements from suppliers. Thus, every financial transaction, regardless of how informal, should produce some sort of written record.

Books of original entry. These books, also called journals, are used to record the initial transactions and their supporting information. *Journal entries* provide a permanent chronological record of the financial transactions. These journal entries are the first and most important original record that is a part of the financial transactions history. They should be carefully maintained and up to date at all times.

Ledger accounts. Ledgers contain summary accounts that are used to record the increases or decreases in a particular category of items such as assets, liabilities, capital items, income, or expense. The business will create and use as many ledger accounts as are necessary to properly summarize each of the various accounts. As a business grows, it is

Figure 15–1
Debit and credit entries (double-entry accounting system

Type of account	If the transaction *increases* the account, enter it as a	If the transaction *decreases* the account, enter it as a	Typical balance
Asset	Debit	Credit	Debit
Liability	Credit	Debit	Credit
Capital	Credit	Debit	Credit
Income	Credit	Debit	Credit
Expense	Debit	Credit	Debit

desirable to add more detail to the accounting system, so that accounts will be divided and subdivided, each part being assigned its own new ledger account number.

The balance sheet and income statement. These two financial statements, which are defined and explained in later sections of this chapter, derive from the information that was originally recorded in the journal entries. Although the journals yield the basic data for the income statement, preparation of the balance sheet requires that financial transactions also be posted in a general ledger of asset and liability accounts. Each transaction is entered in the general ledger as both a credit and a debit, according to the rules of double-entry accounting.

These two financial statements serve as the basis for analyzing the firm's performance over a period of time, as well as for determining the financial condition of the firm as a particular point in time. The income statement and balance sheet are the two documents that individuals outside the firm usually request in analyzing the firm's performance.

The sales and cash receipts journal. The general format of this journal is shown in Figure 15–2. Information is normally entered each day in this journal. Each column is marked debit or credit to indicate the typical entry. If it is necessary to make a credit entry in a debit column, or a debit entry in a credit column, the entry is circled. Total sales, charge sales, collections on accounts, and total cash receipts can all be entered on the same line of the journal.

The cash disbursements, purchases, and expense journal. All disbursements for whatever purpose should be entered daily in the cash disbursements, purchases, and expense journal. Most expenditures should be made by drawing a check, and each check should be entered in this journal. Figure 15–3 shows the column headings of this journal.

Entries in the merchandise purchases column need no explanation. The general ledger columns of the cash disbursements journal are used only for the entries that directly affect the assets, liabilities, and capital of the business as recorded in the general ledger. Typical examples are purchases of furniture or equipment, payment of bank loans, and withdrawals of funds by the proprietor or partners.

THE INCOME STATEMENT

The income statement is a summary of sales revenue and expenses over some period of time. The period can be a month, a quarter, or a year. For tax purposes it must be produced annually, but in practice it will also be developed at in-between periods to reflect the ongoing activity of the firm. It is useful to express the figures in the income statement as percentages of net sales. A comparison of these percent-

Figure 15–2
Sales and cash receipts journal

Date 19—	Description and/or Account	Total Sales (Credit)	Charge to Customers (Debit)	Collections on Accounts (Credit)	Miscellaneous Income and Expense Entries		General Ledger Entries	
					(Debit)	(Credit)	(Debit)	(Credit)

Figure 15–3
Cash disbursements, purchases, and expense journal

Date 19—	Payee and/or Account	Check No.	Amount of Check (Credit)	Merchandise Purchases (Debit)	Payroll Deductions		Miscellaneous Income and Expense Entries		General Ledger Entries	
					Income Tax (Credit)	Social Security (Credit)	(Debit)	(Credit)	(Debit)	(Credit)

ages (commonly known as operating ratios) on a month-to-month basis is a vaulable means of analyzing performance.

A typical income statement is shown in Figure 15–4. It is to be read from top to bottom, starting with *sales revenue* and ending with *net income, after income taxes*. As you read down the income statement, each successive category is totaled and subtracted from the preceding amount. Thus *cost of goods sold* reflects the adjustments in inventory to yield gross margin. After that, expenses are listed, totaled, and subtracted from *gross margin* to yield *operating profit (or loss)*. Following this, taxes are subtracted to show *net income*.

The income statement is as reliable and valid as the figures used. It may, however, not show some operating transactions that might be desired. More will be said about this later.

The net profit or loss result derived in the income statement can be checked by balancing the general ledger. After all the entries have been made in the general ledger for the month, the debit balances should be totaled and the credit balances should be totaled. The difference

Figure 15–4
Income Statement

THE MILE-HI SYSTEMS COMPANY
Income Statement
For the Month of _____ 19_____

	Amount	Percent of sales
Net sales.	$_____	100
Less cost of goods sold:		
Beginning inventory	_____	
Merchandise purchases.	_____	
Merchandise available for sale . . .	_____	
Less ending inventory.	_____	
Cost of goods sold	_____	_____
Gross margin	_____	_____
Less expenses:		
Salaries and wages.	_____	_____
Rent	_____	_____
Utilities	_____	_____
Supplies.	_____	_____
Advertising.	_____	_____
Depreciation	_____	_____
Taxes	_____	_____
Insurance.	_____	_____
Interest	_____	_____
Delivery expense.	_____	_____
Bad debts	_____	_____
Other expenses	_____	_____
Total expenses	_____	_____
Operating profit (loss) before owner's withdrawals and income taxes	$_____	_____

between these two results should equal the *bottom line* figure on the income statement.

THE BALANCE SHEET

The small business owner should also prepare a monthly balance sheet. Recall that the balance sheet is simply a summary of the balances of the general ledger accounts, and in contrast to the income statement, shows conditions in the business as of a specific date. For validity and correctness, the balance sheet is prepared as of the close of the period reported in the income statement.

Construction of the balance sheet

The balance sheet is divided into two categories. On one side or at the top are the assets, balanced off on the other side or at the bottom by the liabilities plus the owner's equity.

Neither the income statement nor the balance sheet tells you a great deal about the origins of the figures shown. It is therefore necessary to examine the original source documents and journals to find out what the individual transactions involved.

Balance sheet account listings

Each section of the balance sheet represents a special part of the business in terms of functional and operational purpose. It is useful to examine each of these parts to understand what each particular category is called and what is its particular relationship to the business.

The first entry on the asset side of the balance sheet is *current assets*. Current assets include cash and those assets that will be converted to cash during the normal course of the business within a year. The cash account includes both petty cash and cash on deposit in a bank.

Accounts receivable include amounts due for merchandise or services purchased but not yet paid for by customers. In reporting this balance, an allowance is made for that portion of accounts receivable that is estimated to be uncollectible. The allowance is usually estimated as a percentage of the average balance of accounts receivable, or as a percentage of net credit sales for a period, based on previous years' experience.

The final entry in current assets is inventory. In a retail business, inventory consists of merchandise owned by the company, either on the shelves or in storage, and listed at cost or market value, whichever is lower. In a manufacturing concern, the inventory account is broken down into raw materials, goods in process, and finished goods. At this point, a figure for total current assets appears on the balance sheet.

Figure 15–5
Balance Sheet

THE MILE-HI SYSTEMS COMPANY
Balance Sheet
At June 30, 19X0

Assets

Current assets:
  Cash
    Cash in bank. . . . . $_____
    Petty cash . . . . _____ $_____
  Accounts receivable . . . . _____
    Less: Allowance for doubtful accounts . . . _____   _____
  Inventories. . . . . _____
        Total current assets. . . . . $_____

Fixed assets:
  Land . . . . _____
  Buildings. . . . . _____
  Delivery equipment. . . . . _____
  Furniture and fixtures. . . . . _____   _____
    Less: Allowance for depreciation. . . . . . . _____
        Total fixed assets . . . .   _____
Total assets. . . . . $_____

*Liabilities and Capital**

Current liabilities:
  Notes payable, due within one year . . . . . . $_____
  Accounts payable . . . . _____
  Accrued expenses . . . . _____
        Total current liabilities. . . . . $_____

Long-term liabilities:
  Notes payable, due after one year . . . . _____
        Total liabilities . . . . $_____

Capital:
  Proprietor's capital, beginning of period . . . _____
  Net profit for the period . . . . _____
  Less proprietor's drawings† . . . . _____
  Increase in capital. . . . . _____
      Capital, end of period . . . .   _____
Total liabilities and capital . . . . $_____

*For partnership or corporation, see footnotes to Figure 13–3.
†If the business suffers a loss, the proprietor's drawings will be added to the net loss to give the total decrease in capital.

The next general grouping of balance sheet accounts is *fixed assets.* Fixed assets are those items used in the business operation that are not intended to be resold. Typical fixed assets include land, buildings, machinery, trucks, automobiles, and furniture and fixtures. In contrast to accounts receivable and inventories, which produce income by being converted into cash, fixed assets produce income indirectly through their use in operations.

The final entry in this section of the balance sheet is allowance for depreciation. All the fixed assets but land will eventually wear out; in recognition of this fact the owner periodically makes an allowance for depreciation, thereby reducing the stated value of the assets. Current and fixed assets are totaled, and the asset side of the balance sheet is complete.

The first entry on the liability side of the balance sheet is *current liabilities*. Current liabilities include all debts due within one year. Typical current liability accounts include notes payable, accounts payable, and accrued expenses. A typical note payable is the sum of principal payments on a bank loan that falls due within one year. Accounts payable include those monies the company owes to suppliers and other business creditors for such things as materials, merchandise, and insurance. And finally, accrued expenses indicate such things as wages, interest, and other amounts owed but not yet paid by the business as of the date of the balance sheet (and for which bills or invoices will not be received).

The *long-term liabilities* include those debts or parts of debts that are not due to be paid within a year. The most common entries in this category are long-term mortgages on property owned, long-term loans, and long-term purchase contracts. The loan account shown in Figure 15–5, notes payable, would typically represent principal payments on a bank loan due after one year. Current liabilities plus long-term liabilities equal total liabilities, and the second major grouping of accounts on the balance sheet is complete.

The last major section of the balance sheet is the *capital account*. If the business is a single proprietorship, the proprietor's capital at the beginning of the period is entered; net profit for the period is added; any withdrawal are subtracted; and the result is capital at the end of the period. On the other hand, in a corporate organization, the capital section of the balance sheet will include such entries as common stock, preferred stock, earned surplus, capital surplus, and possibly one or two reserve accounts representing earned surplus that is earmarked for a particular purpose.

The traditional summary accounting statements of the past have been the income statement and the balance sheet. Today, however, it is not sufficient in controlling a business to examine only such summary statements. The analyst must examine the cash flow to identify the sources of cash and the ways in which cash was used during the year.

In Figure 15–6, the sources and uses of cash are shown in a tabulation taken from a leading book on the subject entitled *How to Read a Financial Report*.[1] An examination of the various line items in Figure 15–6 shows that the analysis of cash flow starts with the net income figure shown on

---

[1] John A. Tracy. *How to Read a Financial Report* (New York: John Wiley & Sons, 1980), 156 pp.

Figure 15–6
Sources and uses of cash during first year

Cash impact of net income		
Net income, from income statement		$ 150,000
Changes in operating assets during year (Increase = Demand on cash; Decrease = Release of cash):		
Accounts receivable	+ $486,000	
Inventory	+ $702,000	
Prepaid expenses	+ $ 90,000	
Fixed assets—Depreciation expense	− $116,000	($1,162,000)
Changes in operating liabilities during year (Increase = Release of cash: Decrease = Demand on cash):		
Accounts payable	+ $270,000	
Accrued expenses	+ $117,000	
Income tax payable	+ $ 30,000	$ 417,000
Cash inflow (outflow) from net income		($ 595,000)
Other cash sources:		
Stock issue	$933,000	
Borrowing:		
Short-term debt	$220,000	
Long-term debt	$300,000	$1,453,000
Cash uses		
Cash dividends	$ −0−	
Fixed asset purchases	$696,000	($ 696,000)
Increase in cash during year		$ 162,000

Source: John A. Tracy. *How To Read A Financial Report* (New York: John Wiley & Sons, 1980).

the income statement. The remaining analysis reveals the flow of cash through the business over time.

In general, examination of the cash flow of the business seeks to detect causes and effects, and to measure the time lag involved between each cause and its effect. As an example, if sales are made on credit, some time will elapse before the resulting accounts receivable are collected. The duration of time needed to collect accounts receivable requires an investment of cash in the goods that were sold if they had been bought for cash prior to sale. If the goods sold (inventory) have not been paid for, then the examination focuses on the comparative times of cash payments versus cash receipts and the amount of cash tied up until collections are made.

In turn, each operating condition that has an effect on cash flow is examined and related to the accounting period. Typically these are cause-and-effect relationships that *are not equal over some short-run period* or through a time period that moves from one accounting period to the next. It is the fact that cash is absorbed or utilized for various periods until the cause-and-effect transaction is liquidated that leads to cash flow problems.

Further information about the nature of cash flow analysis should be obtained by the small business manager. In most instances this information should relate to the needs of the particular business. Some accounting systems, such as those referred to at the end of this chapter, may provide the format for such analysis.

SPECIAL TYPES OF ACCOUNTING RECORDS

In addition to the more significant accounting records that have been described, there are a number of other record forms that are useful in a typical small business. These are not always necessary but are mentioned here as a means of alerting the manager to their possible use in a firm.

The first of these is the detailed record of *accounts receivable.* Two important benefits of such a record are: more accurate billing procedures

and ready information for evaluating the firm's credit and collection policies. For example, if receivable turnover is declining and the average collection period is increasing, an accurate, detailed accounts receivable record should indicate the particular customer accounts causing the problem.

A detailed and separate *inventory record* is also helpful. Accurate inventory records not only are essential to the control and security of inventory stocks, but also they provide information necessary for purchasing decisions and for the evaluation of inventory policies.

It may prove valuable to organize *accounts receivable* information in a separate set of records. Such detail can protect the credit standing of the firm by indicating such things as available cash discounts and final payment due dates.

Often a detailed *sales record* will aid in the analysis of such things as the effectiveness of advertising, market coverage, and the profit derived from certain customers. Furthermore, sales records are needed to provide the basis for compensation of salespeople.

A final item is detailed *tax records*. These are necessary to maintain the proper payment schedules and to generate the information for the detailed statements filed on personal and/or corporate income.

Other records may be important for a given business. The manager or owner must recognize what is necessary, to create the system to generate such documents or information, and to then utilize it. If and when the record is no longer needed it should be terminated.

MANAGING THE RECORD-KEEPING FUNCTION

An accounting system is only as useful as it is up-to-date and accurate. To prevent errors and to safeguard the assets of the business, the accounting system must provide for certain internal checks. A standard method for protecting against errors or fraud is to have two or more individuals involved in the record-keeping function. The obvious approach if the small business owner is familiar with general accounting practice and theory is for him or her to design an accounting system. In doing this, however, care should be taken to avoid oversimplifying the system by failing to provide adequate checks and balances to protect against error.

Sources of help

An alternative approach to ensuring accuracy is to employ the services of a public accountant or a bookkeeping service that caters to small businesses. Data are normally submitted by mail, and periodically the service provides financial reports by mail. Assistance will also be provided by a bookkeeping service agency in filling out tax returns and in making periodic audits.

Still another approach to handling the accounting function is to purchase one of a number of simplified bookkeeping systems that have been prepared for use by small businesses. Such systems are ideal for the business owner who knows little about accounting or finds a bookkeeping service too expensive.

Several commercial agencies produce simplified bookkeeping systems that may be purchased in most office supply stores. An appendix at the end of this chapter provides specific information on the names, prices, and sources of specific systems designed for use in any retail or service establishment. The Small Business Administration can also be helpful in locating the source of a record-keeping system for a particular type of business.

Use of the computer in small business record-keeping

The use of electronic data processing is rapidly becoming feasible for the small business. At present, a retailer with annual gross sales of $100,000 or more who is willing to spend around half of 1 percent of gross sales in processing fees can instantly acquire much of the accurate up-to-date information that would take many hours or even days to assemble.

Two major problem areas in which use of the computer proves valuable are inventory control and accounts receivable management. The following comments indicate the types of service that are presently available for these two purposes.

Coding on cash register tapes. Information on inventory and accounts receivable can be recorded as a code on cash register tape at the point of sale. Cash registers designed to record information on computer-readable tape as daily transactions are rung up can be leased for $50 a month and up, or purchased for $2,000 to $5,000. Usually on a weekly basis, the tape is removed from the machine and mailed to a data processing center. A few days later, the manager gets back a computer printout with as much detailed information as he or she needs, desires, or can afford.

Coding on adding machine tapes. Computer-readable tapes can also be used in conjunction with an adding machine instead of a cash register. The machine is similar to a regular adding machine but has a device attached that punches a paper tape as entries are made. Operation of the machine requires no special training and these are available at costs below $3,000.

The following example illustrates how a punched-tape accounting system works. The small business owner identifies all checks and deposits by assigning general account numbers and enters the cash items and necessary adjusting journal entries on the tape adding machine. Each entry includes a reference number, general ledger account number, and a dollar amount. The average tape machine operator can enter 250–300 transactions an hour—much faster than making such records by hand.

The punch tape is then mailed to a service center, where the information is transferred to punched cards used to produce the necessary records. Within a few days the service center produces and returns printed journals, a general ledger, and financial statements. Thus, the function of making journal entries, posting to a general ledger, and constructing the financial statements is accomplished efficiently with a high degree of accuracy.

Packaged programs. Computer service bureaus or data processing centers can usually provide packaged programs for both accounts receivable and inventory management. Because these ready-made programs are easily adapted to any small business, the initial conversion fee may be as low as $200. The monthly processing fee is generally based on the number of items processed and lines printed on each report.

Computer consultants. Many accountants and management consultants are familiar with computer programming techniques. These individuals can assist in setting up retail programs, but will generally refer the actual processing to a computer service bureau. Normal consulting fees for such services start at about $20 an hour.

The banker's computer. Commercial banks throughout the country own or have access to computer facilities. The ones that maintain their own equipment are usually willing to assist small business in a widening range of record-keeping functions, including the management of accounts payable and accounts receivable, as well as payroll and inventory management.

APPENDIX

Accounting systems designed for use in any retail or service firm

Most of the record-keeping systems listed below are available from local stationery stores. If a particular system is not available from your local retail store, you may contact the publisher at the address given with each entry.

Dollartrak Systems. General Business Services, Inc., 51 Monroe St., Rockville MD 20850. The Dollartrak Systems are designed for retail businesses, a professional service system, a computer system, form system, and Business Counselor system.

This company does not sell directly to the public, but through Business Counselors, who operate under a franchise arrangement with the parent company. The systems are designed to provide a simple and easily maintained set of accounts for use in preparing initial records, information for profit and loss statements, all forms of tax liability records that are needed, and other data.

The company guarantees that the data prepared and later submitted to any taxing authorities will be accurate and acceptable. If not, the resulting penalty or interest will be the responsibility of General Business Services.

This firm also provides several different types of pegboard, one-write bookkeeping systems.

Greenwood's Approval Business and Income Tax Record. The Greenwood Company, 411 S. Sangamon St., Chicago IL 60607. System No. 212 provides the records for a complete bookkeeping system, which includes the daily entry forms as well as the various summary forms and statements needed for the preparation of tax returns, final year-end statements, etc.

A number of other special packages are available for perpetual stock records, sales tax records, real estate firms, garage and gas stations, restaurants and cafes, and records for truckers.

McBee Folding Bookeeper. McBee Systems, Route 50 East, Athens OH 45701. This bookkeeping system is a complete one-write system that completes all the records needed for a transaction through the use of carbon copies. It is available in versions adaptable to a variety of retail businesses, professional offices, laboratories, etc. A typical system handles payroll, disbursements, receivables, payables, and receipts. The company provides the form packages that are applicable to a given type of firm.

Kolor-Key. Moore Business Forms, Inc., P.O. Box 5252, Eastman Station, Oakland CA 94605. The Kolor-Key system provides the forms necessary to handle the records needed in buying, receiving, stockkeeping, production, selling, delivery, billing, collecting, and disbursing. It is a very versatile system and can be adapted to almost any small business activity.

The system is available through the Moore business representatives throughout the United States and Canada.

Ideal Business Accounting Systems. Symo Visual Systems, Inc., P.O. Box 1568, Augusta GA 30903. The Ideal systems have been marketed in the United States for several years and will probably be available in Canada before long. There are 20 specialty systems, designed for the following businesses:

1. Apartments, motels, and hotels
2. Attorneys
3. Beauty and barber shops
4. Beer, wine and liquor stores
5. Service businesses
6. Contractors
7. Doctors and dentists
8. Farms and ranches

9.	Garages and service stations	15.	Professional services
10.	Cash basis businesses	16.	Real estate
11.	Grocers	17.	Restaurants and cafes
12.	Insurance agents	18.	Service stations
13.	Manufacturers	19.	Taverns and cafes
14.	Merchants	20.	Jewelers and watchmakers

In addition to the above listing the company provides special record systems for activities such as inventory management and equipment control. The forms provided make it possible to record all the transactions involved in proper business operation. Other forms maintain the records needed for tax obligations.

Dome Simplified Monthly Bookkeeping Record #612; Dome Simplified Weekly Bookkeeping Record #600.   Dome Publishing Co., Dome Building, Providence, RI 02903. Available in stationery stores and chain stores. Contains the following forms sufficient for recording the results of one year's business: monthly record of income and expenses; annual summary sheet of income and expenditures; weekly payroll records covering 15 employees; individual employee compensation records. Also contains general instructions, specimen filled-in monthly record of income and expenses, and a list of 276 expenses that are legal deductions for federal income tax purposes. This record was designed by a CPA and fits every type and kind of business.

Other packaged accounting systems

Numerous other accounting systems are available for use in specific retail and service trades. A listing of these appears in Small Business Bibliography No. 15, which may be obtained from the Superintendent of Documents, U.S. Government Printing Office, Washington, D.C.

In addition to the systems listed, some trade associations, manufacturers, and wholesalers offer specially designed record-keeping systems to their dealer customers. These systems are prepared to meet the general record-keeping needs of a large variety of retail and service trade establishments. On the other hand, the owner of a small business may find it advantageous to have a system adapted to his or her special requirements by a trained public accountant.

The installation of accounting systems and the preparation of tax returns is a service commonly rendered by public accountants. These professional men are listed under appropriate headings in the yellow pages of any local telephone directory. For complete listings, you may request membership rosters from the American Institute of Certified Public Accountants, 666 Fifth Ave., New York, N.Y. 10019, and the National Society of Public Accountants, 1717 Pennsylvania Ave., N.W., Washington, D.C. 20006.

Public accountants also render many accounting services, such as auditing, preparation of reports for government agencies, tax planning, analysis of financial reports, and a variety of specialized management advisory services.

Many of the Small Business Administration's management publications discuss the necessity for keeping adequate records and the services available from public accountants. Most of these publications are slanted toward a certain phase of business operation or a specific kind of small business. Examples are:

1. *A Handbook of Small Business Finance,* Small Business Management Series No. 15.
2. *Financial Recordkeeping for Small Stores,* Small Business Management Series No. 32.

These two booklets may be ordered from the Superintendent of Documents, U.S. Government Printing Office, Washington, D.C. 20402.

QUESTIONS

1. What are the three basic objectives of a workable system of accounting and financial controls?

2. Define the terms *asset, liability,* and *capital,* and identify the *accounting equation.*

3. Discuss the financial records that serve as a basis for any good accounting system.

4. Differentiate between the balance sheet and the income statement.

5. On the income statement, what is the difference between gross profit and operating profit?

6. What types of information are entered in the sales and cash receipts journal?

7. Discuss three situations in which some particular special type of accounting record may be useful and necessary.

8. What suggestions would you have for the small business person that would protect against errors in the accounting records and safeguard the assets of the business?

9. Discuss the uses of electronic data processing in performing the accounting function.

10. How can integrated data processing be used by a small business without heavy investment in physical facilities?

PROBLEMS

1. Contact a public accounting firm in the community, and discuss the services it provides to small business persons as well as the fees for such services.

2. Obtain a copy of one of the many bookkeeping systems that have been prepared for small businesses, and analyze it in terms of its advantages and disadvantages.

3. Interview a number of the more successful small business persons in the community regarding the use of integrated data processing, and prepare a report on its feasibility and acceptance.

BIBLIOGRAPHY

Pyle, William W.; John Arch White; and Kermit D. Larson. *Fundamental Accounting Principles.* 8th ed. Homewood, Ill.: Richard D. Irwin, 1978.

Thacker, Ronald J. *Accounting Principles.* Englewood Cliffs, N.J.: Prentice-Hall, 1976.

Tracy, John A. *Fundamentals of Financial Accounting.* New York: John Wiley & Sons, 1974.

_____*How to Read a Financial Report.* New York: John Wiley & Sons, 1980.

The titles of these books indicate what particular areas of accounting they deal with. The two books by John Tracy are particularly good as comparison texts for a beginning small business owner or manager.

16

Materials management and inventory control

Every business must operate with a steady input of goods or materials. If the firm is a small manufacturer, there will be the continuous flow of various types of input items such as raw materials, purchased components, and parts of all kinds. If the firm is a service organization, the quantity of parts or materials handled will be a great deal less, but some quantity of materials or supplies will be necessary to produce the services being rendered. Typically, in a hospital there would be substantial quantities of drugs, food items, and surgical dressings.

WHAT MUST BE CONTROLLED AND WHY

No business can hope to survive for very long without an effective program of controls over the parts and materials that are used in producing the final goods or services of the firm. Therefore, each and every step of the operation must include a control point that allows the manager to know the status of such things as the following:

1. Materials and goods on hand at the beginning of the business cycle. This is a starting balance or position upon which to build subsequent activities.
2. Additions and deletions that change the stock levels for reasons other than use or consumption.
3. Goods being used at each stage of the business process.
4. Goods and materials on hand within each department during stages of completion—the so-called goods in process or stock-on-hand inventory.
5. A perpetual inventory system utilizing some recorded form of running total.
6. Periodic physical inventory counts to verify the accuracy of the recorded systems information.
7. An accurate method of adjusting inconsistent data reflecting changes in inventory levels, prices and values from start to finish.
8. The condition of the inventory as to age, appropriateness for use or sale, deterioration and obsolescence—in other words, any changes not reflected in the normal recording processes.
9. A means of developing internal data that will alert the manager to the approach of a condition that will cause a problem; e.g., a stepped-up pace of usage that requires a change in lead time for the replacement order.
10. A way of establishing the costs of each phase of materials and inventory management, so that no method of control costs more than the benefit is worth.

MATERIALS MANAGEMENT

This chapter is concerned with the overall tasks that are involved in the management and control of all physical items that are used or consumed in a business firm. Thus, our concern is broader than just inventory control: it includes the total management of all items that are used and consumed by the firm. Materials management is also needed in conjunction with the output functions as shown in Figure 16–1, which illustrates the various materials activities that are involved throughout the entire organization.

It is apparent that there are many functions that are a part of materials management. Each is a specialty that contributes to the effectiveness of the total materials program. Inventory control, which will be discussed later, is a more limited group of activities primarily concerned with the handling of merchandise and materials on hand within the firm. Another distinction is that many retailing firms are primarily concerned

Figure 16–1
Operational functions relating to materials and inventory

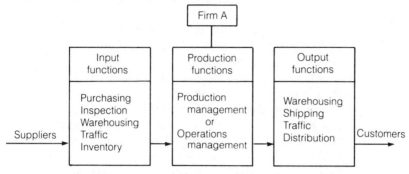

with inventory controls and do not require extensive materials management activities.

Let us now consider the nature of materials management and examine the series of functional activities that service the materials needs of a given firm.

Purchasing and buying are vital activities for any business. If the business is a manufacturer, it is likely that the purchasing department will account for more than 40 percent of the firm's total expenditures. These purchases are negotiated and contracted for as needed, so that the prices paid are the result of market factors and purchasing skills. The purchasing agent is thus very important to the firm in that the exercise of judgment can result in substantial cost savings for the firm.

If the firm buys merchandise, the person assigned such job will probably be called a buyer and will proceed to exhibit his worth to the company by acquiring good salable items for resale at the right price and on the right terms of quality, delivery, etc.

The accomplishments of a good purchasing agent or buyer are just as important to the business as any other aspect of the materials control system. Refer to Chapter 17 for additional explanation.

Inspection is often considered to be primarily related to manufacturing, and for the most part it is. In recent years, however, consumer protection laws have become more prevalent, and additional responsibilities have been placed on retailers and service organizations. As a consequence, it is important that all incoming goods or merchandise be carefully inspected to confirm that the quality is satisfactory and that the specifications of purchase have been met. A disregard for inspection is apt to commit the firm to a bad purchase that otherwise could be detected and corrected promptly. As time passes it may be difficult to get correction or a settlement from the supplier.

Warehousing is the physical storage and protection of all forms of items used in a business. These may be raw materials, parts, and merchandise as well as the supplies used to support an ongoing manufacturing or merchandising operation.

Efficient warehousing operations call for a series of logistical decisions. How do you move it? Where do you put it? How do you number it? How much does it cost to move it?

Many individuals have little concept of what it takes to do a good job of warehousing. It is just as vital to the servicing of customers as it is in providing goods for manufacture or merchandise for sale.

Traffic management is the total job of purchasing transportation for the materials or goods acquired by or shipped out by the firm. The total traffic function will include the selection of transport companies, determining the proper quantities to be shipped in carload or lesser quantities, packaging, routing, and other related matters.

Traffic management is significant because it is concerned with expenditures that are to some extent controllable. For example, truckload shipment will typically cost only 60 percent of the amount charged to transport the same weight of goods in less-than-truckload lots.

Scheduling of traffic movements to take advantage of warehouse space and the replenishment rate dictated by the production schedule reduces the total amount of warehouse space needed.

The smaller business will probably want to experiment with the services provided by different carriers if there is a choice available. Deregulation trends in the trucking and air-cargo industries have changed much of the previous pricing structure, but it is still important to determine whether the services provided by one carrier are clearly better than another.

Useful logistical comparisons can be based on differences in price of equivalent goods at various points, transportation costs, delivery time, and invoice payment schedules. In such comparisons the objective would be to determine the most attractive or least-cost combination of factors which would best service the business. A typical trade-off might involve a lower price offered by a more distant supplier offset by a slightly higher cost of inbound transportation and better and more reliable delivery direct from the manufacturer or principal wholesaler.

Shipping and distribution are primarily associated with shipments by the firm to someone else. Such shipments to customers require the right inventory variety and levels and the ability to make direct shipments or replacement stock shipments to warehousing locations from which further shipments are made to ultimate customers.

The ability to provide proper service to the customers starts at the plant, where the whole production process is made possible by the right materials at the right time at the right place.

Customers can be very demanding, and much of what the shipping and distribution personnel will be able to do depends on effective materials management. Competition also requires that the business provide more options for customers, increasing the complexity of the materials management functions.

Variations in shipping and distribution range all the way from attempts to service all customers directly from a central production point or warehouse to the operation of one or more intermediate storage and supply points. A number of larger firms are becoming more integrated in that they own their own warehouses, trucks for over-the-road hauls, and city delivery equipment. A smaller firm should analyze its own situation and incorporate combinations of public, contract, and self-owned vehicle services. Maintaining a responsive and efficient service for customers is one area where the smaller business should be able to do at least as good a job as its larger competitors.

INVENTORY CONTROL

Inventory control should be considered a part of materials management, at least as it is being considered here. Control over inventory implies that there is in fact an inventory and that it is in possession of the firm so that it can be controlled. The main task is to develop processes and techniques that will maintain the right inventory levels and also provide physical protection until the stock is sold or liquidated. When designing and implementing an inventory control system it is important to establish certain guidelines for the controlling people. Some procedures useful in this regard include:

1. The division of inventory into price or value classes—the so-called ABC system.
2. The formulation of policies governing the practices and objectives of those who buy for the firm.
3. Decision as to whether or not the firm intends to employ an economic ordering quantity where appropriate.
4. Establishment of the degree of slack or variance in the actual inventory (as compared to the running records) that management will tolerate.
5. Assignment of the role of transport costs and services that management desires for its inventory programs.
6. Choice of whether management will be very rigid and picky regarding inventory control or amenable to reasonable deviations as being more workable.

Each of these will be discussed as a means of showing how inventory control mechanisms can vary substantially from one firm to another.

Like many other things that depend on human interpretation, control means different things to different individuals.

ABC: The vital few and the trivial many

The law of the vital few and the trivial many states that there is a maldistribution of importance of all items of inventory—that some items are vital while others are trivial. This idea originates from the philosopher Wilfredo Pareto. While this principle has been directed to many generalities, its relevance has long been recognized in respect to inventory control. Business managers in general have come to consider their inventory items to be of two different types: some inventory is of a vital nature and requires that records must be kept; while other inventory is of a trivial nature and the cost of the record-keeping is more than the cost of any pilferage, breakage, or other loss of goods.

In current practice, the principle of the vital few and the trivial many has evolved to what is frequently called ABC inventory control. Under this method, all inventory items are designated as either A, B, or C.

The *A group* will consist of a few expensive items. Perhaps 60 percent of your total inventory dollars will be tied up in only 10 percent of your physical stock. The *B group* will be the middle range, both in terms of dollar investment and physical stock. A typical relationship would be 30 percent of the dollar investment and 20 percent of the physical stock. The *C group* are the low-cost items that you keep on hand in large quantities. 70 percent of your total inventory stock may only take up 10 percent of your total dollar investment.

An uncontrolled inventory is too much inventory. The second maxim of inventory control is that any inventory that is uncontrolled is bound to be too large. Elementary as this saying may be, it is often ignored because at first glance it appears to contradict the idea behind C items in ABC inventory control. However, in actuality the deliberate lack of control is some control, and therefore even C items cannot be called uncontrolled inventory items. More important than the academic argument, however, is the principle behind this adage on uncontrolled inventories.

Not only are truly (not deliberately) uncontrolled inventories extremely expensive because they tie up money and space and cost money in insurance and taxes, they also represent a hidden danger simply because they have a built-in attraction to small business managers. That is, an uncontrolled inventory situation is a comfortable (if not desirable) position to be in and one toward which the typical small business operator will gravitate. Perhaps this principle can be more succinctly stated as "Most people are pack rats." Most people—small business operators included—have the built-in desire to store a little away for the future. Because of this they will often stock more items than they need, or order ridiculous quantities because of some appealing but unrealistic quantity discount.

The point is that when inventories are not controlled, they will practically always be too large. Salesman are always interested in taking orders, and having too much inventory is always more appealing to the small business operator than too little, even though it is expensive. Ample inventory eliminates the worry caused when new supplies don't come in on time; production can always proceed on schedule; and customers never have to wait for a finished product.

The aim of inventory control is perfection. The third adage of inventory control is that perfection in the supply of inventory items is the aim of inventory control. If a business has a perfect supply of an item, it should never run out of anything and at the same time never have anything on hand and never have to pay high prices because of buying in small quantities.

Of course, it should be obvious to anyone that such perfection—as in anything else—is, for the most part, unattainable. However, realistic appraisal of the inventory process dictates that this perfection must be a continuous goal if anything like perfection is to be attained. This statement takes the form of an adage because many people throw up their hands in despair and quit trying when they recognize the fact that perfection can never be attained. They will not even try to achieve perfection unless there is some easy, mechanical way to attain the objective. Therefore, this maxim is necessary because it gives a vote of confidence in maxim Number 1—the law of the vital few and trivial many. What it really states is that the small business (1) should try to attain perfection, but (2) if it does not attain perfection, it should not be discouraged.

One fourth of any inventory is waste. The fourth adage of inventory control is that it can be assumed that one fourth, or 25 percent, of the value of inventories is eroded by the various costs of carrying the inventory for a year. This feature of inventory control is altogether too commonly misunderstood or ignored by small business operators. In general, the problem is that inventory costs continue whether merchandise is sold or not. Usually small business persons overlook inventory costs because they do not pay them all at once. For example, they pay their taxes on inventory on one day; they pay their rent for space occupied by inventory on another day; and they seem never to recognize that the reason they are short of money and must borrow from the bank is pre-purchased, unneeded inventory. Frequently small business operators will argue that while they are cognizant of these costs, they can justify carrying a seasonal item of inventory from one year to the next because they already have the space and the item has already been purchased. They rationalize away the need to move the merchandise, saying that those costs to be incurred have already been paid. The truth, however, is that some costs have been incurred, but not all. When next year's season rolls around, those items of merchandise that are stored may be so deteriorated because of dust, sunlight, and careless handling that they will be worthless. Statistically, the business would be as well off to sell an item of merchandise at 25 percent off cost than to store the item for one year. Thus, the small business, be it a manufacturer, retailer, wholesaler, or service business, is better advised to sell off seasonal or other items that will be stocked for periods upwards of a year at cost or even 25 percent below cost rather than store the item.

Buying policies and practices

The way in which the buyers and purchasing managers conduct their activities will determine to some extent the nature of internal inventory control. If the buying program is hand-to-mouth with frequent orders, the additional work involved creates added costs and chances of mistakes. It also requires a greater amount of emergency adjustment of records to accommodate tardy orders and emergency shipments. When

buying is conducted on longer lead times, the adjustments can be made within liberal time periods as required.

Economic order quantity

The replacement or replenishment of inventory stocks will usually require placing an order with an outside supplier; the goods are bought, shipped, and received according to the needs of the company and its established inventory policies. There is, in general, an economic order quantity, which balances the *costs of acquisition* against the *costs of holding* inventory to arrive at some optimum total which combines the two at least cost.

Review the following example:

Acquisition costs	Typical cost
Requisition	$1
Purchase order.	3 to $50
Transportation	Open
Receiving and inspection	$5 and up
In-plant handling	$3 and up

Holding costs	Percentage of dollar value
Interest.	10 to 20%
Insurance	1 to 3%
Taxes	1 to 3%
Warehousing (Storage)	1 to 3%
Loss, pilferage, theft, obsolescence.	3 to 15%

The firm will usually compare the costs of acquisitions (orders) and deliveries, on one hand, with the costs of holding inventory on the other. In a year's time, which is usually the longest interval within which EOQ analysis is practical, the typical firm may place 1 to 12 orders and receive 1 to 12 deliveries. Holding costs are a composite of time, insurance costs, obsolesence and inventory losses in dollar amounts calculated against the dollar quantity of inventory held.

The common formula used is

$$EOQ = \frac{2 \times D \times C_p}{V \times C_n}$$

where

EOQ = Economic order quantity, the order size that minimizes total costs of acquisition and holding;

D = Expected usage per time period;

C_p = Cost to place an order;

V = Value of the item;

C_n = Holding cost as a percentage of the value per time period.

The formula utilizes the minimum number of conditions that will give the answer that is desired.[1] Additional factors, such as variations in prices due to discounts and volume transportation costs, require modification of the formula. It is sufficient for our purposes to understand that the two classes of costs can be offset to achieve an optimum of combined *order frequency* and *quantity* that is most advantageous.

Perpetual inventory versus actual inventory

The running record kept on paper or perhaps stored in a computer memory is commonly known as the perpetual inventory record. It is the running total that is adjusted by each successive addition or deletion from the total, *as an adjusted calculated record only*. Without a periodic physical review of the actual inventory item in question, there is no way to know how accurate the calculated record will be. Needless to say, enlightened inventory managers have created an endless series of controls and schemes, along with statistical analyses to determine the relative accuracy of the record. Such techniques are helpful, but they cannot substitute for the ultimate physical count and confirmation.

The important question arising from this dilemma is the attitude of managment about the inaccuracy of the stated records. High accuracy will involve constant control and high costs. If high accuracy is not needed, then little control requires little expense.

A small business owner should assess the risks involved, the costs of correction, and the gains achieved, according to the needs of the business. Unfortunately, the decision is often made by one person without regard for the economics of the situation.

Transportation

Transportation was discussed previously in connection with materials management. Its importance regarding inventory control depends on the strategy employed by the business to maintain the proper quantities of goods in inventory. Typical trade-offs arise between regular shipments, with supplemental premium transportation (air freight and United Parcel Service), or a higher continuous level that requires no supplemental shipments.

Small business managers frequently are not well informed about the costs associated either directly or indirectly with transportation. It is an area that should be examined carefully for several reasons.

Deregulation of the trucking industry, which is occurring, as of 1980 in the United States, is creating a change in the transportation pricing

---

[1] F. G. Moore and T. Hendrick, *Production/Operations Managment* (Homewood, Ill.: Richard D. Irwin, 1981).

and shipping options for all of business. Particular opportunities should be investigated. Lease and rental of transport equipment should be investigated for possible usage. Consolidated or pooled shipments can also be arranged often at more frequent intervals and in lower quantities than direct shipments by a single firm.

Management attitude about inventory control

As a final item in this listing, it is necessary to look boldly at what the small business owner really wants from an inventory control system. This is a much broader question than the question of physical inventory count versus the perpetual inventory records dealt with previously. That condition will always exist and can be handled separately and directly. *Management attitude is considerably different.* It is reflected in the decisions of management as to whether to inspect incoming goods at all—many do not. Some managers write off overstocks or obsolescence without much resistance, as long as the condition is not extreme. Others will tolerate very little without some direct action. Some employers tolerate some theft by employees; others do not.

The control measures for a small business must reflect such variances and be set and adjusted to the style and objectives of the owner or manager.

INVENTORY CONTROL SYSTEMS

It is not necessary to outline in detail any particular kinds of inventory control systems. These are generally of the following types:

a. Hand-copied records—Tallies, prices, etc.
b. Machine records and summaries—Cash register tapes, sales tickets, bin tags, etc.
c. Visual displays—Display tube, printouts from a computer run, summary paper copies, microfilm, etc.
d. Stored data—In some form of machine storage available for retrieval.

Items a and b are old traditional ways that are still useful and valid for the smaller firm. If the small business manager does not want to be bothered with much record keeping, these systems can be very simple. Items in c and d are somewhat more costly but not to the extent that they should not be considered.

Technology has moved so rapidly that the 1980s are providing computer record keeping and analysis capability at a fraction of the costs common in 1975.

INVENTORY CONTROL IN YOUR KIND OF BUSINESS

Basically, the methods of inventory control are the same in all businesses. However, the needs of the various types of business dictate differences in the techniques of inventory control methods. Therefore, the following is designed to highlight some of the basic differences in techniques used in retailing, service, manufacturing, and wholesaling operations.

Retailing

It can safely be said that the key to inventory control for the small retailer is to keep inventory well balanced at all times. The first requirement for keeping a well-balanced inventory is that the retailer stock only the proper sizes, colors, styles, and price lines. The second requirement is that all high-turnover items never be out of stock; and thirdly, stock turnover should be as rapid as possible. Therefore, the typical retailer must deal with a myriad of facts and figures. For example, it is not sufficient to have sports jackets that are in high demand if they are all of the wrong size or wrong color; rather, there must be sufficient numbers of the popular sports jackets in the commonly demanded sizes and colors.

In order to be able to meet all specifications in the myriad of items (which sometimes will run up to 15,000 or 20,000) carried by the typical retail store, the retailer must be able to accurately predict needs in high-demand items from the standpoint of size, shape, color, and texture and stock this merchandise accordingly. Therefore, the retailer's inventory problem basically centers on the ability to keep accurate records of what is sold. For this reason, there are a variety of techniques that are designed to eliminate the guesswork and memory element of inventory control for the retailer. These techniques of inventory control include: (1) personal observation, (2) physical counts, (3) the on hand–on order–sold record, and (4) the perpetual inventory.

Each of the above methods of inventory control used by small retailers can be very effective in the proper circumstance and thus merits some elaboration.

1. Personal observation. As the name implies, personal observation is the personal inspection of inventory by the retailer. The manager inspects stock to see what is moving slowly, what is moving fast, what he or she is out of, and what is on order. Obviously, this technique is not very scientific nor accurate unless pencil and paper are used, which limits it to a small store with a small variety of merchandise. Of course, if the small retail store has a relatively constant rate of sales and the owner or manager is always on the premises, the accuracy of the technique will be increased. However, the personal observation technique is not recommended for the usual retail establishment.

2. Physical check.   The second basic technique used by retailers to control inventory is the physical check. Similar to the personal observation technique, the physical check consists of a personal investigation by the small business manager as to the varieties of merchandise on hand. However, in the physical check technique, a deliberate count is made of all items of merchandise on hand and on order instead of simply observing the inventory situation. Technically, a physical count is conducted by two people going from item to item (usually over a weekend or some other time when the store is not open for business) with one person calling off the name of the item, the number of items on hand, and the value of the item while another person records this information. The use of two people working in tandem ensures greater accuracy, honesty, and completeness under this technique.

Of course when a physical count is made by the small business manager and an assistant, they are apprised in one formal report of the precise conditions, status, and value of all the inventory on hand. By comparing one physical audit with the preceding audit and the amounts of merchandise ordered during the period, a precise profile of what merchandise is selling and what is not can be developed.

3. On hand–on order–sold record.   The third technique commonly used by retailers in inventory control is what is commonly called the on hand–on order–sold record. This record is a device that, although time-consuming to keep, is extremely helpful to the retailer in determining what sizes, colors, and styles are being purchased. Figure 16–2 illustrates how the on hand–on order–sold record shows precisely and instantaneously the amount, size, color, and style of merchandise on hand, on order, and recently sold

Obviously this type of record is very flexible and adaptable to all types of goods handled. However, such records rapidly become bulky and hard to maintain. Therefore, unless keeping such a record is imperative, careful consideration should be given to the relative merits and demerits of other techniques before any retailer decides to use it.

4. Perpetual inventories.   Perpetual inventories are very similar to the on hand–on order–sold record. However, in the perpetual inventory, records are kept of each item of merchandise as it is brought into the store, stocked, and sold. Obviously, it is hard to justify the time and expense in keeping perpetual inventories, and they rapidly lose their enchantment to the harried business manager. Thus, usually the perpetual inventory technique is limited to only very costly and important lines of goods that warrant very strict control. "A" items of inventory are of this nature. The advantages of the perpetual inventory method

Figure 16–2
On hand–on order–sold record

ITEM: ALP SHOES Name of supplier: Jones, Inc. Street address: 1419 Pine City and state: Uptown								ON HAND–ON ORDER–SOLD RECORD
	Size	2–13 On hand	Rec'd 2–16 On order	Sold	2–27 On hand	Rec'd 3–4 On order	Sold	3–13 On hand
White Arctic	8	3	5	2	6	0	2	4
	8½	1	4	2	3	1	2	2
	9	6	0	2	4	0	1	3
	9½	2	1	0	3	0	1	2
Brown Arctic	8	4	6	3	7	0	3	4
	8½	2	4	2	4	1	3	2
	9	5	1	2	4	1	1	4

Explanation: On hand—goods on hand on that date; On order—goods on order; Rec'd—date merchandise on order received; Sold—inventory on hand on first date, plus goods on order that were received, minus number on hand on next date.

are that the retailer knows at all times the amount of goods that he or she has on hand and their dollar value, as well as the style, size, shape, color, and texture.

Service industries

The nature of service industries permits small business operators engaged in providing services to maintain much more accurate records of inventory while at the same time spending much less time at record-keeping. This is because the service industry usually must keep records only of materials and supplies purchased that are expended by way of providing the service. Therefore, a TV repairer need only account for parts purchased for repairing TV sets, while a seamer needs to account only for materials purchased for sewing, and the woodworker need account only for parts used in manufacturing the products. The service person's job is simplified by the fact that practically all the parts bought will be of common, ordinary bulk sizes and quantities and can be easily recorded simply by costing out items used on a job once the job is finished.

Therefore, because of the nature of the service industry, the only record-keeping necessary is general control over inventory received for stock, and accurate records showing when stock items are drawn for use in providing the service. Thus, it should be obvious that in the service industry, ample record-keeping involves use of the principle of ABC inventory control, supplemented by job costing of parts. Thus, most items purchased for stock can be rated as either A, B, or C items and reordered accordingly, while as the various jobs occur, items used can be simply noted on an attached job ticket. In this way inventory items are reordered as needed, while particular customers are billed for items used in servicing their apparatus. (See Figure 16–3 for a sample job ticket.)

Manufacturing industry

Manufacturing concerns face problems unlike retail and service industries. Manufacturers transform raw materials and parts into finished products; retail, wholesale, and, for the most part, service industries simply act as middlemen. Therefore, the manufacturing manager is concerned with four inventory problems: (1) ample raw materials and supplies to keep the manufacturing process going; (2) the control of work in process in an effort to eliminate theft, pilferage, and deterioration; (3) the control of finished goods until they are shipped to retailers, wholesalers, or service establishments; and (4) the purchase of new and up-to-date raw materials.

Since an outage of an important production part could make it necessary for a manufacturer to shut down operations, it is essential that the manufacturer either engage in some kind of perpetual inventory control or some basic reorder-point strategem that signals (a) the need to reorder stock and (b) the fact that if more is not reordered an outage can

Figure 16–3
Job ticket

Customer Name: <u>Sam Jones</u> Order No. 00630				
Address: <u>496 Grape</u>				
City, state: <u>Uptown</u> Zip Code: _____				
Nature of repair: <u>TV is blurry</u>				
Quantity	*Article*		*Price*	
1	X3294		4.50	
1	X3295		2.19	
1	ZG solenoid		.15	
	Labor		21.00	
	Subtotal		29.84	
	Tax		1.40	
	Total		29.24	

occur. Maintaining a perpetual inventory has already been discussed and therefore does not need further elaboration here. However, the use of reorder points does need more explanation because it is the device commonly used by manufacturing enterprises, and it is probably the safest, least expensive, and least time-consuming technique to use.

Using this technique is not at all difficult for the small business manager once he/she has an understanding of the principle behind reorder points. This can most easily be shown graphically as illustrated in Figure 16–4.

In the diagram of reorder-point inventory control in Figure 16–4, it can be seen that the quantity of stock on hand is plotted along the vertical axis and a curve is drawn to represent the increase and decrease in materials on hand as stock is used and replenished. It will be noted that as time progresses, the material-on-hand curve goes down, indicating the gradual use of this raw material in the manufacturing process. If no additional goods are reordered, ultimately the material on hand will be depleted to zero. However, the material-on-hand curve takes on a sawtooth appearance because when new stock that has been ordered is received, the material-on-hand curve will instantly jump up, displaying the increase in stock on hand. Thus, the height of the sawtooth will represent the quantity reordered. The reorder point occurs when the manufacturing manager knows that if material is not reordered the business will likely run out because of the time that will elapse between the placement of the order and the receipt of the material.

Figure 16–4
Diagram of reorder point inventory control

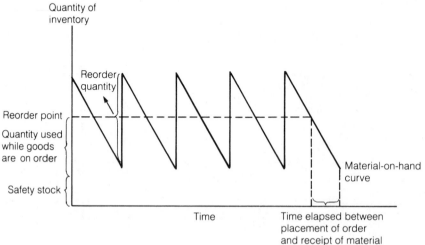

Ideally, of course, the reorder point should be a quantity at which the manufacturer is just running out of material on hand as the new order is received. Practically speaking, however, this is impossible because of delays that can occur in placing an order or transporting the materiel from the supplier. Therefore most manufacturers also include a buffer, cushion, or safety stock, which they always retain on hand just in case their reorder-point calculations or delivery-time calculations are off. Therefore, this safety stock is not considered in planning when to reorder a particular raw material; rather it is just assumed that this material is always on hand as a safety supply to prevent a production-crippling outage from occurring.

In using the reorder-point inventory control device, the small business manager should (1) calculate how long it takes to order raw materials and have them delivered, (2) calculate how much material will be used during this time, (3) add in a safety-stock factor, and thus (4) determine the minimum quantity of inventory that the company can have on hand before that particular merchandise must be reordered.

The quantity of merchandise that the manufacturer reorders when the reorder point is reached, of course, must be sufficient to restore the stock to the reorder-point level. However, most managers find it expedient to reorder amounts greater than are needed to restore stock to the reorder point, because otherwise they would be perpetually reordering as soon as raw materials are received.

Basically, the *economic lot* concept states that the amount of material reordered is that quantity that gives the manufacturer the lowest cost per unit for that merchandise. That is, the economic lot concept recognizes the following facts: (1) processing frequent orders costs money, (2) carrying excessive inventory is also expensive, and (3) buying in large quantities enables the manufacturer to purchase raw materials at some quantity discount.

Wholesaling industry

The wholesale industry inventory control problem is not altogether different from those of the retailing and service industries. Fundamentally, the difference is that, typically, wholesalers buy in larger lots and carry larger inventories than do retail and service industries. In fact, it is not uncommon for some wholesalers to carry half or more of their total assets as investments in inventory. Because such a large percentage of the wholesaler's operating capital is tied up in inventory, it might be said that although the wholesaler's inventory problem differs little from those of retail or service establishments, it is more critical toward the success or failure of the business. Any mistake made in inventory handling will represent a much more serious problem. Therefore, accurate records are imperative for the wholesaler. The techniques are the same as those used by the retail and service industries; the emphasis is merely greater.

It is heartening to note that most small wholesalers are becoming increasingly aware of this phenomenon and are attempting to avoid the problem. There appears to be a widespread acceptance among wholesalers today of the principle of low gross margin and high turnover as a way of operation. To remain in business the wholesaler must be able to compete with low-margin competitors, and it merely stands to reason that the only way to make a satisfactory profit from low-margin items is by selling in high volume.

Rather than pursue this particular subject further, we suggest that the reader contact an office and/or business systems firm for additional details. Many excellent systems are available or can be designed for a particular customer. Money spent for them may prove to be a very sound investment because in the final analysis inventory control is just that—control. It does not generate business nor produce the product, it only keeps records that require action.

No manager should spend more time with it than necessary. The important point, however, is *that every manager must know the status of the business and that can only be gained by reviewing and digesting the records that are developed.* Producing the records means nothing, but what they show and the action taken is what really is important.

QUESTIONS

1. What are the objectives of inventory control? Explain why each of these is important to the small business operator.

2. What is the law of the vital few and the trivial many? Of what use is this law to anyone concerned with inventory control?

3. Can you support the statement: "An uncontrolled inventory is too much inventory"? How is it possible to have too much inventory?

4. Why is the traffic function so important in today's inventory control systems?

5. What is the purpose of the economic order quantity as applied to inventories?

6. What are the particular shortcomings of a perpetual inventory record system?

7. What is the special inventory problem of the typical retailer? Why is it generally unique to retailing? Explain in detail.

8. How does the inventory problem of a service industry differ from that of retailing? Of wholesaling? Of manufacturing?

9. What is safety stock? Is the safety stock concept relevant to the economic lot concept? How? Explain in detail.

10. Explain the concept of the economic lot.

PROBLEM

Jack "Spider" Webb, in his day, was one of the best downhill racers in the country. Many a cup he had won—he even had had the privilege of having one of the major ski manufacturers name one of its better lines of skis after him.

Unfortunately, Spider wasn't quite as good a businessman as he was a skier. When he finally broke his leg in a freak accident (he slipped and fell in his living room testing the release tension on a ski binding he was planning to test for the manufacturer the next day) he had to quit skiing. That was when he decided to take his winnings from his career on the pro circuit and open his own ski shop at one of Colorado's newest and best areas.

It seemed that all was a disaster for Spider. He had sunk all his money, plus all he could borrow from family and friends, into a loser. Spider's bookkeeping service had just informed him that he had lost another $3,000 last month (October) during a time when sales should have easily caused a monthly profit, if not offsetting some of the earlier month losses (May, June, July, August, and September), which are normal in the off-season. His bookkeeper told him that his losses were due to inventory shrinkage, whatever that meant.

a. What might Spider's bookkeeping service have meant by inventory shrinkage?

b. What might be the cause of Spider's inventory shrinkage? List at least five logical causes.

c. What might Spider do about the five causes enumerated in answer to the second question to eliminate future shrinkage? Explain in detail.

BIBLIOGRAPHY

Baty, Gordon B. *Entrepreneurship; Playing to Win.* Reston, Va.: Reston Publishing, 1974. An excellent book that relates to complex business operations.

Moore, Franklin G., and Thomas Hendrick. *Production/Operations Management.* 8th ed. Homewood, Ill.: Richard D. Irwin, 1980. An excellent book on all phases of production and manufacturing activity, including the problems relating to inventory.

Tracy, John A. *How to Read a Financial Report.* New York: John Wiley & Sons, 1980. Required reading to understand the importance of inventories and their relationship to cash flow.

17

Pricing of products and services

Pricing is one of the principal factors that management uses to ensure an adequate return for productive effort. All products and services must be offered for sale at prices that reflect a wide assortment of circumstances affecting both buyers and sellers. Every transaction between buyer and seller involves a price—a price, it is hoped, that will amply reward the seller for his contribution.

THE FRAMEWORK OF PRICES

No system of establishing a single price or an entire line of prices can be set up in a vacuum. A series of reference points, comparisons, and judgments must be considered together to provide some idea of the right initial price for the particular product or service being offered. If no sales are made at the initial price, it can be argued that the price was right, but nobody understood the correctness of the price. But a better approach has to be that a price is set in order to sell something. The inherent fairness or validity of a price is really not a very useful criterion.

The product or service offered. Many products or services are capable of providing very similar end results to the customer. Other items may be highly unique and capable of yielding specialized results. The basic nature of a product or service furnishes the opportunity to achieve prices that will vary under different circumstances. Changes can deliberately be incorporated that differentiate products, often at very little additional cost. Services can include a wide variation in accommodation. In fact, personal services provided by the small business should be superior if accomplished by knowledgeable and capable people. The combination of administrative backing and personal service by the owner at the point of final sale is the real strength of the franchise system.

As differences in products or services become more evident, larger adjustments of prices become possible. Trade-off analysis will show where differentiation can be used and whether it is justified.

Environment of sale. The environment in which a sale takes place has a very definite effect on what price can be charged. The right environment should permit the seller to sell at a higher price than under less favorable conditions. Travelers will often pay prices in specialty shops that they would never pay at home. In recent years, restaurants featuring an unusual decorative theme or locale have become very popular even though they charge higher prices for the food and service offered.

If the right environment does not exist initially the entrepreneurs should provide it. Color schemes, art work, a particular motif, or background music may all be inexpensive environmental features that can justify higher prices.

Reputation. The reputation of the company may be exploited in the prices that it charges. Reputations have been based on customers' collective opinions that prices were right, about right, or not right. A study conducted by one of the authors revealed that customers in general felt that the prices of retail merchants in their particular community were too high. Customers of the same merchants from two neighboring communities thought that in general the prices were low. A reputation that provides the opportunity to adjust prices in favor of the firm should be turned to account at every opportunity.

Competition. The efforts of competitors and competitive products will set the prices of many products and services. Inflation of the 1970s has made buyers much more price-conscious than they have been for many years. Certain industries and particular kinds of business have become much more competitive. Some of them have engaged in confrontations, naming each other in TV commercials and making head-on very direct comparisons of their products; other sellers have tended to be much more subtle and indirect.

Most small businesses are competitive to a degree, but try to avoid competition with larger firms in price and selection alone. The effects of competition can be diluted or side-tracked by changing the total sale package in one or more ways to avoid the impression of offering something interchangeable with the competitors' wares. Services and accommodation are two things that small businesses can provide effectively and they should be promoted. The total package is what counts in the ultimate sale.

Value.   A particular product or service always has something that determines its value to those who own it and those who want it. The important thing about value is that there may be an overall value which is created by a composite of sellers and buyers and which is recognized by a particular individual at some point in time. Value is reflected in price: the going market price for a product or service and the price which a given individual is willing to pay. The seller must be willing to accept that price.

The smaller business is uniquely equipped to utilize value in connection with pricing. By modifying the product or service (often at little cost) to suit the wishes of the customer its value for that customer can be increased. Often the product or basic service does not have to be changed; other things can be done that add value to the regular transaction.

The conditions under which the sale is made also affect value. The idea that the customer is always right is not to be ignored or ridiculed. The purchaser spending money is entitled to expect or demand something for it. Here, again, is an area where the smaller business can profit from smallness. Decisions can be made on the spot to accommodate particular situations. The big company attempts to reduce action to a prescribed checklist; this format is often inappropriate and frustrating to the customer, but the resourceful smaller business can easily improve on it.

Timing.   Timing is another factor that favors the small business in its pricing structure. Many products and services go through life cycles, as well as seasonal variations in demand and periods of over-supply or shortages. Considerable study is needed to find out what timing factors are important as to price; if the effects of competition are subtle it is difficult to assess correctly the effect of timing. On the other hand, the price of a recreational motel unit or service feature may be adjusted to fit a single situation by the small entrepreneur, whose hands are not tied by inflexible company policy.

The nature of timing is very significant in certain well-defined types of business. Convenience food stores and plumbers who will make calls on weekends are two examples of unconventional hours that provide business, but also permit upward adjustment of prices.

Price timing is also closely related to the action of competitors.

Smaller businesses may choose to be leaders or followers in setting prices that vary over an extended time period. Newspaper advertising often reveals the similarity of price timing that occurs when competitors are aware of each other's actions.

PRICING RELATED TO COSTS

Pricing and the volume of sales are two important factors in developing cash flow for the business. Cash inflow must exceed cash outflow in order for the business to profit. Every owner and/or manager of a business must know and understand in detail the factors that influence costs and how these can be adjusted to reflect differences in demand and salability at differing prices. Costs of producing a product or service, in most cases, do not by themselves determine the selling price. They must, however, be taken into account; otherwise the business has no chance of establishing prices that will result in profitable sales.

Buying costs. Proper product selection and effective buying are absolute musts for a retail business firm. Service firms may not put much reliance on products, but their managers should think in terms of the talents that they are offering. Have they hired suitable employees and provided them with proper technical training?

The trade-offs in buying merchandise or purchasing materials are generally related to quantity. In either case, ordering larger quantities results in lower unit costs. The difficulty is in balancing the savings of additional purchases with the anticipated sales levels that follow.

Misinformation and poor forecasting may impair decisions regarding buying expenditures or the quantities to buy. Most small businesses should adopt a conservative position on cost-volume trade-offs until substantial experience is gained in what may happen.

Selling costs. Costs associated with selling constitute a sizable portion of the ultimate price. These costs are usually those of the physical facilities for selling, direct sales expense, advertising and promotion, along with credit, delivery, and other personal services for the customer.

As a product or a service involves more and more middlemen, the selling costs rise. The final seller may reduce ultimate costs by consolidating or eliminating middleman functions.

Each of the costs of selling should be studied to determine whether it has added real value, can best be provided by the established businesses, and how it affects the present cost and yield structure.

Preparation and conversion costs. Before something can be sold it must be prepared for sale. Transportation, warehousing, financing, and inspection are all a part of this process. The costs of these activities taken together are apt to constitute a considerable percentage of the price at which a profitable sale can be made. No good method is ordinarily available to a small busines that can keep such costs as low as those paid for corresponding activities by a larger-scale operation. Constant effort and surveillance are required to make selling costs consistent with the quality of products or services offered.

Overhead costs. Overhead costs are separate from buying, conversion, and selling costs; they usually are not directly associated with the product or service but are a necessary part of getting the job done. They cover items such as light, heat, and water. Accountants will distinguish overhead as being separate from direct labor and material in a manufacturing concern, or as being distinct from sales costs in a merchandising concern.

Overhead will vary substantially from one small business to another and from one business operator to the next. This is one category of costs where the small business person may have substantial advantages over larger businesses. He/she may be able to hold down the overhead and spread it very efficiently throughout the operation. On the other hand, business volume may not be steady enough for the small business person to predict the costs of overhead consistent with the needs of the business.

Discounts. Costs of salable items bought at wholesale are subject to discounts, which take two common forms: (1) trade discounts and (2) cash discounts.

Trade discounts are deducted by the manufacturer from established list prices and allow middlemen (the initial buyers) to make a profit as they move the merchandise on to the final customer. Trade discounts increase if the volume purchased is increased or if the buyer can exert some other form of bargaining power. Lower prices for volume buyers *if justified by lower costs to the seller* are not a violation of the Robinson-Patman Act. However, lower differential prices set without regard to volume or cost-price relationships are unlawful. *Negotiation to establish a price permits considerable freedom to both buyer and seller.*

Cash discounts are provided on the manufacturer's invoice and given to the merchandiser as a reward for payment within a stated period. They are an inducement to the buyer to pay bills promptly and thus improve the cash flow position of the seller. Ordinarily cash discounts are not confusing except when they are in some way substituted for or made a part of trade discounts. The discount offered to consumers should not be construed as either a trade or cash discount.

The entrepreneur must understand the various discount structures, know how to obtain the maximum discount on any given purchase, and take advantage of the effect such discounts should have on selling prices.

COSTING-OUT FOR PRICING

When the various costs have been analyzed; the firm can adopt the most appropriate methods to establish the prices on its end products or services.

Markups

Adding a percent of the total costs related to the thing being sold is markup. For services this may work well, but for products it may be difficult or awkward because of competitor's prices or a complex mix of products being sold. A percent of cost or selling price can be used and has the advantage of maintaining some consistency based on costs. It is also defensible in relationship to the costs of doing business.

As volume increases, along with lower costs, markups may be decreased. The great weakness in the markup system is that it is based on predicted costs and sales volumes. Varying levels of activity dictate different prices—a situation that customers may not appreciate and be willing to live with.

Average costs

Fixed and variable costs can be computed at various levels of sales or output, and prices then set at a level related to the average cost. If sales levels approximate predicted amounts or increase, the method is a good one for maintaining an advantageous price structure. If sales are very unpredictable, then this method is not too good. It also poses problems when the pricing levels need to be changed for one reason or another—particularly when the changes are based on different volume levels.

Return on investment—time or money

Another method of establishing a pricing structure is to relate to the investment that is made. For a service business where personal time and effort are the measurement of what is being sold, the pricing can be based on the amount of time involved. All the peripheral costs will be assumed to be a direct function of the charges being made by the individual. This is standard practice for auto repairs, service charges for plumbers, and most professional services. This method is simple, direct, and easy to maintain. Some adjustment may be necessary to camouflage hourly rates, if customer resistance develops. Low-cost extra services may be included to lessen the impact of a higher per-hour or task charge.

Return on capital investment should always be a criterion for computing prices. Dun & Bradstreet or other data sources can be consulted to find out what rate of return is being developed by businesses in various industry classifications and also how those rates vary with the volume of business (sales) being generated.

Smaller business managers and owners often do a very poor job of setting prices that will produce a fair return on their investment. Some individuals fail even to recognize the going value of time or money. It is one thing to make a temporary sacrifice to develop a later advantage, but quite another to be ignorant of what return is justified on a given investment.

Break-even analysis

Figure 17–1, illustrates how the break-even technique can be used to analyze various alternatives. It may be used for the analysis of production output or the sale of merchandise by a retail firm. In fact, any form of activity for which costs of production and selling prices can be determined can make use of break-even analysis. If costs and prices change at various levels of activity, some of the decisions become a little more difficult.

The entrepreneur or manager should develop experience in using break-even analysis and be able to compute rather quickly the changes in break-even point (BEP) that occur when costs and prices change. Persons approached for support for a business, such as financiers or bankers, will require break-even analysis figures along with information

Figure 17–1
Break-even chart (units or dollar value of units)

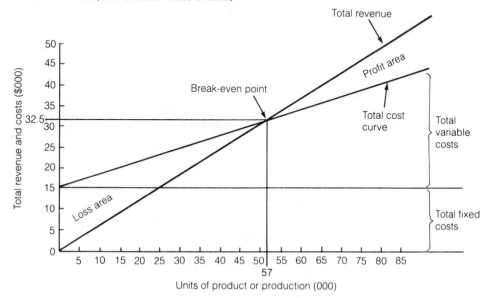

Units of product or production (000)

on budgets and return on investment. Facility in using this technique will be a persuasive factor in gaining support for the business.

The two basic formulas used are:

$$Units \text{ BEP} = \frac{\text{Total fixed costs}}{\text{Fixed cost contribution per unit}}$$

$$Dollars \text{ BEP} = \frac{\text{Total fixed cost}}{1 - \left(\dfrac{\text{Variable cost/unit}}{\text{Selling price/unit}} \right)}$$

Additional formula information is given at the end of this chapter.

Marginal costing

The question that leads to the idea behind marginal costing as a means of setting prices is what is the cost of producing one more unit of product or service? It is particularly useful in analyzing services such as transportation, where additional cargo beyond a minimum or average can be handled at virtually no additional expense. In manufacturing, quantities beyond a certain point can be produced at an attractive (that is, small) additional cost.

This method of analysis is useful if the business can divide its productive results, either products or services, in such a way that additional small increments can be produced and perhaps priced so as to develop sales that would otherwise be lost. Working with quantities and costs set up in a table or on a graph, the marginal costs at various operational levels can be determined.

This section attempts to give some ideas that are useful in relating the costs of a business to its pricing program, while disregarding or minimizing outside influences. It is very seldom that the outside forces are not a part of any inquiry, but costing-out must be done first to really know what figures are valid prior to moving to the other features to be considered. Review of a good basic marketing or accounting textbook will provide more detailed information about the costing-pricing relationships.

PRICE SENSITIVITY

The small business person must understand that every individual has sensitivities; and in the case of customers, many of them have the same sensitivities. *Price sensitivity* means that a small increase in the price of an item may cause a large decrease in its sales. The operator of a business will do well to determine which pricing areas are most sensitive to customers, and what can be done to minimize this feeling and its effect on business.

The average person is being offered many more products and services every year than were previously available. As an example, at the time of the advent of the supermarket, a store might have stocked no more than 3,500 items, whereas today large markets offer nearly 12,000 items. In other product and service lines similar growth is taking place. The question then is, What knowledge do customers have of the products themselves, and to which products are they particularly price-sensitive? A number of grocery items will be sensitive, but not a sizable number. Some grocery marketers have stated that the sensitive items number no more than 50, although these may be different from one locality to another; all that is necessary to be competitive is for grocery marketers to remain competitive in these 50 items, along with an otherwise efficient operation.

It is important to investigate any particular business and determine what customers know about the products, what type of a pricing pattern they expect, and what products are available from competitors with established prices. Knowing this, the business person is faced with the problem of either meeting competitors' prices or attempting to skirt around them in some fashion. For nonsensitive products the small business person has latitude in the price itself, and can make up for a higher price with the service aspects. Some products are traditionally price-sensitive, whereas others may be sensitive from time to time, but not necessarily continuously. Efforts are made on the part of merchandisers and manufacturers to establish markets or to increase sales potential with the use of price alone; this may result in a price awareness on the part of the customer, forcing the competition to adopt comparable price levels.

Standard and well-advertised products frequently support a higher price; lesser known products may have to be priced lower. This again has nothing to do with quality or value but rather the sensitivity element, established on the basis of judgment that the standard, well-advertised product is the premium product. Numerous similar examples could be given indicating that an area of sensitivity is present; price sensitivity must be recognized for what it is worth, and efforts made to minimize its effect.

CLASSIFICATION OF PRODUCTS OR GOODS

One step in the pricing analysis process is the examination of products or goods to determine what characteristics tend to place these items in one category or another. Every business owner or manager must view the goods in terms of how they are so classified and why. This process will help the seller to understand more about the inherent nature of goods and why this makes a difference as to how products are priced and how they are sold.

Suggested-price items.   Some goods carry prices suggested by the manufacturer or distributor. The retailer is expected to use and follow this present pricing structure. There may be no method of legal control or restriction on the ultimate seller if he or she chooses not to comply with the manufacturer's suggested prices. Many products in this category are sold through exclusive sales outlets, and failure on the part of the merchandiser to respect the suggested selling price may result in the loss of that particular product to his or her operation.

Leaders or loss leaders.   Leaders are items within the product mix that are sold at low markup or low price as a means of developing business. Some state laws restrict the selling of products below costs; but generally speaking, enforcement is enacted only on the complaint of a competing merchant, and it is very difficult to determine the individual costs of any particular operation for the purpose of injunction or damages as a result of leader pricing.

Convenience goods.   Convenience goods are fast-moving items with wide distribution and available for sale in a great many outlets. They will consistently have fairly low markups, and frequently be carried as a convenience for customers without any particular contribution to profit being expected by the merchant.

Fashion goods.   Fashion goods possess features that are generally somewhat extreme and possess a short life. These will be shopped for by particular groups of people and will ordinarily carry a high initial markup. Over the salable period of their life, they will gradually depreciate in value, and ultimately if they are not sold, they may have to be disposed of at considerable markdown. Goods that have seasonal characteristics are also generally classified along with fashion goods and sold at prices that allow for some ultimate markdown of unsold stock.

Specialties.   Specialties have unique characteristics that allow fairly high initial markups, which are reduced as competitors recognize their market acceptance. Novelty characteristics are often featured in specialties, although items in this category need not be thought of as special products but rather as special, fast-moving products that enjoy a high degree of popularity for a limited period of time. The Frisbee is a good example of a specialty.

Shopping goods.   Goods possessing certain characteristics that make them unstandardized items that change with the times are rather carefully shopped for by the prospective buyer and called "shopping goods." Varieties of clothing, furniture, automobiles, and certain other items carry a relatively high price, and they create a combination of conditions that cause the buyer to be somewhat more deliberate in his or her investigation and purchase of such items. These are slower selling than other items, develop rather low turnover, and carry fairly high markups to cover additional costs of merchandising.

Aspinwall's characteristics of goods. A former professor at the University of Colorado, Leo Aspinwall, has developed some ideas regarding characteristics of goods and their movement through the markets. He classifies goods in terms of the following factors:

1. *Replacement rate:* the rate at which goods are purchased and consumed.
2. *Gross margin:* difference between cost and realized sale prices.
3. *Adjustment:* services applied to meet the exact needs of customers.
4. *Time of consumption:* the time during which the good gives up the utility desired.
5. *Searching time:* the time needed to find a suitable item.

He then proceeds to classify goods into three categories which he designates as red, orange, and yellow. As an example, red goods have a high replacement rate and are low in margin, adjustment, time of consumption, and searching. Orange and yellow goods possess other combinations of the five characteristics. The gist of his analysis is that goods possess consumer characteristics in addition to the nature of the goods themselves, which must be analyzed by the seller, for him or her to better understand how to merchandise the mix of goods which are carried in his or her establishment.[1]

PRICING POLICIES

Policy, which is a guide to action, will apply just as much in guiding the analysis and creation of a pricing program as in any other operating phase of a business. The important thing is to take the time to analyze factors that will affect pricing and establish prices for goods or services that are appropriate to maintain continuity of the business operation.

Activity within any business operation will result in the production of either goods or services, or perhaps both, to be sold by the business to one or more groups of customers. Before policy formation it is advisable to analyze the three divisions of business activity regarding the relationship to price: The first product group is goods *manufactured* and sold that will reach the ultimate buyer through one or more middlemen. These

---

[1]Leo V. Aspinwall, *Four Marketing Theories* (Boulder: Bureau of Business Research, University of Colorado, 1959).

goods are made up from various raw materials and components with the ultimate end product being something different from those items originally bought. The second category of goods and merchandise involves those things that are bought and later resold in the same form, which is a typical activity of the average *final sale merchandising organization,* which sells something produced by someone else. The third category involves the *sale of services,* which may be wholly controlled by the seller or made available by him or her in conjunction with some other organization, such as a franchise service firm.

Marketing channels.   If the products or services generated by the firm are sold to customers who are located away from point of production, a marketing channel for distribution is needed. Channels can be direct to the consumer, through one or more middlemen, or perhaps some variation involving two or more methods.

Middlemen are not always popular. Ever since the days of Theodore Roosevelt they have been accused of being "nonproductive parasites," who add very little value to the transaction and extract high prices for what they provide. For many smaller businesses, the choice of a marketing channel is often difficult. Small businesses usually represent small and limited output. Middlemen are reluctant to handle small-volume business and charge a high price to do so.

The small business person should investigate the channels of distribution to determine what they provide for his or her particular business and whether or not there is any possibility of circumventing middlemen to reach a customer. Similar opportunities can exist in buying for manufacturing or buying goods for resale. Opportunities to eliminate middleman functions are perhaps more prevalent today than some years ago because of substantial changes in the previously established methods of distribution. Methods of distribution are changing, and "who sells what" is no longer predetermined. Careful analysis and understanding of the function of marketing channels will be a worthwhile investment.

Competition.   A pricing policy must consider the prices charged by competitors. The small business entrepreneur may wish to go his/her own way in setting prices and may actually do so, but is more likely to review the competition and try to figure out what policy is best, based on what is found.

Many existing firms will react to a new firm by cutting prices in an attempt to discourage customers from patronizing the new firm. This may continue for some time until it is obviously futile. Other tactics, such as increased advertising, may be used.

It is probably well for the newly established business to expect that competitors will initiate a direct or indirect price campaign. Some allowance must be made to carry the loss of sales revenue until this period is over.

Market share.   The market for any given product or service is only so big, and ordinarily if a new firm enters the market it must take away business from someone else. There are always a certain number of new products that provide the opportunity for developing a new market. These new products, however, may be incorporated into the sales pattern of an already established market. Pricing is *extremely persuasive* in developing a share of the market, and numerous experiments and studies have been conducted to determine the effect of *price and advertising* in developing market share. A difficult problem is trying to divide the impact of market penetration between advertising and pricing, and to determine just how much one is independent of the other. If the demand for a product is elastic, and reducing price increases volume, it is important to know how far to go with price reductions in trying to build additional volume and market share. Some theories can be developed about this, but it would probably require trial and error on the part of a business person to determine the limits of his/her own potential.

As a means of making a quick entry into the market, some share of the market for a service business is frequently established by using prices below those of competitors. It is apparent that particular market areas are highly individualistic in terms of the pricing structure for services; these pricing levels can be readily determined by a check of the particular market area. The difficult task is for the small business person to decide what can be gained by using differential prices and service patterns to acquire a market share and what the retaliatory effects of these tactics will be.

Goals of the entrepreneur.   Independent business managers and owners will tend to project a good deal of their own personal ideas into the pricing structure that they establish for their businesses. This personal influence is related to how a person views the role of an entrepreneur or business operator, and is a projection of individual business ethics. A large business is much less personal, and the influence of one person seldom dominates.

There are several ways that the goals of the individual may affect the pricing structure. The person may not wish to gouge customers and take advantage of any situation in dealings with customers or clients. On the other hand, the choice may be to charge the infrequent or transient customer a higher price. An individual may view the business as a means of making a reasonable living and not charge a higher price even though the market permits it. The prices set may be considered to be fair and bear no relationship to what the market will bear or to the action of competitors. In some cases a price may be set by pure intuition.

Expansion or change from a previous format. When a business is scheduled for a substantial change from its previous pattern of operation, it may be time to overhaul the pricing structure. A definite change in the product lines or a change in the "thrust" elements of the business are ample reasons for considering some changes.

Making the price changes may not be as difficult as planning the strategy of justifying the changes in the minds of customers or clients. One technique is to eliminate previous points of reference as to product mix, selection, and shelf-space allocations. Another would be to change the assignments of products to departments and the arrangement of display and shelf space.

The expansion or change may actually be a new "thrust" factor that needs to be highlighted. Pricing is a part of this change in emphasis and should be highlighted to take advantage of a time when such price adjustment can actually be implemented. Prices may or may not be cut. Different price combinations may be established and fit well with the other changes.

Services. The pricing of services poses problems that are different from the traditional markup, or pricing to the prices of competitors. It is apparent that many small business owners are not particularly astute in establishing pricing policies for their services.

Certain lines of business adopt uniform or agreed-to prices. These might be unlawful for larger businesses engaged in interstate commerce, but are seldom resisted by legal action at the small enterprise level. The fact that they are agreed to "along Main Street" does not necessarily make them unfair. Common, standard tasks may be listed in flat-rate manuals. These manuals rate a job in time units, which are then multiplied by an hourly rate to set the price for a given job. Customers will probably complain if the job time is shortened, resulting in a higher effective rate per hour, but it may be the only reasonable way to justify service rates so that they have a degree of consistency.

Service pricing is difficult and subject to a great deal of customer criticism. The small business owner-manager should think seriously of policies that add extras or "sweeteners" to blunt the impact of the price itself. One successful service-business owner describes his policy as "Smother them (customers) with kindness and charge like hell."

PRICING STRATEGY

Following the consideration and adoption of basic pricing policies, the next step is to set up the strategy to be used in the actual pricing programs. The process at this point is to set the prices so that the objectives of the business are met. Considerable change and adjustment will take place before the best workable combinations are found. Some suggestions and ideas about strategy follow.

Leaders. A leader, or formerly a loss leader (before resale price-maintenance laws), is just what the name implies—a low-priced product or service intended to attract customers, who will then purchase other offerings. The leader mechanism is well known and can be examined easily by anyone.

Random discounts. Some smaller businesses have had success with marking down products and merchandise on a purely random basis. To be successful, this policy must apply to good, salable items, and it must be executed on a big enough scale to make it pay. Customers attracted by the policy will search for the reduced items and in the process become potential buyers of other items.

Low-cost extras. A number of small business enterprises have been very successful in providing an image of higher value with low-cost features. This is particularly true in service businesses, where a little extra effort and expense can greatly enhance the value in the mind of the customer. A free newspaper or free coffee in the morning might allow a motel operator to charge a high price.

Bargain pricing. One strategy in pricing is to rely on the fact that all people love a bargain. The fact that a customer thinks he or she bought at a bargain price is often more important than the price itself. This permits the entrepreneur to demand a higher price if the image can be conveyed that the price is still a bargain. Discounts from list prices have probably lost their novelty, although they are still being used. Prices lower than any competitor's, or membership club prices, are examples of bargain pricing.

The strategies suggested are a few that have been used with success in the past. Variations and other strategies will occur to alert entrepreneurs as they see what others are doing.

Small business owners usually are able to develop their own strategies because they operate from flexible positions. They can experiment on a short-run basis, react to conditions as they develop, and establish their own style and methods which are consistent with their own philosophy of how to price.

PRICES AND THE LAW

Because it is small and has little influence, the small business is not often challenged on the pricing of its products or services, although some state regulatory agencies try to prescribe prices.

As a business becomes larger, and particularly if it engages in interstate commerce, its prices may be subject to scrutiny and challenge as to their legality.

State laws such as unfair practices acts or resale price maintenance acts are designed to put a floor under prices, including some reasonable percentage as a markup. The laws vary, but their purpose is to prevent pricing below cost as a sales inducement and to prevent price wars, which are considered unfair and ruinous competition.

The Robinson-Patman Act, which applies to goods sold in interstate commerce, provides that a seller may not discriminate in prices between buyers if the goods are the same.

These practices of deceptive pricing have been attacked by the Federal Trade Commission in the Wheeler-Lea Amendment of 1938 and in later guidelines brought out in the 1950s and 1960s. Most actions under these guidelines have taken the form of warnings requests that private trade organizations police their own membership.

Colorado has had a Fair Trade Act, an Unfair Practices Act, a Deceptive Trade Act, and a Restraint of Trade Act. Owners and managers in other states should find out whether similar laws in their own states affect their pricing policies.

SUGGESTIONS FOR PRICING

For the small business, a number of things associated with pricing may be different from what they are for major manufacturers, retailers, or service enterprises. The following suggestions may prove helpful to the small entrepreneur as an aid in setting prices:

1. Never assume that any price established on a product is necessarily correct, or that the product is priced "right."

2. Be willing to experiment with prices and to change them to an extent that is not inconsistent with company policy or likely to affect customer goodwill.

3. Try to avoid head-on price competition with larger companies or others who are better able to achieve a lower pricing structure.

4. Study markets, products, and people continuously and carefully to determine what will work, under what conditions it will succeed, and how it can be incorporated into the goals of the organization.

5. Be realistic as to price changes of products and services over time, and the necessity of setting a pricing structure that allows for reductions necessary for the movement of the goods at the end of seasonal periods. Prepare to meet the pricing of competitors from time to time. Apply the idea of balancing or compensating over the entire range of products and

services offered to develop and maintain some average gross margin that is consistent with the needs of the business.

6.   Constantly supplement products with service to achieve competitive advantage. Nothing will support a price as well as accompanying it with service. Many small business services can be provided with very little cost. In fact, a smile, addressing a customer by name, some conversation, and showing an interest in customers may be all that is needed to win and hold them.

7.   Make use of the flexibility available to most small businesses. React to changes and make adjustments. Capitalize on developing opportunities and fill voids that have been created, or in some other way prepare for new opportunities and move quickly when they present themselves. Later, if larger competitors move in, or cutthroat competition develops, the opportunist will be mentally prepared to move out of his or her present operation into something else.

8.   Examine all phases of the business constantly in regard to the effect that pricing has on the operation. Examine product sales by individual product, by departments, by seasons of the year, by customers and class, by amount of sales transactions, and any other yardstick that makes sense. In other words, be a leader and an innovator rather than a follower, who must do business on somebody else's terms.

9.   Analyze the relationship that credit and installment selling have on the pricing structure. Many times a price is meaningless unless the item or service is available for sale over time or on credit terms.

10.   Use your customers as a sounding board to find out what they think about your prices and also your competitors' prices.

FORMULAS TO AID IN PRICING

Every business manager should be able to perform several calculations related to pricing.

1.   *Stock turnover:*
   a.   Cost

$$\frac{\text{Cost of goods sold}}{\text{Average inventory at cost}} = \frac{\text{Stock}}{\text{turnover}}$$

   b.   Price

$$\frac{\text{Net sales}}{\text{Average inventory at selling price}} = \frac{\text{Stock}}{\text{turnover}}$$

c. Units

$$\frac{\text{Sales in units}}{\text{Average inventory in units}} = \frac{\text{Stock}}{\text{turnover}}$$

2. *Cost of goods:*

$$\frac{\text{Cost of goods}}{\text{Selling price}} = \text{Percent of sales}$$

3. *Gross margin:*

Net sales—Cost of goods sold = Gross margin

4. *Markup on cost:*

$$\frac{\text{Dollar markup}}{\text{Cost}} = \text{Percent markup}$$

5. *Markup on selling price:*

$$\frac{\text{Dollar markup}}{\text{Selling price}} = \text{Percent markup}$$

6. *Capital turnover:*

$$\frac{\text{Net sales at retail}}{\text{Capital investment}} = \frac{\text{Capital}}{\text{turnover}}$$

7. *Break-even points:*

a.
$$\text{Units BEP} = \frac{\text{Total fixed cost}}{\text{Fixed cost contribution per unit}}$$

b.
$$\text{Dollars BEP} = \frac{\text{Total fixed cost}}{1 - \left(\dfrac{\text{Variable cost per unit}}{\text{Selling price per unit}}\right)}$$

QUESTIONS

1. Why should each category of costs be analyzed separately before a decision is made on the sales prices of a firm's products or services?

2. What kinds of information about discount structures help the small business to buy more advantageously?

3. Are there ordinarily direct relationships of price and quality over the range of a product line? Why or why not?

4. In theory are all costs variable in the long run?

5. How should a business entrepreneur attempt to find out the price sensitivities of customers?

6. Do inflation and rising prices tend to change a customer's attitude about the value that a particular purchase represents?

7. What is advantageous about a small entrepreneur setting prices to some extent on the basis of a feeling as to what is "right"?

8. How much justification and evidence of costs should be provided to a customer when a price is quoted or stated?

9. How does the smaller business decide what is the best price for a rather different or unique service?

10. What is the advantage of adjusting prices frequently (up and down) instead of maintaining considerable price stability?

PROBLEMS

1. Study the newspaper advertising of three or four directly competitive retail firms. Compare the prices of the firms over a six-week period on items that are the same or comparable. Attempt to answer the following:
   a. Is there really price competition?
   b. Are the same items repeatedly being featured and priced below the regular prices?
   c. What pricing images are conveyed by the advertising of each establishment?

2. Using the Yellow Pages select five service firms and place calls to price a particular well-known type of service job. Carefully note what statements are made in connection with the price quoted by each firm.

3. Contact a wholesale firm and inquire about its pricing policies. Try to avoid particular details and names that are apt to be sensitive. Try to establish the following:
   a. Do they use a list price less a discount as a method of pricing?
   b. What conditions warrant differing discount prices?
   c. How do this firm's prices compare with those of other competitors in the area? (This may be only an opinion or conjecture.)

4. Select a small manufacturing firm and make an appointment with the purchasing agent or whoever buys materials and components for the firm. Ask questions that deal with the following circumstances:

   a. What circumstances relating to price uncertainty, shortages, and other problems of the 1970s have continued to make the buying programs of small businesses difficult and costly?

   b. In what areas have tighter standards of liability tended to raise prices?

   c. How should the buying program of a small business be changed during a period of larger and more frequent price increases than prevail during more normal times?

5. Review the laws and statutes of your state relative to control of businesses through administrative boards and agencies. Contact two or three agencies of your choice and inquire whether the prices within the area of agency regulation are actually controlled.

BIBLIOGRAPHY

Baumback, Clifford M., and Kenneth Lawyer. *How to Organize and Operate a Small Business*. 6th ed. Englewood Cliffs, N.J.: Prentice-Hall, 1979, chap. 19.

Frantz, Forrest H. *Successful Small Business Management*. Englewood Cliffs, N.J.: Prentice-Hall 1978, chap. 11.

Moreau, James F. *Effective Small Business Management*. Chicago: Rand McNally College Publishing 1980, chap. 4.

Redinbaugh, Larry D., and Clyde W. Neu. *Small Business Management*. St. Paul, Minn.: West Publishing, 1980, chap. 7.

18

The management of credit sales

An extremely perplexing problem for the small business manager is whether customers should be offered credit. The answer depends on a number of factors surrounding the firm's operation. The first factor is whether credit sales are customary in the firm's particular line of business. If so, failure to offer credit could put the business at a competitive disadvantage.

Other important considerations involve the investment necessary to carry credit sales, the type of credit terms to offer, the type of credit analysis to be used in the selection of credit customers, the levying of service charges, and the establishment of a systematic and efficient collection system. This chapter considers these various questions and provides a practical approach to managing a credit sales program.

THE CREDIT SALES DECISION

Primarily, any decision to offer credit involves comparing the earnings on working capital tied up in credit sales with the earnings the funds would produce if they were invested elsewhere. The credit

317

program can be justified only if the benefits exceed the costs. The costs of credit must include the interest charge on any borrowed funds tied up in accounts receivable, as well as the cost of administering credit policy.

When the question of cost versus benefit is considered, many small businesses may be unable to offer credit. For instance, the manager may find it impossible to maintain adequate working capital to support desirable inventory levels and support a credit sales program at the same time. In such a case it may be illogical to cut back inventory stocks to finance credit sales.

If the decision is made to establish a credit sales program and the funds are available to finance it, the problem is determining the appropriate credit terms. This involves determining the credit period and the desirability of offering discount terms to customers for early payment. In deciding what credit terms to offer, it is important to consider the nature of the product or service.

The desirability of a service charge is also an important question. How will a service charge influence sales volume? Will any loss of credit sales because of the service charge be offset by the income resulting from the service charge, plus the earnings on the working capital released from accounts receivable?

Each of the above factors demands serious consideration before the credit decision is made. Although some control over the level of receivables is possible through credit rejection and acceptance procedures and through efficient collection procedures, once the decision has been made to offer credit it is difficult to reverse.

Controlling the level of credit sales

Controlling the level of credit sales involves determining the quality of credit applicant to accept and the investigative procedures to be used in examining each applicant.

First, consider the quality of the credit applicant to be accepted. As credit customers are accepted, each makes some incremental addition to income and to expenditures. Thus, the added income must be compared with the added costs. The costs include additional production, administrative, selling, and collection expenses resulting from the credit sales. The increase in costs may be significant, based on the assumption that total demand will increase if credit sales, as well as cash sales, are made.

In theory, credit sales should be added as long as the marginal benefit exceeds the marginal cost. This principle is applied by first determining the amount of additional sales that are produced by accepting a particular group of credit customers, minus the percent of bad debts generated within the group. This result equals the additional revenue produced by the group. Next, additional production, administrative, and selling costs, plus any collection expenses, equals the additional expenditures. The additional revenues minus the additional expenditures equal the net incremental income resulting from the credit sales.

A word of caution is appropriate at this point. Although the marginal principle sounds good in theory, its application is somewhat subjective and requires sound judgment and experience in the analysis of customers. In addition, one or two more subtle questions must be answered in deciding the quality of credit applicant to accept. One is to determine the level of operations necessary to support a particular volume of credit sales and also any costs that may be associated with increased sales. For instance, in manufacturing there are different sets of incremental or marginal costs at different levels of production. In retailing there are the costs associated with hiring additional sales personnel as credit sales expand, and additional investments in inventory and space.

This means the credit policy of the firm should be flexible, and vary with the level of sales activity. As sales volume decreases in a recessionary period, the manager may approve the marginal credit risk to maintain an acceptable sales volume. On the other hand, as economic conditions improve and sales volume approaches capacity, the manager can be more selective in accepting credit customers.

TYPES OF CREDIT ARRANGEMENTS AND CREDIT TERMS

The credit investigation procedure used to determine the credit worthiness of applicants depends on the type of credit being extended. There are two classes of credit: *consumer credit* and *trade credit*. Trade credit is extended by manufacturers and wholesalers to retail establishments and involves the financing of goods for resale. Consumer credit is granted by retailers to the consumer, who is purchasing for personal or family use. The type of credit being offered is important because it dictates the kinds of information available and desired for an adequate evaluation of the credit applicant.

Trade credit

On the *trade credit* side, goods are usually purchased on an open-book basis, subject to specific terms of sales such as 2/10 net 30. This means that a 2 percent discount is given by the seller if the buyer pays within 10 days. Failure to take the discount within the first 10 days makes the full amount of the invoice due within 30 days. (Many buyers *don't* pay their bill in 10 days and take the discount anyway—a practice that in the 1980s has become progressively harder to eliminate.) Other discount arrangements in common use today appear in Figure 18–1.

Another type of trade credit involves the use of extended datings, common in seasonal selling. By using extended dating, the manufactur-

Figure 18–1
Trade credit sales terms

Sales term	Explanation
3/10, 1/15, n/60	Three percent discount for the first 10 days; 1 percent discount for 15 days; bill due net on 60th day
2/10, n/30, ROG	Two percent discount for 10 days; bill due net on 30th day—but both discount period and 30 days start from the date of receipt of the goods, not from the date of the sale.
2/10, n/30, MOM	Two percent discount for 10 days; bill due net on 30th day—but both periods start from the 15th of the month following the sales date.
2/10, n/30, EOM	Two percent discount for 10 days; bill due net on 30th day—but both periods start from the end of the month in which the sale was made.
2/10, 60 EX	Two percent discount for 10 days; bill due date extended for so many days after the 60-day term allowed.
2/10, PROX	Terms of 2/10, PROX in reality are no different from 2/10 EOM. EOM is used as the designation of such terms in the textile industry, while PROX is more generally used in the wholesale grocery line and in the sale of automobile tires.
MOM	Billing will be on the 15th of the month, including all purchases made since the middle of the prior month.
EOM	Billing at end of month, covering all credit purchases of that month.
COD	Amount of bill will be collected upon delivery of the goods.

er gives the retailer time to obtain funds for payment through resale of the goods. An extended dating program also eliminates the problem of inventory storage at the manufacturing site. An extended dating arrangement simply defers the buyer's payments. For example, payments due on an invoice may be 10 percent after 30 days, 20 percent after 60 days, and the remainder after 120 days. Or, the terms may be 2/10 net 30 with dating from 90 days after the date of sale.

The particular trade credit terms used by the manufacturer depends on the type of product; competitive conditions; and the buyers' and sellers' circumstances. The credit period will normally vary directly with the length of the buyer's inventory turnover period, which depends on the type of product. However, if the seller determines the individual sales terms of each customer, the larger the customer's order and the better the credit standing, the more generous the sales terms. Of course, the seller's sales terms are limited to some extent by financial strength and the liquidity of working capital.

Generally speaking, the manager cannot afford to allow competition to have the best terms. Furthermore, in many product lines, credit terms are so firmly set by tradition there is little choice other than to conform.

Consumer credit

There are four major types of *consumer credit* accounts offered at the retail level: the *ordinary charge account,* the *installment account,* the *budget account,* and the *revolving credit arrangement.* In any particular case, the most desirable account to use will depend upon the type of merchandise, the customer's financial position and income, and the customer's ability to budget expenditures.

Ordinary charge.   An ordinary charge account involves charging for merchandise when purchased, with payment due when the bill is sent to the customer. Typical terms call for payment at the end of the month; but a longer period is allowed if the customer desires an extended payment period. Normally 30-day cash terms are offered; and if the account goes beyond, a service charge is assessed. The ordinary charge

322

account is best suited for frequent family purchases in department stores.

Installment account. The consumer installment account is most often used in large purchases, such as automobiles, appliances, and furniture, where payment must be spread over a long period of time. A down payment of 10 to 30 percent is normally required, and service charges are added to the cost. The payment period usually extends from 90 days to 36 months, but longer periods are becoming more common. A service charge of as much as 1½ percent per month on the unpaid balance is typical.

In selling on the installment basis, the credit is usually secured by a chattel mortgage or a conditional sales contract. Both of these arrangements permit the seller to repossess the goods if the customer defaults a payment. Under a chattel mortgage, legal title to the goods passes when the sale is made, but is subject to the seller's lien. When a payment is defaulted the seller can then take court action to repossess the goods. Under the conditional sales contract, legal title does not pass until the buyer makes the last payment; hence, immediate repossession is possible when a payment is defaulted.

Budget account. The consumer budget account is a short-term installment account resulting from charge purchases in amounts typically ranging from $100 to $200. Payment is ordinarily spread over 60 to 120 days, and a service charge is normally added to the price.

Revolving credit account. Finally, the consumer may be offered a revolving credit account, which is simply another variation of the installment account. A line of credit is granted up to $1,5000 or $2,000, and the customer can charge purchases at any time, if the total purchases do not exceed the credit limit given. The buyer must pay a specified percentage of the outstanding credit balance monthly, and the interest charge is computed on the unpaid balance at the end of each month. The revolving credit account forces the consumer to budget and limits the amount of debt to be carried.

INVESTIGATION OF THE CREDIT APPLICANT

The credit investigation procedure involves an analysis of costs and benefits. The manager must decide how much time and effort can be spent in analyzing credit worthiness. In adopting a format for analysis, an important relationship exists between the time and cost of the analysis, and credit losses. Furthermore, in conducting each investigation the manager must recognize the great importance of time to both parties.

Sources of credit information

A number of sources of credit information can be used in making the credit decision. Their use will depend upon the time and money available for the investigation.

First, consider the sources of credit information that apply in the extension of consumer credit. In retailing, the first step is to develop a credit application form. An example appears in Figure 18–2.

The credit application will provide all of the basic information necessary for an analysis of the applicant's financial responsibility, and together with information from a local credit bureau or from the customer's banker, will make up the data to be used in the final decision.

The information acquired in the credit application needs no explanation. It is appropriate, however, to discuss the services that a local credit bureau can offer. The credit bureau is an organization supported by its members, who are usually retailers. The basic objective of the credit bureau is to summarize the credit experience of the various bureau members with particular consumers in the community. In addition, the local bureau may be affiliated with either the National Retail Credit Association or the Associated Credit Bureaus of America, and thus be able to offer credit information on persons who move from one city to another.

One of the important functions of the local credit bureau is to provide credit reports. The report will normally contain a listing of the credit accounts maintained by the applicant, the length of time these accounts have been maintained, the date of the last purchase, the balance due, and the promptness of payment. In addition, the report will indicate the applicant's income and income sources, whether the home is owned or rented, employment data, and a character evaluation.

Another function of the credit bureau is to investigate newcomers to the city, in anticipation of requests for credit data. Notification service is also provided to the member firms that warns them against certain customers that have become poor credit risks in the community. Finally, the local credit bureau can offer valuable assistance in tracing local debtors who have moved from the city without leaving forwarding information, and it can assist in the collection of past-due accounts. Most of these local credit bureau services do not require membership for use, but the fees charged for services to nonmembers are considerably higher than those charged to members.

The other source of credit information that usually proves valuable is the banker. This source may be limited, however, because not all bankers will supply credit information about their depositors and

Figure 18–2
ABC store credit application form

NAME_____Phone_____

ADDRESS_____City and State_____ Years at This Street Address____

Previous Address_____City and State_____ Years There____

Age__Married__Single__Divorced__Widowed__Dependents__ Wife's or Husband's Name_____

Nearest Relative Not Living with You_____Relation_____Address_____City and State_____

EMPLOYED BY:_____ Position_____ No. of Years_____
            (If in business for self, give firm name)

Address_____ Immediate Superior_____Phone_____

Previous Employer_____Address_____From_____To_____

INCOME: Salary $_____Week Month . . . Other Income $_____Week Month . . . Source_____

Wife's or Husband's Income $.. ___Week Month . . . Employed by_____Phone_____Years There_____

* OBLIGATIONS: I owe the following banks, mortgage companies, loan and finance companies, and store accounts, medical and other bills and NO others: (If
none, so state)

To Whom Owing	Address	Unpaid Balance	Monthly Payments	Amount to be Paid by this Loan
_____	_____	$_____	$_____	$_____
_____	_____	_____	_____	_____
_____	_____	_____	_____	_____
_____	_____	_____	_____	_____

* (If no obligations are owing, give three references above with whom you have had credit
dealings, preferably installment credit.)

Real Estate Owned_____Title in Name of_____

Present Value $_____ Total Mortgage $_____Held by_____ Monthly Payments . $_____

Rent from_____Address_____ Per Month . . . $_____

Bank with_____Checking Savings . . . Life Insurance Carried $_____Cash Value $_____

Automobile Owned: Year_____Make_____Owing $_____To_____

I am not now a co-maker or endorser on any other loans except_____

I have had no suits, judgments, garnishments, or other legal proceedings, except_____

I have not obtained credit, nor intend to obtain credit, elsewhere to make the above purchase, except_____

Send Mail To:

Residence_____ Business_____

First Payment

To Start_____

I hereby certify that the above statements are true and
correct and are made to obtain a loan from this store. I
agree to notify the store concerning any material change in
my financial condition. I authorize you to obtain any information you may require, and agree that this application
shall remain the property of the store whether the loan is
granted or not.

☞ SIGN HERE_____

CREDIT BUREAU REPORT FINDINGS_____

TRADE REFERENCES_____

SALES TERMS_____

324

borrowers. Many feel such information is confidential and should not be disclosed.

In the extension of trade credit, much more detailed information about the credit applicant is available. First, there are a number of privately operated trade credit agencies that collect credit information on business firms. These data are analyzed and evaluated; then the agency publishes credit ratings that are available to subscribers for a fee. A credit agency may be involved only with a particular line of business, or may be more general in nature, such as Dun & Bradstreet.

Dun & Bradstreet is the best-known credit concern in the United States, with over 100 years of experience in the field of credit reporting. Of primary importance among its many services are its reference books and written credit reports. The reference book is published six times a year. Through a system of letters, numbers, and symbols, it provides credit information and Dun & Bradstreet's estimate of the credit standing of the firm.

If additional material is needed, a credit report is obtained. It provides detailed information on the payment record the prospective customer has established with other suppliers; the highest amount of credit that a particular supplier has extended; the amount currently owed to each particular supplier; the promptness with which the customer is making payments; and whether or not the prospective customer has been discounting. The data provided in the written credit report are based on the ledger experience of creditors of the particular company in question.

Data and materials supplied by a local credit bureau may also help in making a trade credit decision. The National Association of Credit Managers operates a credit interchange service. Participating firms provide their local bureaus with listings of their customers. Then when an inquiry is received about the payment habits of some particular company, the bureau acquires reports from each of the firm's suppliers and prepares a summary. The reports are available on both a local and national level.

The banker may be a valuable source of credit information at the trade credit level also. Through the correspondent banking system, commercial banks throughout the nation regularly exchange credit information. For example, suppose a small firm in Denver receives an order from a new customer in Phoenix. Desirous of credit information on the Phoenix customer, the Denver manager requests the Denver bank to contact the bank's Phoenix correspondent. It is very likely that credit information on the Phoenix firm can be secured through the correspondent bank network. In fact, firms in smaller communities often can get credit information by using their local bank to go through a chain of four or five banks. The availability of this type of service is another reason why a good banking relationship is so vital to a small business.

It may be that salespeople, with proper training, can be relied upon to provide useful credit information. They may be asked to make periodic reports concerning particular customers as they see them. For instance, by observing the various brands stocked on the retailer's shelves, the salesperson can provide the names of other suppliers. These suppliers can then be contacted to learn of their credit experience with the customer.

In the extension of trade credit, an analysis of financial statement information is important. The latest balance sheets and income statements should be obtained directly from the customer. If the customer is hesitant in offering the information, the manager should explain that the firm refuses credit to any concern that does not provide its financial statements upon request. In collecting financial information, the most current statement is not enough, because much of the analysis is based on a comparison of values appearing in the balance sheet and income statement from one period to another. Thus, it is appropriate to obtain the financial statements of the last three or four periods.

A spread sheet will put the financial statement information in a more workable form. An example appears in Figure 18–3. The spread sheet provides space for both recording and analyzing financial information. The spread sheet illustrated is rather detailed, and a more simplified statement may be adequate in some cases. However, regardless of detail, the objective remains the same: to adopt a basic format in the organization and analysis of credit information.

Finally, the manager may find useful credit information from such sources as Better Business Bureaus, Chambers of Commerce, attorneys, trade associations, and the nationally published investment manuals. But regardless of the type and number of sources used, the time and effort expended in the credit analysis function must be consistent with the benefits of the credit analysis program.

Other credit analysis information

If the manager finds that a large percentage of total sales involve a relatively few customers, a more extensive analysis of each customer may be desired. The following paragraphs illustrate the types of information that may be valuable:

1. Organization and history. The legal form of organization may be important. Is the customer's business a sole proprietorship, partnership, or corporation? If it is corporation, the number of shareholders and the distribution of ownership among the shareholders may be important. In a partnership, any formal agreements between the partners and the names of the principal officers and partners are important. In addition to the form of organization, it may be wise for the manager to request a brief history of the firm.

Figure 18–3
Credit information spread sheet

ASSETS	Date Source							
Cash								
U.S. government securities								
Accounts receivable—trade								
Reserve for bad debts								
Net receivables								
Total Quick Assets								
Inventory								
Cash value life insurance								
Other current assets								
Total Current Assets								
Land								
Buildings								
Leasehold improvements								
Machinery and equipment								
Reserve for depreciation								
Net Fixed Assets								
Prepaid items								
Investment and advances affiliates								
Intangibles: Goodwill, etc.								
Other noncurrent assets								
Total Assets								
LIABILITIES								
Notes payable banks								
Current maturities—long-term debt								
Notes payable—other								
Notes payable—officers and employees								
Accounts payable trade								
Accrued expenses								
Federal income tax accrual								
Total Current Liabilities								
Long-term debt								
Total Liabilities								
Net worth—partnership or proprietor								
Capital stock—preferred								
Capital stock—common								
Capital or paid-in surplus								
Earned surplus								
Treasury stock								
Total Net Worth								
Total Liabilities and Net Worth								
Current assets								
Current liabilities								
Net Working Capital								
Current ratio								
Quick ratio								
Net Worth to debt								
Sales to receivables								
Cost of sales to inventory								
Percentage earnings to beginning net worth								
Net sales								
Net profits								
Annual provision for depreciation								
Officers' salaries								
Dividends or withdrawals								
Contingent liabilities								

Figure 18–3
(continued)

	Date									
	Source									
ANALYSIS WORKING CAPITAL										
Beginning balance working capital										
Net profit (loss)										
Depreciation, amortization, and depletion										
Increase long–term debt										
Other factors										
Total additions										
Dividends: Withdrawals										
Additions to fixed assets										
Reduction long–term debt										
Other factors										
Total deductions										
Net increase or (decrease)										
Working Capital End of the Period										
ANALYSIS EARNED SURPLUS										
Balance beginning of the period										
Net profit (loss) for period										
Total additions										
Dividends—preferred										
Dividends—common										
Total deductions										
Net increase or (decrease)										
Balance End of the Period										
INCOME STATEMENT (DOLLARS)										
Gross sales										
Returns and allowances										
Net sales										
Cost of sales										
Gross profit (loss)										
Operating expense—selling expense										
gen. and admin. expense										
officers' salaries										
Total operating expenses										
Net profit (loss) from operations										
Other income										
Other expense										
Net profit before federal income tax										
Federal income tax										
Net Profit (Loss)										
Dividends—withdrawals										
INCOME STATEMENT (PERCENT)										
Net sales										
Cost of sales										
Gross profit (loss)										
Operating expense—selling expense										
gen. and admin. expense										
officer's salaries										
Total operating expenses										
Net profit (loss) from operations										
Other income										
Other expense										
Net profit before federal income tax										
Federal income tax										
Net Profit (Loss)										

2. Production. The manager should be familiar with the particular products or service offered by the prospective customer. In addition, the names of other suppliers may be important. Finally, the manager may be interested in the prospective customer's physical plant and equipment, whether it is owned or leased, and whether insurance coverage is adequate.

3. Sales. The prospective customer's sales experience is important. This involves a familiarity with the applicant's marketing area, the number of customers, and the sales volume with the largest customers. Also important may be the terms of sale offered by the applicant, the backlog of orders, and the lead time necessary to fill an order.

4. Reputation and prospects. The prospective customer's position in the industry and the competition he or she faces may be important. Also of interest are industrial trends in new product development and the growth potential of the prospective customer. Although the applicant's initial purchases may not be large, increases in sales volume may be anticipated as new products are developed and the business grows.

5. Management. When one customer represents a relatively large percentage of total sales, the experience of the customer's managerial staff is important. Who are the major officers in the firm, what is their background, and has the question of successor management been resolved? Also of interest is the number of employees, their union affiliation, and the status of the union contract.

6. Finances. In addition to an analysis of the information gathered from the financial statements, there are a number of other financial questions to answer before making the credit decision. It may be important to know whether the assets are pledged or assigned; the data of the last federal tax clearance; the names of the prospective customer's accountant, banker, and attorney; and whether the prospective customer is affiliated with any other business firms.

The foregoing discussion suggests a rather detailed approach in reaching the credit decision. Although this was intentional, the manager must decide how much time and effort can be spent with each individual applicant in determining the organization and format to be used in gathering credit information.

THE SUBJECTIVE SIDE OF THE CREDIT DECISION

Once all the information and data desired about the prospective customer have been gathered, the credit decision depends on analytical ability and good judgment. In making the decision, the manager must keep one point in mind: People, not dollars, pay bills. Thus, some attention should be given to examining the credit applicant in terms of what are known as the four C's of credit: character, capacity, capital, and the conditions of business.

In naming the factors essential to a satisfactory risk, most experienced credit analysts cite character as the most important. There must be a willingness to pay as well as a determination to pay; the determination to pay varies directly with character.

Character alone, however, is not sufficient for the extension of credit. Character is a moral endowment, incapable of doing more than directing the force found in capacity and capital. In attempting to appraise character, the manager usually ends up looking at the customer's reputation. The distinction between the two, however, is considerable. Character is within the person, while reputation is in the minds of others. The danger, then, is that those who are responsible for the person's reputation may have erred in their appraisal.

In summary, the best advice is to learn everything possible about the prospective customer's past. Personal habits, manner of living, amusements, environment, and the person's business code of ethics are important.

Capacity, like character, is an intangible factor for which there is no unit of measurement. The appraisal of it, therefore, is comparable. In a sole proprietorship, capacity of the firm may be found solely in one person; but in a partnership or corporation, the managerial ability of many may be considered.

Capacity is both physical and mental. The age of the credit applicant is significant, for it indicates both physical stamina and experience. Energy, aggressiveness, ambition, shrewdness, and judgment should be taken into consideration in evaluating capacity. Also, important are executive ability, general education and training, and general business methods.

In terms of capacity, there are two basic classes of credit applicants: those who have demonstrated their capacity or lack of it, and those who are just beginning in business and have yet to reveal their capacity to run a firm. In summary, capacity and character go hand in hand. The person who possesses character, having a will to pay and capacity, will find a means to pay.

The capital factor is typically given more attention than the character and capacity factors because capital is tangible and subject to measurement. Capital means the financial strength of the credit applicant. Capital is the amount of money the applicant has at risk in the business. Not only is quantity important, but the nature of the assets in which the capital is invested is also significant.

Capital is the money the prospective customer holds out as a guarantee that a credit transaction entered into will be redeemed. Capital represents the extent to which losses resulting from error in business judgment, or adverse business conditions, can be absorbed. The extent of the applicant's capital as well as how it was acquired are important. Was it acquired through the successful operation of the business or by some other means?

In addition to the consideration of character, capacity, and capital, general business conditions must be reviewed. The amount of credit a seasonal business may advantageously use varies with the time of the season.

In considering changes in economic conditions, the manager must look at the general movement of business, as well as the status of the particular business or industry under review. Credit conditions may be generally good on a particular firm, while the status of the industry as a whole may be bad. Or conditions in a certain industry may be good, when general economic conditions are poor.

MAKING THE CREDIT DECISION

Foremost in the mind of the person involved in the credit decision should be that time is of the essence. This is true for both parties. Once all the necessary information has been collected, the manager owes it to the credit applicant to reach a decision within a short time.

In the case of rejection, it may be that alternative credit terms to those that were applied for can be offered. A clear understanding of the decision by the applicant will avoid stirring up resentment in a credit rejection. Once the decision has been made, the manager must abide by the decision and not be swayed by the prospective customer's pleas for reconsideration.

COLLECTION PROCEDURE

A systematic means of collection is just as important as a systematic approach to the credit investigation. Once again it is a cost-benefit type of analysis. Ten dollars should not be spent in the collection of five dollars. The problem is determining just how much pressure should be exerted on customers who are slow in paying. Furthermore, the effect of collection procedures on future sales must be considered. Regardless of the collection procedures employed, the manager must avoid becoming known as a "soft touch." The solution is to formulate a clear-cut reasonable collection plan to be followed in every case without exception. The following discusses such a plan and the various collection tools that have been found to be most effective.

The customer invoice

The collection procedure should begin with the mailing or billing of the customer invoice at the time the goods are shipped or delivered. The invoice informs the customer of the exact amount of total charges and the due date. If a discount is offered on the merchandise for early payment and taken, or if the invoice is paid at maturity, no other collection instrument is necessary. However, the purchaser may not recognize the customer invoice as a collection instrument; hence, the next step in the collection procedure may be necessary.

The statement

The second step consists of mailing a statement of account to the customer. The statement serves as a reminder to the customer of payments due, and also reconciles the records of the seller and the buyer.

There are three generally accepted methods of handling the statement. First, it may be sent to all customers once a month, regardless of whether there are items due. A second approach is to mail the statements on the first of the month only to those accounts that are already delinquent. A third plan is to mail monthly statements only to those customers who request it.

If the statement is to be used as a payment reminder, it should be mailed on the first day of the month to secure the best results. Furthermore, as an inducement to pay promptly, the terms of payment should be printed prominently on the statement. If an account is delinquent, it is quite a common practice to add a collection appeal by means of a rubber stamp or gummed reminder such as "past due," "please remit," or "kindly send us your check."

The collection letter

If the customer invoice and the statement of account fail to bring payment, it becomes necessary to use some sort of collection letter. The collection letter is probably the most-used tool in the collection procedure and the most economical and satisfactory method of collecting past-due accounts.

The manager must avoid being offensive in the latter but at the same time indicate the intention to collect. Regardless of how the collection letter is composed, it has two basic objectives: (1) to let the debtor know the bill must be paid; and (2) to retain the debtor's goodwill. Some creditors use a series of three letters. The first is a reminder; the second more firm; the last promises drastic action.

Collections and the telephone

If the collection letter fails, consider direct contact by the telephone. The telephone has certain distinct advantages as a collection instrument. First, it is more definite than the letter, because it brings an answer. The letter can be ignored, but the debtor can hardly refuse to promise a check or give a reason for not doing so over the telephone.

The primary disadvantage of the telephone is that the manager must still rely on the debtor's promise. The second disadvantage is the difficulty that may be encountered in contacting the debtor who simply refuses to talk on the phone.

The telegram

A number of businesses have been successful in using the telegram as a collection tool. The telegram implies some degree of urgency and has the distinct advantage of getting the debtor's immediate attention. Furthermore, by the time the manager gets to the point of using a telegram, he/she will probably want to use a much stronger appeal. Thus, it is customary to state that the account is overdue and will be referred to an attorney, or even to threaten a civil suit. The telegraph company can suggest wording available for collection appeals.

The personal contact

If all collection tools fail, an attempt should be made to establish personal contact with the debtor. If the volume of slow-paying accounts is large enough, the manager may hire an individual solely for the purpose of making these contacts. Although the personal call is often effective, it has the disadvantage of being expensive.

If the manager cannot afford the services of a personal collector, salespeople may be used if properly trained. In fact, in some lines of business, it is almost imperative that salespeople act as collectors. For instance, the wholesaler selling to retail grocery stores sometimes will place full responsibility for collections on the sales force. The salesperson calls on the customer once a week, and the goods bought one week are paid for the next. If payment is not forthcoming, credit is discontinued. This plan has worked well because the individual placing the order is the same individual who writes the check.

Placing the salesperson in the role of collector does have certain disadvantages. First, the salesperson may feel that chances of selling a customer lessen if he/she also plays the part of collector. Furthermore, the salesperson may feel less welcome because the customer has in mind the debt due. This may lead to more conservative buying and thus lower sales volume.

The collection agency

Once the manager has exhausted all internal efforts to collect, the account should be referred to a collection agency or an attorney. Both use basically the same procedure.

The advantage of using a collection agency is largely psychological. Debtors who are habitually slow-paying know that creditors themselves are rarely in a position to force collections. Thus, as long as the account remains under the creditor's control, the debtor has nothing to fear. But the situation changes once the account passes to a third party. The debtor knows that the collection agency's only interest in the account is to get payment and earn the commission. Thus, referring an account to a collection agency or an attorney is the creditor's ultimatum. All friendly relations are terminated.

Care should be taken in the selection of a collection agency. The laws relating to collection agency practices do not offer much protection to the creditor, and an agency that is temporarily hard-pressed for funds is tempted to use the creditor's money. Two safeguards that are commonly used in working with the collection agency are (1) to be sure that the

monies collected be carried in a separate bank account from the private funds of the agency, and (2) to insist that the agency be adequately bonded.

The local attorney is often used by collection agencies in smaller communities where the agency does not maintain an office. The usual procedure is for the collection agency to make attempts to collect via the mails. When these efforts fail, the account is forwarded to a local attorney who continues the pressure by letter, by telephone, or by personal contact. The local attorney has an influence not possessed by the creditor or the collection agency. Because the lawyer is in a position to start suit at any time, the debtor senses the harm that may be done to his credit reputation.

When the account is forwarded directly to the attorney by the collection agency, the manager will have no direct contact with the local attorney. On the other hand, a lawyer may be used to collect under the direct supervision of the creditor. An advantage of dealing directly with attorneys is that they may work harder for collection because they receive the full fee. When a claim is relayed through a collection agency, the fee is split. The one disadvantage in using an attorney is the cost involved.

The charge-off of bad debts

Considerable difference is found among firms in the practice of charging off customer accounts never collected. The problem is to determine those accounts that are to be considered as lost. Who within the business firm is to decide when an account is uncollectible, and when the charge to bad debts should be made? The person best qualified is the credit manager. Regardless of the procedure used, accounts receivable should be cleared of all bad accounts before the books are closed for the period.

SMALL BUSINESS AND THE CREDIT MANAGEMENT FUNCTION

As previously noted, in the small business firm the volume of credit sales may not justify a full-time credit manager. However, in those cases where the position of credit manager exists, there must be a clear definition of functions. If the credit manager is responsible to the treasurer of the firm, sales volume and profits may suffer because treasurers, being conservative, are too cautious in extending credit. On the other hand, making the credit manager responsible to the general sales manager often proves undesirable because the sales manager tends to be optimistic about borderline credit risks. The preferred arrangement is for the credit manager to be in an independent position in order to be objective and impartial in decisions about credit risks.

QUESTIONS

1. Your text says that "primarily, any decision to offer credit involves comparing the earnings on working capital tied up in credit sales with the earnings the funds would produce if they were invested elsewhere." Explain what is meant by this.

2. How does one go about controlling the level of credit sales?

3. Identify the different kinds of credit arrangements and credit terms explained in your text.

4. What are the four major types of consumer credit?

5. What is meant by MOM? EOM?

6. What are the sources of credit information that your text lists?

7. What does your text mean by the "subjective side" of the credit decision? Explain in detail.

8. How does one go about making a credit decision? Explain in detail.

9. How is a collection letter used?

10. How is a collection agency used?

PROBLEMS

1. Go to a local merchant in the community in which you live or in which your school is located and fill out a credit application. This should be a company that carries its own credit. While filling out the form, ask if you might have a copy of the form to present to your class. If you can obtain one, critically analyze the format compared to the sample form in the text and discuss any differences you find.

2. Telephone a collection agency in the community in which you live or go to school and ask them to explain to you the procedures they use in collecting past-due accounts for their clientele. Report to your

class on the findings and critically analyze why the collection agency does what it does and suggest things that the collection agency does not do they that they might. Explain to your class how these suggestions might be used.

BIBLIOGRAPHY

Abrams, Don. *The Profit Taker*. Somerset, N.J.: John Wiley & Sons, 1980. A practical book on how to make money and make sure that cash is received when it should be.

Gibson, Charles H., and Patricia A. Boyer. *Financial Statement Analysis*. Boston: CBI Publishing, 1978. This book presents an organized, realistic, and balanced approach to financial statement analysis through the extensive use of actual situations and cases. Explains carefully how cash flow can be enhanced.

Nickerson, Clarence B. *Accounting Handbook for Non-Accountants. 2d ed.* Boston: CBI Publishing, 1979. This book is an absolute must for those who need to understand cash flow management, ratio analysis, cash flow analysis, funds flow analysis, and analysis of financial transactions.

Schollhammer, Hans, and Arthur H. Kuriloff. *Entrepreneurship in Small Business Management*. Somerset, N.J.: John Wiley & Sons, 1978. This book covers in detail not only how to start a business but how to run a business. It emphasizes how to avoid many of the cash pitfalls which can entrap a new or small business. Includes real-life cases to illustrate strategic issues.

Tracy, John A. *How to Read a Financial Report: Wringing Cash Flow and Other Vital Signs out of the Numbers*. Somerset, N.J.: John Wiley & Sons, 1979. A short, nontechnical, practical guide that explains, step by step, the basics of the three key statements in financial reports—the balance sheet, the income statement, and the cash flow statement—and the relationships between them. A realistic, practical company example illustrates each key point.

Westlin, Bertil. *New Financial Planning Opportunities for Owners of Closely Held Corporations*. New York: Boardroom Books, 1979. A comprehensive treatise on how owners and managers of closely held corporations can enhance their cash flow position.

Case Study

Deutsch Electrical

Al Fredericks was just getting into his car after having shared a rather prolonged luncheon with Bob Deutsch. Bob was one of the "new period" electrical contractors in the local area (at least, that is what Al called them). What Al meant by the new period was the late 1960s and early 1970s, when many of the youngsters in the field of electrical contracting had taken their apprenticeship.

Actually, Al thought, Bob Deutsch isn't a bad type, but he certainly has gotten himself into some difficulty. When Al began to reflect upon Bob's entry into the business, he realized that it had been inevitable that Bob would someday become an electrical contractor. Bob was an ambitious fellow, serious and genuine, and was an extremely good electrician. Bob had three children and a wife who liked nice things, and the whole package just added up to the circumstance that Bob Deutsch, the minute he got a few bucks together, would start his own electrical contracting firm.

And that is the problem, thought Al. Seems like anymore *anybody* can get into the electical contracting business. In Bob's case, Al knew, his grubstake came two years ago, when Bob's father had died and left him $50,000. Bob had immediately taken the $50,000 plus most of his own savings and set up his own little operation at the edge of the new shopping district. And now, thought Al, as is so typical of the guy who has a little ambition, inherits a little dough, and sets about establishing his own business, Bob is in financial straits and Al was betting that Bob couldn't pull out of his trouble.

Al has suspected for some time that Bob was getting in over his head, but it wasn't until today that Bob had called Al and asked to have lunch with him. Al knew something was up when Bob suggested lunch because Bob just wasn't the kind of guy who did that very often. They had gone to lunch at the steak house, which was a nice comfy little out-of-the-way restaurant with a passable bar. When they had sat down, Bob had immediately ordered himself a martini, which was unusual. He then looked at Al and had said, "I guess you're wondering why I asked to get together with you? Well, the answer is that I am in real trouble. I am in such a financial bind that I am afraid I am going to lose my business." Al looked at Bob and said, "Bob, why don't you tell me all about it and I will see if I can be of any help."

The story of Deutsch Electrical

"Well," said Bob, "things had been going along pretty good for me over the past two years since I opened up my operation, at least up until this recession started. As you know, I got that one home project down south of town, and I really thought I was going to make a bundle on that. And I guess I would have made a bundle if it hadn't been for a few problems like skyrocketing material costs and now that damned Bill Jones (the general contractor on the project) is holding up final settlement with me. Well, as you know, it is kind of tough not to get some money that you are counting on. That $15,000 would go a long way toward helping me pay some of my bills. I don't know what I can do about Bill Jones and make him cough up; I sure am sorry that I bid on that job now."

"Well, it's all water under the bridge now," said Al, "but you know that Bill Jones is considered a rascal by most of us in the electrical contracting business in our area. You know I didn't even bid on that job, just because I didn't want to have to work with Bill. But that doesn't help your situation now. However, I don't imagine that that is your only problem. What else seems to be going wrong for you?"

"You're right, Al," said Bob, "that $15,000 from Bill Jones isn't the only money that I haven't received that I have been kind of counting on. In fact, I was talking to Shirley—my bookkeeper—yesterday afternoon and it looks to me like everybody in this whole city owes me money and I don't know how to get it out of them. In fact, right now, I have accounts receivable of about $50,000. I took a friend of mine's advice about a week ago and reviewed some of my accounts receivable, and do you know that I have $24,300 worth of accounts receivable that are more than 60 days past due. How do you handle your accounts receivable, Al, and is that out of line?"

"Well, it sounds pretty high to me," said Al, "but I don't think that it would be your only problem. Why don't you go ahead and explain some of the other difficulties you said that you were having."

"Well, another problem I have," Bob continued, "is that of keeping my help, or at least keeping those that are good employees. I don't know what it is—whether it is my leadership style or just what—but it seems like whenever I get a guy who really works effectively with the tools, he leaves. In fact I don't have anybody who has been working for me longer than four and a half months, and I'm beginning to think that something is wrong in that department."

"I know from my own experience it is hard to make it when you have got new people working for you all the time," said Al. "I know I couldn't make it if I didn't have Brad, Cletus and Ed. You know Ed has been with me now for going on 15 years and that continuity of employment certainly has been valuable to me."

"I don't know what it is that I am doing wrong," said Bob. "After all, we pay all our people the same rates, and I don't think I am that tough of a guy to work for. Oh, I'll admit I get a little bit uptight sometimes when I find these guys doing sloppy work. I guess the thing that I really worry a lot about is the material that some of the guys carry home with them—not to mention the tools. It always seems like every job that I bid on takes 10 percent more of everything than the specs seem to have provided for, and all I ever get from my people is 'it was damaged' or 'broken' or 'someone else must have walked off with it.' I read my guys the riot act occasionally, but I don't think I get anywhere with it."

About that time the waitress brought the food that Bob and Al had ordered and they began eating. The subject changed for a few minutes, but then Bob had another thought: "Al," said Bob, "you know I have another problem with my people, come to think about it. It seems like every project engineer I have ever had—and you know I have had four of them in the last two years—always fouls me up in scheduling. I am beginning to wonder if it is my fault. You know it seems like when I bid a job, I've got a pretty good idea of how long it should take to do the various things and I've got a real sound image in my mind as to the sequence of work. But it seems like when we actually get started on the job, things never work out quite right. Either I or my supervisor have a breakdown in communications or something, but anyway it seems like we never have the material ordered on time or at least never seem to have the material needed on the job when we need it. It always seems like things happen—like just the other day, when I sent Claude out on one of those residential jobs, I outlined the job for him and told him all that he would need to take. Well, he got there and come to find out he didn't have enough boxes with him to finish the job. So what happened? He drove clear across town to my shop to pick up the boxes he needed and drove clear back. It took him better than an hour to do it. I would have been happier if he had just walked into your office and bought some boxes from you and paid full retail price for it. It would have been cheaper in the long run. You know, Al, I have been exposed to some of this fancy planning stuff like PERT and critical path method that some of the general contractors fool around with, but i never put much stock in it. But there must be something to the technique, or at least they seem to have fewer problems like that than I do, or I don't know how they can stay in business."

"What do you think you are going to do now," asked Al. "Do prospects look so bleak that you think you are going to have to fold up or do you think you can pull out of it?"

"There is no question about one thing," said Bob, "I have to get some money in somehow. I have been thinking about bidding on that new housing project over in Watham Hills. You know that is 125 units and if I went in real low, I am pretty sure I can get it and that will get some cash coming in. I don't know, Al, what do you think?"

Exhibit 1

DEUTSCH ELECTRICAL
Profit and Loss Statement

Sales			$440,000
Less:	Materials	$237,500	
	Direct labor.	108,600	
	D.J.E.	21,900	
	All others	5,700	
	Total prime cost.	373,700	
Gross profit			66,300
Less: Overhead expenses			60,300
	Total operating profit (loss) before taxes		$ 6,000

Exhibit 2

DEUTSCH ELECTRICAL
Balance Sheet
Assets

Current assets:	
Cash	$ 4,000
Inventory	18,000
Accounts receivable	50,200
Other	3,000
Total current assets.	75,200
Fixed assets less depreciation:	
Land and building	34,200
Equipment	25,100
Trucks	21,000
Total fixed assets	80,300
Total assets	$155,500

Liabilities

Current liabilities:	
Accounts payable	$ 33,000
Notes payable.	22,000
Accrued expenses	2,100
Accrued wages	2,400
Taxes	700
Interest	300
Long-term due	200
Total current liabilities	60,700
Long-term debt:	
Notes payable.	5,000
Other notes	2,600
Total long-term	7,600
Total liabilities	68,300
Stockholders' equity	87,200
Total stockholders' equity and liabilities.	$155,500

QUESTIONS

1. You are Al Fredericks. What will your advice be to Bob Deutsch?
2. What additional information would you need before you could effectively advise Bob?
3. How would you use this information if it were available to you?
4. Do you think Bob will be able to borrow any money from the usual sources of credit for someone in a business like his?

19

Planning for managing

To plan means to make a detailed program of action, involving the selection of objectives, policies, and procedures. There should be little confusion as to what is meant by planning and little doubt in the small business person's mind about the importance of planning. Planning is needed for the successful operation of any business, hence the ability to plan is one of the essential elements of small business leadership.

Despite the wealth of evidence in support of the fact that planning should, and does, pay off in successful business operations, lip service is often all that is paid to that need by small business people. Therefore the importance of planning to the success of the small business cannot be overemphasized. Planning is necessary at all levels of management, particularly the top level.

MANAGING FOR RESULTS

In recent years the concept of management known as "management by objectives" or "management for results" has emerged as a useful tool for the small business person in establishing performance goals and

343

objectives for the business operation. The concept of management by objectives was originated by Peter Drucker in his book *The Practice of Management,* published in 1964.

Although the concept of management by objectives is relatively well known, many people who own and/or manage small businesses are not aware of what the concept truly means. It is one thing to say that one should establish performance objectives as an integral process of making and executing business plans. It is something else for someone to genuinely understand what establishing these performance goals and objectives means. Management by objectives does not mean such things as writing out job descriptions for employees; nor does it mean a technique to use in measuring a subordinate's performance. Management by objectives concerns itself with establishing specific performance goals and objectives for various parts of the organization. If the business is truly small—say, five people or less—management by objectives might involve a single policy statement that specifies what the business expects to do in terms of growth, developing its share of the market, and meeting a target return on investment. If the business is larger, however, the statements of objectives assume a different character. In a larger business with various operating departments or units, objectives will be stated for the overall corporation as well as for each department or major subunit of the business firm.

Establishing objectives

Establishing performance goals and objectives for a going small business is not an easy task. However, there is a rather common sequence or routine that can be followed. The sequence includes the following steps:

Step 1. Set up a policy committee, establishing who will serve on the committee (this might be the board of directors, or only the owner if the business is extremely small); define its duties; determine the completion date for the statement of objectives.

Step 2. Assign members of the policy-making group their various duties in developing their ideas and/or outlining what the policies and objectives of the business ought to be with respect to specific functions within the organization.

Step 3. Have the policy maker(s) review the policy statements outlined by the various individuals and assess the effect of the individual policies on mutually dependent functions.

Step 4. Agree to the policy to be established and reduce that policy to written form.

Step 5. Assign individuals within the separate functions of the organization to outline detailed operating plans and objectives that they will use in implementing the policies and accomplishing the objectives agreed on in step 4.

Step 6. As a committee, review the overall policy manual, by function, to correct any errors or omissions that may have occurred.

Step 7. Implement the stated policy and objectives.

The procedures involved in establishing the business policy manual should be carried out methodically. Common sense, of course, prevails, for it is a simple planning function that is to be carried out: making sure that the plans are thorough and concise and then implementing the plan. However, one thing must be pointed out clearly. All of the various functional areas within the business must be considered in establishing the plan. Thoroughness is probably more important than any other factor in establishing the goals and objectives of a business firm.

What goes into business objectives

Business objectives can encompass many things. However, the following items are usually considered in establishing overall objectives by most small businesses.

1. Financial objectives.
2. Personnel objectives.
3. Customer and public relations objectives.
4. Advertising objectives.
5. Accounting objectives.
6. Production objectives.
7. Credit and collection objectives.
8. Purchasing and inventory control objectives.
9. Sales objectives.
10. Profit objectives.
11. Legal objectives.
12. Security objectives for the organization.

In very small businesses many of the above functions cannot be clearly separated from each other and many of the areas may overlap. Nevertheless, it is incumbent upon the small business manager to establish operating goals and objectives in each of these specific areas.

How one plans and manages by objectives

In a functioning system of management by objectives, the senior operating executive must necessarily establish overall goals and objectives of the business. He or she should do this through a committee of people who know what is going on in the operation.

Many small business managers have found that there is a cycle in the establishment of *performance* goals. Essentially the cycle—Phase 1—

begins when the overall policies and objectives are established for the business. Then, in Phase 2, the small business person allocates portions of the objectives to subordinates, who actually are responsible for achieving them. These individuals are then set free in Phase 3 to take appropriate action in their departments to obtain the desired goals.

Phase 4 in the cycle of management by objectives is accomplished when, after the subordinates have had sufficient time to execute their assignments, a review is made to compare the results with the original goals. At this stage, a formal assessment is made of progress, and then the cycle starts all over again. Thus, Phase 5 is simply a repeat of Phase 1 (in which the manager of the business establishes new objectives to be obtained by the organization). These new objectives are based on the degree of success or failure that subordinates have had in reaching the original objectives. Thus Phase 5 might include the renewal of some of the original objectives of Phase 1, if they were not realized.

REQUIREMENTS FOR PLANNING

The fine art of managing any small business necessarily requires that the small business manager be adept at planning. But what kinds of planning does a small business manager engage in? Does one actually differentiate in the types of plans that one makes? Exactly what are the requirements for effective planning in a small business?

These questions must be answered if one is to become an effective manager of a small business. There are certain capabilities required for good planning in any small business and these essentials include:

Seeing the situation as a whole

A primary ingredient of effective planning in the small business is that the small business person see the situation as a whole. This is why it was emphasized in the first portion of this chapter that overall goals for the business must be established. This is true whether the business is very small or quite large. The overall goals must be seen before the subordinates' goals and objectives can be established for each operating department or unit.

Dividing the whole into workable parts

Once the manager has taken an overall view of the objectives, he/she must be able to break the whole situation into workable parts. This is why it is so important that the various categories of objectives be clearly developed in the overall corporate policy statements. Each of these statements then can be broken down into parts for production operations, financial control, advertising plans and strategies, and other purposes.

Using constructive imagination

Many people do not use imagination constructively in trying to establish performance goals. Wishing something so does not make it so, but trying to define where one wishes to go with one's business is not wishful thinking if it is based upon realistic, concrete, obtainable, and measurable performance objectives. Thus it is imperative that the small business person try to define what the performance goals of the business will be, in terms of the quantity of business expected, the quality of work expected, the time budget within which the goals are to be realized, and the corresponding financial budget. In fact, these four criteria—quantity, quality, time, and cost—are the only constraints upon any small business person in trying to be constructively imaginative in determining goals for each major operating unit within the business organization.

Being objectively analytical

The small business manager will be ineffective at planning if he/she is unrealistic in establishing performance goals. Necessarily, therefore, effective small business managers are objectively analytical in assessing what they intend to do in each forthcoming period. They do not expect to reach the unreachable or obtain the unobtainable. However, they do necessarily attempt to challenge their organizations to perform to their capabilities. This requires a very realistic and honest assessment of what the expectations for the business can actually be.

Measuring the effect of the plan

Yet another dimension essential to planning at the small business level is a capability to measure what is happening when the plan is being implemented. It must be recognized it is is possible to overplan or underplan for any business. Just so, it is also possible to overcontrol or undercontrol the implementation of that plan. Many small business persons plan, but fail to set up ways to measure the implementation of the plan. Others set up excessive control devices that are a hindrance to thorough and accurate implementation of the plans. Realism again becomes the key. In this case, however, the key to success concerns realism in the measurement of the performance of the plan as it is being implemented and not the realism of the plan itself.

Avoiding getting bogged down in details

Some people become emotionally attached to the irrelevant. Many small business managers, in attempting to establish operating plans for their organization, get bogged down in detail and never truly define an overall statement of plans for the business. Getting bogged down in the details of planning is a result of failure to keep attention focused on the task at home. It is imperative to realize that the primary purpose is to establish the plan.

Working with many unknowns

Another essential requirement for effective planning upon the part of the small business person is the ability to operate in the face of uncertainty. More attention will be devoted to this later in the chapter, but it must be realized that this ability to face uncertainty is indispensable to effective planning.

ESTABLISHING PLANS OF OPERATION

The first section of this chapter was designed to explain the use of the concept of management by objectives in planning for the overall operation of the small business. Now it is necessary to probe into some refinements of the planning function. This and the following sections will be devoted to that task.

One of the primary jobs of the small business manager is the establishment of a master or long-run plan of operation for the firm. Master planning should, ideally, be complete before the firm is a going, operating concern. Unfortunately, many small businesses are started without benefit of a master plan of operation. Thus, many small business managers find that even though their concerns are rolling merrily along, they have no long-run plan of operation. Whether the small business person is planning to start a business or has a going concern that he/she wants to perpetuate, the principles of establishing such plans are the same.

The time to dream and the time to be conservative and realistic

One of the fundamental principles of establishing a master plan of operation is recognition that there is a difference between dreaming and realistic planning. Plans very definitely should not be based on wishful thinking about things that can never be accomplished. By way of example, General Motors will not be replaced in the near future, no matter how carefully plans are made by anyone now starting an automobile manufacturing firm. The same thing can be said for any of the firms that rank among the 100 largest in the United States.

The foregoing is obviously a truism. No small business manager is going to displace one of the corporate giants existing in the United

States today. Yet, businesses do not grow by chance; they are *caused* to grow by entrepreneurs who establish plans that push and stretch the company's abilities within reasonable limits. Although small business managers are wasting their time and money when they make plans that overreach their capacity and abilities, they are being realistic and striving for success if they are designing plans that stretch their capabilities to their limits. One needs to know the capacities and capabilities of one's company. One needs to know whether one's people will be able to produce or sell according to plan. One needs to know one's resources, and how much money can be spent.

Strategies and tactics of master planning

The strategies and tactics of making a master plan of operation for a small business firm are as much an art as a science. In developing such plans of operation, small business managers are formulating and directing their own futures. But, as was pointed out above, the manager is possibly limited by two serious factors: uncertainty and lack of imagination.

Uncertainty. Planning, to be realistic, has to deal with uncertainty. Lack of certainty about future events limits one's ability to plan, but the one's mere existence of uncertainty is not always a disadvantage for the small business planner. The reason is that uncertainty also exists for one's competitors. Although the small business person cannot predict the future, neither can competitors. Further, the small business person can even capitalize on the existance of uncertainty. There is little question that those companies that forecast and plan well for the most likely eventualities are better prepared than those which do not plan and are caught by surprise. Thus, the planning small business manager can work the negative features of uncertainty to advantage simply by facing the issue squarely.

Imagination. Planning requires imagination, and most people don't possess much imagination. Thus, limited imagination can pose a problem for the small business in planning where the firm will be 5, 10, or 15 years.

The successful small business planner is one who possesses the imagination to foresee the future with some degree of accuracy. Naturally, some people are more adept at this task than others. Everyone possesses some imagination and however limited, it should be put to use in speculating about the future.

Benefits and advantages of long-run and master planning

There are some positive aspects to the task of master planning. One of these positive aspects is that the planning centers on a subject with which the small business manager is familiar. This lightens the task considerably, for it is much easier to plan the future when one knows the market in which one is operating.

A second advantage to small business persons in practicing the art of master planning is that they are making plans that will affect themselves. This means that the small business person has the opportunity to reject committing the business to those things that he/she does not want to do or does not feel capable of doing. At the same time, the manager can attempt to commit the business to things that are felt to be desirable. This is not always possible for the professional manager hired by a large corporation.

Normally, when one plans, certain courses of action are established while others are precluded. Precluding certain courses of action takes away much flexibility that would be available were the plans not made, and thus the plans can become a disadvantage if they are followed even though events take an unexpected course. This does not have to be the case in master planning, however, because the strategy of the master planner can be designed along the lines of making plans that can be changed at reasonable cost and in reasonable time should the situation require it. In other words, the small business person can plan to avoid crises and their high costs. This sometimes requires that the small business manager lay two sets of plans: one to be followed when things go right, and the other to be used if things go wrong.

Formalizing the plan

Once a master plan of operation has been developed, it should be formalized. Concrete plans are usually accomplished; vague ones are not. For example, the difference between the following two proposals is apparent: "I really need to start an investment program; I think I'll buy some property" and "I made a bid on the corner lot of Broadway and Pearl consistent with my overall investment plans of buying one acre of commercial property this year." Obviously, the person in the first situation really has nothing more than wishful thoughts, perhaps a good idea, and probably little likelihood of ever investing in real estate. But the second person has taken formal action consistent with a definite plan. Obviously the second person is more apt to invest in real estate.

Analogous to the foregoing example, the small business manager who formulates clear, concise plans and spells them out in detail is much more apt to develop better plans than is the individual who simply speculates from the comfort of a rocking chair. Put simply, so long as a plan is nothing more than a vague idea, it is not much of a plan; formalized plans that have been put down in writing are much

more likely to be carried out, and the desired results are much more likely to be obtained.

The advantages of formalizing a master plan are so great that doing without one is foolish for any small business manager. In operational terms, these advantages include the following:

1. Master planning helps direct the efforts of the organization into new growth areas, thus avoiding stagnant and/or low profit areas.
2. Master planning not only shows the areas of operations which the firm should go into in the future, but also discloses when action must be taken to get into those specific business areas.
3. Master planning helps the manager take stock of business operations and identify the sources of strength and weaknesses in the organization.
4. Master planning highlights various future needs such as additional manpower, subordinate managers, machinery, new facilities, and new locations. It helps give stability to the firm, particularly in the

short run, because it serves as a source of perspective as to how particular short-run plans fit into the overall scheme of things.

OTHER PLANNING METHODS

Short-run planning

Master and long-run planning is concerned with the entire foreseeable future; short-run planning applies to the more immediate time period of three to six months, or, at most, a year. Thus, although short-run planning deals with the future, it does not permit total reshaping and redirection of the firm. It requires much more careful and specific formulation.

Short-run planning is essential to the day-to-day success of the small business. It involves the small business person with specific problems and issues that cannot always be anticipated in long-run planning. By way of example, one small business manager failed to recognize in her long-run plan that property that she held had some commercial value. However, due to the rerouting of a road the property's commercial value increased considerably, and in the short run the small business person had ample time to capitalize on the increased value of her land holdings.

Thus, the nature of short-run planning emerges. It gives the small business person the opportunity to work within the framework of long-run and master plans, but it also allows the implementation of long-run and master plans in the most efficient and effective way possible. Short-run planning permits the vague, ambiguous areas of the long-run plan to crystallize into shape. In the short run, small business managers are better able to see the situation that is developing as a whole. Thus, they can be more objective and analytical in evaluating the situation and can avoid getting bogged down in details which are meaningless. Finally, the short run gives the manager more rapid feedback on the efficacy of the plan and how it may be changed to promote effectiveness.

Planning for special events

Another kind of planning in which the small business person will frequently engage is planning for a special event. This is often called task-force management or project management. But it is really no different from any of the other types of planning. However, the importance of integrating the special events plans with the long- and short-run plans of the firm cannot be overemphasized. The problem is that many times small business managers find themselves in the position of not seeing the forest for the trees. They fail to recognize the ramifications and implications of following a particular course of activity in implementing a special project, and as a result, they end up encumbering—if not destroying—the rest of the operations.

One example of this problem that comes to mind is the case of the once-small business operated by Henry Ford:

> Henry Ford made a relatively inexpensive automobile available to the American public through his production genius—and made barrels of money in the process. Yet, because of his disregard for the marketing function, company dealers, competition and customers, he succeeded in piloting his company from an undisputed and unchallenged first place in the auto industry in 1927 to a miserable and challenged second place in 1928. He did this by closing shop for six months to introduce his Model A, and because of his short-sighted plan succeeded in pushing his company from the class of one of the greatest money makers to one of the greatest money losers of that time.[1]

Thus, by becoming engrossed in the changeover from producing the Model T to producing the Model A, Ford nearly destroyed his whole enterprise.

Crisis planning

Another planning situation that the typical small business person is faced with is the business crisis. As mentioned above, although planning helps avoid most crises, some will arise no matter how well plans have been formulated. If a decision must be made in the face of a crisis, the following guidelines should be used:

1. The manager should get into a relaxed frame of mind and try not to decide anything under stress or without sufficient time, but should concentrate on the problem at hand and exclude other things for the time being.
2. The manager should not try to anticipate all eventualities. Not only are there entirely too many things that could happen, but such an effort may prevent focusing on the logically predictable effects of any decisions.
3. The manager should not expect to be right all of the time. In a crisis, the successful manager is probably right only a little more often than wrong.
4. The manager should not be afraid of failure. Fear of failure is one of the biggest causes of failure and creates additional mental tension, which tends to muddle one's thoughts.
5. The manager should act decisively. Indecision itself creates tension,

---

[1]From an unpublished paper by Lawrence L. Steinmetz on the Ford Motor Company.

while tenacity of purpose will make up for minor shortcomings in the plans formulated.

6. When a true crisis arises, the manager should decide how to act and not put off making the decision. Procrastination will only increase the difficulties.

7. The manager should try to develop alternative solutions if conditions warrant, but by the same token must be willing to stick by the original decision rather than continually mulling over it and trying to modify it. The manager must recognize that it is more important to be decisive than to have the right plan—that alternative plans should be invoked only upon total failure of the original plan.

PERSONAL PLANNING—AN EXAMPLE OF THE PROBLEMS ENCOUNTERED IN PLANNING FOR THE DAILY OPERATIONS OF THE SMALL BUSINESS

Indivisibility of employees

Personnel planning is one of the most trying situations that a typical small business manager will encounter. The major problem with personnel planning is that, unlike many other things, people are not divisible. The small business manager can buy things, build things, and otherwise establish things pretty much in units of a size that will best fit his/her needs. But in the case of personnel, this is not possible to the same degree, particularly in the very small firm. People are people, and they must be hired, one at a time. Of course it is possible to hire people part-time, but only in exceptional circumstances are good, qualified, valuable employees obtainable in this way. Most qualified people who want to work want full-time employment. The one exception to this is the person who because of health, family, or other reasons, desires a limited work load. Such situations, although permitting the hiring of a part of a person, usually are not satisfactory because they often end up with the small business person creating unnecessary work for the part-time employee during slack periods—an expensive proposition. The indivisibility of people is even more of a problem when hiring managerial personnel. Most small businesses have one, two, or three subordinate managers who control the various functions of the operation. Many times, such a firm is large enough to hire the exact amount of of rank-and-file help needed, but not big enough to hire the exact amount of high-level managerial talent needed.

This problem is more severe than the one of indivisibility of rank-and-file employees because of the higher salaries paid to managers and the scarcity of qualified part-time managerial help. For example, as can be seen in Figure 19–1, it might be possible for the Kis Company to hire as many rank-and-filers as needed in each of its three plants, but a whole manager must be hired for each plant—even though the operations at plant 3 amount to only half the magnitude of the work at plants 1 and 2 and require only half as many employees. The ideal solution to this situation is to hire half a manager, which is impossible. What does happen is either the hiring of excessive managerial talent or the stretching of limited managerial talent. In either case the result is an expensive mismatch between managerial ability and the requirements of the position.

Lack of facilities for developing managers

The indivisibility of employees is further compounded by the fact that most small business firm's lack funds to properly recruit, select, develop, and train personnel. But even if money is not a problem, there is still the indivisibility problem, which shows up on two counts. First is the indivisibility of the employees being recruited, selected, developed, and trained; second is the indivisibility of the people who are actually performing the personnel function. General Motors can have several personnel departments across the country, but the Kis Company can logically have only one. This means that the Kis Company may be adversely affected in its personnel functions because of the need to spread the personnel manager's efforts around to three different plants.

Lack of economies of scale

The third problem that complicates the personnel-planning aspect for the small business firm is lack of the usual economies of scale that larger business firms can capitalize on in dealing with their employees. One such diseconomy comes from the compensation aspect of employing

Figure 19–1
Kis Company organizational chart

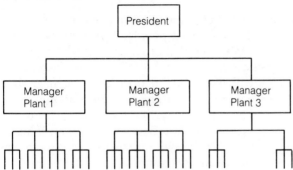

people. The bookwork process required is the same, whether 25 or 2,500 people are paid. Though the process is repeated several additional times in the larger corporation, the same kinds of books and records must be kept by all. Whether the records are many or few, they incur certain fixed costs that are disproportionately large for the small business.

Another lack of economy of scale arises in the administration of fringe benefits to small business employees. For instance, both small and large corporation usually provide sickness and accident insurance for their employees. However, large corporations get breaks on their expenses for these fringe benefits because they can enroll their employees in company group plans. Most small businesses are not large enough to compose a "group" and therefore must enroll in one of the many commercial group plans, paying a higher rate. The rate is higher partly for statistical reasons, but also because the large corporations can often reduce their premiums by keeping a staff nurse and/or a staff physician on the corporate payroll to treat employees for minor injuries. Obviously a small business the size of the Kis Corporation cannot hire a physician to be in residence at its plants. Therefore, the cost of any insurance plan per employee would be higher for the Kis Corporation than for the large business firm.

Personality complications

Another problem in personnel planning is the possible conflict of personalities that can be anticipated but cannot be predicted by a small business manager. The problem is that in the small business everybody knows everyone else. This can create a situation involving a great degree of harmony and unison of action with complete accord on the part of all employees. However, it can just as easily cause a great deal of discord. This disharmony will work to the detriment of the small business firm because one disgruntled person represents a much larger percentage of the total work force in the small business firm than in the larger firm.

The chore of planning

Personnel planning can be one of the most trying of all small business planning efforts because of the nature of people. Not only are people indivisible, they also tend to talk back and often have opinions of their own. Thus, any small business manager who fails to plan in terms of staffing the establishment will likely fail in operating the firm. It is essential that the small business manager think in terms not only of the short run ("Who will be my fry cook today?") but also in the long run ("Who will be my maître d' five years from now when I've hit it big?") and even in the longer run ("Who will ultimately replace me as president and general manager of my restaurant chain?").

People-planning problems are not the only sticky problems that the small business must face. Many other planning problems are just as critical and difficult. Therefore, it is necessary for the small business manager to learn to plan. Plans must be made for the long run and the short run, the crisis, and for special events. Logically, this can all be accomplished by incorporating the concept of management by objectives, which not only gives completeness to the planning but also gives timely and accurate feedback, as required, particularly for short-run plans.

PLANS THAT FAIL

Before we leave the topic of planning, one other element must be considered. Planning for success does not guarantee success; sometimes plans fail. The most common reasons for failure include misguessing, failing to assess the public's reaction properly, or failing to foresee certain events as being probabilities.

Thus, the small business manager should accept the likelihood of failure at some time or other in attaining the goals that have been established through careful planning. However, such a result should not cause a great deal of concern. To begin with, this is not an uncommon phenomenon. But more importantly, to have plans go awry does not mean complete failure, nor that the small business planner is worse off than there been no plan at all. Planning, whether the plans are realized or not, will help shape the direction, goal, and ultimate destiny of the firm. If the firm is anywhere near being well conceived and well founded, the plans should have helped it realize better results. It might be well to keep in mind the advice of the Cheshire Cat in Lewis Carroll's *Alice's Adventures in Wonderland:* If you don't know where you're going, any path will take you there.

QUESTIONS

1. Explain the concept of management by objectives.

2. Can the concept of management by objectives be used in evaluating the efficiency of a small business? Of a part of a small business? How?

3. Explain how to establish objectives in a going concern, being careful to trace through the whole process.

4. What is meant by a master plan of operation? Must all small businesspeople concern themselves with such plans? Why?

5. Explain the role of uncertainty in the function of planning. Can uncertainty be used to the advantage of the small business?

6. What are the advantages to long-run planning? Any disadvantages?

7. What is the difference between long-run and short-run planning? Are both important? Why?

8. When is crisis planning appropriate? How should it be done by the small business if it is to be successful?

9. Develop some of the planning problems you think are peculiar to small business operations.

10. What should the small business planner do if he or she fails in carrying out his or her plans?

PROBLEM

Dick Tutton picked up his cup of coffee, took a big gulp, and told Fred Rose that he had to get back to work. Fred said, "You're always strung out, Dick. You need to get better organized."

Leaving the coffee shop on his way back to his office supply company, Dick reflected on Fred's comments. "I know my work seems disorganized, but what could I do differently?" he thought. "I tell people what to do and then watch them mess it up. I was told it was bad management strategy to just do what one's subordinates can't do. But what other way is there? It certainly seems that there ought to be a better way of doing things. But I sure don't know what it is. I wonder if Mr. Byte, the banker, could help me?"

You are Mr. Byte.

a. What would you tell Dick?
b. Are there any systems of management that Dick should know about? What are they? How do they work?
c. What three important management tips might you give Dick?

BIBLIOGRAPHY

Baumback, Clifford M., and Kenneth Lawyer. *How to Organize and Operate a Small Business.* 6th ed. Englewood Cliffs, N.J.: Prentice-Hall, 1979, chaps. 12 and 13.

Drucker, Peter F. *Managing for Results.* New York: Harper & Row, 1964.

Frantz, Forrest H. *Successful Small Business Management.* Englewood Cliffs, N.J.: Prentice-Hall, 1978, chap. 13.

Moreau, James F. *Effective Small Business Management.* Chicago: Rand McNally, 1980, chap. 7.

Redinbaugh, Larry D., and Clyde W. Neu. *Small Business Management.* St. Paul, Minn.: West Publishing, 1980, chap. 3.

20

Management of the organization

The basic process of management is concerned with planning, organizing, directing, and controlling work. That is, the manager must be able to conceive the total operation in order to plan what and when things will be done; to organize employees, machinery, and material around these plans; to direct the performance of the plans through organization; and to maintain adequate control over the entire operation.

This chapter deals first with the nature of management, then with those things that are related to the organization; i.e., those who are managed and how management implements its decisions through subordinates and the organizational structure.

PART I—MANAGEMENT

To be successful as a small business manager, one must instill in one's subordinates a degree of entrepreneurial spirit and feeling. This first of all means that the small business manager must understand what is meant by "entrepreneurial spirit" or personality. Basically the successful entrepreneur is one who possesses a hardworking, middle-class set of social values but little desire to move up the social ladder or to become socially prominent. This is, in turn, coupled with an unremitting, unyielding desire to achieve and accomplish certain objectives.

Developing such a spirit in a subordinate is not a simple task, particularly since the small business person many times may personally display little respect for lines of authority and control and is sometimes accused of being unable to achieve satisfactory relationships with subordinates except on a partriarchal or patronizing basis. Thus a dilemma arises: Although instilling entrepreneurial spirit in one's subordinates is essential to developing a winning combination of people, material, machines, and money in the business world, the very personality pattern that will foster success in small business management sometimes tends to conflict with achieving such success. How, then, does one solve this dilemma and create a strong management team?

HOW GOOD MANAGERS SUCCEED AT MANAGING

The foregoing highlights the fact that small business managers have their work cut out for them if they are to develop a winning combination among subordinates. This is true whether the small business organization is composed of two persons or two hundred: the fact remains that the manager is responsible for developing the people in the organization. Fortunately, there are some guidelines that can be used by the small business manager in making things happen in the desired manner. These guidelines are concerned with a way of thinking about managing and, therefore, cannot be compiled like a grocery list. Thus, each will be discussed in turn rather than merely listed.

The good manager makes things happen. Nicholas Murray Butler, former president of Columbia University, once said that there were three kinds of people: people who make things happen, those who watch things happen, and those who don't know what has happened. Effective small business managers not only know what is happening but also make things happen. They make their own decisions to increase sales, to develop new products, to cut costs, to improve quality, to tap new markets, or to expand plant or facilities. Further, once these managers have determined what they intend to make happen, they will put all of their brains, leadership, and drive into making it happen. The manager who engages in making things happen is, of necessity, a dynamic, driving individual, one who is unaswering and unremitting in the pursuit of shaping not only the company but the total business environment.

The vital shift from doer to managers. A second guideline for the effective small business manager is to be a manager rather than a doer. This requirement is becoming even more necessary today than it was several years ago.

A manager is an expert in analyzing situations, in classifying problems, seeing cause and effect relationships, and in identifying and pursuing the proper course of action. This, of course, requires that the successful small business manager be a creative thinker who can predict and foresee unfortunate or troublesome circumstances before they arise. Such creative thinking requires that the small business manager work *smarter* rather than *harder* and think along broad lines rather than along lines of specialized, limited procedures.

People and management success. The third requirement for successful small business managers is that they not go out of their way to be "nice," or a friendly competitor, a swell boss, or otherwise popular individual. This doesn't mean the small business person should have Scrooge as a model (although Scrooge *was* a *financially* successful small business manager). It does mean, however, that it is not essential to be the most popular boss in three counties to be the successful manager of a small business.

The principle behind this requirement is that no one person will be liked by all people, and that persons who attempt to or endeavor to be liked by all people will necessarily alienate some people. One anonymous expert on the management of people described his own experiences in this regard in the following manner:

> I once believed that a leader could operate successfully as a kind of adviser to his organization and could avoid being a "boss." In doing so, I suspect I hoped to duck the unpleasant necessity of making difficult decisions and taking the responsibility for one course of action among many uncertain alternatives. I couldn't have been more wrong, but it took a couple of years to realize that a leader cannot avoid the exercise of authority any more than he or she can avoid responsibility for what happens to the organization.

Being results-oriented. A fourth guideline for successful small business management is to be results- and responsibility-oriented. This means that the small business manager must know precisely what results to expect from the plans he/she has made. This also means that small business managers will be responsible for their actions in achieving these results. The ends do not necessarily justify the means, but the end result does have to be clearly defined. Take, for example, the commonly sought results of profits and growth of the firm. These results cannot be accomplished without full regard for the rights of all individuals affected in the organization. Extracting profits and developing a growing organization based on unethical conduct or shady means will not result in a well-founded and firmly established, continuing enterprise, or one that has a strong team. Yet, by the same token, if the organization *is* composed of subordinates who are aware of the ordinary standards of fair play and good conduct and who are *also* clearly results-oriented, the ethical small business manager will likely attain the desired results.

The effective small business manager works through the organization The final guideline that the small business manager can use in developing an effective and winning combination is to work through the organization and efforts from that organization rather than alone. This maxim should be obvious, yet it is an often-ignored principle. The fact is simply this: *Once a small business gets of sufficient size, one person can no longer operate that business.* This means that the manager must develop subordinates, and as the organization continues to grow, must develop large numbers of subordinates.

The development of subordinates requires that the manager be effective at delegating responsibility and authority for various tasks. This requires that the manager relinquish direct control over the performance of the job. Unfortunately many managers seem unable to comply with this final maxim.

WHY SMALL BUSINESS MANAGERS FAIL AT MANAGING

The preceding section has served to point out the need for managerial expertise in building a strong team. Each business has unique problems of its own, but several common pitfalls confront small business managers often result in poor managerial practices. The following sections of this chapter will discuss these pitfalls and how they can be avoided.

Wasting time. Wasting time is one of the most common hazards to good management. It is often difficult if not impossible for the small business manager to determine why time is being wasted. Most managers will feel that everything they do is absolutely essential for satisfactory management of the business.

Despite this attitude, many of the "essential" tasks that managers feel they must accomplish are not only unessential but they are completely superfluous. Although such a statement is likely to be laughed off by the manager (or to cause downright indignation that such an accusation might be made) the truth is that laughing it off or becoming indignant doesn't diminish the pathetic consequences that result from the knowing or unknowing waste of time.

Many managers of small businesses waste more time than they

should. For example, Clark C. Caskey, a noted managerial consultant, found that the reasons managers don't get things done is because they put off, postpone, or otherwise procrastinate in doing things they dislike, find difficult to do, have experienced failure at, do not see as being critical, or feel a lack of opportunity or capability to perform. On the other hand, he found that the things managers spend their time doing are things they like to do, do well, have experienced success at, or have perceived as being absolutely critical. Unfortunately, however, those things that the manager likes to do and is good at do not necessarily carry top priority in *needing* to be done. Thus managers do things that don't need doing and put off doing things that need to be done.

Avoidance of certain duties.   It becomes obvious that the nemesis of many managers is their inability to differentiate between what functions *have* to be performed and what functions are pleasant, fun, or otherwise nice to perform if they have time. Overcoming this pitfall is not easy for small business managers, but it can be done if they will first recognize that many of the activities that take their time do so because the managers are not effecitve in budgeting their time. Difficult as it may be, however, the task of good management is to recognize activites for what they are—necessities or nonessentials.

To help the small business manager analyze his/her own activities and their relative usefulness to the goals and objectives of the business, the following questions need to be asked:

1.   Can this activity be *eliminated* or *delegated?*
2.   Can this activity be *combined* with others?
3.   Can the time required to perform the activity be *reduced?*
4.   Can the sequence of activities be *changed?*

The answers to these questions should provide the small business manager with a great deal of insight as to whether or not particular activities are "fun things" or essential, productive, profit-contributing activities.

Inability to assign work.   Inability to make effective work assignments is another failing of many small bsuiness managers. Such inability can be extremely detrimental because it not only serves as a bad example to the subordinates but also gives them license to fail in performing their jobs. Delegating work effectively permits the supervisor to devote time and attention to other, more critical tasks. Furthermore, it is often an important training device for developing subordinates and building their morale.

The basic reasons that managers fail to delegate work fall into one of the following categories:

1. They are little Napoleons who must satisfy their own ego by keeping all authority.
2. They feel that they can do it better themselves, and they refuse to permit others to do it in a substandard manner.
3. They are unable to communicate to their subordinates precisely what it is that they want done, when, where, and how much.
4. They lack confidence in their subordinates' abilities to do the work that should be delegated to them, because:
   a. They are afraid the subordinate will miss the main point.
   b. They are not sure of the subordinates' judgment in the unusual or uncommon situation.
   c. They feel the subordinates do not follow through on ideas that are given them.
   d. They feel that the subordinates are too young to command the respect of other employees, customers, or clients with whom they will be working.
5. They are afraid that their subordinates will "outshine" them or otherwise prove that they know as much or more about the job than the boss.
6. They are afraid to trust anyone besides themselves.
7. They suffer from a martyr complex—because they desire to have people feel sorry for them, they refuse to delegate work that logically could be done by other people.
8. They are possessed by a "guilt drive"—they feel guilty if they have nothing to do, and delegating work to others leaves them in that awkward position.

The above reasons are basically shortcomings on the part of the small business manager and are easily corrected once they are recognized. Specific actions to take include the following:

1. You must delegate. Managers must recognize that even though all their subordinates look up to them because they control all the puppet strings in the organization, they will not *continue* to control the organizational strings if they do not delegate work to their subordinates. The only small business that can survive as a one-person operation is the small business that is so small it employs only one person.

2. Don't do the job too well. It must be recognized that the "I can do it better myself" fallacy is, in fact, a fallacy. Even if a manager can do a job better than subordinates (which research shows is less often true than the boss usually believes), he or she must nevertheless delegate it to someone who can do the job *well enough.* It is possible to waste time and money by doing some jobs too well, thus jeopardizing the entire operation.

3. Communicate. Inability to communicate to subordinates is a block to effective delegation that can be easily overcome. All that is required is that the boss learn to make an effort to apprise subordinates of plans and objectives and assign responsibilities to them. This can best be done by using a system of "management by objectives," which is a well regarded management technique.

4. *Choose intelligent subordinates.* If the manager lacks confidence in the present subordinates he/she should determine whether or not the subordinates are so ignorant that they often miss the main point of ideas, whether they display poor judgment in crises, and whether they have the ability to follow through on ideas. Any subordinate that fails to pass these tests should be discharged. However, if the problem is the fact that the person is considered too young to command the respect of clients, customers, or co-workers, this mental block should be viewed as precisely that—a mental block. Experience shows that young, knowledgeable, competent people quickly gain the respect of others because of their knowledge and ideas.

5. *Use the management-by-exceptions principle.* The solution to the problem of control is relatively simple. Control means feedback, and feedback can be gained through written or oral reports, periodic observations, or the employment of the management-by-exceptions principle, whereby the manager prescribes rules to cover all usual situations so that subordinates can decide all routine cases by applying these rules. Exceptions—nonroutine situations—are not decided by subordinates but are taken to the manager for resolution.

6. *Recognize your weaknesses.* Fear of being shown up should not be a reason for inability or reluctance upon the part of a manager to delegate work. The sign of a good manager is ability to recognize that his/her abilities lie in certain areas and that there are some areas in which others can do a more effective job. For example, a good manager might be an incompetent bookkeeper. Recognizing this, he/she would do well to hire the best bookkeeper available and take pride in the ability to hire good people and use their talents.

7. *Take a chance on subordinates.* Fear of taking a chance can be a serious detriment to a manager when it comes to delegating work. Certainly the manager would not want to entrust his or her business to a subordinate if a decision might be made that could ruin the business firm. However, this is not the kind of fear that tends to make managers reluctant to delegate. More commonly, it is a simple mental aversion to taking any kind of a chance. This can be overcome, perhaps, by the recognition that operating a business in and of itself requires a certain degree of risk-taking. If the manager is unable to take any risks, he or she should not be trying to operate a business.

8. *Don't be a martyr.* Those managers who enjoy playing the role of the martyr must recognize that the sympathy they enjoy is usually

shortlived and seldom results in admiration. Since recognition is their true goal, they can overcome the martyr complex once they realize they will receive more recognition through a job well done—in this case, the successful management of their business.

9. *Overcome the guilt drive.* The guilt drive, like the martry complex, can easily be overcome once the manager accepts it for what it is—an obstacle to the successful operation of the business. Leisure time is a perfectly ordinary, legitimate, and common goal for which most people work. Furthermore, it is not only a legitimate goal but also a necessary one in terms of physical health.

10. *Recognize that real respect comes from being well organized.* No one who knows what must be done in a business will be accused of being unreasonable as a taskmaster. People who are disorganized or who demand things be done when there is insufficient lead time or unrealistic time constraints become ineffective supervisors. Managers who are well organized practically always are respected and have the reputation of being astute executives.

11. *Recognize that there is seldom sufficient time to do by oneself all the jobs that one wants to do.* Any person running a small, dynamic business will find that there are many things he/she wants to do. But endeavoring to do them all is seldom possible. Thus, priorities must be established and some of the less vital things must be eliminated or assigned to others.

12. *Understand the difference between managing and doing.* Anyone intending to own, operate, and manage a small business must be fully cognizant of his/her obligation to *manage,* leaving the *doing* to subordinates. A manager must plan, organize, direct, control, motivate, communicate, and delegate. He/she has only secondary responsibilities to lift, carry, sort, wrap, disassemble, etc.

Being a leader, not a follower. The lucky manager is the manager who makes things happen. One executive who has given advice as to how managers can make themselves lucky says that the key ingredient is a long-range frame of mind. This frame of mind is based on: (1) application of knowledge, (2) study of all angles that must be considered, (3) direction of brain power toward the qualitative and quantitative aspects of managing effort, (4) the will to plan, and (5) communications ability. Put in more functional terms, this means that managers who are endeavoring to create luck will (1) possess know-how; (2) be alert to changes in taste of consumers, trends, locations, competitive products, and services that are being produced, and trade connections that they can develop to enhance their position; and (3) map a strategy toward ameliorating any undesirable developments. If such activities are undertaken by small business managers, there is no reason for them to be beset with misfortune or bad luck.

PROVIDING LEADERSHIP—KEY TO MANAGEMENTS SUCCESS

Managing personnel.   One common failing of small business managers is their general lack of ability at managing their personnel—at providing leadership for their people. Small business managers tend to fail in this respect even though today a wealth of available knowledge exists in respect to the management of subordinates. It is often as near as the closest public library, and a great deal of it is written in a very readable and entertaining style. Yet many small business managers fail to avail themselves of such information—particularly those who have not extended their formal education or whose education has been primarily in scientific or technical fields.

Not only has such education by means of self-study been avoided, but other, even easier ways of learning have also been ignored by small business managers. For example, throughout the country executive development and training programs are conducted with the sole intent and purpose of training managers to handle employees. But most of the people who attend such training sessions come from the giant corporations.

Many times the reason an effective small business operation is not developed to its full potential is that the manager lacks the information and knowledge to do it. It is not a lack of ability to learn on the part of either the small business manager or the employees; the simple fact is that small business managers have not acquired the knowledge which they need and can use in developing an effective work team.

Knowing one's leadership characteristics.   Anyone can be a leader. Everyone who owns a small business (or is considering starting one) possesses the leadership characteristics and abilities requisite for successful management, regardless of personality, traits, quirks, and idiosyncrasies. It is entirely possible for the small business manager to make a success of an operation irrespective of personal quirks and idiosyncrasies because there is no one best style or technique of leadership; rather there is an infinite variety of managerial or leadership techniques that can be successfully utilized by the right individual. Furthermore, it is often difficult to emulate a certain leadership style, for what works for one person may not be suitable for another.

Three interlocking variables determine how successful one will be as a leader in a small business. One of these factors is the personality and charisma of the small business manager; one is the attitude, personality, and charisma of the people the manager is bossing; and one is the situation itself. For example, one small businessperson might be a thorough, firm, demanding person and be successful, while another might be just as successful by being soft-spoken, even bashful—but they must have the right kinds of people working for them. While it is true that some approaches to leadership are more appealing than others (especially in terms of a nice-person approach) it is not true that the best results are always attained from such strategies. Today's modern theories argue that all people *can be* effective leaders if they work at it. On the other hand, many will probably not be very effective.

The problem of leadership, therefore, is not which leadership style is the best and must be used; rather, it is a question of identifying and being aware of one's own style and finding subordinate employees who will respond effectively to the style that one happens to possess. Thus, being a good, effective, *and successful* leader depends upon picking followers who will work well with the leader; poor leadership and failure are associated with incompatible followers.

PART II—ORGANIZATION

In Part I the job of management was examined from the standpoint of the individual who is the manager. Management is a process, but it must be implemented by the people who are the managers. In order for the managers to be effective in their role of managing, it is necessary to establish the proper organizational structure. We now consider organization in Part II.

ORGANIZING AND ASSEMBLING RESOURCES IN THE BUSINESS

In the field of business management, it is axiomatic that nothing will get done until there is management, that organizations must be designed to accomplish the goals or objectives for which they are established. But the goals or objectives of any organization are never stagnant, and they do not lend themselves to any definitive listing. They are always changing, and therefore designing the proper kind of an organization for the small business is an ever-changing part of the process of management. Fortunately, however, there are some guidelines that can be developed for meeting these ever-changing requirements.

How size of business relates to organizational form.

It can be said that very few small business managers have mere existence as their goal. In fact, simple existence is a stagnant philosophy. Rather, the typical small business person wants his/her company to grow from a small operation into a large operation, if not into a giant in

Figure 20–1
Organizational chart for a very small firm

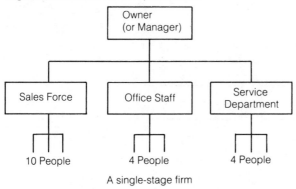

A single-stage firm

the field. Therefore, one of the problems that the small business person has is developing an organization that will do the desired things for the firm.

Organizational structure is originally a question of the size of the organization in terms of the numbers of people working in it. If the number of individuals is no more than 20 to 30, then the manager deals directly with each person. There is no need for intervening levels of supervisors or submanagers. Typically such a size is represented by Figure 20–1. In this stage, even though there may be nominal submanagers for certain given tasks, the manager deals with all persons, organizes all the jobs, and is in direct contact with and control over every aspect of the operation.

As the business grows to larger size—beyond 25 to 30 people—it will become necessary to move to a dual-stage organization, as shown in Figure 20–2.

Only when the business grows to 250 to 300 employees—a process that takes a while—will it become necessary to move to a multiple-stage organizational structure.

In the multiple-stage organizational structure (see Figure 20–3) the manager will supervise the first level of subordinates, who in turn supervise another level of intermediate supervisors, who in turn supervise the direct operative workers. In this case, there are three levels of supervision.

The multiple-stage structure will probably work for a small business until its size exceeds 1,000 employees. At that time the business is no longer small. When such a size is reached, the business will probably be restructured into a form that involves the further separation of the higher-level management positions into product-line divisions. When this is done, the functional activities of manufacturing, sales, office

Figure 20–2
Organizational chart for a medium-sized smaller business

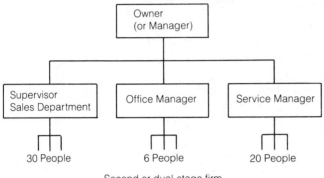

Second or dual-stage firm

service, etc., are realigned and incorporated into a managerial structure that will serve each division along with the needs of the main business or corporate headquarters.

Rationale underlying organizational structure

The ultimate objective of any organizational structure is to provide a means of utilizing, in an effective fashion, the total number of employees of any given firm. Organization is a means of dividing and subdividing both management and operative workers in a pattern that is appropriate to the total mission of the firm.

In general, the objectives are best accomplished if the following rules are observed:

Figure 20–3
Organizational chart for a larger small business

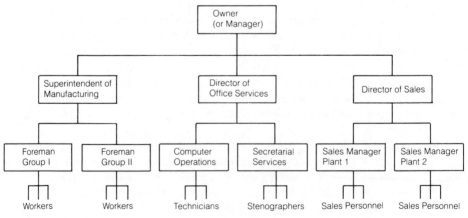

A multiple-stage firm

1. Vertical separation along functional lines—i.e., sales, production, finance, etc. These would normally be called divisions.
2. Horizontal separation into levels that allow the building of a pyramid-shaped organization from top to bottom.
3. Creation of individual job segments in accordance with each job and its relationship to all other jobs that interface with it.
4. Limits on the amount of separation, both vertical and horizontal, holding divisions and levels to a minimum, consistent with what is best for each given situation.
5. A proper balance between the number of managers and/or supervisors and the number of workers directly supervised.

To sum up the above listing, organization is a means of dividing the total amount of work and necessary managerial tasks in an efficient way. No more separation should take place than necessary, but there must be enough to provide an orderly block of assigned duties so that each employee can perform the job effectively. This presumes job assignments that are in line with the tasks to be performed and the ability of the average workers who perform such jobs.

IMPROVEMENTS ON THE BASIC ORGANIZATIONAL STRUCTURE

The organizations outlined and illustrated previously are the traditional line organizations. We now move to some desirable improvements on this basic structure.

Kinds of formal organization

So far, the various stages of growth of organizations and some fundamental principles of effectively organized work have been discussed. Now it will be beneficial to discuss the various forms that formal organizations might take. These various forms are *functional, line,* or *line-and-staff.* Organization charts are presented to help visualize these ideas.

Functional organizations. The functional form of organization is an extremely old concept, having little popularity today. However, the small business person must understand the principle of the functional organization because most small businesses *start* as functional organizations and *then grow into* organizations that are either line or line-and-staff. What is meant by the functional organization, at least in the traditional sense, is that each supervisor is in charge of a specific function, rather than in charge of specific workers. For example, assuming that there might be eight functions that are being performed in a small business, there might be one supervisor in charge of each function. Thus, you might find a supervisor in charge of all operations having to do with inspection, another in charge of all operations concerning rework, and another in charge of all operations concerning the order or sequencing of work. Each of these supervisors would have the final say in respect *to some particular function.*

Normally, the business that is just starting will have only a few people working in it, therefore only a few people will be in charge of all functions. This means that as any one employee moves from function to function, he/she works for a different supervisor. And this is a source of trouble with the functional form of organization. People become confused when they work on more than one function and therefore work for more than one boss. Not only do job responsibilities get extremely confusing, but it becomes very difficult for a supervisor to observe the performance of the function when there are large numbers of people to supervise—say, 100 or more. Therefore, the functional form of organization is appropriate only to the very small organization. However, because small businesses tend to start small, the small business person should be aware that in all likelihood, the first kind of organization that will be utilized will be the functional organization.

The line organization. The pure line organization is the second form of organization, but it, too, is not in great use today. The line organization should be thought of as one primarily concerned with the company's main product or service. In the line organization there is limited use of such things as staff specialists and/or staff departments. There may be departments that do different things, but in each department one person is directly in charge of another who is directly in charge of yet other people who are providing the company's main products or services. The line organization differs from the functional organization in that each supervisor, rather than being in charge of a specific function, no matter who executes it, is in charge of a specific operational unit and the people who are assigned to work in that operational unit. For example, in the military a platoon sergeant is in charge of the men and women in a platoon, no matter what their assigned objective. Similarly, in a small business that makes tents and awnings the owner or manager is in charge of all the people who perform the various jobs of making tents and awnings. When the tent and awning manufacturer becomes big enough there will be a supervisor of tent makers and a supervisor of awning makers, just as when there are enough platoons to make a company, each platoon leader will supervise one platoon in accomplishing a specific job.

The line-and-staff organization

A special illustration for small business is shown in Figure 20–4. This classical line-and-staff organization is appropriate for a small manufacturing firm. Using this as a base model, let's now move to a special variation.

In several other places in this text it has been pointed out that a small business person needs outside help in areas where the particular talent needed is too specialized and too expensive to justify a full-time employee. One desirable form of organization that accommodates these requirements is shown in Figure 20–4.

In this case the organization of the small manufacturing firm has been changed to a more general form. The important point is that the owner is now provided with a staff that comes from outside the organization and provides the expertise that is needed. Inasmuch as the staff people do not take a direct part in the supervision of other employees *in the line part of the organization*, it is not necessary that they be regular employees of the firm.

In this way the lawyer, accountant (CPA), banker, and insurance agent can serve as staff, probably paid for their services on a retainer basis, and provide necessary additions to the talents of the owner. Such an arrangement can have other possible combinations of full-time and part-time staff personnel with talents in addition to those shown. The imporant point is to have the talents available as needed.

The informal organization

No textbook discussing the formal organizations of business would be complete without at least passing mention of the phenomenon called

Figure 20–4
A line and special staff organization

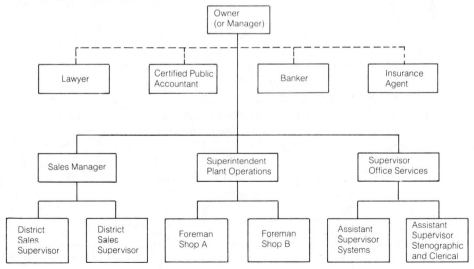

the informal organization. The informal organization cannot be seen, but it certainly can be felt by the small business person. Unfortunately, the small business person can do little or nothing about the informal organization other than recognize the fact that everyone is a part of it, and that it can work both to his advantage and to his disadvantage.

The informal organization is nothing more than the informal system of employees and employee interactions that develop in any work environment. Whereas the formal organization can be charted on a graph showing direct lines of authority and responsibility between superiors and subordinates, the informal organization cannot be charted nor can any direct lines of authority be established. Rather, the informal organization is a myriad of interpersonal relationships that arise on the job between people who must work together. These relationships arise as a result of friendship and other associations that develop both on and off the job and represent the fact that employees affect each other informally as well as formally. The informal organization is frequently led by the "natural-born leaders," who may either benevolently or maliciously influence employee behavior on the job. The job of the small business manager is to recognize the fact that the informal organization does exist, that natural-born leaders will emerge in any situation, and that the leader of the informal organization can work either to the small business's advantage or detriment, depending upon the attitude and aspirations of the informal leaders.

SUPERVISING AND DIRECTING ORGANIZATIONAL EFFORTS

The job of the small business manager is not only to plan what actions will be taken by his organization and to design an organization capable of enacting these plans, but to direct the enactment of the plans that have been established for the organization. This means that the small business person must be adept at communicating with, counseling, motivating, and disciplining the efforts of the employees, as well as organizing the use of material, machines, and money.

Communicating with subordinates

Communication, like the weather, is very much discussed, but very little is ever done about it. Most managers recognize the need for effective communication; however, very few recognize the fact that they are poor communicators.

The very essence of directing employees at their jobs is the ability to communicate. But there is a great disparity between what should be done and what is done. For example, studies have shown that in the average business, typical workers understand and comprehend only about 20 percent of what top management thinks they understand, and the general foremen may grasp only about 30 percent or so. Further, not only do typical workers understand only about 20 percent of what top level management thinks and hopes they understand, but because of this lack of understanding, the typical worker is not equipped to be an effective subordinate who can accomplish the job.

Communication—a two-way street. At the outset of any discussion of communications as a tool in effectively directing work, it should be recognized that communication is a two-way street: that is, effective communication requires that the small business person be able to communicate ideas to a subordinate, but by the same token, it also means that the subordinate should be able to communicate ideas to the boss. Therefore, any small business person who is effective not only knows how to *talk to* subordinates, but also how to *listen to* subordinates.

In communicating with one's subordinates, it is essential that the small business person understand the principles of effective communication. They can be put into practice in these ways:

1. Have a precise idea in mind of what the message is that is to be communicated to the subordinate.
2. Have a plan as to how the message can be most effectively communicated to the subordinate; i.e., what mode of communication will best reach a subordinate.
3. Understand the subordinate's background and experience and what might help the subordinate to understand the information that is being communicated.
4. Understand the personal values of the employee and what personal appeals might be used in making the communication more effective and meaningful.
5. Be aware of the mental and physical state of the subordinate who receives the message.
6. Understand what the subordinate expects and wants from the small business manager as a result of the communication.
7. Understand what his/her *own* personal motives and goals are and what he/she intends to gain from communicating to the employee in the manner elected.
8. Think through a proper timing, sequence of thoughts, locale, and style of delivering the message.
9. Follow up promptly with whatever action must be taken if any action was indicated in the communication.
10. Check on whether or not the subordinate clearly understood the message, either by asking questions or observing the subordinate's immediate and subsequent performance on the job.

Compliance with the above rules for effective communication should help the small business person in conveying messages to subordinates. However, that is only half the battle. The other half is whether or not the small business person permits subordinates to communicate with him or her—i.e., whether or not the small business person effectively listens to subordinates. The essence of this problem primarily resides in the fact that it is altogether too common for people to "listen" without hearing what they are being told. Ten bad habits that are typical of small business people and preclude them from being effective listeners are:

1. Not being interested in the subject.
2. Criticizing the manner of delivery (rather than what is being said).
3. Getting overstimulated because of emotional bias at things the subordinate says.
4. Listening for facts rather than ideas.
5. Insisting on logic instead of ideas.
6. Faking attention to the subordinate and thinking about other things.

7. Tolerating (and/or creating) distractions while the subordinate is talking.
8. Evading or avoiding anything difficult or complex that the subordinate has to say.
9. Submitting to emotional words or phrases used by the subordinate rather than concentrating on the message.
10. Wasting thought power by failing to utilize the capacity of the mind to think faster than a human being typically speaks, thereby not trying to integrate the message with the overall situation.

These bad listening habits obviously apply to the small business person in the workaday life not only in managing subordinates but also in relation to customers, clients, sales reps. etc. That is, people are either good listeners or bad listeners, and people who are bad listeners tend to be bad listeners all the time, not just part of the time. Obviously the bad listener and the unorganized or disorganized speaker cannot be effective managers of subordinates. They will not be able to communicate orders, nor will they be able to understand why various jobs are left undone and why many things that are done are done wrong.

CONTROLLING THE ORGANIZATION

The word control has a variety of meanings. Therefore, it is absolutely essential to have a clear understanding of what is meant by the concept of control in respect to a small business operation. Control means the force that guides a business to a predetermined objective by means of implementing predetermined policies and decisions. Control also may not require action, but it frequently compels the small business manager to instigate action by turning a spotlight on the pertinent facts of any circumstance. It might be said, therefore, that control of the small business is a three-stage process: the first stage is the adopting of the plan; the second is the reporting of *actual* performance of the small business as compared with the *plan* for performance; and the third is making decisions and taking any required corrective action.

Different forms of control

Controls exercised by the owner of a small business may assume a number of different forms. To choose a given course of action and to pursue it in whatever manner is appropriate is a form of discretionary control. More likely, however, controls involve monitoring, evaluating, and making necessary changes in the ongoing activities of the business.

Staff and directorial control

As pointed out earlier in this chapter, the small business operator will very likely utilize the services of voluntary or paid staff assistants. As the owner utilizes their ideas and puts them into effect through his own top-level position, the group is indirectly exercising a form of control.

Likewise, the board of directors of a smaller business can operate in a similar capacity. They can influence the owner, who in turn implements their ideas. In theory, the board of directors actually controls the owner (or president) of a firm, but as a practical matter, business uses boards of directors more as a help in decision making, and thus control, than in the role of dominating and controlling the owner or president.

Daily operating control. The second form of control that might be invoked in the successful small business is that of the workaday operating control required. That is, it is necessary for a small business person to establish, coordinate, and maintain an integrated plan for the conduct of operations in the small buisness. This plan must provide cost standards, expense budgets, sales forecasts, profit planning, programs for capital investment and financing, and any other necessary procedures to implement the operating plans. Establishing such plans however, does not ensure that the small business person will have adequate control of operations. In controlling a small business there is a duty not only to establish operating plans but also to measure performance against those plans and to take corrective action when it is determined that results are not in compliance with the plans. Therefore, the small business person must recognize that the larger and more successful the business becomes, the more necessary it becomes to be able to control the organization from a remote position. *This means, in essence, that the manager must be able to maintain control of operations by the use of reports that subordinate managers submit rather than by direct observation.*

Report for information and control

Reports—oral or written, formal or informal—will become an increasing element for review and control by a small business manager. Machines now record, store, and summarize a vast assortment of necessary managerial information. Also, as a business grows, the owner-manager will need to place an increasing dependence on printed reports as a means of making judgments about the firm.

Control must follow the delegation of authority, which assigns the duties to be performed and the people to direct the performance. A report back from a person to whom authority has been delegated should indicate the degree to which the authority has been used; most commonly we would say that we are measuring the extent to which responsibilities have been discharged. Following this review, the necessary control measures can be formulated and delegated to those whose actions need a change or modification.

1.   Reports must cover separate organizational units (i.e., reports must cover only single organizational units; all other reports are unacceptable). It is undesirable and, in fact, useless to lump the performance of several operating units together in one report. Such a report will not permit the manager to isolate and understand which units are performing adequately and which are not.

2.   Reports must update the manager's information, and under no circumstances should late reports be tolerated. This is a simple matter, yet it is often ignored. Any report that reveals a bad situation six months after that bad situation began is entirely worthless in today's dynamic business world. Reports must be prompt and up-to-date if the manager is to have any control over the work that is being done, particularly if remedial action is required. The manager must know when a bad situation arises or when a bad situation is getting worse in order to take the required action in time to alleviate matters.

3.   Reports must not be designed to make anyone look good. The fundamental content of a report is facts—not an effort to make everybody look good. The small business person should recognize that many subordinate managers, because they want to look good to the boss, often permit their subordinates (or themselves) to make reports that tend to hide or otherwise modify bad or poor performance.

4.   Reports must always include notes with respect to actions that are taken and/or planned. If the manager intends to have control over the organization, he/she must design reporting procedures that not only highlight things that are getting out of control or bad situations that are developing but also give some idea of what is being done to remedy these situations. Knowing what, if any, action has been taken by the subordinate manager will permit the small business person to determine whether he/she personally needs to take any action or that the subordinate's actions are sufficient. If a subordinate manager recognized a bad situation, assumed some initiative, and engaged in some remedial activity, the small business manager may not need to act. On the other hand, a small business person who deems the remedial activity taken by the subordinate as insufficient or incorrect may want to act.

5.   A final rule is that reports must be designed to highlight comparisons of performance between various organization units and/or individuals within the organization. The small business manager who hopes to evaluate the performance of subordinates individually or in units must have reports that highlight critical elements in each individu-

al's or unit's performance. Thus reports must underscore those elements of performance that can be compared and that are meaningful. They should not be designed to hide, cover up, or otherwise embellish poor performance or force the small business person to compare apples with bananas.

QUESTIONS

1. Describe what is meant by "entrepreneurial spirit." Can the small businessman instill such spirit in his subordinates? How?

2. What is meant when it is stated in the text that a good manager is a generalist rather than a specialist? Do you agree with this statement? Why or why not?

3. Can small business managers expect to be both successful and popular with their employees? If so, explain how it is possible; if not, explain why not.

4. What is meant by being "results- and responsibility-oriented?" Should small businessmen be results-oriented, or should they be people who are willing to "wait and see" what happens? Why?

5. The text states that many managers seem unable to effectively delegate work to subordinates? Do you agree? Why or why not?

6. One problem for many small business persons is the fact that they waste their time on "essential" tasks? Can this be possible? Why? Explain in detail.

7. Discuss the various stages of growth experienced by most successful small businesses.

8. Discuss what you believe to be the five most important principles of organization listed in the text.

9. What is meant by control? How is it obtained by the small business person?

10. How can a person running a small business use reports to insure effective managerial control?

PROBLEM

The production in your small operation has been steadily decreasing, and you strongly suspect that the men have deliberately organized a slowdown. You question several of your good workers, and they admit that they are being pressured into holding back production, but they refuse to incriminate any of their fellow workers by naming the ringleaders of the slowdown. When you ask the cause of the slowdown, they tell you that the cost of living is increasing and that they need to make more money by working more overtime.

You believe that right now there is no justification for more overtime. In addition, you feel that if you submit to this type of pressure, you will lose control over your group.

a. What are the possible solutions to this problem?
b. What are some of the possible consequences of the above solution?
c. How can the situation be prevented from recurring?
d. What leadership characteristics do you need to develop? Explain.

BIBLIOGRAPHY

Anyon, G. Jay. *Entrepreneurial Dimension of Management.* Wynnewood, Pa.: Livingston Publishing, 1973. Discusses the nature of entrepreneurial behavior.

Hagberg, Janet, and Richard Leider. *The Inventurers: An Excursion in Life/Career Renewal.* Reading, Mass.: Addison-Wesley Publishing, 1978. A book aimed at the career renewal process. A good source of ideas for small business management as a second career.

Mancuso, Joseph. *Fun and Guts—The Entrepreneurs' Philosophy.* Reading, Mass.: Addison-Wesley Publishing, 1973. Just plain interesting reading on the trials and tribulations of small business managers. An excellent book.

Case study

West Fork Bicycle Shop, Inc.

In 1976, Sig Neilson and Stan Abernathy had opened a small bicycle sales and service shop in a city of some 40,000 in the southwestern United States. Originally the firm was created to sell a limited variety of bicycle brands—one domestic and three foreign—and to conduct repair work on a rather limited scale. The firm was small and furnished only part of the livelihood for both Sig and Stan. They each spent considerable time with the business, although Sig was a resident property manager of an apartment complex and Stan worked as a fireman for the city. They ran the business with the help of two part-time employees.

The shop had been opened because the local community did not have what Sig and Stan thought was a good, well-managed bicycle shop. A building that was suitable was available at $310 per month on a straight year-to-year lease with a $30 per month increase each year. The location was on a well-traveled arterial street through the city, across the street and down one block from a fairly substantial shopping center. The building had no private parking, but the street was metered and there were other private parking areas within one block that had served adequately for the needs of West Fork.

The initial capital investment was $10,000 by each owner. The firm was incorporated with Sig and Stan each taking 45 percent of the stock and their wives each taking 5 percent to comply with the state incorporation laws as to the required number of stockholders. The business barely broke even in 1976, but the firm only operated for eight months that year. In 1977, the firm did $120,000 in gross sales, split 60 percent to bicycle sales and 40 percent to service. On this amount there was a gross profit before taxes of $17,500. Additional borrowing had been necessary to the extent of $20,000, primarily for the purchasing and carrying charges on new bicycles.

In 1978, there was further improvement in sales, up to $142,000 for the calendar year, but not nearly what had been expected. In looking back, the owners realized that they had actually opened on the tail-end of the bicycle boom in the United States and had been building their business through a period of resurgence since the time when the sales of new bicycles had reached a low point in 1975. The industry improvement from 1975 had been slower, however, than the growth in the early 1970s, which reached its peak in 1973.

Now that 1979 had arrived it was time to assess the firm and decide what to do with it. The two owners sat down together and began the task of planning primarily for the next year but also for at least another three to four years. The first order of planning was an assessment of the business as to a few key features; these are summarized as follows:

1.   *Location and layout.*   The present location is adequate, but cannot accommodate any further expansion. Space is tight and needed storage and shop space could not be conveniently taken from the selling area without a serious effect on sales. Layout is OK, but again not subject to any change to facilitate additional business.

2.   *Market share and sales vitality.*   Sig and Stan had been fortunate in taking on a good U.S. bicycle line but on this they made very little profit. However, this manufacturer's line gave them an entry wedge into the market that was new and developing among older, or perhaps first-time, purchases. These people were willing to shop for quality as well as price. The lower-priced lines are dominated by U.S. manufacturers, whose products constituted 75 percent of the market and are sold through large discount chain and mail order stores. At the present time West Fork has good lines (some had been dropped), a market share that is satisfactory for its size and the community size, and a passable service operation that carries a fairly good inventory of parts.

Very few accessories, including a few saddlebags, chains, and padlocks, and some clothing, have been stocked in the store.

3.   *Reputation and image.*   A rather informal survey of some 150 customers had been conducted at the end of the summer of 1978 to determine the general customer attitude toward the firm and what good and bad features were apparent to this group. Even though this survey had been done in the shop, it was considered to be reasonably objective as to the general opinions given. The procedure was to ask customers to fill out a rather general two-page questionnaire and then to call them back or talk to them about their comments.

It was the owners' opinion that West Fork came out all right, but certainly did not have a clearly superior image. They received middle-of-the-road comments on service, product lines, and other features such as sales effectiveness; follow-up contacts with the customers ranged from inconclusive to unsatisfactory.

4.   *Management.*   The owners attempted to assess their own managerial abilities. They seemed to rate about average on most counts. It was the opinion of both that the business had not been given as much attention as was justified, partly because they had other jobs. Also, the shop had not previously offered enough potential profit to generate enthusiasm and good effort on their part. It was their further opinion that their attitudes would have to change for the better or they should sell the business and go on to something else.

5. *Financial stability.* The business had not been spectacular as to profits (far from it), but it was certainly not about to go broke. The firm had a good line of credit at the local bank and had done well enough that there should be no trouble with the bicycle distributors or equipment suppliers they had been dealing with.

6. *Future prospects.* All the indicators that Sig and Stan reviewed seemed to indicate that the overall future in bicycles was good. Domestic manufacturers were planning expansions for 1980. Automobile fuel prices seemed likely to rise in the future, a condition that in previous years had helped bicycle sales. Their community was growing and was in a geographical area where bicycling was a pleasant activity throughout the year.

In total, the owners of West Fork Bicycle Shop Inc. could see nothing within a two or three year period that would threaten their established business position.

QUESTIONS

1. If West Fork, as a firm, would be moved physically to a better location with more floor space, what should the firm do to enhance the image of the company?
2. What kinds of changes in management would be most beneficial for a small business of this type in support of a move to a new location?
3. Would you recommend that West Fork expand into a more extensive assortment of products related in some way to bicycling?
4. Do you think that the sponsorship of a bicycle racing team and/or a local intercity race with substantial prize money would be a feasible promotional activity for the firm?

21

Personnel and employee relations

For the small business manager an important area of involvement is the field referred to as employee relations or personnel management. Most people today instinctively know what is meant by personnel management, but many small business people minimize or completely neglect employee relations as part of their job.

The basic job of personnel management is to recruit, select, develop, train, and maintain a stable work force. But this checklist is meaningless unless the small business person understands the importance of the personnel function.

THE PERSONNEL FUNCTION

The need for the personnel manager—or at least for someone who performs the job duties of the personnel manager—arises from what is called the black-box phenomenon. Of all the factors of production employed by the small business person, only one has an unpredictable control device that the small business person cannot see into, take apart, rewire, reprogram, or otherwise alter to ensure performance to his/her liking. That black box is the human mind.

The personnel function results from the unpredictability of the black box, that is, differences in the ways various people think and react. For example, it was stated above that personnel management's function is to recruit, select, develop, train, and maintain a stable work force. That seems a simple requirement at first, but it is not so simple if one considers that what may be an effective recruiting device for one potential employee (e.g., an offer of a good position, responsibility, and the possibility of advancement) may not appeal at all to another individual, who is interested in pay, working conditions, and liberal company benefits. The job of the personnel manager is to know these differences in attitude and reaction and to use the appropriate appeal in recruiting employees. But once this is done (which is not as easy as said), there is the problem of selecting the right person from among those recruited. Now the following questions occur: Which one is a hothead? Which one will come to work regularly and on time? Which one will be a know-it-all? Which one drinks too much? Which one has severe problems at home? *Which one will, all things considered, be the best employee?*

Once the best employee is selected, he/she must then be developed into a qualified employee, must be trained to do the jobs expected, and finally, must be encouraged to remain with the company. However, remaining with the company involves the satisfactory—both from the company's viewpoint *and* the employee's viewpoint—resolution of any problems regarding such things as absenteeism, sickness, vacations, safety issues, suggestions, and grievances. In short, the function of the personnel manager is a never-ending, yet essential, job if the small business is to prosper and grow. This does not necessarily mean that a full-time personnel manager is needed, but it does mean that the small business manager will have to be adept at handling employee relations until the organization becomes large enough to hire a personnel manager.

Unfortunately, many small business people are not good at handling employee problems for a variety of reasons: they simply don't know what is involved; they feel their firm is too small to have personnel problems; they feel, because the firm is small, they can have personal daily contact with their employees and eliminate personnel problems; they feel their informal, open-door policy will alert them to any serious personnel problems; or they think they possess the insights needed to hire the kind of employee who never creates personnel problems.

In short, it might be said that ego and ignorance in the hiring and managing of employees are common sources of personnel difficulties. It is simply not true that all people are honest and straightforward. Although the large majority of people will do an honest, capable day's work for their employer, some people either will not or cannot. The problem occurs in both large and small businesses, but the problem is more acute for the small business manager. If a large business with 10,000 employees has 100 incompetent workers, these employees account only for $\frac{1}{100}$ of the total, but a small business with 25 employees can't afford to have even one incompetent employee on the payroll because it would mean that $\frac{1}{25}$ of the labor force was ineffective.

FINDING EMPLOYEES

One of the first things the small business person must learn as a personnel manager is how to recruit employees. Many small business owners don't know how to go about finding qualified people to fill the jobs they offer. Furthermore, the problem of not knowing where to go to find someone to fill a job is often accompanied by the feeling of not being able to afford some of the more commonly used devices to recruit employees.

There are two fundamental sources of personnel: internal and external. A study of these sources should help the small business owner solve the recruitment problem.

Internal recruiting methods

Internal recruitment of employees is the simplest and best way to find a person to fill a job. Promoting someone from within carries the advantages of already knowing the person's strengths and weaknesses. Furthermore, a policy of promotion from within is good for the morale of the employees because it offers them *all* the possibility of advancement.

There are two potential disadvantages to promoting from within. First, the jealousy of those not promoted; and second, the possibility that no one currently employed by the company is capable of filling the vacant job (or is willing to take on the increased responsibilities of the new job).

But all employees are new at one time or another. Therefore, even though internal recruiting is probably best, it may be necessary to consider some of the external sources that can be used in finding employees.

External recruiting sources

There are a variety of external sources that many small business managers use in finding needed employees. They include:

1. Newspaper advertising.
2. Trade paper advertising.

3. Radio advertising.
4. Telephone solicitation of leads given by other employees.
5. Display signs.
6. Checks with personnel managers of other companies.
7. Employment agencies, both public and private.
8. Rehabilitation centers.
9. Draft boards and veterans bureaus.
10. Customers and suppliers.
11. High school, college, and university placement and counseling offices.
12. Trade schools, business colleges, and night schools.
13. Labor unions.
14. Churches and social groups.
15. Business executives' clubs.

Each of these sources may be more or less effective, depending upon the kind of employee sought. For example, a college or university placement office is a good place to find a managerial trainee, but a labor union hiring hall or trade school is not. Thus, it is up to the small business person first to decide what kind of talent is needed and then choose the sources most likely to produce such talent.

Some of the recruitment sources listed above are free, while others involve a cost. Furthermore, there is not always a direct relationship between the cost and the result. For example, public employment agencies are free and often are excellent sources for finding employees for lower-level jobs, while newspaper advertisements cost money and may not be effective if poorly written. Finally, some thought should be given to getting broad coverage of job openings to avoid possible claims of discrimination in hiring practices. Thus use of several sources of finding applicants may be advisable.

SELECTING EMPLOYEES

Once the manager of the small business has determined how to recruit the required personnel, attention must be devoted to the question of how to select the best applicant for the job. The personnel selection devices available fall into four groups: (1) the application blank (used at the time the person applies for the job—it may include a physical examination); (2) the interview (used to estimate the applicant's personality and attitudes toward working); (3) various tests and examinations (to determine the applicant's proficiency, skills, aptitude, vocational interests, and other job-related capabilities); and (4) checks of the individual's prior work record.

Even though the above techniques have been available to small business managers for decades, they have been seldom used. Perhaps that is because they are often misunderstood. Although entire books are available explaining these devices, the following brief explanation will give the reader an idea of their simplicity, ease, and inexpensiveness.

Application blanks

Anyone who has ever applied for a job has probably had occasion to complete an employment application form. One study found that 70 percent of the companies with more than 10 employees used some sort of application blank.

Although application forms come in a variety of sizes and shapes, they all should ask the kinds of questions that provide the employer with a summary autobiography of the candidate, as well as a sample of the applicant's neatness, thoroughness, and ability to answer questions. If necessary, the form can go further and give a physical report and perhaps some facts about the applicant's family.

Figure 21–1 indicates the variety of information that can be obtained

Figure 21–1

Name Last First Middle	Describe the type of work you want:

KIS CORPORATION
EMPLOYMENT APPLICATION FORM

INSTRUCTIONS
1. Type or print CLEARLY in INK.
2. Answer each question FULLY and ACCURATELY. Use additional sheet if necessary.
3. Do not include information regarding race, color, age, creed, or national origin.
4. Sign and date application on reverse side.

Address Number Street City State Zip	Telephone	Social Security No.	
( ) Single ( ) Divorced ( ) Married ( ) Widow(er)	No. of dependents (include yourself)	Ages of children	If married woman, give maiden name.
U.S. citizen? ( ) Yes ( ) No	Health ( ) Excellent ( ) Good ( ) Fair ( ) Poor	Height	Weight
Minimum rate expected: $ per	What shift do you prefer?	List handicaps, chronic ailments, serious illnesses, operations:	
Do you object to working nights? ( ) Yes ( ) No			
		Have you ever received workmen's compensation payments? ( ) Yes ( ) No If yes, explain.	

In case of emergency, notify:	Name (last, first, middle)	Telephone
	Address Number Street City State	Zip

EDUCATION (include all U.S. Military Service Schools)

	Name and Address	From	To	Course	Graduated
Elementary					
High School					
Other					

EXPERIENCE (include all U.S. Military Service, summer and part-time jobs—AND ALL PREVIOUS KIS EMPLOYMENT)

Employer's name and address (list last employer first)	From mo., yr.	To mo., yr.	Salary per wk. or wage per hr.	Occupation	Brief description of duties	Specific reason for leaving

by using an application blank. However, job candidates should not be asked to fill out such forms unless the information is truly important in assessing the applicant's suitability for the job.

Interviews

More use is made of the employment interview than any other screening device, and this is as it should be. It is easily the single best screening process. The basic purposes of the employment inverview are as follows:

1. To evaluate the applicant's appearance, speech, mannerisms, etc.
2. To gather factual information about the applicant and his/her background and experience.
3. To provide the applicant with information about the company and the job.
4. To size up the applicant's attitudes, personality traits, goals, and expectations.
5. To secure sufficient information from the applicant so that an intelligent investigation of the applicant's background and capabilities for the position can be made.

Tests and examinations

The use of tests and examinations have long been considered by many to be of some value in the selection process. However, there is some question as to when they should be used, as well as to the legality of the use of certain tests. Psychological testing, for example, is a sensitive area, and personality tests should be avoided because their legality is in question.

Reference checks and similar reports

A final technique used in screening applicants is that of the reference check. This technique is often misused because people who use it tend to think of it primarily as a way to check on the honesty of the individual. Actually, the reference check has a threefold purpose:

1. To verify the truth of what the applicant has said in his or her resume, application blank, or interviews.
2. To expose possible omissions of information supplied by the candidate and to clarify unclear points.
3. To help determine the applicant's ability to handle the job for which he/she is being considered, by answering questions as to whether the candidate has exhibited the necessary skills, frame of mind, attitudes, etc., on previous jobs.

Thus, the reference check is a good device for securing additional information about the candidate that might indicate his/her probability of success on the job. In fact, some people consider this to be the basic purpose of the reference check.

TRAINING AND DEVELOPING EMPLOYEES

Once a person is selected for employment, there is still the problem of training the person to do the job required. Many small business managers tend to overlook this function and take too much for granted. Some think a stock clerk should automatically know how to reorder merchandise. But this is not the case, and sometimes the problem is far more complicated (for example, the manager of the small business usually must train people to do certain specific actions in sequence). Seldom does a new employee arrive on the job with complete knowledge of the duties and obligations involved. Providing the knowledge and information required to do the job is the process of training and development. Training and developing an employee should, however, be distinguished from "educating" an employee. Education is knowledge that the individual should have gained in grade school, high school, or even college, such as how to add, subtract, read, and write. On the other hand, the purpose of *training* is to improve the employee's abilities in on-the-job skills and requirements. Education, therefore, is normally of little *direct* use so far as the job is concerned, while training is specifically designed to help the employee perform the job. The overall objective, then, of a good training program (be it formal or informal) is to make the worker equal to the job to be performed.

How much to train

Training is an investment in one's ability to do a job, but like any investment, there is necessarily a cost involved. The training costs may be large or small. For example, training a janitor usually does not involve a great deal of cost, while training a person to be an efficient forklift operator in a warehouse can be quite expensive. Therefore, the question of the business's ability to afford the needed training may be as important as recognizing the need to train. But it must be remembered that an employee who is not well trained will probably be a more costly employee in the long run than the individual who is adequately trained, even though the training may be costly.

DEVELOPING A STRONG WORK FORCE

Promoting employees

The question of promoting employees was touched on previously in this chapter under the general topic of recruiting from within. However, it should be recognized that although recruiting from within is a good policy, not all people want to be promoted. Many people are not anxious to become higher-level personnel in any given organization, and some refuse to accept the added responsibility that usually comes with moving up.

In light of these facts the small business manager should categorize personnel into three different groups: those who are not interested in any kind of advancement or promotion, those who are interested in rising only "so far" and then staying there, and those who are interested in working their way to the top, even becoming a partner or shareholder in the firm. Except in the very smallest of businesses, there is room for all three kinds of employees.

Promoting an employee has certain advantages. It instills a feeling of pride and accomplishment in the person receiving the promotion. It may stimulate the employee to greater effort and encourage the employee to develop even greater capacities. It may keep the employee from seeking other employment opportunities. Finally, it usually builds the morale of the employee and promotes a feeling of closeness and kinship to the organization.

There are also certain disadvantages to promoting an employee from within. No "new blood" is introduced into the organization, thus, no fresh viewpoints or ideas are produced. The possibility exists that the employee will not succeed when promoted, thus creating a serious personnel problem if he/she must later be discharged or demoted. Finally, disappointment, jealousy, and charges of favoritism may be generated by the people who feel passed over. This may lead to a general loss of morale within the organization if the boss's "pet" is promoted.

How to pay people

In addition to the question of promoting an employee, the small business manager must decide how much to pay employees. Should they all be paid the same or should they be paid differently on the basis of differences in the kind of work? What about pay increments for such things as length of service or cost-of-living adjustments? The whole question of remuneration is as important in the small business as it is in the large corporation.

The question of how much to pay an employee is more than a simple dollars-and-cents problem. There are esentially two forms of compensation that people look for in a job: monetary and nonmonetary. The nonmonetary compensations (sometimes referred to as *psychic income*) include such things as advancement, recognition, responsibility, a feeling of achievement, and the pleasure of doing the work. These factors should be evident in the job, but they have little relationship to the hard facts of paying an employee. In other words, recognition and responsibility should be given to the employee whether or not they are specifically reflected in his or her salary or wages.

The aspects of psychic income will not be considered here, for they more rightly belong under the heading of employee motivation. What will be considered here, however, are the two aspects of monetary compensation that must be considered by the small business owners— absolute and relative.

INSURING FAIR PAY FOR GOOD WORK

Absolute income

In determining how to compensate employees, the first step is to determine the total or absolute amount of money to pay in wages or salaries, and then consider how to divide this absolute amount of money in a fashion that will be acceptable, on a relative basis, to the employees. The basic issues that must be considered under the heading of absolute income for employees include the following:

1. The effort factor.   All people like to think that they are being paid directly in proportion to the physical and mental efforts they make on the job. Thus, in establishing the absolute amount of money to be paid to a specific employee, the small business manager must think in terms of the cold, hard facts of how much is being demanded in terms of physical or mental work, and what the employee will expect to receive for this work.

2. Time.   Rank-and-file employees, in particular, feel that they should be paid for their time whether or not it is productive time; down time is considered just tough luck for the employer. Being paid for one's time is ingrained in our economic history. This is not only a standard-ized assumption behind the principle of wages from the employee's viewpoint, but employers themselves think in terms of billing for time spent. Therefore, in determining the absolute amount to pay an employ-ee, the small business manager must think in terms of the time demanded of the employee on the job.

3. Ability of the firm to pay.   Some businesses certainly have more ability to pay than others, for some firms are far more profitable than others. The ability to pay is often the overriding factor in determining the amount to pay, but this is inconsistent with sound wage theory. The small business owner who pays on an ability-to-pay basis should recognize that if all employers followed this practice, the best employees would end up with the most profitable firms.

4. The cost of living.   If the cost of living in the area of the small business operation is extraordinarily high, the business will necessarily have to pay employees more than if it is in a low cost-of-living area. Furthermore, many employees are more than aware of the cost-of-living index published by the government, and unions are constantly trying to tie the level of wages in their contracts to the rising costs of living as reflected in the index.

5. Legislation. There are laws that establish minimum wages to be paid employees, the hours for which overtime must be paid, etc. The small business must necessarily comply with this legislation to the extent that it covers its employees. Thus, federal, state, and possibly city laws may help determine the absolute level of wages to be paid by the small business.

6. Role of the union. No business is immune from having its employees organize into a labor union, and to the extent that the small business is either unionized or *is threatened* to be unionized, the union wage scale may have a bearing in determining the absolute amount of wages to be paid employees.

7. Supply and demand. The final factor that must be considered in determining the absolute amount of wages to pay employees is the old economic principle of supply and demand. To most small business owners and the bulk of the population, this concept is nebulous at best, yet it clearly operates in the labor market. The supply of labor available in an area compared to the demand for such labor will influence the amount of money that this labor receives. For example, it is commonly observed that unskilled laborers consider themselves underpaid. One of the reasons they are underpaid is that the supply of such workers exceeds the demand. For example, construction firms always seem to find enough unskilled labor at the low wages they offer. If they increase their wages (as do some of the companies in the larger cities), they will discover that they have more than enough people who will work at the higher wages. Therefore, with the demand for laborers relatively fixed in number at any given time, the supply of laborers determines the wages that will be paid.

The principle of supply and demand works in the same way for the business that must determine how much it is willing to pay employees. If there is a good supply of employees and very little demand for their services (similar to the situation in construction), the small business person can establish a relatively low wage and find sufficient people to work. On the other hand, if there is a low supply and a high demand for employees, the small business owner will have to pay a higher wage to attract employees.

This concludes the discussion of factors important in determining the absolute amount of wage a small business must pay employees to keep them on the job. However, recall it is also important that employees be paid a fair amount on a relative basis. The following section of this chapter considers how the small business owner might make sure of paying employees a fair wage or salary on a relative basis.

Relative income

In reflecting on the general acceptance of individualism, it is fair to say that people are not so much interested in being paid equal income, as they are in being paid *unequally for unequal* work. In other words, most people recognize that some jobs are harder than others, require more skill, and demand more of the employee by way of responsibility than do other jobs. Therefore, most people will agree that the question of equal pay for equal work is more a question of making sure that people are paid unequally for unequal work on a fair and equitable basis. This, in short, is the requirement that must be met if the small business owner is to succeed in paying people on an acceptable relative basis. Fortunately, some guidelines have been established to help determine a fair and equitable basis for unequal pay for unequal work. This system is called job evaulation.

The importance of job evaluation. Job evaluation determines the value of one job as compared to other jobs. A job evaluation alone is not a completely satisfactory answer to all questions of employee remuneration because it does not help determine the *absolute* pay level for employees. But it does provide a sound basis for making decisions and formulating wage policies so that different employees are paid a fair relative wage for the work they perform.

Job evaluation does this by seeing to it that people are paid on the basis of the total contribution they make to the business. Job evaluation requires that all the factors entering into accomplishing a given job are considered in determining the wages for that job, including skill, educational requirements, and mental effort, along with physical requirements of the job.

Conducting a job evaluation for a small business involves the collection of the details involved in doing all the jobs involved in the operation. Collecting these facts can help the employer not only in determining how much to pay employees, but also in (1) simplifying work methods; (2) assigning tasks to jobs; (3) training new workers; (4) selecting, promoting, and transferring employees; and (5) improving working conditions and preventing accidents. Thus, a good job evaluation program gives a sound foundation on which to set wages, cut down wage inequalities, and help make the difficult decisions of selecting and promoting employees. It does so by forcing a thorough evaluation of all jobs performed in the firm and specifying the requirements for successful performance of these jobs.

Other advantages also arise from the use of job evaluation in the small business. Labor turnover may be reduced and employee morale heightened as a result of job evaluations and the fact that employees believe they are paid fairly for unequal work. Further, a job evaluation program will facilitate recruiting new workers because the employer now knows exactly what to look for in a person recruited for a given job. Furthermore, training is facilitated because the specific requirements of the job are known and written down. Another important aspect of the job evaluation program is the help it gives employers in dealing with unions. Because job evaluations are the base for establishing wage rates, many unions use the findings from a job evaluation study as a groundwork on which to discuss major and fundamental wage issues during negotiations and collective bargaining negotiations.

Therefore, a job evaluation program is exceedingly important to the small business manager, particularly once the business becomes of sufficient size to have experienced real difficulty in determining how much to pay whom, and when. Although the cost of a job evaluation program may seem high, in the long run it generally will pay for itself many times over in decreased costs and other efficiencies.

The assignment of absolute and relative wages

Once the job evaluation process is complete, the small business person will know which jobs are worth more, which jobs are worth less, and which jobs are in between so far as their value to the business is concerned. Then the small business person can look at the absolute pay scale and determine how much to pay for a given job, in terms of a rate that is reasonable both absolutely and relatively. However, anyone who knows the intricacies of operating a business knows that a business person rarely has a free hand in establishing wage levels. For example, wages cannot be established freely if the firm is unionized, no matter how accurate the job evaluation system and regardless of the ability to pay. Furthermore, there are laws and other regulations that may force the small business person to pay more or less money for specific jobs.

The manner in which employees are paid must also be considered. That is, the small business person must decide how much to pay employees in wages and salaries and how much to pay in the form of fringe benefits such as sickness and accident insurance, life insurance, vacation and holiday pay, severance pay, company-paid pension plans, compensation for tools or clothes, profit sharing, and even possibly stock-purchase plans. Many good books are available in public libraries on the general subject of wage and salary administration that will be helpful in making these fringe-benefit decisions.

UNION-MANAGEMENT RELATIONS

Fewer small businesses than large businesses are unionized. There are a variety of reasons for this. One reason is that small businesses are not particularly appealing to union organizers. In other words, the union organizer would prefer to spend time trying to organize the employees in a 10,000-employee plant than in trying to organize the members in a 10-employee plant. However, even though there is a certain amount of shelter in being small, it certainly offers no immunity from unionization. In fact, there are some unions that specialize to some extent in organizing small businesses, particularly small manufacturers, service firms, printing and trucking firms, and construction crews.

Unfortunately, individuals who have developed their own businesses tend to have rather strong personal anti-union feelings. Part of the reason is that they feel they have made it on their own and that their employees only want to unionize to take their gains away from them. Further, the union itself, by definition, means that an employee is willing to rely on the strength and muscle of others, which would seem the very opposite of the owner's attitude. Most small business owners tend to feel that it is more honorable and respectable to rely on one's own drive and initiative rather than on a group drive or initiative. But employees do join unions; and the small business person must be prepared to face this fact. This is true especially as the small business gets larger or if it trades in interstate commerce.

Unionization of one's small business need not be regarded as a tragedy. Many employers deal quite successfully with labor organizations. In fact, many small business owners—a good example is a man who starts his own construction crew—not only have been unionized the entire time that they have been in small business, but were union members themselves before they started their own firm and still retain their membership in the organization.

Thus, a union does not necessarily spell doom for the small business. However, the small business person who is faced with a union organizing campaign should become familiar with the labor laws and other legislation that governs their organization.

QUESTIONS

1. Why must the small business person be good at personnel management?

2. What are the various sources a small business person might use in

recruiting personnel? Which do you consider the best and worst, and why?

3. Critically analyze the use of the interview technique in screening potential employees.

4. Discuss the various kinds of tests that the small business person might use in screening job applicants.

5. Describe the various kinds of training that the small business person might use to train rank-and-file employees; to train managerial employees.

6. Discuss the problems of paying employees.

7. What is a job evaluation program?

8. Do you feel people want to be paid unequally? Why?

9. Do small business people need to worry about unions? Why?

10. Outline a comprehensive personnel program for a small business with 40 employees.

PROBLEM

Del owns and manages a small business with 12 employees. At work, everything seems fine. Everyone is friendly, the employees do not seem to take themselves too seriously, and things move along smoothly.

Things off the job aren't that good, however. Del knows that four of his best employees are members of a union. Further, he knows they are always talking about the union and what it could do for the other employees. In addition, there are some complaints about pay and other working conditions.

Del doesn't really know what to do about all the complaints. He does know that he is paying as much in wages to some of his best employees as he is paying himself.

a. Does it sound as if Del has a potential problem?
b. What would you do, if you were Del, about the situation?
c. What actions would you expect of Del's prospective union organizers?

BIBLIOGRAPHY

Baumback, Clifford M., and Kenneth Lawyer. *How to Organize and Operate a Small Business.* 6th ed. Englewood Cliffs, N.J.: Prentice-Hall, 1979, chap. 16.

Frantz, Forrest H. *Successful Small Business Management.* Englewood Cliffs, N.J.: Prentice-Hall, 1978, chap. 14.

Moreau, James F. *Effective Small Business Management.* Chicago: Rand McNally, 1980, chap. 8.

Redinbaugh, Larry D., and Clyde W. Neu. *Small Business Management.* St. Paul, Minn.: West Publishing, 1980, chap. 13.

Case study

Wilson Trucking Company

Bob Wilson was born in 1920 and grew up near the shore of Lake Michigan, north of Chicago. His father owned a small trucking company that made short hauls between all the numerous communities on the north shore between Chicago and Milwaukee, Wisconsin, a distance of about 100 miles. After Bob graduated from high school in Libertyville, Illinois, he joined the U.S. Navy and spent the next 10 years as a seaman. He served on active duty during World War II and received various honors for his bravery and dedication to duty.

Bob was a very likable person and made friends easily. After returning from the service in 1948, he started working in his father's trucking firm. His father told Bob that he could take the business over once he learned the ropes. Dad was 60 years old now and about to retire.

Bob did in fact learn the ropes of the trucking business by working all the various jobs in the firm over a period of time. He worked on the loading docks, as a mechanic, in the routing department, and even drove a truck for six months.

In 1950 Bob's father left the business for sunny California and Bob assumed control. Wilson Trucking Company had a fleet of 30 trucks of various sizes, including 10 large semitrailer units. Wilson Trucking employed 48 people on a full-time basis and 16 people part-time.

All of the 16 part-time employees were navy personnel from the Great Lakes Naval Training Station, who would work 10 to 20 hours a week to make a little extra spending money. Bob was very happy to be able to help out a few young seamen while they were in training camp. Furthermore, he was able to hire the young men from Great Lakes at a considerable savings over what he paid his full-time personnel.

Bob Wilson was an excellent manager and produced good profits in the business for the next 25 years. His was kind and thoughtful to all his employees and they all liked Bob very much. He provided each full-time employee with a two-week paid vacation each year. In addition, each full-time worker was provided with a good medical insurance plan, some group term life insurance, disability insurance, five days of sick leave each year, and a profit-sharing plan that produced an annual bonus for each person at Christmas time.

The part-time workers were not provided with the same benefits because of a very high turnover rate. Most seamen spent only 10 to 12 weeks at

Great Lakes and then moved on to another assignment. Bob did, however, give the part-time personnel paid sick leave if needed.

Wilson Trucking Company prospered under Bob's guidance. By 1978, the firm had doubled in size to a fleet of 60 trucks and a labor force of nearly 125. It was then that a serious problem arose.

Bob was working in his office one Monday morning in July when three men entered and announced they were representing the local truckers' union. They informed Bob that some of his part-time employees from Great Lakes felt they were being underpaid. Furthermore, they were not happy with the lack of fringe benefits for part-time employees.

The union representatives criticized Bob for being unfair to the part-time workers and announced that they were going to organize Bob's entire labor force. Bob was shocked. He suddenly realized that if the union was successful, his wage costs would at least double and severely reduce profits. He went home that night in a daze and tried to figure out how to handle the situation.

QUESTIONS

1. What would you recommend Bob do at this point?
2. What response should he make to his employees concerning this development?
3. What should he say to his part-time work force?

Help Bob organize his thoughts and prepare to meet the problem head on.

22

Research—how it fits into
small business

Research is an essential element of successful small business management. Nevertheless, many small business people are skeptical of its
values, while others just don't know what it is. Thus, because of the
skeptics and because of ignorance, research is not a commonly used tool
of the small business. Much like the element of planning, research is a
veritable panacea for the businesses which do employ it, not because the
results are always so informative but because the business's competitors, for the most part, fail to use it.

Research can be defined as the gathering, recording, and analyzing of
factual information relating to the transfer and sale of goods and
services for the business. Obviously, any definition of research is very
broad.

Perhaps more important than a definition of research is an understanding of the need for research upon the part of small business
managers. It can be argued that the consumer is king; when sale of
merchandise begins to slacken, businesses must get out and sell.
However, the admonishment to sell must be backed up with know-how.
Selling is half the battle. But knowing what the customer wants, and
when, and how, is an additional problem. It is the task of reserach to
give the necessary insights into a complex picture.

405

What are the problems research should answer? First, there is the problem of finding out what the customer wants. This involves not only ascertaining preferences among existing products and services, but also discovering what new or improved products and services are to be designed. Also, how the customer wants or needs to have this product delivered is important.

There is also the job of informing the consumer of products that might better serve his or her needs. This requires, among other things, a better-informed sales organization, fully aware of buying intentions and motives in addition to the likes and dislikes of the customer. Thus, the need to engage in some kind of marketing research emerges because of the need for the small business to know (1) what the customer wants, (2) how to inform the consumer of the products and services that the business has for sale that might better serve the customer's needs, and (3) how to optimize the efficiency of the distribution process.

SOURCES AND USES OF MARKET RESEARCH INFORMATION FOR SMALL BUSINESSES

Sources of information

Primary information collection. There are a variety of sources of information about the market and the small business's customers. These types of information take the form of unpublished data and published data. Unpublished data is information that the small business itself generates. Usually this requires that the small business manager collect information (or that someone collect the information for him/her on a payment-for-services-rendered basis). It is not really important who collects the data, so long as (1) it is reliable and accurate, and (2) it is concerned with the sale or distribution of the products or services of the small business. Examples of such data might include very elementary things such as determining the kind of customers the business serves by analyzing credit information, or determining what geographical area the customers come from by noting the location of the banks on which they draw their checks or the counties in which their automobile license plates are issued. No matter how the small business assembles such data, such sources of information can be invaluable toward informing the manager about the clientele, where they live, what they do, and so on. Further, no matter how such data is collected, whether it is by formal random process or by an informal process, one thing is certain: such information is generally accurate and fairly reliable because the studies are made by the business manager (or an agent) and the information is gleaned from actual customers. Thus, a great amount of reliable, timely, and accurate information can be amassed by the use of primary information-collection techniques.

Secondary information collection. While the primary sources of information are invaluable to a small business, there are other sources of good information, many of which are very inexpensive and can be quite reliable and valid. These sources are termed the secondary sources of information, and they include such things as general economic base studies for communities, information from trade associations, U.S. Census reports, and published market analyses.

Secondary sources of data can be very valuable to a small business, but they can also be next to useless or, in some cases, even *worse* than useless. The problem with secondary sources of information is that often they are not readily available, and many times when they are, they are either too comprehensive to be of real benefit to a specific retailer or manufacturer or they are so highly specialized (which often is the case of trade association data) that they are too narrow in their application for a particular small business.

Probably the greatest source of difficulty found in using secondary data comes from using data that are too comprehensive. This tends to lead the small business manager down the primrose path to believing that the information is complete, accurate, and relevant to some particular problem, when it may not be. The manager is then lulled into a sense of security that is often false. Less critical, but sometimes as serious, is the reliance on too well-refined or too narrowly applicable information. In this case, the small business operator is not lulled into a false sense of security, but, by contrast, is driven out of a particular market or business endeavor by fear of a lack of need for the service or product he/she provides or intends to provide.

Because of the microscopic and macroscopic error element in much of the published information available to the small business, it is not highly recommended that managers rely extensively on such secondary sources of information. Such information, however, can be immensely useful to the small business, and if the business is in a well-defined activity and has trade association data, such material can be invaluable to the manager. The small business operator should be alert to the fact that many times this information is not relevant or appropriate unless it is combined with other data, which he/she collects or has an agency collect; still it can be quite useful.

Collection of information that is not primary or secondary

There is still another source of published information available to the small business—information which is usually published in almanacs, statistical abstracts, and current business surveys. However, such data is practically always of a general-purpose character, and rarely, if ever,

does it have any specific benefit or meaning for the small business in respect to its particular market or clientele. The only advantage to such information is that it is plentiful and cheap. Thus, the small business manager who finds these sources of information relevant to the business is wise to use them.

Using research information

Some of the uses to which the small business manager can put research data collected from primary, secondary, or other sources include price decisions, product decisions, promotional decisions, and place decisions. Inasmuch as price, product, promotional, and place decisions are the main points on which most businesses compete, research provides the small business with help in areas where the manager needs it most.

Research answers the questions of why customers buy what they buy and how they are influenced to buy. In seeking answers to the question of why people buy what they buy, the usual practice for the small business manager is to break the research project into one of three kinds of research: motivational research, advertising research, or product research. Because advertising research was dealt with in Chapter 9, only motivational research and product research will be considered here.

WHY PEOPLE BUY

Doing research on buyer motivation

One of the first uses for research is to lend insight into the reasons people buy the products that they do—that is, what are their motivations for purchasing the various items which they buy? Many small business managers feel that people buy products merely because of price. They feel that if a product is priced accurately, it will be purchased. However, such an attitude about people's motivations for purchasing is about as archaic as the concept of the "economic man."

People are motivated to purchase products by a variety of impulses, even though they are price-minded. Research of the motivational variety is concerned with the total mix of the motives that people have for buying products or services, be they rational or irrational, emotional or calculated, conscious or subconscious. After all, if price were the only reason anybody bought anything, only one supplier would sell all there is that is sold of that item.

Getting a fix on why people buy

Motivational research information lends decisiveness and assurance to otherwise uncertain and confused situations concerning the operation of a business. For example, research into the motivation and buying habits of consumers tells the manager of a retail store that it is wise to place impulse items on shelves at eye level rather than floor or ceiling levels, because it is known that people only see merchandise at eye level unless they are specifically looking for the product.

For example, a grocery store, if wisely managed, will stock high-margin, profitable items (such as light bulbs, hair spray, etc.) at eye level so that the shopper, who usually doesn't think of such items in a grocery store, can be reminded by impulse that this is something he/she needs. At the same time the same grocery will stock staple items that carry lower profit margins at the lower levels of various shelves, knowing that the shopper will deliberately seek out such things as canned vegetables, eggs, and milk. The idea is to rely on the fact that the staple items attract customers into the store, but that additional sales and revenue are generated by communicating the impulse to the customer to purchase other luxury, convenience, or spur-of-the-moment items.

Knowledge such as the above "shopper's-vision" phenomenon has been developed through years of extensive motivational research. Practically speaking, the information that shoppers have only a limited field of vision, that they buy things in gaily colored or bright packages, or that they are inclined to purchase an ostensibly new product, has been gleaned through years of research conducted by larger businesses and the nation's colleges and universities. Many small business managers do not develop such information on their own because they have neither the time, the financial resources, or the knowledge. But mere lack of time, money, and know-how is no excuse for the really competitive small business manager to neglect doing research.

By now it should be obvious that the owner or manager of a small business can develop valuable information about why people buy what they do and can test this information by way of a new floor layout, clientele approach, or product or service. All that the small business manager really needs to know are the fundamentals of consumer buying behavior as developed by the many motivational research studies. If one strategem or technique, layout, or design fails, others can quickly be tried until the right one is found. In short, a little knowledge of people's motivational drives, coupled with a willingness to arrange and rearrange formats or layouts, can allow the small business manager to capitalize on knowledge that the consumer buys products and services for reasons other than price. Some of those reasons, of course, are quality of products, how the product is advertised, and such things as convenience.

Understanding customer buying habits

There are a few principles of motivational behavior that have been developed from extensive research. These are, of course, not complete and therefore tend to be very general. But they are sufficient for use by small business managers in developing ideas and approaches as to how to capitalize on the fact that customers purchase things because of a variety of motivations, both conscious and subconscious. These principles include the following.

1. A customer's behavior is a function of his or her attitude, plus the facts of the situation. While the facts of the situation (the price of the product, the extent of the service rendered, etc.) are known and valid, the behavior of the customer is going to vary because of his/her attitude.

People's attitudes represent an expression of how they feel about particular factors and, therefore, determine the extent to which they accept or reject the factual circumstances of the product. Attitudes are extremely important in attempting to elicit the desired behavior of the customer, and it is important that the small business manager understand that attitudes are rarely, if ever, all positive or all negative.

No product or service will be pleasing and appealing to all customers, and thus the small business operator should try to reach only a particular segment of the market. Further, small business operators should concentrate their conjectures and speculations on the attitudes that the customers display toward their product or service rather than the facts of the situation.

2. Customers rely on reference points for decision making. Any person will store information learned from living and will use such information as reference points for accepting or rejecting ideas. Thus, people will decide to buy or not to buy a particular product or service on the basis of interpretations that they give to their need for that product or service.

Understanding and applying this principle of customer motivation requires that the small business manager recognize that it is far more important to have a knowledge of the assumptions or beliefs held by customers or clients rather than to attempt to tell them how they should perceive the business's product or service. Of course, it must be recognized that assumptions and beliefs often are hard to measure because of customer rationalization. Some people, for example, will hire a gardener because they have convinced themselves consciously that they do not have time to tend their own gardens; however, the real reason may be that they need or want the prestige that having a gardener implies. But whether or not customers rationalize openly about their underlying assumptions and beliefs is immaterial so long as the small business manager *knows* the customers and utilizes this knowledge of their fundamental assumptions and beliefs.

3. Physical sensations frequently trigger customer behavior. Physical stimuli such as smell, sound, taste, a touch, or sight frequently trigger impulsive or spontaneous behavior upon the part of customers or clients. This principle is commonly put to use in various forms: a candy store may make candy within sight of the front window; a grocery store may put the bakery near the front of the store so that the smell of freshly baked goods surrounds customers as they enter; or the record store may play music that the manager feels will appeal to those entering the store.

Small business operators, in utilizing this principle of motivation, can promote impulse sales more effectively by solidifying, materializing, or personifying their product or service in order that it will be convenient, handy, and readily accessible to the various physical sensors of customers or clients. Such ready access to the actual product or service can many times trigger immediate purchase or order action by a client, while inaccessibility or lag time might leave the customer without any immediate feeling of need for the product or service.

4. Images, while intangible, give customers very concrete feelings. While the image that a customer or client holds of a firm, product, or service is wholly intangible, it is nevertheless a very real, solid, concrete sensation—much like frightening dreams that a small child experiences. Therefore, to invoke the principles of customer motivation and enhance the success of a firm, the small business manager must be cognizant of the very real nature of both the corporate and personal image and the impact this image will have on the desire of prospective customers and clients to buy the business's product or service.

5. People have a variety of motives, but more often than not they are not aware of the real motives that impel them to action. Customers and clients are always motivated in their actions by some want or need, even though they do not always recognize or understand those wants or needs.

The use of this principle in attempting to direct customer behavior is limited by the fact that there cannot be a complete inventory or catalog of motives that trigger human activity. However, even though the real motives for individual activity may not be known to the individual, let alone outsiders, the fact is that a knowledge of general sociopsychological human motives may be beneficial to the small business person in determining crucial aspects of the motivation of people.

The psychologists tell us that the desire and need for ego staisfaction underlies practically all basic motives that people have. Thus, ego satisfaction becomes a primary source of motivation for people, and oftentimes it is the real (versus rationalized) motive for a particular action or activity. Assuming that people in general (and customers in particular) are striving to satisfy their own egos can, and should, be a fundamental building block in establishing a way to advertise a product, lay out a store, serve a customer, or elicit the desired activity on the part of others. The drive for ego satisfaction constantly asserts itself in connection with all people's desire to gain social acceptance or approval, in their desire to feel superior or to be different, and in their attempts to satisfy various ambitions. Because ego satisfaction, or the drive for it, plays such a significant role in the basic motives of people, the small business operator should design advertising and promotional efforts to take advantage of this knowledge.

Buying habits and the small business

In summary, the foregoing section has been designed to help small business managers gain a knowledge of what motivates people to buy and so establish their own (nonscientific but practical) motivational research program. It pointed out that motivational research is designed to discover why people buy the things they do, but at the same time it recognized that the typical manager has neither the time, money, or knowledge required to make a full-blown study of customers' psyches.

Suffice it to say that with the knowledge of the practical limitations imposed upon a small business in doing motivational research, a business *can* test consumer motivational patterns and buying habits in an effort to determine roughly what motivates customers to buy, how better to lay out a store or an operation, assemble merchandise, and present ads. Although this type of motivational research is at best only a trial-and-error method, it can be an immense aid in determining the habits and buying patterns of customers and clientele. The final fact emerges that, unscientific as it may be, some idea of what motivates customer action is better than no knowledge whatsoever. "'Tis better to try and fail than not to have tried at all."

PRODUCT RESEARCH: WHAT CAN AND CAN'T BE DONE

What product research is

As differentiated from motivation research, product research is something that the small business can engage in and successfully master with little investment. The need for product research is just as important, if not more important, than the need for motivational research on the part of the small business. While motivation research does give answers to why people buy implusively, product research is needed to help determine what to offer for sale.

Because of the nature of product research and its more readily quantifiable features, product research can be more scientifically designed and more readily adapted to the capabilities of most small business managers. For example, most product research requires the following steps:

1. Recognizing that a problem needs resolving.
2. Mapping the strategy to be used to solve the problem.
3. Gathering whatever factual information is available.
4. Interpreting the information that is gathered.
5. Making a decision.

Let us review each of the above, in turn.

1. Recognizing that a problem needs resolving. Product research necessitates first the recognition that a problem exists and needs researching. In other words, the small business manufacturer must know whether to continue making existing products, change the existing products slightly, add new products, drop old products, or develop an entirely new line.

2. Mapping the strategy to be used in actually researching the recognized problem. This step should involve discussion with potential customers or clients, reading trade publications, studying competitor's products, and sampling consumers' opinions.

3. Gathering whatever factual information is available. This is the key to product research because it requires the amassing of *objective* and *pertinent* information that will help resolve the problems which exist. Numerous techniques can be used in fact gathering; most of these entail the actual engagement of the strategies decided upon in Step 2 above.

4. Interpreting the information that is gathered. Many times small business managers are duped into thinking that the gathering of the factual information has been informative enough to give a solution. Often, however, the really wise solution is not obvious from the factual information gathered. That is, careful interpretation of the information will often disclose much better solutions than snap judgments.

5. Making a decision. Decision making can be a chore, and deciding whether to sink a large investment in a new product, develop a new line, or provide a new service can be a real headache to small business operators. Forcing oneself to be decisive and to act on a decision helps eliminate this headache. However, it should be realized that the key to successful decision making in product research, even that which is carefully carried through the first four steps, is to be *decisive* and *forceful* in the implementation of a decision. There is never absolute certainty that the correct decision has been made, even if the information available is generally accurate and timely.

Thus, although decisiveness and forcefulness of implementation have long been recognized as essential ingredients in decision making by business leaders, many small business managers become procrastinators when faced with a decision that concerns much time and money investment on their part.

How to do product research

Although product research can be greatly beneficial in the direction and operation of any firm, many small business managers are reluctant to engage in this activity. Many times they feel it is a frill that only the giants can afford, or they think they're too inexperienced and un-schooled in the statistical methodology required for such research. Such an attitude is unfortunate indeed.

While it is true that highly involved product research requires some statistical sophistication, it is also true that many of the giants of industry who have product research departments staffed with hundreds of employees are fond of stating that their product decisions are right only 52 percent of the time. The point is that even with very sophisti-cated methodology and research design, all that product research provides by way of information to any business is a guesstimate of what decision to make. It is then up to the business managers to see to it that this guesstimate is accurate enough to work. The small business manager is therefore advised to accept the fact that, although he/she is not a $35,000-a-year research manager for a giant soap manufacturer, he/she may be able to muster the wherewithal required to evaluate whether or not to manufacture both genuine and imitation leather jackets, just one, or neither. Further, the manager should have some confidence that if the research is based on a good sample of intelligent people, it will be almost as accurate as that of the $35,000-a-year researcher.

How to conduct product research

Product research and its use by the small business manager might best be demonstrated by a specific problem. Product leadership is one example of the problems analyzed by product research techniques. Many small business managers have no idea whether to engage in a policy of product leadership or whether to wait and see whether a particular product that hits the market is acceptable to the consumer. In other words, it is the age-old problem of deciding whether to be a leader or a follower in the manufacturing of a new product. In designing a research experiment to shed light on this particular problem, a small business manager should take the steps previously outlined as follows:

1. Recognition of the problem. A new product (or the possibilities of introducing a new product) may occur to the small business. Question: Should that product be offered for sale (or produced)?

2. Planning the investigation. Once the problem is recognized, a plan must be designed to determine whether or not product leadership is warranted. All relevant information that will be desired or needed must be outlined, and a plan must be formulated for gathering such information. Relevant information desirable in such a situation might include:

1. Prospective customers' preferences and purchasing power.
2. Stability (or lack of it) of the small business's competitive position.
3. The leadership and prestige sought by the business.
4. The possibility of filling an unmet need.
5. Utilization of some excess production capacity or floor space.
6. Possibility of utilizing waste products or personnel who otherwise have nothing to do for part of the day.
7. Possibility of utilizing materials for a higher-value use.
8. The possible retaliatory reaction of competitors.
9. The ability to secure supplies needed to make or market the product.
10. The general practice of the trade as to the frequency of introducing new models.
11. Availability of the necessary channels to distribute the new product.
12. The ideas suggested by potential customers or clients.

All of the above topics should be investigated in determining whether or not the small business should be a product leader.

3. Information gathering. The third step is to gather the information that will answer (or at least shed light on) the foregoing problems. This involves talking with suppliers to find out whether supplies are or can be made available, sampling the customers or clients to find out whether there would be a demand for the product, evaluating operations to find out whether the productive capacity and personnel are available, and evaluating personal desires as to whether it is preferable to be a leader (and possible failure) or a follower (and possible Johnny-come-lately).

4. Interpretation of the data. The fourth step requires that the information gained from customers, suppliers, in-house personnel, and others, be arranged so that it is meaningful to the small business manager and then evaluated to determine the desirability of introducing the new product or service and the degree of confidence in the decision.

Let us consider what might happen here. It might be discovered that the prospective buyer of the new product is highly desirous of purchasing such a product but the feasibility of making the product is low because of raw material supply. Confusion then reigns in the manager's mind unless he or she is able to determine whether the lack of materials outweighs the degree of desire for the product or vice versa. Thus, it is important that the information be given rank order during step 3 of the operation.

5. Making a decision.   At step 5 the small business manager makes the decision whether or not to be a product leader. If the research has been successful, it will lead to some conclusion. It is possible that uncertainty will still reign, but at least the manager will know more than he/she did at the beginning of the investigation, and this best guesstimate should be better informed than a random hunch. At this stage, however, the small business manager must decide whether to go ahead. Refusal to make a decision is, in fact, a negative decision. The decision should follow logically from the interpretation and reasoning involved from the preceding steps, even though there would still appear to be several intangibles, such as the weight of one group of facts compared with another.

The reader should be aware, by now, that in determining whether or not to introduce a new product by means of the formal steps of product research, the small business manager will never have certain knowledge of what to do but will be in a much better position to make a decision than before. This circumstance is very similar to the situation that large businesses gravitate toward in making their decisions. While it may be true that large businesses will have much more refined data based on larger samples, they will not necessarily have any more definite an idea of the correctness of their decision than will the small business operator. Only time will tell whether the decision was a good one.

FORECASTING SALES

It has been stated above that the small business should engage in research to determine why people buy what they do. The logical extension and application of such information is to be able to project or predict sales and customer behavior in the future. After all, research information should not be collected for its own sake.

Having good information about why people buy what they buy unfortunately does not ensure that good sales forecasts are made. The reason is that market research fundamentally is historical, while sales forecasts are predictive. That is, motivational, product, and advertising research tells why people are buying what they buy now, not what they will buy in the future. Sales *forecasting,* however, by its very definition, means making an estimate of *why* people will buy *what* in the future. Thus, the sales forecast is a guess about the future, and it is an educated guess when it is based on solid market research information.

Making the sales forecast

Good sales forecasts are immeasurable in value to the small business for they help in determining what is to be done, when, and by whom. Good sales forecasts, furthermore, are based upon good market information. Therefore, good sales forecasts are made by (1) analyzing what market information is available as a result of the various marketing research projects conducted by the small business and (2) estimating, on the basis of such analysis, what amount of a product or service will actually be sold over some defined period in the light of existing marketing methods.

There is no problem in analyzing the available data generated by the marketing research project. Thus, step 1 of making the sales forecast is simple, but limited to the thoroughness and accuracy of the marketing research job. However, step 2—making the actual estimate—is far more difficult.

Normally, one of two methods are used to make the actual estimate of projected sales.[1] One of these is what is called the *unit forecast* procedure, the other is called the *overall forecast* procedure.

The unit forecast

The unit forecast procedure of sales forecasting is most often used by manufacturers and sellers of items of high unit cost. Therefore, the unit forecast system is not applicable to many areas of small business operation such as retail stores. However, the small business manager who is operating in a high-unit-cost field should be familiar with the technique.

The unit forecast procedure is nothing more than an estimate, based on marketing research information, about how many units of a given item will be sold. An example of the user of the unit forecast procedure might be an automobile dealer. The dealer will try to predict how many units (automobiles) will be sold in an upcoming period. The dealer will do so by identifying, on the basis of market research information, the types of people who buy cars, evaluating these groups as to their potential for buying a car from that dealership, and making an estimate of how many will actually buy a car in the period. Thus it might be said that the unit forecast procedure is nothing more than the adding up of the number of buyers the small business expects to have, based on

---

[1] It should be recognized that some (often sloppy) sales forecasts are made on the basis of estimates or preceding years' sales. These methods are not included because (1) sales people are notorious for the overoptimism and (2) preceding years' sales are far less valuable as a guideline than is research information, particularly valid research information designed to elicit buyers' future intentions. Nevertheless, these methods can be and are being used—sometimes with great success—and thus merit mention for sake of completeness.

market information as to why people buy what they buy when they buy it.

The overall forecast

The overall forecast procedure is nearly the exact opposite of the unit forecast procedure. That is, whereas the unit forecast can be considered additive, the overall forecast might be considered subtractive or deductive.

The overall forecast procedure starts with an analysis of overall business conditions. That is, an estimate is made for, say, the total market for automobiles in a particular price range, based on expected business conditions. Then an analysis is made of how much or what percentage of this total market the individual dealer might be able to get. This analysis is based, again, on the market research information gleaned by the small business as to who are the prospective buyers, where they come from, what they buy, why they buy it, etc.

Obviously the unit forecast procedure is better for some businesses than is the overall forecast procedure. Basically, which is best depends upon the value of the average unit of sale. Estimates of sales of high-unit-cost items are more likely to be accurate using the unit forecast procedure; low-unit-cost item sales are best projected by breaking down the overall sales picture. Whichever method is used, however, the small business manager must be cautioned to recognize that its accuracy and usefulness will correspond to the care used in assembling the market research information.

RESEARCH: SMALL BUSINESS'S BOON OR BANE?

So far, this chapter has been designed to give the student of small business operations an idea as to the use of research to obtain information on how the small businessperson should act in running a business. However, the small business manager obviously cannot conduct market research continuously. Thus, it is important to know when one is really in need of research information, and when such information is nice to have but rather superfluous.

When research is a necessity

There are numerous times when additional research information must be gleaned by the small business. In fact, one might logically argue that whenever a decision must be made by the small business, market research information would be highly beneficial to that decision. The question then becomes one of relative necessity.

It is, of course, difficult to say for sure when something is an absolute necessity and when it would just be convenient to have. However, several situations can arise in which additional information in respect to the market is needed. These instances might include times when the small business is faced with determining whether or not to produce a particular product; whether to develop or expand into a particular market or market area; whether to produce a product that will require an extremely high investment, inventory, or distribution costs; whether or not to expand production capacity; how to allocate advertising and other promotional efforts; how to determine the proper channels of distribution; or how to allocate or control sales personnel.

The foregoing list is not complete and should not be used as an absolute guide toward determining when a small business should engage in either motivational research, product research, or advertising research. However, those are the areas in which small businesses seem to have the most difficulty and in which they tend to lose their shirts when they make a bad or poor decision. For that reason it would appear that in making decisions relevant to the above question, the small business might consider some marketing research effort as a necessity.

When research is superfluous

Since it has been indicated that market research is necessary when the decision involves significant cost or other serious implications for the small business, it is easy to assume that any other research information sought by the small business is unnecessary and perhaps superfluous. However, such a statement gives little or no guide to the manager who is trying to determine whether or not to spend time and money in research activities.

Most superfluous research activity *becomes* superfluous because of the attitude assumed by the small business researcher. That is, many small business managers get enamored with researching projects and engage in the research merely for the fun of researching rather than for the information obtained. Clearly, such activity is superfluous. However, there are other times when the research appears unessential. This can happen if the researcher is totally ignorant of the principles of research design. For example, some pseudo researchers have been known to engage in completely unscientific product research. A notorious example is one restaurant owner who had *his* family sample *his* wares in an effort to determine whether or not the general public would enjoy them. Obviously, the results of such study are wholly unreliable and invalid because of bias and familiarity.

Time can also have a bearing on the necessity of marketing research activities. If there is not adequate time to conduct a research project in totality, the research is completely invalid. Engaging in a half-baked plan is fruitless and may lead to erroneous conclusions and decisions.

Superfluous research also results if insufficient funds are available to do the project properly. Again, the results of an improperly funded research study can be misleading and, therefore, damaging. Another instance of worthless marketing research may occur if the small business manager fails to consider the scope of the research project; the manager may be unaware of how much area the study should encompass, or how many people, or how many suppliers.

A marketing research study would also appear pointless if the researcher is limited by personal characteristics or by the characteristics of assistant researchers. For example, caution is the watchword of the successful market researcher, but many times the inexperienced or uninitiated willingly jump into water over their heads. A good researcher will make no predictions until relatively sure of the information. However, the poorly trained or uninitiated researcher might antagonize the respondents to a questionnaire or quickly gloss over salient facts in a report because of being in too big a hurry to reach a conclusion.

Marketing research is likely to be unrewarding if the very objectives of the research project are limited. Such a situation rises when the researcher engages in the research task with foregone conclusions or objectives. Thus, while the small business manager may be working to gain knowledge of information as to what to do or how to act, he/she may have decided subconsciously or covertly what the outcome of the research will be. Obviously the results of such research are worthless.

SUMMARY

Marketing research can be highly useful to the small business if the researcher has a fundamental knowledge of the various sources of information available and knows how these sources of information can be used. In most cases, the small business manager is not a sophisticated researcher and does not have the funds and time available to test various ideas that might enhance business operations. However, even though the small business operation cannot be expected to compete effectively with big business when it comes to sophisticated research design, it is still not precluded from effective utilization of general knowledge that exists in respect to motivation research and product research. From the standpoint of motivation research, the small business manager should simply be willing to experiment with the general principles of motivation that years of experience have developed in motivational research studies. In product research all that is needed is a working knowledge of the five steps of information gathering and decision making involved in testing a product.

While the small business manager is therefore well advised not to be too cautious in conducting research experiments in order to uncover knowledge needed to make business decisions, he/she should also be apprised of the fact that there are times when research is essential and other times when it is basically nonessential and can be damaging. Most of the dangers involved in engaging in research arise because of various limitations on time, money, know-how, and attitude of the researcher rather than because research knowledge itself is unneeded. It must be recognized that some research is *not* better than no research. Rather, any research study must be clearly thought out and actively pursued from start to finish if it is to be of merit. A sloppy, haphazard research project does more harm than good.

QUESTIONS

1. Why must an owner/manager of a small business know something about doing research? Explain.

2. What are the primary sources of information for the owner/manager of a small business? Explain.

3. Why is it important for an owner/manager of a small business to get an idea on why people buy? Explain.

4. What does your text mean by understanding customer buying habits? Explain.

5. What is meant by product research? Explain.

6. What is meant by sales forecasting? Explain.

7. What is necessary to make a good sales forecast? Explain.

8. What is meant by the unit forecast procedure? The overall forecast procedure? Explain.

9. When is research a necessity for an owner/manager of a small business? Explain.

10. When might an owner/manager of a small business consider doing research as a superfluous activity? Why?

11. Write an essay about the statement "Some research is no better

than no research." Point out in your essay whether you agree or disagree with the statement.

PROBLEMS

1. Develop statistics to evaluate the idea that the town in which your school or college is located needs one of the following businesses: (1) a Rolls Royce distributorship, (2) a new motel, (3) a kite shop, or (4) a toy store. Be sure to give detailed data as to the volume of business that could be expected, what competition is in existence or potentially exists, and what that competition might be expected to do. Also, assess what and how prospective customers might react to the new business.

2. Visit a local small manufacturer and discuss with the company's representative what their company has done in the area of product research. Be cautious not to suggest that, if the company has not done anything, that the company itself is somehow remiss. After all, success can be obtained without doing all things "by the textbook."

    If you find a firm that has done some product research, analyze what it did, why it did it and how it was beneficial.

    If you find a firm that has not done product research, analyze what you think you might do to try to develop information concerning the manufacturing firm's product and how it might even more successfully operate its business.

BIBLIOGRAPHY

Brown, W. E. "Research Project Selection: Part III". *The Creativity Review* 15, no. 3 (August 1973): 2–14. A study of the differing attitudes toward research in smaller companies.

Molloy, John T. *Live For Success*. New York: William Morrow, 1981. A book that explores very productively how research is accomplished effectively to ascertain what is going on in smaller business operations.

Ries, Al and Jack Trout. *Positioning: The Battle For Your Mind*. New York: McGraw-Hill, 1981. The authors are advertising executives who give a tremendous amount of insight into the research necessary for a business to know adequately what it is doing and to accomplish its marketing goals and objectives.

Wheelright, Steven C., and Spyros Makridakis. *Forecasting Methods For Management*. 3d ed. Somerset, N.J.: John Wiley & Sons, 1980. This book has been revised and expanded to include the newest forecasting methods and actual advice on how to apply them to solve problems and plan more effectively in the small business. The book avoids theoretical and technical stumbling blocks that plague some not-very-well-organized researchers.

23

External sources of help toward better management

At some point, usually very early in the formative period of a business, it will become necessary to make contact with professional experts. The services of these professionals will be needed in varying amounts throughout the life of the business. The selection of the right type of persons and the right professional arrangement as to services provided is an important decision for the prospective business owner.

There is not much question about the need for these professional services. The difficulties involve the selection of the right individual or firm and the type of payment or fee schedule to be used to pay for the services rendered.

It is of the utmost importance that the professionals contacted be more than just people who will provide professional services. They should be individuals who have a personal and professional interest in the well-being of the firm and a willingness to assist in the success of the enterprise. This means that the small business person should probably spend some time finding out what firms or individuals would be most likely to be the most beneficial to the firm's operation. Personal contact will then be needed to express the needs of the firm and the necessity for a continuing relationship. This might be a difficult proposition if the prospective owners are starting in a new community where they are not acquainted. It will then take longer to conduct the search process.

There is no guarantee that any professional chosen to help the firm will in fact do what the management would like to have done. If the initial choice is not a good one, for one reason or another, then the owner should terminate the relationship and seek help elsewhere. In this regard it is important to not be put in a position of obligation to the professional, so that anytime that the services rendered are not satisfactory the owner can look elsewhere.

The attorney

Conducting a business in today's world requires the combined efforts of many people. Even in a smaller business there are important decisions that the untrained person is not competent to handle. Other sources of possible difficulties are the numerous laws, regulations, ordinances, etc., that the small business person may not be aware of. A competent attorney whose practice involves business operations will be in a position to know what kinds of circumstances require caution or, on the other hand, positive action at the right time.

Many attorneys will work on a retainer basis. When on retainer, the retained individual agrees to handle the legal matters of the firm at some stated amount per month, such as $100 or perhaps $150.

This is a minimum fee for office or consulting time and does not include any time in court, filing of legal papers, or the like. This provides an opportunity for an owner to be able to phone or personally contact the attorney on questions with legal overtones, without having to pay $30 to $35 per hour or office visit.

A common part of this arrangement is that the attorney will take part of his/her professional fee in the form of stock if the firm is incorporated. Another relationship involves the role of the attorney as an estate advisor, which would encourage the attorney to perform services at a reasonable fee for the firm, with the expectation that if the business is a success, increasing and substantial fees will come later.

The accountant

The investment of time and effort in a good accounting system rewards the manager on a continuing basis by providing accurate and up-to-date accounting information. Inadequate and ill-kept accounting records represent one of the principal causes of small business failure.

These observations point up the need for the services of a competent certified public accountant to establish an efficient record-keeping system, to review the system regularly, and to prepare periodic financial statements. If need dictates, a CPA may be hired on a full-time basis. In most cases, however, the certified public accountant should be hired on a retainer basis. As in the case of the attorney, this is usually more economical than seeking the service only when accounting problems arise.

The insurance agent

Chapter 11 stressed the importance of an adequate insurance program. Insurance is a highly technical topic, and the advice and service of a reliable insurance agent is needed. Insurance agents, both in property and life insurance, are always willing to appraise the need for insurance and recommend the insurance coverage most appropriate.

In the small business, the free advice of an insurance agent should be adequate. However, in some cases the services of an insurance broker are warranted. Acting as the agent of the small business firm, the insurance broker will appraise the risks, make recommendations as to the type of policies that appear necessary, and then go to the market and acquire the coverage at the lowest possible cost. The only real difference between the services of a broker and an insurance agent is that the agent may underwrite policies for only one or a few companies, which may limit the types of coverage available. The broker, on the other hand, is able to place insurance with a number of companies, and thus may be able to offer more complete service in cases of unique or unusual risks.

The banker

Besides the professional staff, there are people in the community who may be able to provide valuable advice and guidance. Probably the most important person in this category is the local banker. The importance of a favorable banking connection cannot be overemphasized, for the commercial banker offers the most complete financial service at the least cost. In establishing a working relationship with the small business, the banker will avail himself of complete financial information about the business, and be in an excellent position to offer advice on financial matters and management policy. Furthermore, through correspondent relationships with banks in other communities, the banker is a valuable source of credit information on customers.

Management consultants

In selecting a management consultant, the manager should assess the services offered by the firms in the area. The lawyer, accountant, banker, or supplier may be helpful in making recommendations. Furthermore, the local chamber of commerce or the Association of Management Consultant Engineers in New York can provide information regarding the reliability and competence of particular consulting organizations. The important questions that must be answered before selecting a consulting firm include the following: How long has the consulting firm been in business? What business firms have they served? How have the firms they have served reacted to their recommendations? Do they get repeat business from these firms? Who are the principal individuals involved in the firm, and do the principals go out on the job? Have they had any experience in problems in your particular industry or line of business? Finally, are they financially sound?

In the selection process, the manager should be suspicious of consulting firms that use high-pressure selling techniques and advertising. Furthermore, the manager should be skeptical about the firm that sets a fixed fee before examining the actual amount of work to be done, or the firm that offers cut-rate services that may prove to be inadequate. The manager should also probably avoid management consulting firms that ask for payment in advance, that tie in consulting services with the purchase of certain machines or equipment, or will not be specific as to the costs and charges involved.

As for cost, it will depend on the contract arrangement. For example, a consultant may be put on a retainer basis, as are the accountant and the attorney. In such an arrangement, the consultant would ordinarily visit the firm three or four days a month, and would always be available on short notice to consider problems that may arise. The advantage of the retainer arrangement is that the consultant has a fairly constant control over any changes instituted.

Of course, whatever the manager agrees to pay for consulting services, the total bill will depend on the time spent on the job. The daily fee varies with the person's experience. A daily fee of $100 per individual is probably minimum.

Useful help from trade associations

The large business is able to represent its own interests in relationships with labor, government, the public, and other business firms in or out of their industry. But small businesses are not, and the trade association is a means of joining together for more strength, influence, and protection.

The trade association also offers a variety of services. For example, it may develop accounting and record-keeping systems, organize industry-wide meetings for the interchange of thought and ideas, initiate research in the industry, and keep members informed of legislation, public events, and technical and trade information that affects the industry. It can also offer statistics and specialized data on sales promotion and the markets for the industry's products. Additionally, a number of trade associations organize and administer training courses and seminars for employees, provide credit reporting services, and maintain a clearinghouse for technical advice for small businesses that cannot afford their own technical staffs.

There are certain costs associated with joining a trade association, and the dues vary according to the size of the group and the services provided. Some associations assess a flat, uniform rate, while others base the rate on annual sales volume. Local associations normally collect dues monthly. Nationwide or statewide associations usually collect annual dues.

The use of an advertising agency

The objective of an advertising agency is to study a firm's product or service by surveying the present and potential market. Based on the survey, the merits of using the various advertising media available are considered and an advertising plan is formulated.

The agency then designs the advertising copy, contracts with the media for space, and forwards the approved copy with complete instructions for presentation. In the use of radio and television, the agency will contract the writing of the commercials, hire the technical staff to produce them, buy the time, and supervise the presentation.

In essence, the services of an advertising agency are free. This results from the fact that the various communication media generally charge the agency 15 percent less than the business would have to pay; and this represents the agency's commission. In other words, the manager must pay the full media rate whether or not the agency is used.[1]

In addition to the services that are provided through compensation to the agency by the media, agency services can be purchased on a fee basis. Packaging designs, sales research, the training of sales personnel, designing merchandise displays, and the preparation of sales and service literature are the typical services available.

The problem in selecting an advertising agency is finding one that will get profitable results from what is typically a limited advertising budget. Some feel the smaller advertising agency gives the small account more attention. On the other hand, the manager may need the specialized services of one of the larger agencies if the product or service is of a highly technical nature.

The Standard Advertising Register lists over 2,500 advertising agencies; thus the manager should have little trouble locating one nearby. An agency should be picked that is financially responsible; that has a staff of sufficient size, ability, and experience; that is free from control of any one media owner; and that is recognized by the various media associations (and hence is eligible for the 15 percent discount). Once the selection has been made, the manager should ask for a

---

[1]Where a local rate is in effect, the media are not allowed to pay the 15 percent commission to the advertising agency; hence the small business person in such a case would have to pay a fixed fee to the agency.

demonstration of past work to give some indication of the results that can be expected.

The agency-client agreement should specify the services the agency is to perform; the means of billing the business for the services; some understanding that the agency will not handle advertising for a directly competitive business; and that the client's approval is required for all advertising expenditures. Also included should be the statement that the manager is to pay the published rate of the medium, and that the agency is to keep the commission allowed. Finally, the advertising agency will specify it cannot be responsible for the failure of the media to meet their commitments.

As mentioned above, the various media generally allow a 15 percent commission to recognized advertising agencies, which usually covers most of the services rendered. However, if the small business uses so little advertising space or time that the 15 percent commission is too small to cover agency costs, additional fees may be charged. The normal practice is to agree on a minimum fee. Special handling charges may also be added when it is necessary to purchase materials and outside services. All of these conditions should be spelled out in the agency-client agreement.

EDUCATIONAL OPPORTUNITIES AVAILABLE TO THE SMALL BUSINESS

The typical successful small business manager enjoys hard work and puts in long hours. Another common trait is the high regard for experience and know-how, plus the continuing need to update that experience and know-how through formal and informal educational training.

Although some with limited formal education have been outstandingly successful in business, the number is small. Only through education can the small business manager learn the elements of a successful venture. No one has yet discovered a method for convincing customers to buy, irrespective of product, price, or service. Without a minimum knowledge of business operations, success is nothing more than a matter of chance. The untrained mind is simply not capable of analyzing the problems of operating a small business venture.

To be successful in small business, the manager must be able to identify and evaluate the elements of a problem, then bring them together in a workable course of action. The degree of success the manager has will depend, in large part, on experience, knowledge, and on being conversant with new developments in managerial decision making. Thus, it is important to take advantage of the educational

opportunities a community has to offer and to tap the wealth of information provided by the many libraries, publishers, and government agencies.

Among the many opportunities available, vocational training in business has long been fostered by the U.S. Office of Vocational and Adult Education, a part of the Department of Education. Vocational training is also provided through the various state vocational training supervisors. Furthermore, a program of distributive education can be found today in almost every city and town in the United States. These two avenues are very valuable in training young qualified people for eventual ownership and leadership in small business. Such an opportunity should prove valuable in situations where the owner's son or daughter plans to move eventually into a responsible position in the firm.

For the past 20 years, university schools of business have recognized the value of education for small business management. Traditionally, collegiate schools of business have offered advanced business training at the graduate level, and training at the undergraduate level, for students interested in middle management positions in medium- and large-sized corporations. Admittedly, this is an essential function of the schools, for big business will continue to need better trained executives. On the other hand, the development and training of the small business owner-manager is also becoming an essential function. Thus, most institutions offer at least a basic course in small business, and in some cases, advanced work is available.

Business educators across the country are also beginning to realize a responsibility in adult training for small business. At the present time, through various night programs across the country, tens of thousands of small business owners are taking one or more short courses under the leadership of trained and experienced business teachers. For example, the University of California at Los Angeles and New York University publish a list of courses that small business owners are encouraged to take. Such programs are a principal ingredient in promoting better, more profitable, small business management.

The Small Business Administration has been an important force in encouraging management training for small business through its administrative management course program. It has co-sponsored over 4,000 courses, in some 900 educational institutions, in which thousands of small business owner-managers have participated.

Business-sponsored organizations have also done much to advance the training of small business owners. Furthermore, chambers of commerce and trade associations often encourage local educational institutions to offer management courses for those members who are small business owners.

Professional associations have had an unusual opportunity to help the small business person through research. More and more, professional journals and publications are recognizing the importance of small business in the American economy and have presented research findings and articles that are very helpful.

The Small Business Administration has pioneered in the field of management assistance, with its previously mentioned administrative management courses; workshops for prospective managers; management publications; management research; and related programs. There are close to 100 field offices of the Small Business Administration, where a wealth of information and opportunity is available for the asking. Literally hundreds of management aids and management bulletins published by the SBA are distributed free by the field offices. Additionally, there are some excellent SBA publications for sale through the Superintendent of Documents, Government Printing Office, Washington, D.C.

In conclusion, a wealth of information and research is being published about small business, and numerous opportunities for self-training and formal education are available in most areas. Thus, the small business manager has little excuse for not enhancing his or her managerial ability. The small business world is extremely competitive. Only those individuals with foresight, knowledge, experience, and a never-ending thirst for self-improvement will survive.

THE SMALL BUSINESS LIBRARY

Every person who is associated in any way with the management of a small business needs to have access to information on a current and continuing basis. Business today is nowhere in the world conducted in a vacuum. The mass media, and in particular, television, have penetrated to virtually every part of the world.

To keep up to date, a small business owner-manager needs *his own library*. Starting out, this can be relatively simple and include an assortment such as the following:

1. Basic reference textbooks in the following areas
   a. Accounting.
   b. Marketing.
   c. Management.
   d. Business law.
2. A trade publication covering the type of business being conducted (if one is available).
3. Administrative regulations governing the business, from state, county, and municipal levels.
4. A tax manual such as the *Tax Guide for Small Business* published by the Internal Revenue Service and available from field offices of this agency.
5. A local newspaper that reports business information and provides an ongoing source of business activity.
6. An economic newsletter, published by a commercial bank or some business research agency, such as a member branch of the Federal Reserve System.
7. A business periodical such as *Fortune, Business Week, Forbes,* etc.
8. A business newspaper such as *The Wall Street Journal.*

As the business prospers, the scope of knowledge and information should also expand. The managers then should move to become more knowledgeable in matters involving management development, advertising, financing innovations, new products, marketing techniques, and personal estate matters involving insurance plans, retirement funds, hospitalization plans, etc.

The banking organizations in the United States have been of considerable aid to the small business operator, although the aid sought by any particular firm will require the sponsorship of the firm's local regular banker. The best known formal efforts are those of the Bank of America of San Francisco. Their publications devoted to small business activity are listed in Appendix A following this chapter.

The banking organizations in Canada have developed numerous special materials and programs within the banking system. Again, the initial contact would be made through the firm's regular banker. The publication *Doing Business in Canada*, published by the Canadian Imperial Bank of Commerce, the *Minding Your Own Business* series of pamphlets published by the Federal Business Development Bank, and *Your Business Matters*, a series of pamphlets published by the Royal Bank of Canada, are three examples of special materials that are of direct benefit to the smaller firm. The reader should consult the Appendix B for a the survey of Canadian reference materials.

QUESTIONS

1. Name the three individuals who should make up the professional staff for any small business.

2. What are the advantages of a favorable relationship with a local commercial bank?

3. Describe the functions performed by a management consultant. What are the advantages of hiring such a consultant?

4. Discuss the services that a trade association is prepared to offer.

5. What services are available through an advertising agency? What important problem is associated with selecting an advertising agency?

6. What educational opportunities are normally available in the community that will aid small business?

7. Discuss the functions of the Small Business Administration in terms of educational aid offered to small business.

PROBLEMS

1. Contact a local management consulting firm and discuss the services being provided to small businesses in the community.

2. Contact a local advertising agency and review the services available to small businesses. Also examine the charges for such services.

3. Examine the educational opportunities in the community that are available to aid small business managers in self-improvement.

4. Examine the library facilities in the community and review the availability of literature that would prove valuable to small business.

Appendix A

BUSINESS OPERATING GUIDES AND HANDBOOKS

Handbooks that treat specific phases of business operation often contain practical information. Only a few examples of the many types available are listed below.

Prentice-Hall Federal Tax Handbook—Annual. Has authentic information with tax-control methods for practical and competent guidance to insure effective tax management. Prentice-Hall Inc., Englewood Cliffs, NJ 07632.

Foreign Commerce Handbook, 17th ed., 1976. Chamber of Commerce of the United States, 1615 H St. NW, Washington, D.C. 20006. A guide to sources of information and services for exporters and importers. Gives types of service of U.S. government, intergovernmental and private organizations in foreign trade and related matters. Information sources under 60 major subjects, includes a bibliography of further references.

Marketing Handbook. A. W. Frey, editor. 2d ed., 1974. Ronald Press Company, 15 East 26th St., New York, N.Y. 10010. $25. A comprehensive reference book for persons concerned with marketing goods and services.

Production Handbook. Harry L. Wylie, editor. Ronald Press Company, 15 East 26th St., New York, N.Y. 10010. $31.95. Gives information about plant layout and location, production planning and control, quality control, and manufacturing processes.

Purchasing Handbook. George W. Aljian, editor. 3d ed., 1973. McGraw-Hill Book Company, Inc., 330 West 42nd St., New York, N.Y. 10036. $42.95. Gives thorough treatment of purchasing department organization, management, and operating procedures.

Tax Guide for Small Business. Internal Revenue Service, U.S. Department of the Treasury. Revised annually. GPO or local District Director of Internal Revenue. Designed to assist businesspersons in the preparation of their federal tax returns. Discusses tax problems incident to conducting a trade, business, profession, or acquiring or selling a business.

DIRECTORIES

Business firms often need information concerning products, potential buyers, or trade associations. Directories of various types are available.

The most obvious are telephone books and their classified sections. Many libraries keep some out-of-town telephone directories for business reference. For further listings of directories, consult the following, available at most libraries:

Directory of Corporate Affiliations. Skokie, Ill.: National Register Publishing Company, Inc. Published annually. Directory lists approximately 3,000 parent companies with their 16,000 divisions, subsidiaries and affiliates; an index of "who owns whom."

Moody's Industrial Manual. New York: Moody's Investor Service, Inc., 1974. A brief background, business and products and description, history, mergers and acquisition record, principal plants and properties list for each company. Principal officers and directors are given as well as seven years of financial statements and a seven-year statistical record for each company.

Reference Book of Corporate Managements. New York: Dun & Bradstreet, Inc., 1975–76. Published annually. $95. A comprehensive listing of more than 30,000 executives who are officers and directors of 2,400 companies. The companies listed are those whose revenues equal 80 percent of the Gross National Product and that employ 20 million people.

Commercial Atlas & Marketing Guide. New York: Rand McNally & Co. Published annually. A volume containing statistics and maps that provide data on population estimates, principal cities, business centers and trading areas, county business, sales and manufacturing units, ZIP code marketing information, and transportation data for the United States. General reference maps of Canada and other countries are also included.

Ayer Directory of Publications. 113th ed. Philadelphia: Ayer Press, 1981. Issued annually. A comprehensive listing of newspapers and magazines and trade publications of the United States, by states, Canada, Bermuda, Republic of Panama, Republic of the Philippines, and the Bahamas. Further indexed by more than 900 subject classifications and also the names, addresses, and phone numbers of the editors of the most popular newspaper features.

Directory of Special Libraries and Information Centers. 5th ed., 1979. $90. Gale Research Co., Book Tower, Detroit, MI 48226. Has information about more than 13,000 special libraries, information centers, and documentation centers in the U.S. and Canada, arranged alphabetically by the names of supporting organizations. Gives details on information units operated by businesses, government agencies, educational institutions, and trade and professional associations.

Guide to American Directories. 9th ed., 1975. B. Klein and Co., 104 Fifth Ave., New York, N.Y. 10011. Gives information on directories classified by industry, by profession, and by function. Useful for identifying specific directories to aid in locating new markets or sources of supply.

Standard Directory of Advertising Agencies. Skokie, Ill.: National Register Publishing Co., Inc. Published in three issues with an updating service; $75 annually. A listing of more than 4,000 agencies alphabetically, indentifying their branches, 30,000 personnel, and 60,000 accounts.

ASSOCIATIONS

Encyclopedia of Associations. Vol. I., National Organizations of the United States. Gale Research Co., Book Tower, Detroit, MI 48226. Lists trade, business, professional, labor, scientific, educational, fraternal, and social organizations of the United States; includes historical data.

National Trade and Professional Associations of the United States. Annual. 1980 ed., $30. Columbia Books, Publishers, 917 Fifteenth St., Washington, D.C. 20005. Lists the name, telephone number, address, chief executive officer, size of staff and membership, and year of formation for more than 4,000 national business and professional associations.

FINANCIAL DATA

Dun & Bradstreet Reference Book. Six times a year. Contains the names and ratings of nearly 3 million businesses of all types located throughout the United States and Canada. (Dun & Bradstreet also publishes other specialized reference books and directories, for example, *Apparel Trades Book* and *Metalworking Directory.*)

Moody's Banks and Finance. Annual with twice-weekly supplements. Moody's Investor Service, 99 Church St., New York, NY 10007. Indexes more than 9,700 American banks and financial institutions, listing their officers, directors, and other top-level personnel.

Rand-McNally International Bankers' Directory. Semiannual. Rand-McNally & Company, Box 7600, Chicago, Il 60680. Lists over 37,000 banks and branches, giving their officials, and statement figures. It also includes the ABA check-routing numbers for all U.S. banks, and a digest of U.S. banking laws.

GOVERNMENT

The following references include directories of municipal, state, and federal agencies, their personnel, and functions.

Municipal Year Book. Annual. International City Manager's Association, 1313 East 60th St., Chicago, IL 60637. $27.50. A review of municipal events of the year and a directory of city officials in all the states.

Book of the States. Biennial. Council of State Governments, 1979. P.O. Box 11910, Lexington, KY 40578. Directory of state officials, state legislatures, state judiciary systems. Also has data on current state programs and legislation.

State blue books. Many states publish their own "blue books" or directories. Inquire of your local librarian.

Sources of State Information and State Industrial Directories. Chamber of Commerce of the United States, 1615 H St. NW, Washington, D.C. 20006. Contains names and addresses of private and public agencies that furnish information about their states. Also listed, under each state, are industrial directories and directories of manufacturers published by state and private organizations. Some regional directories are included.

INDIVIDUALS

The following lists only the most general works. Who's Who directories are also available for specific occupations and locations.

Current Biography. Monthly. H. W. Wilson Company, 950 University Ave., New York, NY 10452. Extensive biographical data on prominent contemporary person.

Poor's Register of Corporations, Directors, and Executives. Annual. Standard & Poor's Corporation, 345 Hudson St., New York, NY 10014. Listed by corporation and individual.

Who's Who in America. Biennial. 40th ed. 1978–79. Marquis—Who's Who, Inc., Marquis Publications Bldg., Chicago, Il 60611. Biographical dictionary of notable living men and women.

Who's Who of American Women. Biennial. 11th ed., 1979–80. Marquis—Who's Who, Inc., Marquis Publications Bldg., Chicago, IL 60611. Biographical information of more than 20,000 distinguished women.

World's Who's Who in Finance and Industry. Marquis—Who's Who, Inc., Marquis Publications Bldg., Chicago, IL 60611. Biographical information of men and women prominent in finance, industry, and trade.

MANUFACTURERS

In addition to the directories listed, there are available many state manufacturer's and industrial directories. These are too numerous to list here. Ask your librarian if such a directory is published for the state in which you are interested.

Conover-Mast Purchasing Directory. Semiannual. Conover-Mast Publications, Inc., 95 East Putnam Ave., Greenwich, CT 06830. Alphabetical listing of manufacturers, showing product lines, code for number of employees, addresses, and telephone numbers. Classified section lists products with names and addresses of manufacturers. Special chemical and mechanical sections, and trademark and trade name identification.

MacRae's Blue Book. Annual. 4 vols. MacRae's Blue Book Co., 903 Burlington, Western Springs, IL 60558. Lists sources of industrial equipment, products, and materials; alphabetically arranged by product headings. Separate alphabetical listing of company names and trade names.

Thomas' Register of American Manufacturers. Annual. 8 vols. and index. Thomas Publishing Co., 461 Eighth Ave., New York, NY 10001. Purchasing guide listing names of manufacturers, producers, and similar sources of supply in all lines. Products are classified in six volumes; vol. 7 lists manufacturers, trade names, and commercial organizations; and vol. 8 indexes all product classifications and advertisers.

Trade Directories of the World. In loose-leaf form, kept current with monthly supplements. Croner Publications, 211–13 Jamaica Ave., Queens Village, NY 11428. Lists 2,000 directories from 151 nations that provide primary sources of information. Cross-indexed to trade and professions, countries, and general export-import publications. Lists over 400 trade categories.

ECONOMIC AND MARKETING INFORMATION

The nation's economy and, in turn, its marketing trends are changing constantly. Business persons can keep abreast by using the current books, booklets, and periodicals issued by commercial firms and government agencies. Much of the basic statistical information in the economic and marketing areas is collected by the federal government. Commercial organizations use these data and supplement them with surveys of their own. Listed below are some basic reference publications that present statistical and marketing information; many are issued on a continuing basis.

Business Literature: An Annotated List for Students and Businessmen. Baker Library, Graduate School of Business Administration, Harvard University, Soldiers Field, Boston, MA 02163. Provides a list of books and magazines in the principal areas of business.

Business Statistics. Biennial. U.S. Department of Commerce. Supplementary and historical data for the economic statistics published in the *Survey of Current Business.*

County and City Data Book. Bureau of the Census, U.S. Department of Commerce. Presents statistical information on business, manufacturers, governments, agriculture, population, housing, vital statistics, bank deposits, and other subjects. Issued every several years.

Directory of Business and Financial Services. 7th ed., 1976. Special Libraries Association, 31 East 10th St., New York, NY 10001. $6.50. An annotated listing of several hundred business, economic, and financial services.

E & P Market Guide. Annual. Editor & Publisher Co., 850 Third Ave., New York, NY 10022. Tabulates current estimates of population, households, retail sales for nine major sales classifications, income for states, counties, metropolitan areas, and 1,500 daily newspaper markets. For each area, gives information on transportation and utilities, local newspapers, climate, and employment. Includes state maps.

McGraw-Hill Dictionary of Modern Economics. Douglas Greenwald and Associates, McGraw-Hill Book Co., Inc., 1221 Ave. of Americas, New York, NY 10020. Explains the meaning of more than 1,300 terms currently used in economics, marketing, and finance. It also describes approximately 200 government and private agencies and nonprofit associations concerned with the fields of economics and marketing.

Rand McNally Commercial Atlas and Marketing Guide. Annual (leased on an annual basis). Rand McNally & Co., Box 7600, Chicago, IL 60680. An extensive U.S. atlas presenting marketing data in the form of maps and area statistics.

SM's Survey of Buying Power. Annual *Sales Management,* 630 Third Ave., New York, NY 10017. Gives population, income, and retail sales estimates for state, county, and metropolitan areas (as defined by *Sales Management).*

The Statesman's Year Book. Revised annually, John Paxton, 1975, $15. St. Martin's Press, Inc., 175 Fifth Ave., New York. NY 10010. This book is a storehouse of information on the United Nations, all countries of the world, and each of the 50 states of the United States.

Statistical Abstract of the United States. Annual. Bureau of the Census, U.S. Department of Commerce. GPO. The standard summary of national statistics, including information on the labor force, population, business enterprises, and national income.

Statistical Services of the United States Government. Annual. Bureau of the Budget. 1968. GPO. $1.50. Serves as a basic reference document on U.S. government statistical programs.

Statistics Sources. 9th ed., 1977. $64. Gale Research Co., Book Tower, Detroit, MI 48226. Arranged in dictionary style, it cities periodicals, yearbooks, directories, and other compilations issued by state, federal and foreign agencies, associations, companies, universities, and other organizations.

PERIODICALS—U.S. GOVERNMENT

The following are some of the basic federal government periodicals that contain business and general economic reports and are widely used by business persons for keeping abreast of developments in their specific areas of interest:

Construction Review. Business and Defense Services Administration, U.S. Department of Commerce. Monthly. GPO. Brings together virtually all the government's current statistics pertaining to construction, plus some non-government statistical information.

Federal Reserve Bulletin. Board of Governors of the Federal Reserve System, Washington, D.C. 20551. Has monthly tables of financial and business statistics. Interest rates, money supply, consumer credit, and industrial production are some of the subjects included. Special articles cover the state of economy, financial institutions, statistical methodology.

Monthly Labor Review. U.S. Department of Labor. Monthly. GPO. $22.35 a year; $1.90 a copy. The medium through which the Labor Department publishes its regular monthly reports on such subjects as trends of employment and payrolls, hourly and weekly earnings, working hours, collective agreements, industrial accidents, and disputes, as well as special features covering such topics as automation, and profit sharing.

Monthly Wholesale Trade Reports: Sales and Inventories. Bureau of the Census, U.S. Department of Commerce. GPO. Reports trends in sales and inventories. Also gives some geographic data.

Survey of Current Business. Office of Business Economics, U.S. Department of Commerce. Monthly. Subscription includes a weekly statistical supplement. This periodical includes statistics and articles on significant economic developments. It presents statistics on national income, business population, manufacturers sales, inventories, and orders. Carries special articles on personal income, foreign trade, and other aspects of the economy.

Statistical Abstracts of the United States. Washington, D.C.: U.S. Department of Commerce, Bureau of the Census. Issued annually. A standard summary of statistics on the social, political, and economic organization of the United States, derived from public and private sources.

Statistical Yearbook. New York: United Nations, 1975. Issued annually. A body of international statistics on population, agriculture, mining, manufacturing, finance, trade, education, and so forth. The tables cover a number of years; references of the original sources are included.

GENERAL REFERENCE SOURCES

Information Please Almanac. Simon and Schuster, 6300 Fifth Avenue, New York, NY 10020.

World Almanac. Doubleday & Co., Inc., 277 Park Ave., New York, NY 10017.

Encyclopedias

For information on almost any topic, encyclopedias are readily available. Many contain general information; others are specialized. Often included are illustrations and maps, as well as bibliographies listing standard works on the topic under consideration. They are kept up to date by yearbooks.

Among the encyclopedias available are *Colliers Encyclopedia, Encyclopedia Americana, Encyclopaedia Britannica,* and the *World Book Encyclopedia.*

Specialized encyclopedias

The more specialized encyclopedias include *Van Nostrand's Scientific Encyclopedia, McGraw-Hill Encyclopedia of Science and Technology, Encyclopedia of Banking and Finance, Encyclopedia of Chemistry, Encyclopedic Dictionary of Business Finance,* and *Accountant's Encyclopedia.*

INFORMATION SERVICES

When the information being sought is too recent for inclusion in almanacs and encyclopedias, consult the following services, which are available at most reference libraries.

Bulletin of the Public Affairs Information Service. Weekly. Public Affairs Information Service, Inc., 11 West 40th St., New York, NY 10018. Cumulated five times a year, bound annual volume. This is a selective subject list of the latest books, government publications, reports, and periodical articles, relating to economic conditions, public administration, and international relations. An especially useful feature is the extensive listing of many types of directories.

WHERE-TO-FIND PUBLICATIONS

Facts on File: A Weekly Digest of World Events. Facts on File, Inc., 119 West 57th St., New York, NY 10019. This useful and time-saving weekly index digests significant news of the day from a number of metropolitan dailies. The indexes are cumulated quarterly, then annually.

Funk and Scott Index of Corporations and Industries. Weekly. Funk and Scott Publishing Company, 11001 Cedar Ave., Cleveland, Ohio 44106. Indexes articles appearing in the leading business, financial, and trade newspapers and magazines. This is an excellent source of current information.

Books in Print. Annual. 2 vols.: vol. 1—Author index; vol. 2—Titles and Publishers. R. R. Bowker Co., 1180 Ave. of the Americas, New York, NY 10036. An author and title index to books currently available from major publishers.

Cumulative Book Index. Monthly. H. W. Wilson Co., 950 University Ave., Bronx, NY 10452. A subject, title, author index to books in the English language. Gives price, publisher, number of pages, and date of publication for each book.

Forthcoming Books. Bimonthly. R. R. Bowker Co., (in combination with Subject Guide to Forthcoming Books). This service provides a regular updating of Books in Print.

Subject Guide to Books In Print. 2 vols. Alphabetized. R. R. Bowker Co. Useful reference for identifying books currently available on a specific topic.

National Trade and Professional Associations of the United States and Labor Unions. Washington, D.C.: Columbia Books, Inc., 1981. Issued annually. Lists more than 4,700 organizations, trade and professional associations, and labor unions with national memberships.

Ayer Directory of Newspaper and Periodicals. Annual. N. W. Ayer & Son, West Washington Sq., Philadelphia, PA 19106. Provides a geographical listing of magazines and newspapers printed in the United States and its possessions. Listings are also given for Canada, Bermuda, Panama, and the Philippines. Has an alphabetical index and a classified section that increases its usefulness.

Business Publication Rates and Data. Monthly. Standard Rate and Data Service, Inc., 5201 Old Orchard Rd., Skokie, IL 60077. Contains a descriptive listing of business magazines and latest advertising rates. Indexed by name of magazine and business fields covered.

Encyclopedia of Business Information Sources. 2d ed. Detroit: Gale Research Company, 1970. Two volumes. Edited by Paul Wasserman. A listing of primary subjects of interest to managerial personnel, with a record of bibliographies, directories, handbooks, organizations, periodicals, source books and other sources of information on each topic.

Standard Periodical Directory. 1975. Annual. Oxbridge Publishing Co., Inc., 420 Lexington Ave., New York, NY 10017. Gives comprehensive coverage to periodicals in the United States and Canada. Lists over 53,000 entries, including magazines, journals, newsletters, house organs, government publications, advisory services, directories, transactions and proceedings of professional societies, yearbooks, and major city dailies (weekly and small daily newspapers are excluded).

Ulrich's International Periodicals Directory. R. R. Bowker Co., 1180 Avenue of the Americas, New York, NY 10026. Biennial. Vol. 1 covers scientific, technical, and medical periodicals; vol. 2 covers arts, humanities, business and social sciences. Classified by subject.

Applied Science and Technology Index. Monthly. H. W. Wilson Co. Subject index covering periodicals in the fields of engineering, applied science, and industry.

Business Periodicals Index. Monthly. H. W. Wilson Co. Subject index covering periodicals in the fields of business, finance, labor relations, insurance, advertising, office management, marketing, and related subjects.

Reader's Guide to Periodical Literature. Semimonthly, except monthly in July and August. H. W. Wilson Co. A general index to periodicals such as the New York Times Magazine.

The Wall Street Journal Index. Princeton, N.J.: Dow Jones Company, Inc. An index of all articles that have appeared in the Journal, grouped in two sections: Corporate News and General News.

FEDERAL GOVERNMENT PUBLICATIONS

Libraries usually maintain listings of both state and federal government publications. The following are a few examples of such listings that serve as guides to government publications.

Most of the U.S. government publications are the result of research and activities of various federal agencies. Some are free from the issuing agency, while others cost a nominal fee. Since most of these publications are relatively inexpensive and are usually some of the most recent and authoritative writings in a particular field, this reference material proves most helpful to the public.

By law, the established system of Government Depository Libraries makes federal publications available for public reference. Libraries designated within this system can elect to receive from the Superintendent of Documents, Government Printing Office, those classes of federal publications appropriate to their type of library reference service.

Superintendent of Documents (GPO) also issues a number of *Price Lists* (single copy, free) on selected federal (for sale) publications related to specific subjects. For a complete list of price list subjects, request *How to Keep in Touch with U.S. Government Publications*, free from GPO. Examples of titles that may be of interest to readers of this Bibliography are: *Finance* PL 28, *Commerce* PL 62, and *Census* PL 70. These price lists of U.S. government publications on selected subjects give prices and title of publications and may be consulted in depository libraries.

Most libraries have some federal publication listings to identify currently available materials of most of the federal agencies and they keep some of these publications for ready reference.

Some of the guides to federal publications are:

Monthly Catalog of United States Government Publications. Superintendent of Documents. GPO, Annual. The most comprehensive catalog of government publications. It lists by agency both printed and processed publications issued each month, including congressional hearings, documents, and reports.

Economic Indicators. Washington, D.C.: Superintendent of Documents, Government Printing Office. Issued monthly. A digest of current information on economic conditions of prices, wages, production, business activity, purchasing power, credit, money and federal finance presented in charts and tables. The journal gives monthly figures for the past two years and many that go back as far as 1939.

Publications lists of other U.S. government departments and agencies. Most federal agencies issue, periodically or intermittently, lists (titles of the lists vary) of their current publications. If not available at local libraries, these lists are free from the issuing agency—check with the nearest field office of the government agency. (For local office addresses, look for the agency under U.S. Government in the telephone directory.)

Monthly Checklist of State Publications. Library of Congress. GPO. List by state and agency of the state documents received by the Library of Congress.

SMALL BUSINESS ADMINISTRATION—FREE MANAGEMENT ASSISTANCE PUBLICATIONS, SBA 115A, AND FOR-SALE BOOKLETS, SBA 115B

Complete listings of currently available management assistance publications issued by SBA. Both lists are free from the nearest field office of Small Business Administration, Washington, DC 20416.

These free leaflets deal with functional problems in small manufacturing plants and concentrate on subjects of interest to administrative executives. Request by number and title.

Free management assistance publications

These free publications should be ordered from the following address:

U.S. Small Business Administration
P.O. Box 15434
Fort Worth, TX 76119

170. *The ABC's of Borrowing*
171. *How to Write a Job Description*
178. *Effective Industrial Advertising for Small Plants*
186. *Checklist for Developing a Training Program*
187. *Using Census Data in Small Plant Marketing*
189. *Should You Make or Buy Components?*
190. *Measuring Sales Force Performance*
191. *Delegating Work and Responsibility*
192. *Profile Your Customers to Expand Industrial Sales*
193. *What Is the Best Selling Price?*
194. *Marketing Planning Guidelines*
195. *Setting Pay for Your Management Jobs*
197. *Pointers on Preparing an Employee Handbook*
200. *Is the Independent Sales Agent for You?*
201. *Locating or Relocating Your Business*
203. *Are Your Products and Channels Producing Sales?*
204. *Pointers on Negotiating DOD Contracts*
205. *Pointers on Using Temporary-Help Services*
206. *Keep Pointed toward Profit*
207. *Pointers on Scheduling Production*
208. *Problems in Managing a Family-Owned Business*
209. *Preventing Employee Pilferage*
211. *Termination of DOD Contracts for the Government's Convenience*
212. *The Equipment Replacement Decision*
214. *The Metric System and Small Business*
215. *How to Prepare for a Pre-Award Survey*

Small business bibliographies

Topic listings

For-sale booklets

These publications should be ordered from the Superintendent of Documents, Government Printing Office, Washington, DC 20402. Prices shown were in effect as of April, 1980.

Small Business Management Series. The booklets in this series provide discussions of special management problems in small companies.

452

No.		Stock Number	Pages	Price
1.	*An Employee Suggestion System for Small Companies* Explains the basic principles for starting and operating a suggestion system. It also warns of various pitfalls and gives examples of suggestions submitted by employees.	045-000-00020-6	18	$1.10
9.	*Cost Accounting for Small Manufacturers* Assists managers of small manufacturing firms, producing a broad range of products, establish accounting procedures that will help to document and to control production and business costs.	045-000-00162-8	180	4.25
15.	*Handbook of Small Business Finance* Written for the small business owner who wants to improve financial management skills. Indicates the major areas of financial management and describes a few of the many techniques that can help the small business owner.	045-000-00139-3	63	3.00
20.	*Ratio Analysis for Small Business* Ratio analysis is the process of determining the relationships between certain financial or operating data of a business to provide a basis for managerial control. The purpose of the booklet is to help the owner/manager in detecting favorable or unfavorable trends in the business.	045-000-00150-4	65	2.20
22.	*Practical Business Use of Government Statistics* Illustrates some practical uses of Federal Government statistics, discusses what can be done with them, and describes major reference sources.	045-000-00131-8	28	1.40
25.	*Guides for Profit Planning* Guides for computing and using the break-even point, the level of gross profit, and the rate of return on investment. Designed for readers who have no specialized training in accounting and economics.	045-000-00137-7	59	2.50
27.	*Profitable Community Relations for Small Business* Practical information on how to build and maintain sound community relations by participation in community affairs.	045-000-00033-8	36	1.50
28.	*Small Business and Government Research and Development* An introduction for owners of small research and development firms that seek government R&D contracts. Includes a discussion of the procedures necessary to locate and interest government markets.	045-000-00130-0	41	1.25
29.	*Management Audit for Small Manufacturers* A series of questions which will indicate whether theowner-manager of a small manufacturing plant is planning, organizing, directing, and coordinating the business activities efficiently.	045-000-00151-2	44	1.60
30.	*Insurance and Risk Management for Small Business* A discussion of what insurance is, the necessity of obtaining professional advice on buying insurance, and the main types of insurance a small business may need.	045-000-00037-1		3.00

31. *Management Audit for Small Retailers*   045-000-00149-1   50   1.80
    Designed to meet the needs of the owner-manager
    of a small retail enterprise. 149 questions guide the
    owner-manager in a self examination and a review
    of the business operation.

32. *Financial Recordkeeping for Small Stores*   045-000-00142-3   135   4.00
    Written primarily for the small store owner or pro-
    spective owner whose business doesn't justify hir-
    ing a full-time bookkeeper.

33. *Small Store Planning for Growth*   045-000-00152-1   99   2.40
    A discussion of the nature of growth, the manage-
    ment skills needed, and some techniques for use
    in promoting growth. Included is a consideration
    of merchandising, advertising and display, and
    checklists for increase in transactions and gross
    margins.

34. *Selecting Advertising Media—A Guide for*   045-000-00154-7   133   3.75
    Small Business
    Intended to aid the small business person in
    deciding which medium to select for making
    the product, service, or store known to poten-
    tial customers and how best to use advertising
    money.

35. *Training Salesmen to Franchise Index/Profile*   045-000-00125-3   56   2.00
    Presents an evaluation process that may be used to
    investigate franchise opportunities. The Index tells
    what to look for in a franchise. The Profile is
    worksheet for listing the data.

36. *Training Salesmen to Serve Industrial Markets*   045-000-00133-4   85   2.20
    Discusses role of sales in marketing program of
    small manufacturer and offers suggestions for sales
    force to use in servicing customers. Provides mate-
    rial to use in training program.

37. *Financial Control by Time-Absorption Analysis*   045-000-00134-2   138   2.75
    A profit control technique that can be used by all
    types of business. A step-by-step approach shows
    how to establish this method in a particular busi-
    ness.

38. *Management Audit for Small Service Firms*   045-000-00143-1   67   1.80
    A do-it-yourself guide for owner-managers of small
    service firms to help them evaluate and improve
    their operations. Brief comments explain the im-
    portance of each question in 13 critical manage-
    ment areas.

39. *Decision Points in Developing New Products*   045-000-00146-6   64   1.50
    Provides a path from idea to marketing plan for the
    small manufacturing or R&D firm that wants to
    expand or develop a business around a new prod-
    uct, process, or invention.

40. *Management Audit for Small Construction Firms*   045-000-00161-0   53   2.50
    Written to help top executives of small con-
    struction firms to make a self-appraisal of their
    management practices. Recommends ways to
    improve existing practices and introduce effective
    new ones.

Starting and Managing series. This series is designed to help the small entrepreneur in the effort "to look before leaping" into a business. The first volume in the series—*Starting and Managing a Small Business of Your Own*—deals with the subject in general terms. Each of the other volumes deals with one type of business in detail, and their titles are designed to inform of their contents. Available titles are listed below.

No.		Stock Number	Pages	Price
1.	*Starting and Managing a Small Business of Your Own*	045-000-00123-7	97	3.50
20.	*Starting and Managing a Small Retail Music Store*	045-000-00107-5	81	1.30

Nonseries publications.

	Stock Number	Pages	Price
Export Marketing for Smaller Firms A manual for owner-managers of smaller firms who seek sales in foreign markets.	045-000-00158-0	84	$2.20
U.S. Government Purchasing and Sales Directory A directory for businesses that are interested in selling to the U.S. government. Lists the purchasing needs of various agencies.	045-000-00153-9	169	5.50
Managing for Profits Ten chapters on various aspects of small business management, for example, marketing, production, and credit.	045-000-00005-2	170	2.75
Buying and Selling a Small Business Deals with the problems that confront buyers and sellers of small businesses. Discusses the buy-sell transaction, sources of information for buyer-seller decision, the buy-sell process, using financial statements in the buy-sell transaction, and analyzing the market position of the company.	045-000-00164-4	122	3.50
Strengthening Small Business Management Twenty-one chapters on small business management. This collection reflects the experience which the author gained in a lifetime of work with the small business community.	045-000-00114-8	158	4.00
Small Business Goes to College Subtitled "College and University Courses in Small Business Management and Entrepreneurship," this booklet traces the development of small business management as a college subject and provides samples of courses offered by some 200 colleges and universities. It should be useful to educators as well as to counselors who seek sources to recommend for their clients' self-development.	045-000-00159-8	82	3.25

PERIODICALS

These are general information periodicals that are useful for the manager or owner of a small business. They should be read as a source of ideas and information that are on the forefront of current developments in managing and operating a business.

Business Horizons, Indiana University, Graduate School of Business, Bloomington, IN 47401

California Management Review. University of California, Graduate School of Business Administration, Berkeley, CA 94720

Harvard Business Review. Harvard University, Graduate School of Business Administration, Boston, MA 02163

Journal of Small Business Management. National Council for Small Business Management Development, University of Wisconsin Extension, 600 West Kilbourn Avenue, Milwaukee, WI 53203

Management Review. American Management Association, Saranac Lake, NY 12983

Supervisory Management. American Management Association, Saranac Lake, NY 12983

PAMPHLETS

These phamphlets are very useful in showing the background financial data that is developed on a composite basis for a large number of similar type business organizations.

The Business Failure Record. Compiled yearly by the Business Economics Department, Dun & Bradstreet, New York, N.Y.

Cost of Doing Business, Corporations, Key Business Ratios in 185 Lines. Business Economics Department, Dun & Bradstreet, New York, N.Y. 1973.

Cost of Doing Business, Partnerships & Proprietorships, Key Business Ratios in 120 Lines. Business Economics Department, Dun & Bradstreet, New York, N.Y. 1973.

Terms of Sale for 94 Manufacturing and Wholesale Lines. Business Information Systems, Services and Sciences, Dun & Bradstreet, New York, N.Y., 1970.

Venture Capital. The professional journal of the venture capital and SBIC industry, published by S. M. Rubel & Company, 10 South LaSalle Street, Chicago, Ill., 1974.

Appendix B

Canadian materials

GENERAL BUSINESS HANDBOOKS

The Blue Book of Canadian Business. Ed. by Canadian Newspaper Services International Limited, 1976+, 55 Eglinton Avenue East, Toronto, Ont. M4P 1G8. Provides information on Canadian companies that serves to increase knowledge about their social and economic impact and to show the way to expanding that knowledge.

Canadian Business Handbook. 3d ed. Dorothy M. and Jean P. Newman, 1979. McGraw-Hill Ryerson Limited, 330 Progress Ave., Scarborough, Ont. M1P 2Z5. Includes definitions, a few illustrations, forms of address, governmental aids to business, filing systems, etc.

LIBRARY REFERENCE SOURCES

Directory of Special Libraries and Information Centers. Vol. 1—Special Libraries and Information Centers in the United States and Canada, 5th ed. Margaret L. Young et al., 1979. $90. Gale Research Co., Book Tower, Detroit, MI 48226. Has information about more than 13,000 special libraries, information centers, and documentation centers in the United States and Canada—arranged alphabetically by the names of supporting organizations. Gives details on information units operated by businesses, government agencies, educational institutions, and trade and professional associations. Also *Vol. 3—New Special Libraries,* 5th ed. Ed. Margaret L. Young et al., 1979. $80. Gale Research Co.

INTERNATIONAL REFERENCE SOURCES

The Europa Yearbook 1980: A World Survey. Gale Research Co., Book Tower, Detroit, MI 48226, 3,600 pp., $150 set. Two-volume factual survey offers information about every country in the world. Covers statistics, government, religion, the press, trade and industry, etc. Contains data on 1,600 international organizations and describes each group's function, organization, financial structure, and activities. Offers detail of the United Nations structure and activities.

International Postal Handbook 1981–82 Edition. New Harbinger Publications, 624 43rd St., Richmond, CA 94805, 54 pp. $12.50. Guide to international correspondence explains all classes of outgoing and incoming mail including rates, regulations, restrictions, and advantages of each. Lists predominant languages spoken in every country, common addressing formats, postal coding system, prohibited items, package size limits, and local laws governing imports, credit terms, and invoicing. Special topics include international direct mail campaigns, insurance claims, foreign and U.S. customs, cultural idiosyncrasies, and foreign postal terms and abbreviations.

World Product Casts. Predicasts, Inc., 11001 Cedar Ave., Cleveland, OH 44106. A forecast of economic indicators and products based upon historical data.

World Regional Casts. Predicasts, Inc., 11001 Cedar Ave., Cleveland, OH 44106. A forecast of economic indicators based upon historical data.

MARKETING AND TRADE DIRECTORIES

Frasers Canadian Trade Directory. MacLean Hunter, Ltd., 481 University Ave., Toronto, Ont. This directory is laid out similarly to Yellow Pages of the phone book.

F&S Index International: Industries, Countries, Companies. Predicast, Inc., F&S International, 11001 Cedar Ave., Cleveland, OH 44106. An index covering business activity in Canada, Latin America, Africa, the Mid-East, Japan, other Asia, and Oceania.

Market Research Handbook. Statistics Canada, Ottawa K1A OT6 or Publishing Center, Supply and Services, Canada, Ottawa, K1A 059. Developed to provide a convenient source of information and reference for all those who are engaged in analysing the many aspects of Canadian markets on the local, provincial, regional and national level.

Trade Directories of the World. In loose-leaf form, kept current with monthly supplements. $35. Craner Publications, 211–13 Jamaica Ave., Queens Village, NY 11428. Lists 2,000 directories from 151 nations that provide primary sources of information. Cross-indexed to trade and professions, countries, and general export-import publications. Lists over 400 trade categories.

ACCOUNTING REFERENCES

Canadian Accountants Handbook. 3d ed. William George Leonard, 1978. McGraw-Hill Ryerson, 330 Progress Ave, Scarborough, Ont. M1P

2Z5. Gives routine practices and procedures employed by book-keepers and accountants in Canadian commerce and industry. Compares routine practices and procedures with generally accepted accounting principles.

CANADIAN BUSINESS AND ECONOMIC SOURCES

Canadian Business & Economics: A Guide to Sources of Information. Ed. Barbara E. Brown, 1976. Canadian Library Association, 151 Sparks St., Ottawa, Ont. K1P 5E3. Includes English and French indexes.

Canadian Government Publications Catalogue. Information Canada, Vanguard Building, 171 Slater St., Ottawa. A monthly issue with annual cumulations.

Organization of the Government of Canada, 1976. Information Canada, Vanguard Building, 171 Slater St., Ottawa.

FINANCIAL AND BANKING SOURCES

Polk's World Bank Directory. R. L. Polk & Co., Publishers, 2001 Elm Hill Pike, Nashville, TN 37202. Contains list of banks in world communities, population of these communities, and names of managers.

Dun & Bradstreet Key Business Ratios in Canada. Annual, Dun & Bradstreet of Canada Ltd., P.O. Box 423, Station A, Toronto, Ont. M5W 1E2.

Dun And Bradstreet Canadian Key Business Directory, Dun & Bradstreet of Canada, Ltd., Marketing Services Division, 365 Bloor St., East, 15th Floor, Toronto, Ont. M4W 3L4. A complete index of largest businesses in Canada with 17,000 listings, addresses, phone numbers, sales, employees, net worth.

Pick's Currency Yearbook, Pick Publishing Corp., 21 West St., New York, NY. Contains information on monetary legislation, currency values, transfer regulations, and clearing and compensation agreements.

FINANCIAL POST—CORPORATION SURVEYS

Financial Post Corporation Service. The Financial Post, c/o MacLean-Hunter, Ltd., 481 University Ave., Toronto, Ont. M5W 1A7. An up-to-date reporting and reference service covering about 1,000 Canadian companies.

The Financial Post Survey of Funds (formerly *Survey of Investment Funds),* The Financial Post, c/o MacLean-Hunter, Ltd., 481 University Ave.,

Toronto, Ont. M5W 1A7. Being revised under new format. No publications since 1977.

The Financial Post Survey of Industrials. The Financial Post, c/o MacLean-Hunter, Ltd., 481 University Ave., Toronto, Ont. M5W 1A7. Covers all Canadian public industries, corporations, including details of operations, management, financial data, subsidiaries with outlying locations, etc., plus selected financial growth statistics on many investment funds, along with funds eligible for Registered Retirement Savings Plans and Registered Home Ownership Savings Plans. Five-year price ranges of listed stocks and an index of standard industrial classifications.

The Financial Post Survey of Markets. The Financial Post, c/o Maclean-Hunter Ltd., 481 University Ave., Toronto, Ont. M5W 1A7. Contains market data, buying power indexes, provincial and industry data.

The Financial Post Survey of Mines, The Financial Post, c/o MacLean-Hunter Ltd., 481 University Ave., Toronto, Ont. M5W 1A7. A review of the mining and energy industries in Canada, including review of operations, management and financial status of 2,000 mining companies.

BUSINESS FORMATION AND OPERATING DATA

Doing Business in Canada, Canadian Imperial Bank of Commerce, Business Development Division, Head Office, Commerce Court, Toronto, Ont. M5L 1A2. A guide to the incorporation of companies in Canada and Canadian taxes. Covers commencing business in Canada, forms of business organizations, fees for incorporation, provincial and federal taxes as applied to residents and nonresidents, international agreements, labour legislation, and financial services.

Minding Your Own Business, Federal Business Development Bank Management Services, P.O. Box 6021, Montreal, Que. H3C 3C3. The Federal Business Development Bank provides financial and management services to new or existing business anywhere in Canada, particularly those of smaller size. Copies of this pamphlet series may be obtained in English or French without charge from any FBDB office.

No. 1   *Reference Booklets for Small Business*

No. 2   *Giving Credit to Your Customers*

No. 3   *Presenting Your Case for a Term Loan*

No. 4   *Forecasting for an Existing Business*

No. 5   *Managing Your Current Assets*

No. 6 *Forecasting for a New Business*

No. 7 *Managing Your Fixed Assets*

No. 8 *Managing Your Cash*

No. 9 *Working Capital*

No. 10 *Changes of Ownership*

No. 11 *Planning a Motel*

No. 12 *Equity Capital for Small Business*

No. 13 *Paying Your Employees*

No. 14 *Personnel Records*

No. 15 *Planning the Start of Your Retail Business*

No. 16 *Financing for your Retail Business*

No. 17 *Retail Pricing*

No. 18 *Managing Your Retail Inventory*

No. 19 *Attracting and Keeping Your Retail Customers*

No. 20 *Buying a Franchise*

No. 21 *Buying or Starting a Restaurant*

Your Business Matters—A Guide for Independent Business, The Royal Bank of Canada, Royal Bank Plaza, Toronto, Ont. M5J 2J5. A valuable, practical source of information, ideas, systems, techniques, and examples for owners and managers of independent Business.

No. 1 *How to Finance Your Business*

No. 2 *Pointers to Profit*

No. 3 *Good Management—Your Key to Survival*

No. 4 *Exporting—Importing—An Open Door to Additional Profits*

No. 5 *Financial Reporting and Analysis—The Independent Business Way*

No. 6 *Control Over Direct Costs and Pricing*

No. 7 *Planning and Budgeting . . . The Independent Business Way*

No. 8 *Control Over Inventory Investment—The Independent Business Way*

No. 9 *Taxation*

No. 10 *Credit Management and Collection*

No. 11 *Evaluation and Management of Fixed Assets*

No. 12 *Management of Liabilities and Equities*

No. 13 *Management Audit for Independent Business*

Market Planning for Independent Business
Advertising and Sales Promotion for Independent Business

Index

461

466

This book has been set Merganthaler Linotron 606,
in 10 and 9 point Palatino, leaded 2 points.
Chapter numbers are 120 point Optima and
chapter titles are 24 point Optima. The size of the
type page is 30 by 46 picas.